Oracle Database 11gR2 Performance Tuning Cookbook

Over 80 recipes to help beginners achieve better performance from Oracle Database applications

Ciro Fiorillo

[PACKT] enterprise

professional expertise distilled

PUBLISHING

BIRMINGHAM - MUMBAI

Oracle Database 11gR2 Performance Tuning Cookbook

First published: January 2012

Production Reference: 1050112

Published by Packt Publishing Ltd.
Livery Place
35 Livery Street
Birmingham B3 2PB, UK.

ISBN 978-1-84968-260-2

www.packtpub.com

Cover Image by Stanford Murray (stanmoore@live.com)

Credits

Author

Ciro Fiorillo

Reviewers

April C. Sims

Advait V. Deo

Asif Momen

Paolo Napoletano

Acquisition Editor

Dhwani Devater

Lead Technical Editors

Kartikey Pandey

Pallavi Iyenger

Technical Editors

Vanjeet D'souza

Conrad Sardinha

Merwine Machado

Copy Editors

Laxami Subramanian

Brandt D'Mello

Neha Shetty

Project Coordinator

Vishal Bodwani

Proofreader

Aaron Nash

Indexers

Monica Ajmera Mehta

Rekha Nair

Tejal Daruwale

Graphics

Manu Joseph

Production Coordinators

Prachali Bhiwandkar

Shantanu Zagade

Cover Work

Prachali Bhiwandkar

About the Author

Ciro Fiorillo is an IT professional and consultant with more than a decade of experience in different roles (Developer, Analyst, DBA, Project Manager, Data and Software Architect) among software industries. He is an Oracle DBA Certified Professional and he has worked on different technologies and architectures, such as Oracle, SQL Server, Delphi, C# and .NET Framework, C/C++, Java, Flex, PHP, COBOL, Fortran, and Tibco.

He is based in Italy, near Naples, in the beautiful and historic Ercolano.

Ciro is currently employed as Information Systems Manager in a Financial Organization in Italy, and he is in charge of databases and systems management and development, coordinating the IT staff.

As a freelancer, he writes articles for websites and printed magazines about software and computing, participates in workshops, and teaches C++ parallel programming with Intel Software tools.

Ciro can be reached at `ciro@cirofiorillo.com`.

Acknowledgement

Writing a book was my dream and this is the first book I have written, so I would like to thank the entire staff at Packt Publishing, especially Dhwani Devater, who gave me the opportunity to write my first book, and in supporting me during the long way to the publication.

I'd like to thank Vishal Bodwani, the project coordinator, who helped me in following the agreed timeline without too many delays and Lata Basantani, the project leader.

I'd like to thank Kartikey Pandey and Pallavi Iyenger, the development editors, for their guidance and reviews.

I'd like to thank Suzanne Ritter, the marketing executive, for the "Behind the Book" campaign.

I'd also like to thank Vanjeet D'souza, Conrad Sardinha, and Merwine Machado, the technical editors, for their sincere efforts on this book.

A special thanks to the technical reviewers: April Sims, Asif Momen, Advait Deo, and my friend Paolo Napoletano, for reviewing my errors and for helping me provide better content suggesting many improvements and helpful feedback.

About the Reviewers

April Sims is currently the Database Administrator at Southern Utah University and an Oracle Certified Professional: 8*i*, 9*i*, and 10*g* with a Master's degree in Business Administration from the University of Texas at Dallas. Involved as a volunteer with the Independent Oracle Users Group for over seven years, April is currently a Contributing Editor for the *IOUG SELECT* Journal. April is an annual presenter at Oracle OpenWorld, IOUG COLLABORATE, and numerous regional Oracle-related conferences.

Advait V. Deo is a graduate from NIT, Nagpur and a post graduate from Birla Institute of Technology & Science (BITS), Pilani. After graduation he joined TCS and worked there for a couple of years. Later, he joined Oracle Corp. and worked closely with databases.

He's had seven years' experience working in the database world, having spent time on many aspects of database till now starting from Oracle Version 8 until 11*g*. He mainly focuses on database performance tuning, integrating databases with front-end application, scripting, and automation. Currently he is working as a Lead Database Administrator in Amazon.com, Inc. (world leader in retail business), handling a fleet of around 300 production databases.

Currently he resides in Hyderabad, India, with his wife Abha. In his time off from his busy work schedule, he spends quality time with his family, riding a bike, and watching movies.

He updates some of his work and learning on his website at `http://www.avdeo.com`, whenever he gets time.

Asif Momen has been working with Oracle technologies for over 12 years and has expertise in performance tuning and high availability. He has a master''s degree in Software Systems from Birla Institute of Technology & Science (BITS), Pilani.

Asif is an Oracle ACE and is OCP-Certified DBA, Forms Developer, and RAC Expert. He is a speaker at Oracle OpenWorld and All India Oracle User Group (AIOUG). In addition, he is the Editor of *Oracle Connect*—the quarterly publication of AIOUG. His particular interests are Database tuning, Oracle RAC, Oracle Data Guard, and Backup and Recovery.

Asif posts his ideas and opinions on **The Momen Blog** (`http://momendba.blogspot.com`). He can be reached at `asif.momen@gmail.com`.

www.PacktPub.com

Support files, eBooks, discount offers and more

You might want to visit www.PacktPub.com for support files and downloads related to your book.

Did you know that Packt offers eBook versions of every book published, with PDF and ePub files available? You can upgrade to the eBook version at www.PacktPub.com and as a print book customer, you are entitled to a discount on the eBook copy. Get in touch with us at service@packtpub.com for more details.

At www.PacktPub.com, you can also read a collection of free technical articles, sign up for a range of free newsletters and receive exclusive discounts and offers on Packt books and eBooks.

http://PacktLib.PacktPub.com

Do you need instant solutions to your IT questions? PacktLib is Packt's online digital book library. Here, you can access, read and search across Packt's entire library of books.

Why Subscribe?

- ► Fully searchable across every book published by Packt
- ► Copy and paste, print and bookmark content
- ► On demand and accessible via web browser

Free Access for Packt account holders

If you have an account with Packt at www.PacktPub.com, you can use this to access PacktLib today and view nine entirely free books. Simply use your login credentials for immediate access.

Instant Updates on New Packt Books

Get notified! Find out when new books are published by following @PacktEnterprise on Twitter, or the *Packt Enterprise* Facebook page.

To my extraordinary wife, Monica, who helped me to make my dream come true, supporting me even when working late nights and on weekends.

To my children, Miriam and Mario. You are the essence of my life.

Table of Contents

Preface   1

Chapter 1: Starting with Performance Tuning   7
Introduction   7
Reviewing the performance tuning process   12
Exploring the example database   17
Acquiring data using a data dictionary and dynamic performance views   20
Analyzing data using Statspack reports   23
Diagnosing performance issues using the alert log   28
Analyzing data using Automatic Workload Repository (AWR)   29
Analyzing data using Automatic Database Diagnostic Monitor (ADDM)   32
A working example   36

Chapter 2: Optimizing Application Design   41
Introduction   41
Optimizing connection management   42
Improving performance sharing reusable code   48
Reducing the number of requests to the database using stored procedures   54
Reducing the number of requests to the database using sequences   59
Reducing the number of requests to the database using materialized views   65
Optimizing performance with schema denormalization   71
Avoiding dynamic SQL   79

Chapter 3: Optimizing Storage Structures   83
Introduction   83
Avoiding row chaining   84
Avoiding row migration   89
Using LOBs   96
Using index clusters   103
Using hash clusters   109
Indexing the correct way   113

Rebuilding index   **123**
Compressing indexes   **128**
Using reverse key indexes   **130**
Using bitmap indexes   **136**
Migrating to index organized tables   **142**
Using partitioning   **146**

Chapter 4: Optimizing SQL Code   **153**
Introduction   **153**
Using bind variables   **154**
Avoiding full table scans   **164**
Exploring index lookup   **173**
Exploring index skip-scan and index range-scan   **177**
Introducing arrays and bulk operations   **181**
Optimizing joins   **187**
Using subqueries   **192**
Tracing SQL activity with SQL Trace and TKPROF   **201**

Chapter 5: Optimizing Sort Operations   **207**
Introduction   **207**
Sorting—in-memory and on-disk   **208**
Sorting and indexing   **215**
Writing top n queries and ranking   **224**
Using count, min/max, and group-by   **232**
Avoiding sorting in set operations: union, minus, and intersect   **240**
Troubleshooting temporary tablespaces   **248**

Chapter 6: Optimizing PL/SQL Code   **253**
Introduction   **253**
Using bind variables and parsing   **254**
Array processing and bulk-collect   **257**
Passing values with NOCOPY (or not)   **262**
Using short-circuit IF statements   **266**
Avoiding recursion   **269**
Using native compilation   **271**
Taking advantage of function result cache   **276**
Inlining PL/SQL code   **281**
Using triggers and virtual columns   **284**

Chapter 7: Improving the Oracle Optimizer   **291**
Introduction   **291**
Exploring optimizer hints   **292**
Collecting statistics   **298**
Using histograms   **305**

Managing stored outlines | 310
Introducing Adaptive Cursor Sharing for bind variable peeking | 317
Creating SQL Tuning Sets | 327
Using the SQL Tuning Advisor | 331
Configuring and using SQL Baselines | 335

Chapter 8: Other Optimizations | **341**
Introduction | 341
Caching results with the client-side result cache | 342
Enabling parallel SQL | 346
Direct path inserting | 351
Using create table as select | 355
Inspecting indexes and triggers overhead | 359
Loading data with SQL*Loader and Data Pump | 366

Chapter 9: Tuning Memory | **375**
Introduction | 375
Tuning memory to avoid Operating System paging | 376
Tuning the Library Cache | 384
Tuning the Shared Pool | 388
Tuning the Program Global Area and the User Global Area | 396
Tuning the Buffer Cache | 400

Chapter 10: Tuning I/O | **411**
Introduction | 411
Tuning at the disk level and strategies to distribute Oracle files | 412
Striping objects across multiple disks | 419
Choosing different RAID levels for different Oracle files | 422
Using asynchronous I/O | 425
Tuning checkpoints | 428
Tuning redo logs | 433

Chapter 11: Tuning Contention | **437**
Introduction | 437
Detecting and preventing lock contention | 438
Investigating transactions and concurrency | 444
Tuning latches | 452
Tuning resources to minimize latch contention | 457
Minimizing latches using bind variables | 460

Appendix A: Dynamic Performance Views | **469**
ALL_OBJECTS | 469
DBA_BLOCKERS | 470
DBA_DATA_FILES | 470

DBA_EXTENTS	**471**
DBA_INDEXES	**471**
DBA_SQL_PLAN_BASELINES	**472**
DBA_TABLES	**472**
DBA_TEMP_FILES	**473**
DBA_VIEWS	**474**
DBA_WAITERS	**474**
INDEX_STATS	**474**
DBA_SEQUENCES	**475**
DBA_TABLESPACES	**476**
DBA_TAB_HISTOGRAMS	**476**
V$ADVISOR_PROGRESS	**477**
V$BUFFER_POOL_STATISTICS	**477**
V$CONTROLFILE	**478**
V$DATAFILE	**478**
V$DB_CACHE_ADVICE	**479**
V$DB_OBJECT_CACHE	**480**
V$ENQUEUE_LOCK	**480**
V$FILESTAT	**481**
V$FIXED_TABLE	**482**
V$INSTANCE_RECOVERY	**482**
V$LATCH	**483**
V$LATCH_CHILDREN	**483**
V$LIBRARYCACHE	**484**
V$LOCK	**485**
V$LOCKED_OBJECT	**486**
V$LOG	**486**
V$LOG_HISTORY	**487**
V$LOGFILE	**488**
V$MYSTAT	**488**
V$PROCESS	**489**
V$ROLLSTAT	**489**
V$ROWCACHE	**490**
V$SESSION	**490**
V$SESSION_EVENT	**491**
V$SESSTAT	**492**
V$SGA	**492**
V$SGAINFO	**493**
V$SHARED_POOL_RESERVED	**493**
V$SORT_SEGMENT	**494**
V$SQL	**494**

V$SQL_PLAN 495
V$SQLAREA 496
V$STATNAME 496
V$SYSSTAT 497
V$SYSTEM_EVENT 498
V$TEMPFILE 498
V$TEMPSTAT 499
V$WAITSTAT 499
X$BH 500

Appendix B: A Summary of Oracle Packages
Used for Performance Tuning **501**
DBMS_ADDM 501
DBMS_ADVISOR 502
DBMS_JOB 502
DBMS_LOB 503
DBMS_MVIEW 503
DBMS_OUTLN 503
DBMS_OUTLN_EDIT 504
DBMS_SHARED_POOL 504
DBMS_SPACE 505
DBMS_SPM 505
DBMS_SQL 505
DBMS_SQLTUNE 506
DBMS_STATS 506
DBMS_UTILITY 507
DBMS_WORKLOAD_REPOSITORY 507

Index **509**

Preface

People use databases to organize and to manage their data. Oracle Database is the leader in the relational database management systems market, with a broad adoption in many industries. Using the best tool is not enough to be sure that the results of our efforts will be satisfactory—driving the fastest car in a Formula 1 competition, though better than driving the slowest, doesn't guarantee the first place at the checkered flag.

Every developer—and every manager—knows that applications have to be responsive, because users hate to spend their time waiting for a transaction to end, looking at an hourglass. To meet this goal, it's important to adopt a correct tuning strategy, which starts at the same time as the application design, then moves forward together, and will continue even when the application and the database are in production.

Even though this is a cookbook on performance tuning, there are no silver bullets. Every recipe in this book will show us how to solve a problem with the correct approach, so when a similar problem arises in one of our databases, we can apply the correct solution even in different situations than the ones presented in the book.

Before we start a database performance tuning process, we have to define what the tuning goals that we aim to reach are. "As fast as possible" is not a tuning goal. The primary tuning goal, generally speaking, is to reduce the response time or to reduce the resources needed to do a certain amount of work in the same time.

At a lower level, to minimize response time we will try to:

- Reduce or eliminate waits
- Cache the largest number of blocks in memory
- Access the least number of data blocks (from disks)

To increase the throughput and availability we will try to:

▶ Increment hit ratios

▶ Decrease system memory utilization

▶ Eliminate paging and swapping

▶ Reduce recovery time, decreasing the Mean Time To Recovery (MTTR)

▶ Increase load balancing (distributing data files to different disks) to reduce I/O times

▶ Increase scalability

Before starting a tuning session, we have to define which are the goals, in terms of SLA, or define precise and measurable objectives. So at the end of the tuning process, we will know if we have reached the expected results. We will work to reduce the workload—so the same task will consume less resources, allowing other tasks to use those resources—and to minimize the response time.

In this book, we will find many recipes that can help us reach these goals. Have a good read!

What this book covers

Chapter 1, Starting with Performance Tuning will show how to set up the example database, how to adopt a performance tuning process that can help in solving performance problems, and how to collect and analyze data from Oracle Database using various methods.

Chapter 2, Optimizing Application Design presents the most common application design issues that prevent an application from running without performance issues. You will see how to improve database performance by sharing reusable code and by reducing the number of requests to the database by using various database objects.

Chapter 3, Optimizing Storage Structures will show how to optimize the use of different database storage structures, presenting the optimal use for tables, clusters, indexes, and partitioning. You will see how to choose the appropriate structure to improve access time to your data, also analyzing the possible drawbacks in the operations that modify the data.

Chapter 4, Optimizing SQL Code is focused on SQL code optimization. Throughout the chapter you will find many methods to diagnose and solve typical performance problems caused by poorly written SQL code. You will find answers on how (and when) to avoid full table scans, how to use indexes, bulk operations and arrays, join and subquery optimization. You will also see how to trace SQL activity to diagnose problems.

Chapter 5, Optimizing Sort Operations will show the importance of optimizing sort operations to achieve better performance even when you don't see any explicit sort operations in your SQL code. In this chapter, we will see the difference between in-memory and on-disk sort, how an index can improve the performance by reducing or avoiding sort operations, how to perform *top-n* queries, and how to use aggregate functions, and the use of set operations.

Chapter 6, Optimizing PL/SQL Code will show how to optimize PL/SQL code in stored procedures, triggers, and user-defined functions. You will see the advantages of using bulk-collect and array processing, native compilation and function result cache.

Chapter 7, Improving the Oracle Optimizer is focused on how to help the Oracle Optimizer in choosing the best execution plan using various tools, tricks, and tips, to obtain better performance. You will see the use of hints, statistics, histograms, stored outlines, adaptive cursor sharing, SQL tuning sets, and SQL baselines.

Chapter 8, Other Optimizations will show how to use Client Side Result Cache, parallel SQL, CREATE TABLE AS SELECT, and direct path inserting to optimize performance in both queries and DML operations. You will also see how to use SQL*Loader and Data Pump to load data into your Oracle Database.

Chapter 9, Tuning Memory will show how to avoid different memory-related issues, starting with Operating System paging. You will learn how to properly configure the library cache, the shared pool, the Program Global Area (PGA), the User Global Area (UGA), and the database buffer cache.

Chapter 10, Tuning I/O will focus on how to optimize the I/O, learning how to distribute Oracle files and stripe objects on different disks, what RAID level is better for each type of database files. The use of asynchronous I/O, checkpoint and redo logs tuning are also discussed in this chapter.

Chapter 11, Tuning Contention will show how to prevent, detect, and tune contention-related issues. You will see both lock and latch contention, why they occur, and how to prevent and solve any issue related to concurrency and contention in your database.

In *Appendix A, Dynamic Performance Views* you will find a list of the most used dynamic performance views; for each view you will find a brief description and a list of the most useful fields of the view, to be used as a reference in your daily work.

In *Appendix B, A Summary of Oracle Packages Used for Performance Tuning* you will find a brief summary of Oracle supplied packages useful in order to solve performance-related problems.

What you need for this book

You need an Oracle Database 11gR2 instance available on your system; you can download Oracle Software from Oracle Technology Network at the following site:

```
http://www.oracle.com/technetwork/database/enterprise-edition/
downloads/index.html
```

In *Chapter 1* there is a recipe on how to set up the example database to follow the recipes in this book and to use the code presented.

Who this book is for

This book is aimed at software developers, software and data architects, and DBAs who are beginning to use the Oracle Database, and want to solve performance problems faster and in a rigorous way.

If you are an architect who wants to design fast performing applications, a DBA who is keen to dig into the causes of performance issues, or a developer who wants to learn why and where the application is running slowly this book will provide a good start for your career in performance tuning.

Conventions

In this book, you will find a number of styles of text that distinguish between different kinds of information. Here are some examples of these styles, and an explanation of their meaning.

Code words in text are shown as follows: "Drop the MYSTATS table."

A block of code is set as follows:

```
SELECT
   C.CUST_FIRST_NAME, C.CUST_LAST_NAME
FROM sh.CUSTOMERS C
WHERE C.CUST_YEAR_OF_BIRTH = 1949;
```

When we wish to draw your attention to a particular part of a code block, the relevant lines or items are set in bold:

```
SELECT
   C.CUST_FIRST_NAME, C.CUST_LAST_NAME
FROM sh.CUSTOMERS C
WHERE C.CUST_YEAR_OF_BIRTH = 1949;
```

Any command-line input or output is written as follows:

```
CONNECT sh@TESTDB/sh
```

New terms and **important words** are shown in bold. Words that you see on the screen, in menus or dialog boxes for example, appear in the text like this: "From Oracle database 9*i*R2 onwards, **Dynamic Sampling** was introduced."

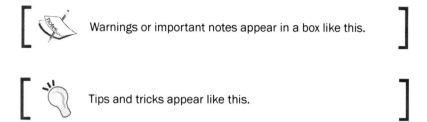

Warnings or important notes appear in a box like this.

Tips and tricks appear like this.

Reader feedback

Feedback from our readers is always welcome. Let us know what you think about this book—what you liked or may have disliked. Reader feedback is important for us to develop titles that you really get the most out of.

To send us general feedback, simply send an e-mail to feedback@packtpub.com, and mention the book title via the subject of your message.

If there is a topic that you have expertise in and you are interested in either writing or contributing to a book, see our author guide on www.packtpub.com/authors.

Customer support

Now that you are the proud owner of a Packt book, we have a number of things to help you to get the most from your purchase.

Downloading the example code

You can download the example code files for all Packt books you have purchased from your account at http://www.PacktPub.com. If you purchased this book elsewhere, you can visit http://www.PacktPub.com/support and register to have the files e-mailed directly to you.

Errata

Although we have taken every care to ensure the accuracy of our content, mistakes do happen. If you find a mistake in one of our books—maybe a mistake in the text or the code—we would be grateful if you would report this to us. By doing so, you can save other readers from frustration and help us improve subsequent versions of this book. If you find any errata, please report them by visiting http://www.packtpub.com/support, selecting your book, clicking on the **errata submission form** link, and entering the details of your errata. Once your errata are verified, your submission will be accepted and the errata will be uploaded on our website, or added to any list of existing errata, under the Errata section of that title. Any existing errata can be viewed by selecting your title from http://www.packtpub.com/support.

Piracy

Piracy of copyright material on the Internet is an ongoing problem across all media. At Packt, we take the protection of our copyright and licenses very seriously. If you come across any illegal copies of our works, in any form, on the Internet, please provide us with the location address or website name immediately so that we can pursue a remedy.

Please contact us at copyright@packtpub.com with a link to the suspected pirated material.

We appreciate your help in protecting our authors, and our ability to bring you valuable content.

Questions

You can contact us at questions@packtpub.com if you are having a problem with any aspect of the book, and we will do our best to address it.

1
Starting with Performance Tuning

Performance tuning is a complex process, which requires a deep knowledge of both physical and logical database structures. In this chapter, we will introduce the process and methodology to adopt in performance tuning an Oracle Database, covering the following recipes:

- Reviewing the performance tuning process
- Exploring the example database
- Acquiring data using a data dictionary and dynamic performance views
- Analyzing data using Statspack report
- Diagnosing performance issues using the alert log
- Analyzing data using Automatic Workload Repository (AWR)
- Analyzing data using Automatic Database Diagnostic Monitor (ADDM)
- A working example

Introduction

There are a wide range of issues that could lead to poor performance. Performance of our Oracle database problems could be related to different areas of the system:

- Application design
- Application code
- Memory
- I/O

- ► Resource contention
- ► Operating System
- ► CPU

When we want to tune a database in a proactive way, we can follow the previous list from the top to the bottom.

Issues in the first two areas generally lead the database to very bad performance and to scalability issues. The most common performance problems in an Oracle database related to application design and coding are as follows:

- ► Incorrect session management
- ► Poorly designed cursor management
    - ❑ Binding variables
    - ❑ Cursor sharing
    - ❑ Non-set operations
- ► Inadequate relational design
- ► Improper use of storage structures

Let's explain each performance problem listed in the previous paragraph. Troubles related to memory, input/output, contention, and operating systems will be explored in the following chapters. A well-tuned application can lead to a significant performance improvement, so it's natural to concentrate the first efforts on performance tuning to application design and coding.

Incorrect session management

Poor session management can lead to scalability problems. For example, if a web page logs on to a database, gets some data, and logs off; the time spent for the log on procedure could be an order of magnitude greater than the time required to execute the queries needed to bring the data which the user has requested.

Poorly designed cursor management

There are different problems related to cursor management.

The first rule in writing applications which connect to an Oracle database is to always use bind variables, which means not to include parameters in SQL statements as literals.

For example, we could code something like the following (using SQL*Plus, connected as user HR):

```
SQL>SELECT * FROM hr.jobs WHERE job_id = 'SA_MAN';
```

This is equivalent to the following:

```
SQL>VARIABLE JOBID VARCHAR2(10)
SQL>EXEC :JOBID := 'SA_MAN'
SQL>SELECT * FROM hr.jobs WHERE job_id = :JOBID;
```

The big difference between the two examples is in the way the database parses the statements when they are called more than once with different values. Executing the statements the second time, in the first case will require a hard parse, whereas in the second case, Oracle will reuse the execution plan prepared at the time of the first execution, resulting in a huge performance gain.

This behavior is due to the way Oracle checks whether a SQL statement is already in memory or needs to be parsed. A hash value of the SQL string is calculated, and is compared to the hash values already in memory. If we supply a different literal value each time, a new hash value will get generated for a SQL statement and hence Oracle has to parse the statement every time.

Using bind variables will not change the SQL string so Oracle has to parse the statement only once; from there on it will find the hash value in memory—if it doesn't age out—thus reusing the execution plan already existing in memory.

Cursor sharing is another problem related to the parse process. We can set the database parameter CURSOR_SHARING to the values SIMILAR or FORCE, to mitigate the drawbacks related to not using bind variables. In this situation, the database will parse two queries with a different SQL text to a single cursor; for example:

```
SQL>SELECT * FROM hr.jobs WHERE job_id = 'SA_MAN';
SQL>SELECT * FROM hr.jobs WHERE job_id = 'AC_ACCOUNT';
```

Both of these statements will be parsed to a single cursor if the parameter CURSOR_SHARING is set to one of the values mentioned.

When a query is dynamically built by the application—for example, to reflect different types of user-defined filters or sorting options—it's important that the statement is built always in the same way—using bind variables, of course—to facilitate the reuse of the cursors, mostly if the CURSOR_SHARING parameter is set to the value EXACT.

Another common problem related to cursor management, is the use of non-set operations. While for the human mind it is simpler to think of an algorithm as an iterative sequence of steps, relational databases are optimized for set operations. Many a times developers code something like the following example code:

```
CREATE OR REPLACE PROCEDURE example1 (
  JOBID IN hr.jobs.job_id%TYPE) IS
BEGIN
  DECLARE
  l_empid hr.employees.employee_id%TYPE;
  l_sal hr.employees.salary%TYPE;
  CURSOR jc IS SELECT e.employee_id, e.salary
    FROM hr.employees e
      INNER JOIN hr.jobs j ON j.job_id = e.job_id
    WHERE e.job_id = JOBID
    AND e.salary > (j.max_salary - j.min_salary) / 2;
  BEGIN
  OPEN jc;
  LOOP
    FETCH jc INTO l_empid, l_sal;
    EXIT WHEN jc%NOTFOUND;
    DBMS_OUTPUT.PUT_LINE(TO_CHAR(l_empid) || ' ' ||
      TO_CHAR(l_sal));
    UPDATE hr.employees SET salary = l_sal * 0.9
      WHERE employee_id = l_empid;
  END LOOP;
  CLOSE jc;
  END;
END;
```

This example is trivial, but it's good enough to explain the concept. In the procedure, there is a loop on the employees of a certain job, which decreases the salaries that are higher than the average for a particular job. The stored procedure compiles and executes well, but there is a better way to code this example, shown as follows:

```
CREATE OR REPLACE PROCEDURE example2 (
  JOBID IN hr.jobs.job_id%TYPE) IS
BEGIN
  UPDATE hr.employees e SET
    e.salary = e.salary * 0.9
  WHERE e.job_id = JOBID
  AND e.salary > (SELECT (j.max_salary - j.min_salary) / 2 FROM
hr.jobs j
      WHERE j.job_id = e.job_id);
END;
```

In the latter version we have only used one statement to achieve the same results. Besides the code length, the important thing here is that we thought in terms of set-operations, rather than in an iterative way. Relational databases perform better when we use this type of operation. We will see how much and why in *Chapter 4, Optimizing SQL Code* and *Chapter 6, Optimizing PL/SQL Code*, in the *Introducing arrays and bulk operations* and *Array processing and bulk-collect* recipes, respectively.

Inadequate relational design

A big issue could be the relational design of the database. Here we are not discussing academic ways to design a database system, because in the real-world sometimes a relational design could be less-than-perfect in terms of normalization, for example, to provide better performance in the way the data is used.

When we speak about bad relational design, we mean problems like **over-normalization**, which often leads to an overabundance of table joins to obtain the desired results.

Often, over-normalization is a problem which arises when we try to map an object-oriented model to a relational database: a good volume and operations analysis could help in designing the logical model of the database. For example, introducing a redundant column to a table can lead to better performance because the redundant data, otherwise, have to be calculated by scanning (in most cases) a big table.

Another big issue in relational design is related to the use of incorrect indexes on a table. Based on the data selection approach an application is going to take, correct indexes should be set on the table, and this is one of the design considerations while creating a relational database model.

Improper use of storage structures

The Oracle database logical structure is determined by the tablespace(s) and by the schema objects. Wrong choices about these structures often lead to bad performance.

While designing an Oracle database, we have a rich set of schema objects, and we have to answer questions like "Which is better, a bitmap index or a reverse key index?", looking at both the application and data.

In the latest releases of Oracle database, many operations to alter storage structures can be performed with the database online, with minimal performance decay, and without service shortage.

We will examine in depth the problems we have just been presented with in later chapters, namely, session management and relational design in *Chapter 2*, cursor management in *Chapter 4*, and storage structures in *Chapter 3*.

OK, let's begin!

Reviewing the performance tuning process

Tuning the performance of an Oracle database is a complex task, which requires in-depth knowledge in different areas. There are a lot of forums, documents, and tutorials online responding to many performance tuning issues related to Oracle Database; often, however, the information gathered from these sources may not be enough to solve the peculiar problem we are experiencing, because of different database versions, different server architectures, and a wide number of variables which make it difficult to find the correct recipe to resolve the symptoms we are facing.

Many would-be DBAs approach a performance problem with a bad attitude; that is, they pretend to solve performance issues without investigating the problem, or with little knowledge about what happens under the hood. Often this approach leads to solutions which don't work or—in the worst case—seem to work temporarily, presenting the same problem or another one after a while.

In the following section, we will see the performance tuning process adopted in this book, which can help us in finding the correct way to diagnose, solve, and prevent performance issues on Oracle Databases.

How to do it...

To solve a performance problem on the database, we need to follow these steps:

1. Elaborate a baseline.
2. Investigate the problem.
3. Assume a solution, a test case, and a rollback strategy.
4. Implement the solution and test for correctness.
5. Test the solution.
6. Compare the results.
7. If the results are not as good as expected, iterate the process.

How it works...

In the first step, we have to elaborate a baseline, because without a comparison element we will not be able to know if the adopted solution really solves the problems we are facing.

The kind of baseline to elaborate depends heavily on the performance issue. There are some performance indicators which should always be checked, while others are more detailed which can be verified only if a previous indicator points to a particular area of the database. After the baseline is decided for the particular problem we are investigating, it is time to automate the process of gathering data, so it is repeatable.

While investigating the problem the process is iterative, so you can return to the previous step to add other elements to the baseline, for final testing of our solution.

When the investigation drives us to assume a particular solution, before we start implementing it on the database we have to list all the changes we are going to do and elaborate a "rollback solution" for these changes. This is especially the case if we don't have the chance to test our solution over a test database similar to the production one which is suffering the problem. If we think, for example, that adding an index IX1 on table T1 could solve our performance problem, we have to prepare a SQL script to create the index, and another SQL script to drop it, in case we want to go back if something goes wrong. In Oracle 11g, we have the opportunity to create an invisible index and check the execution plan of the query, with minimal impact on other sessions.

We might want to prepare a test-case to test the solution we will implement. This task is simpler if we have isolated the problem very well, so we are able to reproduce the issue. If the problem is random, it might be a nightmare to isolate the steps that lead to poor performance. In the latter case, we could evaluate the frequency of the problem, so we could test our solution by measuring the number of occurrences and comparing the results.

After the solution has been implemented, it must be tested with the same process that created the baseline. Check the results of the measure process and decide if the solution has solved the issue. If the results are not acceptable, iterate the whole process until there is a satisfactory outcome.

There's more...

The performance tuning process is a never-ending cycle; even when we solve our performance issue there will be another aspect of the system we can tune to in order to obtain better performance, or we need to satisfy more stringent requirements.

Due to these considerations, the iterative process of performance tuning that will be used throughout the book is represented in the following diagram:

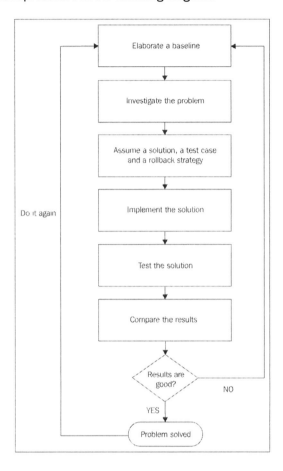

To elaborate a baseline, keep track of how the system—and not only the database—is performing. We need unbiased data to compare before and after different solutions are implemented in the systems.

 Performance of the system here means performance of the server, I/O, network, database, the application, and other factors.

If there is a generic "slow response-time problem", and new hardware resources (CPU, RAM) are added to the database server, this may lead to a situation where it performs worse than before. With a good baseline, before adding more resources, we could evaluate if the problem we are experiencing is related to the lack of enough hardware power—for example RAM—or something else.

To describe a good baseline we need as much data as possible; most are acquired directly from the database itself, as we will see in the next section. There is information from other sources: Operating System logs, performance counters, application logs, trace files, network statistics, and the like.

In today's multi-layered applications, it's simple to say "the database is slow" when an application is suffering poor performance, but there will be many cases when the database is performing very well but the application responsiveness is very weak.

With a solid baseline, we can isolate the layer in which the problem first occurred and concentrate our efforts on that application layer. After a baseline is established, start investigating the problem.

In the rest of the book, we will learn how to interpret the results of the baseline to correctly identify the problem. Sorry, there isn't a bullet list or a magic wand; this phase is based on knowledge and previous experience. If a simple causal-effect was in place, it would have already been coded with an automatic solution or a specific diagnostic advice, implemented in the database itself. There are several automatic diagnostic tuning features in the latest releases of Oracle database; **SQL Tuning Advisor, SQL Access Advisor, Automatic Database Diagnostic Monitor**. These database-centric tools help solve common performance problems, which tend to be easily identified. The real tuning process starts when the magic doesn't work, or they don't work as good as we need them to.

We have seen the most common database performance issues in the previous recipe, divided into several categories to help us in the investigation phase. During this stage, we decide what database area is a bottleneck; for instance, the memory, the I/O, and the SQL code.

Once we have identified and delimited the database area involved in the performance problem, we can assume a solution to the issue. As previously stated, both a test case and a rollback strategy are necessary—the former to check the proposed solution, the latter to revert back if the proposed solution wasn't satisfactory.

Once we have the solution, implementing it is often a trivial task, such as writing a small SQL script to alter a database object or a initialization parameter. Be sure that the solution is implemented using reproducible steps, especially when the task is quite complex or we have to test the solution in a staged database before the production.

At the end of the implementation, we have to test the solution to verify its correctness—probably in a test environment—and to know if the expected performance gain has been reached.

To test the solution there are various scenarios, depending on the work done in previous steps and by the development team. A test case will verify the results; if there are application test sets, they can be used to verify the correctness of the solution, especially if the application logic has changed.

After we have assured ourselves about the correctness of the solution implemented, compare the performance of the database (and of the application) to the baseline gathered in the first step of the process.

If the comparison shows that we have not solved the puzzle, well, let's revert back to the applied solution and start again from the first step, investigating the problem better or assuming another solution. Alternately, if the result is satisfactory, very well, let's start again from the first step to solve another problem. Always remember that the tuning process is something which evolves from the application design and lasts throughout the application life cycle.

In describing the performance tuning process, we have stated a baseline. The Oracle database helps us even in this task, with different tools that we can use to monitor the database itself and to take measurements of various performance indicators.

In the following recipes, we will introduce different tools to acquire performance data from the database, illustrating the guidelines to use them. The diagnostic tools presented are:

- Data Dictionary and Dynamic Performance Views
    - Analyze command
    - Analyze schema and database with `DBMS_UTILITY` package
- `DBMS_STATS` package
- Statspack report
- Alert log and trace files
- Automatic Workload Repository (AWR)
- Automatic Database Diagnostic Monitor (ADDM)

The tools specific for tuning SQL code will be presented in *Chapter 4, Optimizing SQL Code*.

Let's spend some time on **Oracle Enterprise Manager** (**OEM**). It is a graphical web-based application, and it is the main tool the Oracle DBA uses to configure and monitor the database in non-console mode.

In OEM, there is a performance palette which presents a dashboard with many graphs and indicators, all updated live. At the bottom of the page, there are additional links to the most common tasks related to performance tuning.

 OEM itself is not a performance tuning tool, but it's just a front-end to the tools and functions in the previously mentioned list. It's a good idea to familiarize yourself with OEM and its user interface. However, if a DBA knows what happens in the backstage, he/she will be able to do the right thing with any tool, and he/she will not feel lost if his/her favorite tool or GUI isn't up and running (and sometimes this is a real scenario at the customer site).

See also

- ▶ *Acquiring data using Data dictionary and dynamic performance views* recipes in this chapter
- ▶ *Appendix B, Tools and Packages*

Exploring the example database

In this recipe, we will prepare a database to use for our examples.

Getting ready

We need an Oracle Database 11gR2 system up and running to create our database. The host system could be a UNIX/Linux or Windows physical or virtual machine. If you want to use a virtual machine, be sure to follow the minimum CPU and memory requirements for the Oracle installation.

If you have installed the database software along with the **Create Database** option, then you have already set up a database with the necessary schema installed.

How to do it...

We will use the default demo database installed by the default OLTP template of Oracle Database Configuration Assistant (DBCA) for all our examples.

 You can find the official Oracle Database Installation Guide 11gR2 for Linux at `http://download.oracle.com/docs/cd/E11882_01/install.112/e16763/toc.htm`.

1. Log on to the Operating System as a member of the administrative group, authorized to install Oracle software and to create and run database instances.

2. Launch DBCA (for Windows users: **Start | Programs | Oracle – home_name | Configuration and Migration Tools | Database Configuration Assistant**) for *nix systems enter the following command at system prompt:

   `$ dbca`

   Please note that the `dbca` executable is by default in the `$ORACLE_HOME/bin` directory.

3. A welcome screen is shown. Click **Next**.

4. You are presented with some options. Select the first, namely **Create a database**, and click **Next**.

5. You are presented a list of database templates. Choose the first, namely **General purpose / OLTP**, and click **Next**.

6. You are asked for the global database name and SID; enter `TESTDB` in the global database name (the SID should be set accordingly) and click **Next**.

7. In the next screen—shown in the following screenshot—leave the default options selected (OEM configuration). If you wish, you can enable e-mail notifications, checking the corresponding flag and entering the SMTP server to use (something like `smtp.yourdomain.com` or `smtp.yourISP.com`) and the e-mail address where the alerts will be delivered. Click **Next** to go to the next screen.

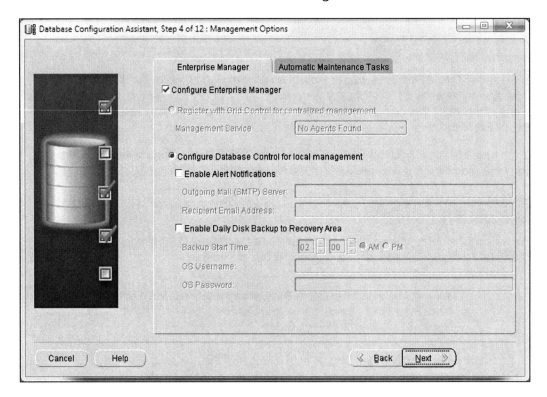

8. Choose to use the same password for all administrative accounts, enter the password you want to use twice, and click **Next**. If you are advised that the password you entered is weak (not responding to the minimum complexity requirements) you can ignore the message and go on. Please note that for a production database these are *very bad choices*, but we are installing a demo database for testing purposes only and don't want to bother with security issues.

9. In the next screen, leave the default option for the files position (**Use Database File Locations from Template**) and click **Next**.

10. Leave the default options for the flash recovery area and click **Next**.

11. In the next screen, check the **Sample Schemas** flag and click **Finish**.

12. You are presented with the operations summary. Click **OK** and wait until the database creation process is finished.

13. At the end of the creation process, we have to unlock the accounts created. In the summary form, there is a **Password Manager** button; click on it, and you will be presented with the list of accounts created.

14. Find the following accounts: **BI, HR, IX, OC, OE, PM, SH** and uncheck the second column (unlocking them). Insert the password for the accounts in the last two columns, setting them the same as the account name.

> You can click on the username column to sort accordingly.
>
> Don't use sample schemas or passwords the same as the username in production databases!

Now our TESTDB database is ready for experimenting.

How it works...

Oracle DBCA lets us create a database using predefined templates. For our examples, we will use the default example schemas provided by Oracle (which are installed in the EXAMPLE tablespace).

The sample schemas are HR (Human Resources), OE (Order Entry), OC (Order Catalog), PM (Product Media), IX (Information eXchange), SH (Sales History), and BI (Business Intelligence). We will use mostly HR and SH schemas.

There's more...

If we want to reset the sample schemas to the initial state, we can use the script mksample. sql located in the $ORACLE_HOME/demo/schema/ directory. This script requires eleven parameters, with the following syntax:

```
SQL>@?/demo/schema/mksample systempwd syspwd hrpwd oepwd pmpwd ixpwd
shpwd bipwd default_tablespace temp_tablespace log_file_directory/
```

> Please note that the log_file_directory is an already existing folder and also the path must be terminated by a slash.

Our database—assuming test as the system and system password—will be reset with the following statement:

```
SQL>@?/demo/schema/mksample test test hr oe pm ix sh bi EXAMPLE
TEMP testlog/
```

Please note that in the default installation of Oracle Database 11gR2 Enterprise Edition the `mksample.sql` script is not present. You can find it in the Companion CD.

Acquiring data using a data dictionary and dynamic performance views

In the Oracle database, there are many views which can be queried to acquire data about the database state. They are divided into **data dictionary views**, with a name similar to `DBA_*`, and **dynamic performance views**, named something similar to `V$_*`.

Getting ready

When we use a standard template in Oracle DBCA to create a database, both data dictionary views and dynamic performance views are in place after database creation. If we prefer to use our own scripts to create the database, we need to launch at least the `catalog.sql` and `catproc.sql` scripts to populate the data dictionary with the views we need. These scripts are located in the `rdbms/admin` subdirectory of the Oracle Home directory.

To collect timing information in the dynamic performance views, we have to set the parameter `TIMED_STATISTICS=TRUE` in the `init.ora` file of our database instance. We can also accomplish this requirement with the following SQL statement:

```
ALTER SYSTEM SET TIMED_STATISTICS = TRUE SCOPE = BOTH;
```

 Please note that the default value for the `TIMED_STATISTICS` parameter is already `TRUE` and that there isn't any perceptible performance gain in changing this default value to `FALSE`.

How to do it...

We can query the data dictionary views and the dynamic performance views like any other view in the database, using SQL statements.

We can also query `DBA_VIEWS`, which is a data dictionary view showing other views in the database:

```
select view_name from dba_views
  where view_name like 'DBA%' order by 1
```

We can query the `V$FIXED_TABLE` view to get a list of all the `V$` dynamic performance views and `X$` tables:

```
select name from V$FIXED_TABLE order by 1;
```

 You can find the definition of each view we will use in the book in *Appendix A*, *Dynamic Performance Views*

How it works...

Data dictionary views are owned by the user `SYS` and there is a public synonym for each of them. They expose data about database objects, for example, tables and indexes.

In Oracle Database 11gR2 Enterprise Edition, the database installed from the DBCA template will have more than 800 data dictionary views available. We will present the data dictionary views that we need in our recipes when we have to query them.

Even dynamic performance views are owned by the user `SYS`; they are synonyms to `V_$*` views. Those views are based on `X$` tables, which are undocumented structures populated at instance start-up. The data dictionary view contains two kinds of data, namely, fields that store information on the characteristics of the object, and other fields that collect information dynamically from object usage.

For example, in the `DBA_TABLES` there are fields about the physical structure of the table (such as `TABLESPACE_NAME`, `PCT_FREE`, `INITIAL_EXTENT`) and other fields which expose statistics on the table contents (such as `NUM_ROWS`, `AVG_SPACE`, `AVG_ROW_LEN`).

To collect these statistical data we have to perform the `ANALYZE` statement. For a table, we will execute the following statement:

```
ANALYZE TABLE hr.employees COMPUTE STATISTICS;
```

To speed up and automate the analysis of many objects, we can use `DBMS_UTILITY.analyze_schema` or `DBMS_UTILITY.analyze_database` to analyze all the objects in a schema in the first case, or in the database in the latter. To analyze the objects of the HR schema, we will execute the following statement:

```
EXEC DBMS_UTILITY.analyze_schema('HR','COMPUTE');
```

 For both the `ANALYZE` command and the `DBMS_UTILITY` functions, we have two choices, which are either to compute the statistics or to estimate these values based on the analysis of a restricted set of data. When `ESTIMATE` is chosen, we have to specify the number of rows to use for the sample or a percentage.

Oracle advises us to use another method to compute statistics, namely, the DBMS_STATS package, which allows deleting statistics, exporting, importing, and gathering statistics in parallel. The following statement analyses the schema HR:

```
EXEC DBMS_STATS.gather_schema_stats('HR');
```

 ANALYZE and the use of DBMS_UTILITY illustrated earlier are supported for backward compatibility only; use the package DBMS_STATS to collect statistics.

Similarly, we can gather statistics on tables, indexes, or database. Even with DBMS_STATS we can use the ESTIMATE method, as in the first of the following examples:

```
EXEC DBMS_STATS.gather_database_stats(estimate_percent => 20);
EXEC DBMS_STATS.gather_table_stats('HR', 'EMPLOYEES');
EXEC DBMS_STATS.gather_index_stats('HR', 'EMP_JOB_IX');
```

Using the DBMS_STATS package we can also delete statistics, as shown:

```
EXEC DBMS_STATS.delete_table_stats('HR', 'EMPLOYEES');
```

To transfer statistics between different databases, we have to use a statistics table, as shown in the following steps:

1. Create the statistics table on the *source* database.
2. Export the statistics from the data dictionary to the statistics table.
3. Move the statistics table (Export/Import, Datapump, Copy) to the *target* database.
4. Import the statistics from the statistics table to the data dictionary.
5. Drop the statistics table.

The corresponding statements to execute on the *source* database are as follows:

```
EXEC DBMS_STATS.create_stat_table('DBA_SCHEMA', 'MY_STAT_TABLE');
EXEC DBMS_STATS.export_schema_stats('DBA_SCHEMA', 'MY_STAT_TABLE', NULL,
'APP_SCHEMA');
```

With these statements we have created the statistics table MY_STAT_TABLE in the DBA_SCHEMA and populated it with data from the APP_SCHEMA (for example, HR).

Then we transfer the MY_STAT_TABLE to the *target* database; using the export/import command line utilities we export the table from source database and then import the table into the target database, in which we execute the following statements:

```
EXEC DBMS_STATS.import_schema_stats('APP_SCHEMA', 'MY_STAT_TABLE', NULL,
'DBA_SCHEMA');
EXEC DBMS_STATS.drop_stat_table('DBA_SCHEMA', 'MY_STAT_TABLE');
```

In the example, we have transferred statistics about the entire schema APP_SCHEMA. We can choose to transfer statistics for the entire database, a table, an index, or a column, using the corresponding import_* and export_* procedures of the DBMS_STATS package.

There's more...

The COMPUTE STATISTICS and ESTIMATE STATISTICS parameters of the ANALYZE command are supported only for backward compatibility by Oracle. However, there are other functionalities of the command that allow validating the structure of a table, index, cluster, materialized views, or to list the chained or migrated rows:

```
ANALYZE TABLE employees VALIDATE STRUCTURE;

ANALYZE TABLE employees LIST CHAINED ROWS INTO CHAINED_ROWS;
```

The first statement validates the structure of the EMPLOYEES table, while the second command lists the chained rows of the same table into the CHAINED_ROWS table (created with the script utlchain.sql or utlchn1.sql.)

See also

  ▶ *Avoiding row chaining* in *Chapter 3, Optimizing Storage Structures*

Analyzing data using Statspack reports

Statspack was first introduced in Oracle Database 8i R8.1.6. We shall now look at how to use this tool.

Getting ready

To use Statspack, we have to set up a tablespace to store its structures; if we don't, in the installation process we have to choose an already existing tablespace—SYSAUX is the tablespace proposed by default. To create the tablespace, we will use the following command (with the necessary change in the datafile parameter, according to the platform used and the database location):

```
CREATE TABLESPACE statspack

DATAFILE '/u01/oracle/db/STATSPACK.DBF' SIZE 200 M REUSE

EXTENT MANAGEMENT LOCAL UNIFORM SIZE 512K

SEGMENT SPACE MANAGEMENT AUTO PERMANENT ONLINE;
```

To collect timing information in the dynamic performance views, we have to set the parameter TIMED_STATISTICS=TRUE, as shown in the recipe about the dynamic performance view.

How to do it...

Follow these steps to make use of the Statspack tool:

1. Connect to the database with a user with the SYSDBA privilege and run the spcreate.sql script from the $ORACLE_HOME/rdbms/adminr directory. This script will ask for a password to assign to the PERFSTAT user.

2. We will then be asked for the tablespace to use. Select the previously created tablespace by entering its name (STATSPACK). When the script asks for the temporary tablespace just press *Enter* to use the default temporary tablespace defined in the system.

3. The script will create the user PERFSTAT, identified by the password provided, and all the objects needed to run the tool.

   After the tool is created, we can collect statistics by executing the following procedure:

   EXEC STATSPACK.snap;

   With this simple command, we have created a snapshot in the Statspack table.

4. When we have at least two snapshots, we can create a report using a pair of them. To do so, we will execute the spreport.sql script.

   The script will show us the completed snapshots and we will be asked for the ID of the two which we want to compare.

5. The script will ask for the name to give to the report—the default will be sp_id1_id2, where id1 and id2 are the beginning and ending snapshots chosen in the previous step.

At the end of the process, we will find our Statspack report.

How it works...

The spcreate.sql script internally launches the spcusr.sql, spctab.sql, and spcpkg.sql scripts. For every script, after the execution, we will find a corresponding file with the extension changed to .lis with the spool of the actions performed. In case anything goes wrong, we can launch the spdrop.sql script to rollback the actions performed by spcreate.sql.

A snapshot of Statspack contains information from the dynamic performance views. As these views are emptied at database start-up, it makes no sense to elaborate Statspack performance reports with the use of snapshots taken before and after a database shutdown.

The tables used to collect the data have names which start with STATS$, and are based on the corresponding V$ dynamic performance views. For example, the table STAT$DB_CACHE_ADVICE has the same columns of the view V$DB_CACHE_ADVICE, with three columns added in front of them, SNAP_ID, DBID, INSTANCE_NUMBER, which are used to identify the snapshot, the database, and the instance respectively.

> If you want to use Statspack in an Oracle Real Application Cluster (RAC) environment, you have to launch STATSPACK.snap connecting to every instance you want to gather data from.

The report is divided into several sections:

- General information about the database instance and the snapshots used
- Cache sizes (buffer cache, shared pool, and log buffer)
- Load profile (instance events per second and per transaction)
- Instance efficiency indicators (buffer cache and shared pool statistics)
- Top five timed events, showing the first five events sorted by total wait time in seconds
- Host CPU and Instance CPU, showing the load on the CPU
- Virtual Memory Paging and Memory Statistics
- Wait events, foreground, background, and both foreground and background grouped together
- SQL ordered by different criteria, by CPU, by elapsed time for DB, by gets, by executions, by parse calls, by sharable memory, by version count
- Instance activity statistics
- Tablespace and file I/O
- Memory, buffer pool, and PGA statistics
- Latch activity
- Dictionary cache statistics
- Library cache activity
- SGA activity
- init.ora parameters

There's more...

We can configure Statspack to collect different amounts of data and to produce a report on specific SQL; we wish to automate snapshot collection, too.

Collecting different amounts of data

We can configure Statspack to collect more or less data. The LEVEL parameter can be used to instruct the tool about the kind of information we want to store in the snapshot. The following table summarizes the available levels (the default level is 5):

Level	Description
0	General performance statistics
5	Additional data: High resource usage SQL statements
6	Additional data: SQL Plans and SQL Plan usage information for high resource usage SQL statements
7	Additional data: Segment level statistics including logical and physical reads, row locks, and so on
10	Additional statistics: Parent and Child latches

We can use a different level parameter for a single snapshot, passing the corresponding level to the STATSPACK.snap procedure:

```
EXEC STATSPACK.snap(i_snap_level=>10);
```

If we want our selection made permanent for subsequent snapshots, we add another parameter to the procedure:

```
EXEC STATSPACK.snap(i_snap_level=>6, i_modify_parameter=>'true');
```

If we want to change the level of the snapshots without taking one, we will use the following statement:

```
EXECUTE STATSPACK.modify_statspack_parameter(i_snap_level=>6);
```

Producing a report on a specific SQL

Statspack provides another script, sprepsql.sql, which allows us to elaborate a more detailed report on a specific SQL statement.

If we find a statement in the Statspack report that we want to investigate deeper, we can launch this script, indicating the beginning and ending snapshots, and the "Old Hash Value" (a pre-10g memory) of the SQL statement on which we want to elaborate the report.

If in our Statspack report (elaborated between the snapshots identified by 2 and 3) we have a row in the **SQL ordered by CPU** section that is similar to the one shown in the following screenshot:

```
SQL ordered by CPU  DB/Inst: TESTDB/testdb  Snaps: 2-3
-> Total DB CPU (s):          51
-> Captured SQL accounts for  126.6% of Total DB CPU
-> SQL reported below exceeded  1.0% of Total DB CPU


    CPU                 CPU per          Elapsd                    Old
  Time (s)  Executions  Exec (s)  %Total  Time (s)  Buffer Gets  Hash Value
---------- ------------ --------- ------ ---------- --------------- ----------
   50.15          1       50.15   97.8     55.77         1,718 3787177051
Module: SQL*Plus
BEGIN Chapter1.Workload2; END;
```

And we want to investigate the related statement, we can launch the sprepsql.sql script and indicate ID 2 as begin, ID 3 as end, and 3787177051 as Old Hash Value.

The script will ask for the filename and will then produce a detailed report for the statement analyzed.

Automating snapshot generation

We can automate snapshot generation in various ways. Besides using a Unix cron job or a Windows Scheduled Task, we can instruct the database to capture the snapshots with a simple job. There is the spauto.sql script in the $ORACLE_HOME/rdbms/admin directory to set up an hourly snapshot. The script uses DBMS_JOB to schedule the snapshots.

Statspack maintenance

We can purge the no longer needed snapshots with the use of the spurge.sql script, indicating the ID of the first and the last snapshot to delete. Before deleting the data, we may want to export the PERFSTAT schema.

The sptrunc.sql script, instead, deletes all the data collected. All the scripts are in the $ORACLE_HOME/rdbms/admin directory.

To completely uninstall Statspack, there is the already mentioned spdrop.sql script, which has to be executed with SYSDBA privileges.

Diagnosing performance issues using the alert log

To diagnose certain performance issues, even the alert log can be used successfully.

Getting ready

There are some parameters to look at in the `init.ora` file of our database instance.

The parameter `BACKGROUND_DUMP_DEST` indicates the directory in which the **alert log** is located. If the parameter `LOG_CHECKPOINTS_TO_ALERT` is set to `TRUE`, we will find even checkpoint information in the alert log. By default this parameter is set to `FALSE`.

Before starting, we can issue the following command:

```
ALTER SYSTEM SET LOG_CHECKPOINTS_TO_ALERT = TRUE;

SHOW PARAMETER BACKGROUND_DUMP_DEST
```

This writes checkpoint information to the alert log and shows the directory in which we will find the alert log file (named `alert_<instance_name>.log`).

How to do it...

The following steps will demonstrate how to use the alert log:

1. In the alert log, we can find information like the following:

   ```
   Sun Sep 19 12:25:26 2010
   Thread 1 advanced to log sequence 5 (LGWR switch)
   Current log# 2 seq# 5 mem# 0: D:\APP\ORACLE\ORADATA\TESTDB\
   REDO02.LOG
   ```

   This informs us of a log-switch.

2. We can then verify the time between log switches.

   If we have set the parameter `LOG_CHECKPOINTS_TO_ALERT` to `TRUE`, we will also see lines like these in the alert log:

   ```
   Sat Sep 25 20:18:01 2010
   Beginning global checkpoint up to RBA [0x16.fd.10], SCN: 1296271
   Completed checkpoint up to RBA [0x16.fd.10], SCN: 1296271
   ```

   Then we can calculate checkpoint performance.

How it works...

The database writes information on the alert log about log switches and checkpoints. We can inspect the alert log to diagnose a possible problem with log files.

There's more...

We can force a log switch by using the following command:

```
ALTER SYSTEM SWITCH LOGFILE;
```

A checkpoint can be forced by using the following statement:

```
ALTER SYSTEM CHECKPOINT;
```

See also

- ▸ We will see the use of SQL_TRACE and TKPROF to generate trace files and the corresponding report over SQL activity of a particular session in *Tracing SQL activity with SQL Trace and TKPROF* in *Chapter 4, Optimizing SQL Code*

Analyzing data using Automatic Workload Repository (AWR)

With Oracle Database 10g, Automatic Workload Repository (AWR) was introduced. It is a tool that extends the key concepts of Statspack.

In this recipe, we will create a manual snapshot, a baseline, and some reports.

Getting ready

To use AWR, the STATISTICS_LEVEL parameter of the init.ora file must be set to the value TYPICAL or ALL.

 With the default setting TYPICAL, all the statistics needed for self-management functionalities are collected, providing best overall performance. Using the parameter ALL the database will collect all the statistics included in the TYPICAL settings, as well as timed operating system statistics and row source execution statistics.

We can change the parameter online with the following statement without shutting down the database:

```
ALTER SYSTEM SET STATISTICS_LEVEL = TYPICAL;
```

How to do it...

The following steps demonstrate use of AWR:

1. To make a manual snapshot using AWR, we use the following stored procedure:

    ```
    EXEC DBMS_WORKLOAD_REPOSITORY.create_snapshot();
    ```

    With the default settings in place, AWR creates a snapshot every hour, and the data collected are stored for seven days.

2. To modify the interval or the grace period of the snapshots, we can use the `modify_snapshot_settings` procedure, as shown:

    ```
    EXEC DBMS_WORKLOAD_REPOSITORY.modify_snapshot_settings(interval =>
    30);
    ```

    ```
    EXEC DBMS_WORKLOAD_REPOSITORY.modify_snapshot_settings(retention
    => 21600);
    ```

3. In AWR, we can also create a **baseline** to compare performances. A baseline is a set of snapshots which will be held to compare with the same kind of data in the future.

    We could have, for example, a baseline for the daily transactional work and a baseline for a batch job or a peak (quarter end). We can define a baseline indicating the start and end snapshots to be used, and we can name it:

    ```
    EXEC DBMS_WORKLOAD_REPOSITORY.create_baseline(Start_snap_id => 1,
    end_snap_id => 11, baseline_name => 'Friday off-peak');
    ```

4. To generate a report, we will use the `awrrpt.sql` script, located in the `$ORACLE_HOME/rdbms/admin` folder. The script will ask to choose the output format (text or HTML) and the number of days to use to filter the snapshots.

5. Then they will be presented the list of the snapshots, according to the parameter chosen in the previous step, and we are asked for the first and the last snapshot to be used. The last question is about the name of the file to generate the output to. The report generated is very similar to the Statspack report.

How it works...

As with Statspack, even AWR collects data and statistics from the database and stores them in tables. With AWR the concept of baseline is introduced.

The baselines can be fixed, moving window, or templates. The baseline we have defined in the previous example is fixed, because it corresponds to a specific time period in the past. The moving windows baseline corresponds to the AWR data within the entire retention period, and it's useful when used with adaptive thresholds. The baseline templates, instead, are created for a future time period, and can be single or repeating.

In the first statement of step 2, we have set the interval between snapshots to 30 minutes; in the second statement the retention period of the snapshots collected is set to 21600 minutes, which corresponds to 15 days.

The adaptive thresholds just mentioned consent to adapt the thresholds of a performance metric according to the workload of the system, eliminating false alerts. From Oracle 11*g*, adaptive thresholds are adjusted based on different workload patterns (for example, a system used for OLTP in daytime and for batch jobs at night) automatically recognized by the database.

We have created a report in the previous example by using the `awrrpt.sql` script. There are other reports available, generated by a corresponding script in the same folder; for example, `awrrpti.sql` is the same as `awrrpt.sql`, but for a specific database instance. `awrsqrpt.sql` generates a report for a particular SQL statement, like the script `sprepsql.sql` for Statspack. The corresponding script `awrsqrpti.sql` prepares the same report for a specific database instance.

There are also compare period reports, which allow us to compare not two snapshots but two AWR reports. If we have a database which performs well in a certain period, and we experiment a lack of performance in another period, we can elaborate two reports for the first and the latter period, and then compare the reports among them, to point out the differences and try to identify the issue.

For example, in step 4, we have created a baseline based on the snapshots with IDs from 1 to 11, and we name it "Friday off-peak".

The timespan of the two reports we are comparing isn't important, because AWR normalizes the data according to the different timeframe.

Compare period reports can be launched from Oracle Enterprise Manager or using the script `awrddrpt.sql` (the script `awrddrpti.sql` to concentrate the result on a single instance).

There's more...

We can specify the adaptive thresholds as a percentage of the maximum value observed in the moving window baseline, or as a statistical percentile, ranging from 0.95 to 0.9999—from five observations expected to exceed the value in 100 to 1 observation in 10,000.

Analyzing data using Automatic Database Diagnostic Monitor (ADDM)

In this recipe, we present the Automatic Database Diagnostic Monitor, a tool which analyzes the data collected by AWR to diagnose the cause of a performance problem, providing advice on how to solve the issue.

Getting ready

ADDM is enabled by default in Oracle Database 11g; it depends upon two configuration parameters of the init.ora file, STATISTICS_LEVEL and CONTROL_MANAGEMENT_PACK_ ACCESS. The value for these parameters should be TYPICAL or ALL for the former and DIAGNOSTIC or DIAGNOSTIC+TUNING for the latter. To show the current parameter values, we can use the following statement:

```
SHOW PARAMETER STATISTICS_LEVEL

SHOW PARAMETER CONTROL_MANAGEMENT_PACK_ACCESS
```

While to set the parameters we can use the following commands:

```
ALTER SYSTEM SET STATISTICS_LEVEL = TYPICAL;

ALTER SYSTEM SET CONTROL_MANAGEMENT_PACK_ACCESS = 'DIAGNOSTIC+TUNING';
```

We are now ready to diagnose a problem using ADDM.

How to do it...

The following steps will demonstrate how to use ADDM:

1. To run the ADDM in **Database mode** (all instances of the database will be analyzed), we will use the following statement where the parameters 3 and 5 in these steps are the numbers identifying the beginning and ending snapshots to be used:

```
VAR task_name VARCHAR2(30);

BEGIN

   :task_name := 'Report for 3 to 5';

   DBMS_ADDM.ANALYZE_DB (:task_name, 3, 5);

END;
```

2. To run the ADDM in **Instance mode** (a single instance of the database will be analyzed), we will use the following statement:

```
VAR task_name VARCHAR2(30);
BEGIN
  :task_name := 'Report for 3 to 5 inst. 1';
  DBMS_ADDM.ANALYZE_INST (:task_name, 3, 5, 1);
END;
```

3. To run the ADDM in **Partial mode** (a subset of all database instances will be analyzed), we will use the following statement:

```
VAR task_name VARCHAR2(30);
BEGIN
  :task_name := 'Custom for 3 to 5 inst. 1,2';
  DBMS_ADDM.ANALYZE_INST (:task_name, '1,2', 3, 5);
END;
```

4. To view the results we will query the DBMS_ADDM.GET_REPORT function, passing the name of the task used in generating the reports:

```
SELECT DBMS_ADDM.get_report('Report for 3 to 5') FROM DUAL;
SELECT DBMS_ADDM.get_report('Report for 3 to 5 inst. 1') FROM
DUAL;
SELECT DBMS_ADDM.get_report('Custom for 3 to 5 inst. 1,2') FROM
DUAL;
```

Each line in the previous code will display the corresponding ADDM report.

How it works...

Automatic Database Diagnostic Monitor runs automatically every time a new snapshot is taken by AWR (by default every hour), and the corresponding report is built comparing the last two snapshots available, so we have an ADDM report every hour.

With the statement presented, we can run a report between snapshots to identify possible problems. The reports can be built, for a Real Application Cluster configuration, with three analysis models: database, instance, and partial. In non-RAC databases, only instance analysis is possible because there is only one instance of the database.

We can see the reports with SQL*Plus using the `DBMS_ADDM.GET_REPORT` function, which returns a CLOB containing the report (80-columns formatted), or we can use Oracle Enterprise Manager to view the reports generated both in automatic or manual mode. In OEM, we can view ADDM findings in the homepage in the Diagnostic Summary information. We can choose **Advisor Central** on the bottom of the page to see a list of the ADDM reports available, as shown in the following screenshot:

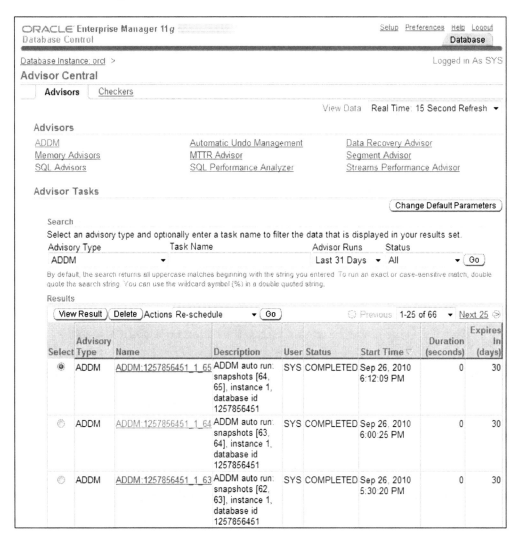

Clicking on the name link in the previous list we can view the corresponding report; in the following screenshot, we can see an example of an ADDM report viewed through OEM:

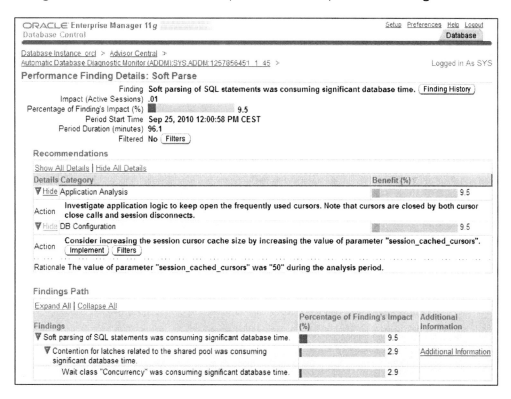

There's more...

The parameter DBIO_EXPECTED influences the ADDM analysis of I/O performance, because it describes the expected I/O subsystem performance, measuring the average time needed to read a single database block. The default value of the parameter is 10 milliseconds, corresponding to the average time of common hard disks. Please note that this measure includes the seek time.

If our I/O subsystem is significantly slower or faster, we may end up with possible false alerts or no alerts at all. We can adjust the parameter issuing the following statement:

```
EXEC DBMS_ADVISOR.SET_DEFAULT_TASK_PARAMETER('ADDM', 'DBIO_EXPECTED',
12000);
```

The numeric value is the time expressed in microseconds.

> ▸ *Analyzing data using Automatic Workload Repository (AWR)* in this chapter

A working example

In this recipe we will present a simple example of a performance tuning session, applying the recipes seen earlier.

Getting ready

The example is based on the SH schema. Be sure Statspack is installed, as presented in an earlier recipe.

How to do it...

The following steps demonstrate a simple example using the SH schema:

1. We assume the user PERFSTAT with the password PERFSTAT and the user SH with the password SH. The TESTDB database is the default instance.

2. Launch SQL*Plus and connect to the SH schema:

   ```
   $ sqlplus SH/SH
   ```

3. Create the package Chapter1:

   ```
   CREATE OR REPLACE PACKAGE Chapter1 AS
     PROCEDURE Workload;
     PROCEDURE Foo(CUSTID IN sh.sales.cust_id%TYPE);
   END;
   /

   CREATE OR REPLACE PACKAGE BODY Chapter1 AS
     PROCEDURE Workload IS
     BEGIN
      FOR i in 1 .. 50000
      LOOP
   ```

```
     Foo(i);
    END LOOP;
   END Workload;
   PROCEDURE Foo(CUSTID IN sh.sales.cust_id%TYPE) IS
   BEGIN
    DECLARE
     l_stmt VARCHAR2(2000);
    BEGIN
     l_stmt := 'SELECT * FROM sh.sales s WHERE s.cust_id = ' ||
     TO_CHAR(CUSTID);
     EXECUTE IMMEDIATE l_stmt;
    END;
    END Foo;
   END;
   /
```

4. Now we create the initial snapshot:

   ```
   CONNECT PERFSTAT/PERFSTAT
   EXEC statspack.snap;
   ```

5. Execute the test workload:

   ```
   CONNECT SH/SH
   EXEC Chapter1.Workload;
   ```

6. Now we can elaborate the end snapshot:

   ```
   CONNECT PERFSTAT/PERFSTAT
   EXEC statspack.snap;
   ```

7. Finally we can launch the report creation:

   ```
   SQL>@?/RDBMS/ADMIN/SPREPORT.SQL
   ```

8. When asked, select the last two snapshots created to produce the Chapter1.lst report (naming the report accordingly).

How it works...

In this simple example, the stored procedure `Foo` inside the package `Chapter1` is executed 50,000 times to query the `SALES` table. We have not used bind variables, and the Statspack report reflects this performance issue:

```
Instance Efficiency Indicators
~~~~~~~~~~~~~~~~~~~~~~~~~~~~~~~~~~
             Buffer Nowait %:  100.00       Redo NoWait %:  100.00
             Buffer  Hit   %:   99.81  Optimal W/A Exec %:  100.00
             Library Hit   %:   91.42        Soft Parse %:    2.92
            Execute to Parse %:   0.50        Latch Hit %:  100.00
Parse CPU to Parse Elapsd %:     97.34      % Non-Parse CPU:   8.42
```

In the highlighted section of the Statspack report, we can see that only **2.92** percent of parses have been "soft", because the `cursor_sharing` parameter is set to `EXACT` and we are not using bind variables.

There's more...

To solve this issue, we can:

  ▶ Change the `CURSOR_SHARING` parameter to `SIMILAR`
  ▶ Recode the `Foo` procedure, introducing bind variables

In the first case, we have to execute the following statement:

ALTER SYSTEM SET CURSOR_SHARING = SIMILAR SCOPE=MEMORY;

Now we can recreate the snapshots:

CONNECT PERFSTAT/PERFSTAT

EXEC statspack.snap;

CONNECT SH/SH

EXEC Chapter1.Workload;

CONNECT PERFSTAT/PERFSTAT

EXEC statspack.snap;

And finally, we launch the report creation:

SQL>@?/RDBMS/ADMIN/SPREPORT.SQL

The newly created report presents a significant change:

```
Instance Efficiency Indicators
~~~~~~~~~~~~~~~~~~~~~~~~~~~~~~~~
            Buffer Nowait %:  100.00        Redo NoWait %:  100.00
            Buffer  Hit   %:  100.00  Optimal W/A Exec %:  100.00
            Library Hit   %:   99.99        Soft Parse %:   99.20
          Execute to Parse %:   99.75        Latch Hit %:   99.99
Parse CPU to Parse Elapsd %:  100.00    % Non-Parse CPU:   99.64
```

Now the **Soft Parse** is **97.84** percent.

We can recode the procedure as well; let's rollback the change in CURSOR_SHARING:

ALTER SYSTEM SET CURSOR_SHARING=EXACT SCOPE = MEMORY;

And let's alter the Foo procedure:

```
CREATE OR REPLACE PACKAGE BODY Chapter1 AS
    PROCEDURE Workload IS
    BEGIN
     FOR i in 1 .. 50000
     LOOP
      Foo(i);
     END LOOP;
    END Workload;


    PROCEDURE Foo(CUSTID IN sh.sales.cust_id%TYPE) IS
    BEGIN
     DECLARE
      l_stmt VARCHAR2(2000);
     BEGIN
      l_stmt := 'SELECT * FROM sh.sales s WHERE s.cust_id = :p_cust_id';
      EXECUTE IMMEDIATE l_stmt USING CUSTID;
     END;
    END Foo;
END;
/
```

Let's launch the snapshots and the report:

```
CONNECT PERFSTAT/PERFSTAT

EXEC statspack.snap;

CONNECT SH/SH

EXEC Chapter1.Workload;

CONNECT PERFSTAT/PERFSTAT

EXEC statspack.snap;

SQL>@?/RDBMS/ADMIN/SPREPORT.SQL
```

The newly created report presents a result similar to the previous execution:

```
Instance Efficiency Indicators
~~~~~~~~~~~~~~~~~~~~~~~~~~~~~~~~~~
            Buffer Nowait %:   100.00        Redo NoWait %:   100.00
            Buffer  Hit   %:   100.00   Optimal W/A Exec %:   100.00
            Library Hit   %:    99.99         Soft Parse %:    99.20
          Execute to Parse %:   99.75          Latch Hit %:    99.99
Parse CPU to Parse Elapsd %:   100.00      % Non-Parse CPU:    99.64
```

There is now a **Soft Parse** of **99.20** percent.

In this simple example, we have seen how to diagnose a simple problem using Statspack; as an exercise, try to use the other tools presented using the same test case.

 To use AWR and ADDM take a manual snapshot before and after running the Workload procedure.

See also

▸ *Using bind variables* in *Chapter 4, Optimizing SQL Code*

▸ *Minimizing latches using bind variables* and *Tuning resources to minimize latch contention* in *Chapter 11, Tuning Contention*

2
Optimizing Application Design

In this chapter, we will optimize the application design, introducing various kinds of issues and hints to improve an application's performance. We will present the following recipes:

- Optimizing connection management
- Improving performance by sharing reusable code
- Reducing the number of requests to the database using stored procedures
- Reducing the number of requests to the database using sequences
- Reducing the number of requests to the database using materialized views
- Optimizing performance with schema denormalization
- Avoiding dynamic SQL

Introduction

It is very difficult to change the application design once the development process begins.

Often the primary aim of a software and data architect is to make things work, but designing applications for optimal performance is not a marginal aspect, many applications need to meet specific timing requirements to be useful.

In this chapter, we will investigate some aspects to keep in mind when designing an application and some tips on specific database features, which can help us in this task.

We will start inspecting the database connection phase, and then move on to general use of SQL statements in our applications for performance enhancement.

Recipes on useful database objects will follow, and the chapter will close with schema denormalization and dynamic SQL.

Optimizing connection management

In this recipe, we will see how to manage a database connection in our application, using Java.

Getting ready

To execute the source code we need the java compiler `javac` and the java runtime environment installed.

Make sure that `jdbc\lib\ojdbc6.jar` is in the `CLASSPATH` environment variable. The `jdbc` folder is located under the Oracle home directory.

To set environment variables in Microsoft Windows environments, right-click on **My Computer**, select **Properties**, then navigate to the **Advanced** button or link—depending on the OS version—and click on **Environment Variables** and find the `CLASSPATH` environment variable. If you don't find it, click on the **New** button and enter the variable name `CLASSPATH` and variable value `%ORACLE_HOME%\jdbc\lib\ojdbc6.jar`. If the variable is already defined, click on the **Edit** button and enter the string `%ORACLE_HOME%\jdbc\lib\ojdbc6.jar` after the current value.

In Linux environments, export the variable `CLASSPATH` using the following command line:

```
export CLASSPATH=$ORACLE_HOME\jdbc\lib\ojdbc.jar
```

You can insert this line in your `.profile` file to avoid manual execution every time you start up.

We need the example database `TESTDB` installed, as explained in *Chapter 1* in the *Exploring the example database* recipe. If we want to use another database, we have to change the value of the connection string to use the correct value. We will use the `HR` schema.

How to do it...

The following steps will demonstrate how to optimize connection management:

1. Create a `OraclePerformanceTuningCookbook` directory and a `chapter02` directory inside it.

2. Open your preferred text editor.

3. Create a class `ConnectionManagement` in the package `chapter02` using the following code and save it in a file named `ConnectionManagement.java` in the previously created `chapter02` directory:

```java
package chapter02;
import java.sql.*;

public class ConnectionManagement {
    private static final String driver =
       "oracle.jdbc.driver.OracleDriver";
    private static final String connectionString =
       "jdbc:oracle:thin:@localhost:1521:TESTDB";
    private static final String user = "hr";
    private static final String pass = "hr";
    private static final int iterations = 100;

    public static void singleConnection() throws SQLException {
        Connection conn = null;
        try {
            Class.forName(driver);
            conn = DriverManager.getConnection(connectionString,
                                               user, pass);
        } catch (Exception e) {
            System.out.println(String.format("Error %s",
                                  e.getLocalizedMessage()));
            System.exit(1);
        }
        try {
            for (int j = 0; j < iterations; ++j) {
                Statement query = conn.createStatement();
                ResultSet result = query.executeQuery(
                                    "select first_name,
                                    last_name
                                    from employees");
                while (result.next()) {
                    String name = result.getString("first_name")
                      + " "+ result.getString("last_name");
                    System.out.println(name);
                }
                query.close();
            }
        } catch (Exception e) {
            System.out.println(String.format("Error %s",
                                  e.getLocalizedMessage()));
            System.exit(1);
        } finally {
```

```
            conn.close();
        }
    }

    public static void multipleConnection() throws SQLException {
        Connection conn = null;
        for (int j = 0; j < iterations; ++j) {
            try {
                Class.forName(driver);
                conn = DriverManager.getConnection(
                        connectionString, user, pass);
            } catch (Exception e) {
                System.out.println(String.format("Error %s",
                                    e.getLocalizedMessage()));
                System.exit(1);
            }
            try {
                Statement query = conn.createStatement();
                ResultSet result = query.executeQuery(
                                "select first_name, last_name
                                 from employees");
                while (result.next()) {
                    String name = result.getString("first_name")
                        + " " + result.getString("last_name");
                    System.out.println(name);
                }
                query.close();
            } catch (Exception e) {
                System.out.println(String.format("Error %s",
                            e.getLocalizedMessage()));
                System.exit(1);
            } finally {
                conn.close();
            }
        }
    }

    public static void main(String[] args) throws SQLException {
        long startTime = System.currentTimeMillis();
        singleConnection();
        long stopTimeSingle = System.currentTimeMillis();
        multipleConnection();
```

```
        long stopTimeMulti = System.currentTimeMillis();
        System.out.println(String.format(
              "Execution with single connection %dms.\n
               Execution with multiple connections %dms.",
              (stopTimeSingle - startTime),
              (stopTimeMulti - stopTimeSingle)));
    }
  }
```

4. Open a terminal and make `chapter02` the current directory.

5. Build the program by using the following command:

   javac ConnectionManagement.java

6. Open another terminal and make `OraclePerformanceTuningCookbook`, the current directory. Run the program from the command line:

   java chapter02.ConnectionManagement

7. The output will be as follows:

   ```
   ...

   Matthew Weiss

   Jennifer Whalen

   Eleni Zlotkey

   Execution with single connection 2863ms.

   Execution with multiple connections 4176ms.
   ```

How it works...

This simple example consists of two methods, `singleConnection()` and `multipleConnection()`, which reads the names of all the employees in the HR schema a hundred times.

The difference between the two procedures is in the way the connection to the database is made. In `singleConnection()`, the connection is opened one time and closed after 100 executions. In `multipleConnection()`, for each iteration we open and close the connection to the database. The only difference in the code is the position of the `for` loops, as highlighted in the source code in step 3.

As we can easily see in the execution time presented in the output, the `singleConnection()` procedure is approximately 30 percent faster than the `multipleConnection()`. Increasing the number of iterations leads to a greater difference, and we consume more resources during the log on and log off processes than while executing the SQL statements.

There's more...

In this recipe, we have seen an example of connection management in action. Let's explore the scenarios, that could occur when we are designing our application, and database architecture.

Dedicated server versus shared server

There are two types of configurations used to connect to an Oracle database: **dedicated server** and **shared server**, called **Multi-Threaded Server** (**MTS**) in previous Oracle database releases.

In dedicated server mode, each client connected to the database will have a separate server process that executes the requests. In a shared server configuration, when a client initiates a connection to the database, the listener process chooses a dispatcher process configured for the database and the dispatcher process passes the request to the least loaded server process, which is already configured for the database, to execute the client request.

The shared server configuration shares a small number of server processes among many users, reducing the resources (RAM) required to serve the user requests.

In a dedicated server configuration, a new server process has to be spawned when a client logs in to the database. However, using a dedicated server is faster than using a shared server configuration, and with memory becoming less expensive it's better to increase the amount of RAM on the database server.

The dedicated server configuration is configured by default in most environments. There are some DBA tasks that cannot be performed with a shared server connection, such as RMAN backup/restore/recovery. Moreover, when a task uses structures stored in the PGA (Program Global Area), the session cannot be migrated to another shared server, this situation can lead to a contention.

Web applications

Web applications pool many users connecting at the same time, and this is the first thing to consider when designing the connection management of our web application.

There are many tutorials about writing web pages which connect to the database, returning data to the user or allowing them to modify and store updated information on the database. These tutorials usually do not consider the correct approach to establishing a database connection, and beyond the programming language used, we have a typical pattern for a web page design:

1. Connect to the database.
2. Query the data and compose the HTML code.
3. Close the connection.

As illustrated in this recipe, this approach is completely wrong, as we don't use connection pooling and waste more time in establishing a connection to the database and then terminating it, than in accessing the data. If connection pooling is in place, instead, we can use this pattern successfully.

There are two things to consider in web applications. First, the application is *disconnected*, so that we can treat each page as a single request disconnected from the previous. Second, with many users, scalability is a goal to keep in mind starting at the first phase of application design.

To meet these requirements, we need to use connection pooling when connecting to the database in our web application. When this is not possible—due to limitations in the language used—we can implement a multi-tier system. Move the data access layer inside web services, which could then use a dedicated connection, shared among many user requests.

This way we have pool connections at the application layer, which then uses a dedicated connection to the database.

Client-server Online Transaction Processing

Client server **Online Transaction Processing** (**OLTP**) is the most common database application.

In this kind of an environment, a dedicated server connection to the database is an easy choice. Estimate the RAM requirement to serve the requests, by multiplying the maximum number of concurrent users with the amount of memory used per Oracle server process.

Due to the nature of transactions involved in this environment—they last for a few milliseconds—a shared server approach could also be used.

For a multi-tier multi-layer application, use connection pooling on the data access layer—as in the Web Application example discussed in the previous section—to save some memory resources on the database server.

Batch processing

Batch processing is a typical activity paired with OLTP applications—often CPU-intensive tasks are scheduled to work in off-peak time, optimizing the resource utilization.

For batch processing, a dedicated server connection is a must, because they often use large queries and updates, which may last for minutes, if not hours on large systems.

See also

- *Tuning the Program Global Area and the User Global Area* in *Chapter 9, Tuning Memory*

Improving performance sharing reusable code

In this recipe, we will see how to share reusable code in our application to improve performance.

Getting ready

To demonstrate the performance gain by sharing reusable code, the following example is written in Java, similar to the one presented in the previous recipe.

How to do it...

The following steps will demonstrate how to share reusable code:

1. Create a `OraclePerformanceTuningCookbook` directory and a `chapter02` directory inside it.

2. Open your preferred text editor.

3. Create a class called `SharedCode` in the package `chapter02` using the following code and save it in a file named `SharedCode.java` in the previously created `chapter02` directory:

```java
package chapter02;
import java.sql.*;

public class SharedCode {
    private static final String driver =
      "oracle.jdbc.driver.OracleDriver";
    private static final String connectionString =
      "jdbc:oracle:thin:@localhost:1521:TESTDB";
    private static final String user = "hr";
    private static final String pass = "hr";
    private static final int iterations = 1000;

    public static void preparedQuery(Connection conn)
    throws SQLException {
        try {
            PreparedStatement ps = conn.prepareStatement(
                    "select first_name, last_name
                    from employees");
            for (int j = 0; j < iterations; ++j) {
                ResultSet result = ps.executeQuery();
                while (result.next()) {
```

```
                    String name = result.getString("first_name")
                      + " " + result.getString("last_name");
                    System.out.println(name);
                }
            }
            ps.close();
        } catch (Exception e) {
            System.out.println(String.format("Error %s",
                        e.getLocalizedMessage()));
            System.exit(1);
        }
    }

    public static void singleConnection(Connection conn)
      throws SQLException {
        try {
            for (int j = 0; j < iterations; ++j) {
                Statement query = conn.createStatement();
                ResultSet result = query.executeQuery(
                        "select first_name, last_name
                          from employees");
                while (result.next()) {
                    String name = result.getString("first_name")
                        + " " + result.getString("last_name");
                    System.out.println(name);
                }
                query.close();
            }
        } catch (Exception e) {
            System.out.println(String.format("Error %s",
                    e.getLocalizedMessage()));
            System.exit(1);
        }
    }

    public static void main(String[] args) throws SQLException {
        Connection conn = null;
        try {
            Class.forName(driver);
            conn = DriverManager.getConnection(connectionString,
                                                user, pass);
            long startTime = System.currentTimeMillis();
            singleConnection(conn);
            long stopTimeSingle = System.currentTimeMillis();
            preparedQuery(conn);
```

```
                    long stopTimePrep = System.currentTimeMillis();
                    System.out.println(String.format(
                            "Execution without prepared query %dms.\n
                            Execution with prepared query %dms.",
                            (stopTimeSingle - startTime),
                            (stopTimePrep - stopTimeSingle)));
                } catch (Exception e) {
                    System.out.println(String.format("Error %s",
                            e.getLocalizedMessage()));
                    System.exit(1);
                } finally {
                    conn.close();
                }
            }
        }
```

4. Open a terminal and make `chapter02` the current directory.

5. Build the program using the following command:

    `javac SharedCode.java`

6. Open a terminal and make `OraclePerformanceTuningCookbook` the current directory. Run the program from the command line:

    `java chapter02.SharedCode`

7. The output will be as follows:

    …

    Matthew Weiss

    Jennifer Whalen

    Eleni Zlotkey

    Execution without prepared query 15198ms.

    Execution with prepared query 13033ms.

How it works...

In this example, we have used the `singleConnection()` method from the previous recipe and prepared a slightly modified version of the routine, called the `preparedQuery()`. The difference between the two methods can be seen in the highlighted section of code, in `preparedQuery()` we use a prepared statement to benefit from parsing the query only once.

The timing presented at the end of the processing shows that the `preparedQuery()` solution is more than 15 percent faster than the `singleConnection()`. Increasing the number of iterations leads to an even greater savings, as it consumes fewer resources than if the SQL statements are only parsed once.

With this example, we have introduced the correct way to use SQL statements in our applications:

1. Prepare the statement.
2. Execute the statement many times (using bind variables).
3. Close the statement.

In this way, the costly hard parse operation is performed only once, that is in step 1.

There's more...

Parsing is a CPU-bound operation (it requires many CPU cycles) that involves latches, hence serialization, and hence waiting. We want to avoid unnecessary parsing.

The parsing process always performs a syntax and semantic check of the statement; after this phase, the database engine first searches for the statement in the shared SQL area. To do so, it calculates a hash of the literal statement, and compares it with the hash of the shared SQL statements. In this way, similar statements, which differ only in whitespaces, in case or in the name of bind variables are treated as different.

To avoid hard parsing, write SQL statements in reusable code sections. Use bind variables and not constants, trying to minimize the number of different queries executed against the database.

I have recommended the use of bind variables and not constants—this is the general rule—but don't overstate it by writing something like `select substr(field, :start, :end) as shortfield, ...` until it's not a requirement (return a variable part of the field).

In this situation, the correct size of `shortfield` is not known to the parser; in situations where bind variables are used in a predicate like `select field1 from table1 where field2 = :value` and `field2` is always "Y" in `table1`, except in some records where it is "N". Different execution plans can be chosen by the optimizer depending on bind variable values. If we query for "Y" records, a full table scan will be more advantageous than an index scan, which is perfectly suited if we ask for "N" records. If a constant is really constant, don't use a bind variable because "it's always better", but think about the drawbacks.

When the same statement is found in a shared SQL area, a soft parse occurs, otherwise a hard parse operation is needed. This requires two extra steps, optimizing and generating the execution plan for the query.

In developing our application, we will try to minimize the number of hard parses and maximize the soft-to-hard parse ratio.

Using the pattern illustrated in this recipe we will reduce the number of soft parses; the statement is parsed only once in this line:

```
PreparedStatement ps = conn.prepareStatement("select first_name,
    last_name from employees");
```

If the same statement had been parsed previously, a soft parse will occur. If the `PreparedStatement` is not closed, it can be executed multiple times—changing the values assigned to bind variables—and only a "light" soft-parse will occur, with no syntax and semantic check.

PL/SQL and parsing

Good news! What we have seen regarding parsing in the previous paragraph is managed automatically by the PL/SQL engine.

In a PL/SQL procedure, we don't need to explicitly prepare a statement before executing it, because the DML statements inside our procedures are automatically parsed once per session, and not once per execution. Subsequent calls use a "softer" soft-parse, which we can call a "light" soft-parse to distinguish it.

For example, if our application is written in Java, we have to parse the `execute` procedure statement once, and subsequent calls to the procedure won't produce unnecessary hard (and soft) parses, but only the unavoidable "light" soft-parse.

Diagnosing soft and hard parsing

Now we know the difference between hard, soft, and "light" soft-parse, and how to design and write our application to reduce parsing.

But can we diagnose a parsing problem, caused by any third-party application, whose sources we cannot inspect?

To find the answer, take a look at the dynamic performance views and monitor the following values—library cache hit ratio and parse count.

Query the `V$LIBRARYCACHE`, using the following statement to view hit ratios related to different areas of the database:

```
SELECT NAMESPACE, GETS, PINS, GETHITRATIO FROM V$LIBRARYCACHE
```

The output will be as follows:

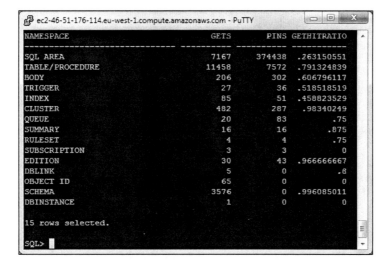

We are interested in the **SQL AREA** values, the first in the response, which indicates a **GETHITRATIO** of 26 percent (poor value) for our example. For an OLTP database, we probably want a value of .99999, while in a data warehouse environment a value above .9 is good.

To investigate parse data in a session, use the following statement:

```
SELECT S.NAME, V.VALUE FROM V$STATNAME S, V$MYSTAT V
WHERE S.STATISTIC# = V.STATISTIC# AND S.NAME LIKE 'parse%';
```

The output will be as follows:

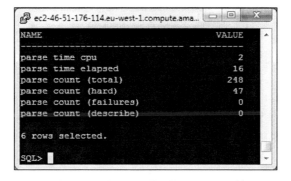

From this query we can see that there were a total of 248 parses, 47 of which were hard and 201 were soft parses.

If for test purposes we want to flush the content of the library cache, we can execute the following statement, which flushes the content of the shared pool (so the library cache):

```
ALTER SYSTEM FLUSH SHARED_POOL;
```

> Please note that flushing the shared pool in a production environment can have drastic effects on the database. We are doing this operation in a test environment.

See also

▸ The *Using bind variables and parsing* recipe in *Chapter 6, Optimizing PL/SQL Code* gives more details on parsing in PL/SQL code

▸ Recipes in *Chapter 7* are focused on the Oracle optimizer

▸ In *Tuning the Shared Pool* and *Tuning the Library Cache* recipes in *Chapter 9,* we will explore the structure used in this recipe in more detail.

Reducing the number of requests to the database using stored procedures

To achieve better performance, we should reduce the number of requests made to the database, especially if those requests have to be routed to a network. There are many strategies to reduce these requests. In this recipe, we discuss the use of stored procedures and packages for achieving this goal.

In this recipe, we execute a simple query in the SH schema. In the first script, we will use SQL*Plus to test the SQL statement and the corresponding stored procedure execution. In the Java program, we will use the same query and stored procedure. For each of these tests, record the execution time.

How to do it...

The following steps will demonstrate how to reduce the number of requests to the database:

1. Open your preferred text editor and copy the following script, and save it as `StoredProcedure.SQL`:

```
SET ECHO OFF

SET FEEDBACK OFF
```

```
SET PAGESIZE 80
CREATE OR REPLACE PROCEDURE SH.SALES_BY_PRODUCT
      (P OUT SYS_REFCURSOR) IS
BEGIN
  OPEN P FOR
    SELECT PROD_ID, SUM(AMOUNT_SOLD) AS AMOUNT FROM SH.SALES
          GROUP BY PROD_ID;
END;
/
ALTER PROCEDURE SH.SALES_BY_PRODUCT COMPILE;
/
ALTER SYSTEM FLUSH SHARED_POOL;
ALTER SYSTEM FLUSH BUFFER_CACHE;
SET TIMING ON
SELECT PROD_ID, SUM(AMOUNT_SOLD) FROM SH.SALES GROUP BY PROD_ID;
SET TIMING OFF
ALTER SYSTEM FLUSH SHARED_POOL;
ALTER SYSTEM FLUSH BUFFER_CACHE;
SET TIMING ON
VAR TEST REFCURSOR
EXEC SH.SALES_BY_PRODUCT(:TEST);
SET TIMING OFF
SET FEEDBACK ON
SET ECHO ON
```

2. Launch SQL*Plus and connect as user SYS:

   ```
   sqlplus /@TESTDB AS SYSDBA
   ```

3. Launch the previous script (we assume the script is in the same directory from which SQL*Plus has been executed):

   ```
   @StoredProcedure
   ```

   The output will be something similar to the following:

   ```
   ...
        126     370204.56
        127    1033311.97
         16     2082330.3
        122      84498.67
        139     244595.65
   Elapsed: 00:00:01.26
   Elapsed: 00:00:00.45
   ```

4. Create a `OraclePerformanceTuningCookbook` directory and a `chapter02` directory inside it.

5. Open your preferred text editor. Create a class `StoredProcedure` in the package `chapter02` using the following code and save it in a file named `StoredProcedure.java` in the previously created `chapter02` directory:

```java
package chapter02;

import java.sql.*;
import oracle.jdbc.*;
import javax.swing.*;

public class StoredProcedure {
 private static final String driver =
  "oracle.jdbc.driver.OracleDriver";
 private static final String connectionString =
  "jdbc:oracle:thin:@localhost:1521:TESTDB";
 private static final String user = "sys as sysdba";

 public static void useQuery(Connection conn)
  throws SQLException {
  try {
   PreparedStatement ps = conn
     .prepareStatement("SELECT PROD_ID, SUM(AMOUNT_SOLD) AS
       AMOUNT FROM SH.SALES GROUP BY PROD_ID");
   ResultSet result = ps.executeQuery();
   while (result.next()) {
    String row = result.getInt("PROD_ID") + " "
      + result.getDouble("AMOUNT");
    System.out.println(row);
   }
   ps.close();
  } catch (Exception e) {
   System.out.println(String.format("Error %s",
     e.getLocalizedMessage()));
   System.exit(1);
  }
 }

 public static void useStoredProcedure(Connection conn)
  throws SQLException {
  try {
   CallableStatement ps = conn
     .prepareCall("BEGIN SH.SALES_FOR_PRODUCT(?); END;");
```

```
   ps.registerOutParameter(1, OracleTypes.CURSOR);
   ps.execute();
   ResultSet result = ((OracleCallableStatement)
     ps).getCursor(1);
   while (result.next()) {
    String row = result.getInt("PROD_ID") + " "
      + result.getDouble("AMOUNT");
    System.out.println(row);
   }
   ps.close();
  } catch (Exception e) {
   System.out.println(String.format("Error %s",
     e.getLocalizedMessage()));
   System.exit(1);
  }
 }

 public static void flush(Connection conn) throws SQLException {
  try {
   Statement s = conn.createStatement();
   s.execute("ALTER SYSTEM FLUSH SHARED_POOL");
   s.execute("ALTER SYSTEM FLUSH BUFFER_CACHE");
   s.close();
   System.out.println("System altered");
  } catch (Exception e) {
   System.out.println(String.format("Error %s",
     e.getLocalizedMessage()));
   System.exit(1);
  }
 }

 public static void main(String[] args) throws SQLException {
  Connection conn = null;
  try {
   Class.forName(driver);
   String pass = JOptionPane.showInputDialog(
     "Insert SYS password:");
   conn = DriverManager.getConnection(connectionString, user,
     pass);
   long startTime = System.currentTimeMillis();
   flush(conn);
   useQuery(conn);
   long stopTimeSingle = System.currentTimeMillis();
   flush(conn);
```

```
        useStoredProcedure(conn);
        long stopTimePrep = System.currentTimeMillis();
        System.out.println(
            String.format("Execution without prepared query %dms.
                \nExecution with prepared query %dms.",
                (stopTimeSingle - startTime),
                (stopTimePrep - stopTimeSingle)));
    } catch (Exception e) {
    System.out.println(String.format("Error %s",
        e.getLocalizedMessage()));
    System.exit(1);
    } finally {
    conn.close();
    }
  }
}
```

6. Open a terminal and make `chapter02` as the current directory.

7. Build the program by using the following command:

   `javac StoredProcedure.java`

8. Open a terminal and make `OraclePerformanceTuningCookbook` as the current directory. Run the program from the command line:

   `java chapter02.StoredProcedure`

   The output will be as follows:

   `...`

   `126 370204.56`

   `127 1033311.97`

   `16 2082330.3`

   `122 84498.67`

   `139 244595.65`

   `Execution without prepared query 1438ms.`

   `Execution with prepared query 1722ms.`

How it works...

Let me explain the script. First we create a stored procedure that returns a cursor, querying the amount of sales of a product. The stored procedure is compiled, so when it is called later, the compilation phase will not be re-executed.

Then we flushed the shared pool and the buffer cache, as it is a good practice to start with an empty working area in a test/development environment—if we don't do so, the first execution will take longer than the subsequent calls because the data will already be in the buffer cache.

The next set of statements will execute the query and the stored procedure, while at the same time measuring the time elapsed.

 The stored procedure opens the cursor and returns it to the caller, while the query actually returns all the records.

The Java class executes the same query and stored procedure. In either case, it executes a loop on the ResultSet to show every record returned; before executing the query and the stored procedure, flush the shared pool and the buffer cache for the same reason as explained earlier.

There's more...

Using a stored procedure improves the performance while executing SQL statements on the database. Another reason to use stored procedures—which are usually grouped in packages—is that they allow the sharing of reusable code, as illustrated in the previous recipe. If we use only stored procedures and packages to manipulate the data, there is a single place that stores all the used statements, which can be easily reused without rewriting. Rewriting similar SQL statements is not only a waste of time, when coding, but can also be a performance issue during the execution phase.

See also

▸ Recipes from *Chapter 6, Optimizing PL/SQL Code*

Reducing the number of requests to the database using sequences

In this recipe, we continue to explore ways to reduce the number of requests made to the database, illustrating how the use of sequences can help us in achieving this as well as improved database scalability.

Sequences are used to assign a sequential number—unique until the sequence is recreated or reinitialized. In many non-Oracle databases, there are tools that allow developers to automatically assign a sequential number to a field—often the primary key—the so-called autoinc fields (Microsoft® SQL Server® and IBM® DB2® can define a field IDENTITY, MySQL™ has the AUTO_INCREMENT attribute, and so on).

Oracle database doesn't have a specific IDENTITY field, to achieve the same result developers have to write a trigger for the table to assign a value to the "autoinc" field, using a sequence. This behavior, however, allows developers to implement whatever policy they want while generating the autoinc field. Sequences can also be used for purposes other than generating the value for an autoinc field.

Without such a mechanism, a common approach to solve the problem would be to maintain a counter in a separate table—when a new sequential number is needed, the user locks the counter table, increments the counter (and uses a new value), and unlocks the counter table. This approach has serious limitations—every request to the counter table is serialized, and if an application keeps many counters in the same table, the serialization generates a new record for every request. If we use the counters to generate the primary key of all (or nearly all) the tables, our database will insert a single row for one table at a time. This is called a bottleneck, because each new insert in each table in the database needs to use the counter table.

In this recipe, we use both the sequence and the counter table approach, populated with a script, to generate the primary keys of a table.

How to do it...

The following steps will demonstrate how to reduce the number of requests to a databse:

1. Connect to SQL*Plus with user HR:

   ```
   sqlplus hr@TESTDB/hr
   ```

2. Create the TRAVEL_SEQ sequence:

   ```
   CREATE SEQUENCE TRAVEL_SEQ START WITH 10000 INCREMENT BY 1
     CACHE 1000;
   ```

3. Create the TRAVELS table:

   ```
   CREATE TABLE HR.TRAVELS (
     TRAVELID NUMBER(9) NOT NULL,
     EMPLOYEE_ID NUMBER(6) NOT NULL,
     LOCATION_ID NUMBER(4) NOT NULL,
     START_DATE DATE,
     END_DATE DATE,
     CONSTRAINT PK_TRAVELS PRIMARY KEY (TRAVELID),
     CONSTRAINT FK_TRAVELS_EMPLOYEES
       FOREIGN KEY (EMPLOYEE_ID) REFERENCES EMPLOYEES,
     CONSTRAINT FK_TRAVELS_LOCATIONS
       FOREIGN KEY (LOCATION_ID) REFERENCES LOCATIONS);
   ```

4. Create and populate a table, and call it `TRAVELS_COUNTER`:

```
CREATE TABLE TRAVELS_COUNTER (ID NUMBER(9) NOT NULL);
INSERT INTO TRAVELS_COUNTER(ID) VALUES (0);
COMMIT;
```

5. Create a trigger to populate the primary key of the `TRAVELS` table using the `TRAVELS_COUNTER` table:

```
CREATE OR REPLACE TRIGGER HR.TR_TRAVELS_INS
  BEFORE INSERT ON HR.TRAVELS FOR EACH ROW
  WHEN (NEW.TRAVELID IS NULL)
DECLARE MYID HR.TRAVELS.TRAVELID%TYPE;
BEGIN
  SELECT ID + 1 INTO MYID FROM TRAVELS_COUNTER FOR UPDATE;
  UPDATE TRAVELS_COUNTER SET ID = MYID
    RETURNING ID INTO :NEW.TRAVELID;

END;
```

6. Populate the `TRAVELS` table for measuring performance:

```
SET TIMING ON
INSERT INTO HR.TRAVELS(EMPLOYEE_ID, LOCATION_ID,
  START_DATE, END_DATE)
SELECT E.EMPLOYEE_ID, L.LOCATION_ID, SYSDATE, SYSDATE + ROWNUM
  FROM HR.EMPLOYEES E, HR.LOCATIONS L;
SET TIMING OFF
```

7. Create a trigger to populate the primary key of the `TRAVELS` table using the `TRAVEL_SEQ` sequence:

```
CREATE OR REPLACE TRIGGER TR_TRAVELS_INS
  BEFORE INSERT ON TRAVELS FOR EACH ROW
  WHEN (NEW.TRAVELID IS NULL)
BEGIN
  SELECT TRAVEL_SEQ.NEXTVAL INTO :NEW.TRAVELID FROM DUAL;
END;
```

8. Populate the `TRAVELS` table for measuring performance:

```
SET TIMING ON
INSERT INTO HR.TRAVELS(EMPLOYEE_ID, LOCATION_ID,
   START_DATE, END_DATE)
SELECT E.EMPLOYEE_ID, L.LOCATION_ID, SYSDATE, SYSDATE + ROWNUM
      FROM HR.EMPLOYEES E, HR.LOCATIONS L;
SET TIMING OFF
```

How it works...

The relevant part of the code is included in steps 5 and 7. The trigger populates the primary key field of the `TRAVELS` table. In the first implementation, we use the `TRAVELS_COUNTER` table to obtain a sequential value, while in the second implementation, we use the `TRAVEL_SEQ` sequence to obtain the next sequential number.

The following contain the timing for inserts in steps 6 and 8:

```
ELAPSED: 1.02
ELAPSED: 0.26
```

It is easy to see that sequence implementation is faster than using the `TRAVELS_COUNTER` table.

There's more...

In the example used, measuring the time elapsed to insert 2461 (107 employees multiplied by 23 locations) records in the table, you may wish to use a Statspack report to get more details from the database statistics. Let's use the following script:

```
CONNECT hr@TESTDB/hr
CREATE OR REPLACE TRIGGER HR.TR_TRAVELS_INS
  BEFORE INSERT ON HR.TRAVELS FOR EACH ROW
  WHEN (NEW.TRAVELID IS NULL)
DECLARE MYID HR.TRAVELS.TRAVELID%TYPE;
BEGIN
  SELECT ID + 1 INTO MYID FROM TRAVELS_COUNTER FOR UPDATE;
  UPDATE TRAVELS_COUNTER SET ID = MYID RETURNING ID INTO :NEW.TRAVELID;
END;
/
```

```
CONNECT perfstat@TESTDB/perfstat

EXECUTE STATSPACK.SNAP;

CONNECT hr@TESTDB/hr

INSERT INTO HR.TRAVELS(EMPLOYEE_ID, LOCATION_ID, START_DATE, END_DATE)

SELECT E.EMPLOYEE_ID, L.LOCATION_ID, SYSDATE, SYSDATE + ROWNUM FROM
HR.EMPLOYEES E, HR.LOCATIONS L;

CONNECT perfstat@TESTDB/perfstat

EXECUTE STATSPACK.SNAP;

@?/rdbms/admin/spreport
```

When requested, use the last two snapshots to prepare the report (using the `TRAVELS_COUNTER` table).

With the following script, we can produce the same report using the sequence to generate the primary keys:

```
CONNECT hr@TESTDB/hr

CREATE OR REPLACE TRIGGER TR_TRAVELS_INS

  BEFORE INSERT ON TRAVELS FOR EACH ROW

  WHEN (NEW.TRAVELID IS NULL)

BEGIN

  SELECT TRAVEL_SEQ.NEXTVAL INTO :NEW.TRAVELID FROM DUAL;

END;

/

CONNECT perfstat@TESTDB/perfstat

EXECUTE STATSPACK.SNAP;

CONNECT hr@TESTDB/hr

INSERT INTO HR.TRAVELS(EMPLOYEE_ID, LOCATION_ID, START_DATE, END_DATE)

SELECT E.EMPLOYEE_ID, L.LOCATION_ID, SYSDATE, SYSDATE + ROWNUM FROM
HR.EMPLOYEES E, HR.LOCATIONS L;

CONNECT perfstat@TESTDB/perfstat

EXECUTE STATSPACK.SNAP;

@?/rdbms/admin/spreport
```

As mentioned earlier, use the last two snapshots to prepare a report.

In the following screenshots, you can identify the difference in elapsed time for the two methods, the TRAVELS_COUNTER table and the sequence TRAVEL_SEQ. In the following screenshot, you can see the results obtained when using the TRAVELS_COUNTER table (see the third line):

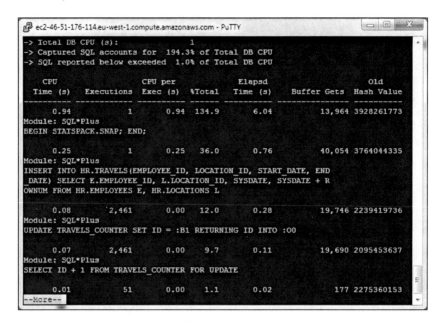

In the following screenshot, we can see the results obtained when using the sequence:

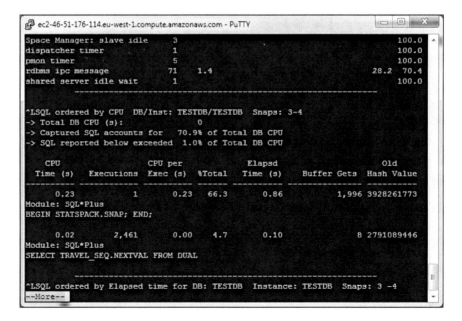

By observation, it is easy to conclude that it consumes fewer resources when using the sequence instead of the TRAVELS_COUNTER table.

Correct definition of a sequence

We have created the TRAVEL_SEQ sequence by using the following statement:

CREATE SEQUENCE TRAVEL_SEQ START WITH 10000 INCREMENT BY 1 CACHE 1000;

It's important to highlight the parameter CACHE 1000, which points out how many sequential numbers the database caches.

To keep track of the current sequence number, the database stores it in the SYS.SEQ$ table. When we indicate a parameter CACHE X, the database updates the SYS.SEQ$ and keeps the current value of the sequence and the high watermark (the last number cached) in the memory, as we have already called NEXTVAL X times on the sequence. When a NEXTVAL is issued on the sequence, the database just increases the counter and if the high watermark is reached, it caches other X numbers in the same manner.

With the NOCACHE parameter instead, for each invocation of the NEXTVAL, a sequential number is generated accessing the SYS.SEQ$ table, increasing the contention on this object and decreasing the scalability accordingly.

> When you are using the CACHE parameter and there are multiple sessions using that sequence, the numbers won't be contiguous and after an instance shutdown or when the sequence is aged out of the shared pool, the cached sequence values are lost.

See also

▶ See *Using reverse key indexes* in *Chapter 3*, *Optimizing Storage Structures* for a hint on using sequential values for primary keys to reduce contention on index leaf blocks

Reducing the number of requests to the database using materialized views

In this recipe, we will see how to increase the performance of the database—especially in a data warehousing environment—but the same recipe can be used with small changes in an OLTP environment as well by using materialized views.

Materialized views can be seen as snapshots of the data in one or more tables, on which a computation has been applied, for example, a join or a group. This summary data can be used to answer client queries readily, instead of reading all the data in the original table(s). An example is worth a thousand words. For example, we have a SALES table in SH schema, containing around 1 million rows, and we want a report of sales by product. We will see how materialized views, in such cases, can help a lot in reducing access to the database, specially the I/O.

How to do it...

We will use SQL*Plus to test a simple script:

1. Connect to the database TESTDB as user SH and execute a simple query on the sales data, collecting statistics, timing, and execution plan:

```
CONNECT sh@TESTDB/sh

SET AUTOTRACE ON

SET TIMING ON

SELECT PROD_ID, SUM(AMOUNT_SOLD) FROM SH.SALES GROUP BY PROD_ID;

SET TIMING OFF

SET AUTOTRACE OFF
```

2. Create a materialized view with the following statement:

```
CREATE MATERIALIZED VIEW SH.MV_SALES_BY_PRODUCT

BUILD IMMEDIATE REFRESH ON COMMIT

ENABLE QUERY REWRITE AS

SELECT PROD_ID, SUM(AMOUNT_SOLD) AS AMOUNT_SOLD FROM SH.SALES
GROUP BY PROD_ID;
```

3. Analyze the materialized view to let the optimizer use it if needed:

```
EXEC DBMS_STATS.GATHER_TABLE_STATS('SH', 'MV_SALES_BY_PRODUCT',
estimate_percent => 100, method_opt => 'for all columns size 1');
```

4. Execute the same query as mentioned in step 1:

```
SET AUTOTRACE ON

SET TIMING ON

SELECT PROD_ID, SUM(AMOUNT_SOLD) FROM SH.SALES GROUP BY PROD_ID;

SET TIMING OFF

SET AUTOTRACE OFF
```

Review the results.

How it works...

The execution plan and statistics of the first query execution are as shown in the following screenshot:

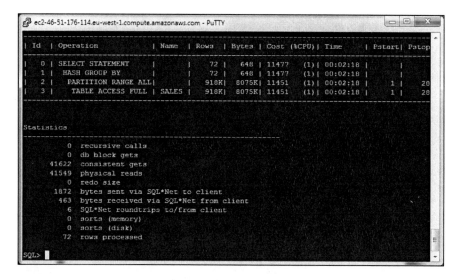

We can see that in the execution plan, there is full table access to the SALES table examining 918K rows and reading 8075 KB. In the statistics, we can see that there are **41549 physical reads** with **41622 consistent gets**, because the data wasn't in the buffer cache before the execution of the query.

The following is the execution plan and statistics for the last query using the materialized view:

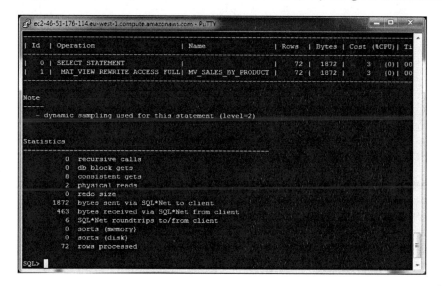

In this case we can see that, even when we have submitted the same query to the database, our query was rewritten to use the materialized view MV_SALES_BY_PRODUCT. This behavior is due to the ENABLE QUERY REWRITE clause in the CREATE MATERIALIZED VIEW statement executed in step 2.

The result is astonishing: the statistics tell us that there are only **8 consistent gets** to achieve the same result. The absence of physical read is due to the fact that the rows of the materialized view are already in the buffer cache from the previous statements. However, from the execution plan, the number of rows processed is 72, and each row is 648 bytes long. The following is the result of the query after flushing buffer cache:

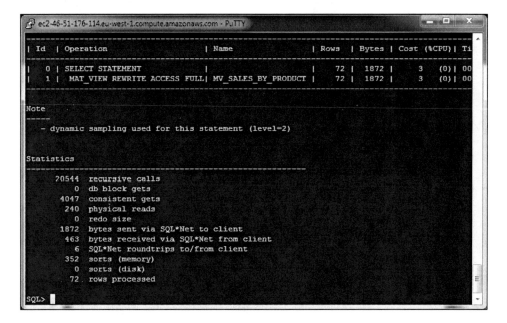

In the latter case, we have **4047 consistent gets** and **240 physical reads**: there is a difference of two orders of magnitude in the physical reads and an order of magnitude in the consistent gets, resulting in a great performance improvement.

The developer may not know that a materialized view is active in the database; this behavior is an interesting aspect of the materialized views. It is easy to identify queries that can benefit from the introduction of a materialized view. The queries will benefit automatically, with the new database object, without changing anything in the original query.

The magic behind this feature is the query rewrite mechanism. When a query is submitted, the parser tries to identify if there is any materialized view that could answer the query, reducing physical reads and response time. If such a materialized view is present, the query is automatically rewritten using the materialized view instead of the base table(s), originally involved. Later, if we drop the materialized view, the query is still functional, although slower than before.

There's more...

Now that we have seen the potential of materialized views, let's take an in depth look at this useful database object. We will also try to answer the frequently asked question "Can I use materialized views in an OLTP environment?"

Materialized views in depth

We have seen how to write a statement for creating materialized views; there are many options that can be used while creating a materialized view, such as the following:

- The BUILD IMMEDIATE clause builds the materialized view immediately when the command is executed. Instead if you use BUILD DEFERRED, the data in the materialized view is populated in the next refresh operation.

- The REFRESH ON COMMIT clause forces the database to refresh data in the materialized view, when a change is committed to one of the base tables. This type of a refresh is FAST (incremental).

- We can also use the REFRESH ON DEMAND clause to instruct the database to refresh the materialized view. Using this command, data is refreshed only when we want—using the DBMS_MVIEW refresh procedures.

- Using the START WITH and NEXT clauses, we can specify when to start the automatic refresh operations and the interval between consecutive refreshes, respectively.

- We can query the DBA_MVIEWS dynamic performance view, to obtain details about all the materialized views available in the database, or the corresponding USER_MVIEWS and ALL_MVIEWS to restrict the results to the materialized views the current user owns or can access. These views contain the materialized view statement and the implementation details.

Materialized views and grants

To create a materialized view there are a few required privileges:

- CREATE SESSION
- CREATE TABLE
- CREATE MATERIALIZED VIEW
- QUERY REWRITE

QUERY REWRITE has to be granted directly to the user who will use the materialized view, not granted to a user through a role.

Database parameters to use query rewrite

To use the query rewrite mechanism, two parameters have to be set in the initialization file or server parameter file. Decide whether to enable it for all sessions, or to enable it for a specific session only. In the latter case, use the ALTER SESSION statement. The two parameters are:

- ▸ QUERY_REWRITE_ENABLE=TRUE
- ▸ QUERY_REWRITE_INTEGRITY

The value for the parameter QUERY_REWRITE_INTEGRITY can be set to one of the following three values, depending on how the query is to be rewritten:

- ▸ ENFORCED: When this parameter is set to ENFORCED, the database guarantees consistency and integrity of the data.
- ▸ TRUSTED: When this parameter is set to TRUSTED, the database can rewrite queries using declared relationships that are not enforced by the database itself. The optimizer trusts that the relationships are correct, so it uses declared but not ENABLED VALIDATED primary or unique key constraints.
- ▸ STALE_TOLERATED: When the parameter is set to STALE_TOLERATED, the queries can be rewritten even if the used relationships are not declared nor enforced by the database, in the presence of data in the materialized views known to be inconsistent with the data in the base table(s).

The last value for the parameter QUERY_REWRITE_INTEGRITY is often used when the materialized views are not refreshed on commit, but on a recurring basis. This is done during off-peak periods. The data is updated to the last refresh of the materialized view, if we are not interested in up-to-date data.

The same parameters have to be enabled to use another functionality, function-based indexes.

The default values for these initialization parameters are ENFORCED for QUERY_REWRITE_INTEGRITY and TRUE for QUERY_REWRITE_ENABLE.

Can I use materialized views in an OLTP environment?

Materialized views were definitely created to help data warehouse queries achieve better performance, and for pre-calculating values to use later.

Surely, if we create a REFRESH ON COMMIT materialized view based on a table involved in OLTP, we might experience very poor performance in our OLTP environment. This is because data in the materialized view is updated for every transaction committed to the underlying tables—the operation is executed during the commit phase—meaning longer execution time, which is unacceptable for OLTP environments.

For example, materialized views can be used in such environments with the REFRESH ON DEMAND clause and execute the FULL refreshes during off-peak hours.

If we have many reports in the OLTP application, it wouldn't matter if reports were from the previous day's data. Against this limitation, which in many cases can be acceptable, the performance gain in the report preparation is often significant.

Optimizing performance with schema denormalization

In this recipe, we will see how schema denormalization can help improve database performance, and what should be done before executing this operation.

Getting ready

We will implement a database schema representing a group of friends and their phone numbers. The following are the requirements for the database:

- For each friend, we want to store the name, surname, and gender
- Each friend may have multiple phone numbers
- For each phone number, we want to know its type of usage (home, work, mobile, and so on)
- A phone number can be shared by more than one friend, for example, Mrs. and Mr. Smith will share the same home number—at least until they get divorced
- For each phone number we want to store, we need to know its availability, that is, working hours, evening, afternoon, weekend only, and so on

The following is the logic schema that we will implement to satisfy the requirements mentioned earlier:

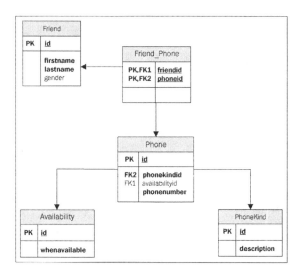

How to do it...

The following steps will demonstrate schema denormalization:

1. Launch SQL*Plus and create the schema corresponding to the logical schema shown in the earlier diagram:

```
CONNECT sh@TESTDB/sh

CREATE TABLE FRIEND (
ID NUMBER NOT NULL PRIMARY KEY,
FIRSTNAME VARCHAR2(30) NOT NULL,
LASTNAME VARCHAR2(30) NOT NULL,
GENDER CHAR);

CREATE TABLE PHONEKIND (
ID NUMBER NOT NULL PRIMARY KEY,
DESCRIPTION VARCHAR2(20) NOT NULL);

CREATE TABLE AVAILABILITY (
ID NUMBER NOT NULL PRIMARY KEY,
WHENAVAILABLE VARCHAR2(30) NOT NULL);

CREATE TABLE PHONE (
ID NUMBER NOT NULL PRIMARY KEY,
PHONEKINDID NUMBER NOT NULL REFERENCES PHONEKIND(ID),
AVAILABILITYID NUMBER REFERENCES AVAILABILITY(ID),
PHONENUMBER VARCHAR2(20) NOT NULL);

CREATE TABLE FRIEND_PHONE (
FRIENDID NUMBER NOT NULL REFERENCES FRIEND(ID),
PHONEID NUMBER NOT NULL REFERENCES PHONE(ID),
CONSTRAINT PK_FRIEND_PHONE PRIMARY KEY (FRIENDID, PHONEID));
```

2. Populate the schema with some data, for example, the following values:

```
INSERT /*+APPEND */ INTO FRIEND (ID, FIRSTNAME, LASTNAME, GENDER)
SELECT CUST_ID, CUST_FIRST_NAME, CUST_LAST_NAME, CUST_GENDER
FROM SH.CUSTOMERS;
INSERT INTO PHONEKIND(ID, DESCRIPTION) VALUES (0, 'HOME');
```

```
INSERT INTO PHONEKIND(ID, DESCRIPTION) VALUES (1, 'BUSINESS');
INSERT INTO PHONEKIND(ID, DESCRIPTION) VALUES (2, 'MOBILE-HOME');
INSERT INTO PHONEKIND(ID, DESCRIPTION) VALUES (3,
   'MOBILE-BUSINESS');
INSERT INTO PHONEKIND(ID, DESCRIPTION) VALUES (4, 'OTHER');

INSERT INTO AVAILABILITY(ID, WHENAVAILABLE) VALUES (0, 'ALWAYS');
INSERT INTO AVAILABILITY(ID, WHENAVAILABLE) VALUES (1,
   'WORK-HOURS');
INSERT INTO AVAILABILITY(ID, WHENAVAILABLE) VALUES (2,
   'AFTERNOON');
INSERT INTO AVAILABILITY(ID, WHENAVAILABLE) VALUES (3, 'EVENING');

INSERT /*+APPEND */ INTO PHONE (ID, PHONEKINDID, AVAILABILITYID,
   PHONENUMBER)
SELECT ROWNUM, MOD(ROWNUM, 5), MOD(ROWNUM, 4),
   CUST_MAIN_PHONE_NUMBER FROM SH.CUSTOMERS ORDER BY CUST_ID;

INSERT /*+APPEND */ INTO FRIEND_PHONE (FRIENDID, PHONEID)
SELECT CUST_ID, ROWNUM FROM SH.CUSTOMERS ORDER BY CUST_ID;
COMMIT;
```

3. Gather statistics related to the tables using the following statements:

```
EXEC DBMS_STATS.GATHER_TABLE_STATS('SH', 'FRIEND_PHONE',
   estimate_percent => 100,
   method_opt => 'for all columns size 1');
EXEC DBMS_STATS.GATHER_TABLE_STATS('SH', 'PHONE',
   estimate_percent => 100,
   method_opt => 'for all columns size 1');
EXEC DBMS_STATS.GATHER_TABLE_STATS('SH', 'AVAILABILITY',
   estimate_percent => 100,
   method_opt => 'for all columns size 1');
EXEC DBMS_STATS.GATHER_TABLE_STATS('SH', 'PHONEKIND',
   estimate_percent => 100,
   method_opt => 'for all columns size 1');
EXEC DBMS_STATS.GATHER_TABLE_STATS('SH', 'FRIEND',
   estimate_percent => 100,
   method_opt => 'for all columns size 1');
```

4. Empty the cache:

```
CONNECT /@TESTDB AS SYSDBA
ALTER SYSTEM FLUSH BUFFER_CACHE;
ALTER SYSTEM FLUSH SHARED_POOL;
```

5. Execute a query to retrieve the data (a simple list of friends with their phone type/number/availability):

```
CONNECT sh@TESTDB/sh
SET AUTOTRACE TRACEONLY
SELECT F.FIRSTNAME, F.LASTNAME, PK.DESCRIPTION AS PHONEKIND,
  PA.WHENAVAILABLE AS AVAILABILITY, P.PHONENUMBER
FROM FRIEND F
  INNER JOIN FRIEND_PHONE FP ON FP.FRIENDID = F.ID
  INNER JOIN PHONE P ON P.ID = FP.PHONEID
  INNER JOIN PHONEKIND PK ON PK.ID = P.PHONEKINDID
  LEFT OUTER JOIN AVAILABILITY PA ON PA.ID = P.AVAILABILITYID
  WHERE F.ID = 29912;
SET AUTOTRACE OFF
```

6. Denormalization, alter the database schema, adjust the data, and gather statistics again:

```
ALTER TABLE PHONE ADD PHONEKIND VARCHAR2(20);
ALTER TABLE PHONE ADD AVAILABILITY VARCHAR2(30);
UPDATE PHONE SET PHONEKIND = (SELECT DESCRIPTION FROM PHONEKIND
  WHERE PHONEKIND.ID = PHONE.PHONEKINDID);
UPDATE PHONE SET AVAILABILITY = (SELECT WHENAVAILABLE
  FROM AVAILABILITY WHERE AVAILABILITY.ID = PHONE.AVAILABILITYID);
COMMIT;
ALTER TABLE PHONE SET UNUSED COLUMN PHONEKINDID;
ALTER TABLE PHONE SET UNUSED COLUMN AVAILABILITYID;
ALTER TABLE PHONE DROP UNUSED COLUMNS;
EXEC DBMS_STATS.GATHER_TABLE_STATS('SH', 'FRIEND',
  estimate_percent => 100,
  method_opt => 'for all columns size 1');
```

7. Empty the cache once more:

    ```
    CONNECT /@TESTDB AS SYSDBA
    ALTER SYSTEM FLUSH BUFFER_CACHE;
    ALTER SYSTEM FLUSH SHARED_POOL;
    ```

8. Execute the same query as mentioned in step 5:

    ```
    CONNECT sh@TESTDB/sh
    SET AUTOTRACE TRACEONLY
    SELECT F.FIRSTNAME, F.LASTNAME, P.PHONEKIND, P.AVAILABILITY,
       P.PHONENUMBER
    FROM FRIEND F
       INNER JOIN FRIEND_PHONE FP ON FP.FRIENDID = F.ID
       INNER JOIN PHONE P ON P.ID = FP.PHONEID
       WHERE F.ID = 29912;
    SET AUTOTRACE OFF
    ```

9. Drop the schema:

    ```
    DROP TABLE FRIEND_PHONE;
    DROP TABLE PHONE;
    DROP TABLE AVAILABILITY;
    DROP TABLE PHONEKIND;
    DROP TABLE FRIEND;
    ```

How it works...

In the example, we first created a small database schema, based on the logical schema presented in the *Getting ready* section of this recipe, which is in 3NF, and then we populated it with some data.

Moving on, in step 3, we gathered statistics on the newly created objects and in step 4, we cleared the buffers and cache.

In step 5, we executed a simple query against this schema, to retrieve the data of a single friend (a common query for OLTP environments). We get the following output upon execution of this query:

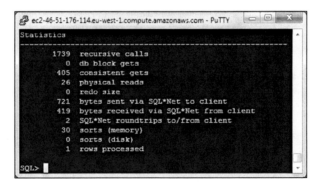

Observe the following statistics:

In step 6, we have restructured the schema applying denormalization, then we integrated in `Phone` table attributes from the lookup tables `Availability` and `Phonekind`, and re-analyzed the table to reflect the changes in the statistics.

In step 7, we cleared the cache; the operation is pointless as we have changed the schema, so the entries in the library and buffer cache are not usable. Then in step 8 we executed a query logically equivalent to the previous one, obtaining the following output:

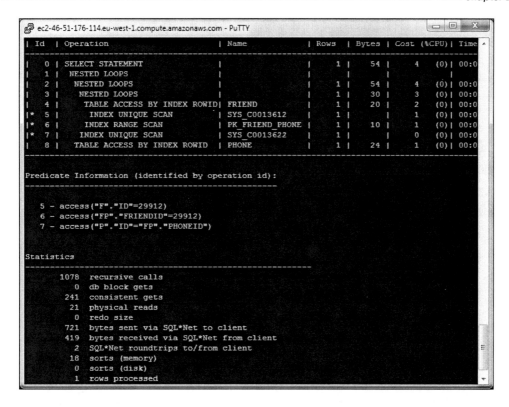

Observe the statistics, and you will notice that we have reduced the number of recursive calls, consistent gets, and the number of the nested loops in the execution plan, the number of sorts has also reduced after denormalization.

> In step 8, we dropped the objects created in this recipe so that the SH schema is in its initial state.

However, there is no such thing as a free lunch, we have introduced redundancy. If the attributes in the lookup tables—which we have migrated in Phone table—change often, to update a single row in the normalized schema, we have to reflect the same update in thousands of records in the denormalized one.

The "rule of thumb", in this case, is to avoid denormalization, when the data is updated often—very common in OLTP environments. We can think about denormalization, when the data is almost fixed over a period of time, for example, to minimize the number of joins, as illustrated in this recipe.

There's more...

In relational database theory, normalization is a mandatory step, in order to minimize redundancy and avoid several anomalies, such as update and insertion and deletion. The advantage of a normalized database, is its general-purpose structure, that is, on a normalized table we can execute any type of query—even those that are least expected at the time of database design.

Several Normal Forms (NF) are defined in relational database theory. Identified by a number and the abbreviation NF, the normal forms with higher numbers are less exposed to anomalies.

The first three Normal Forms were developed by E. F. Codd, and often we say that a table is "normalized" when it is in 3NF, that is, when the following rules are met:

- There are no multi-value attributes
- There are no non-prime attributes, functionally dependent on a subset of a candidate key
- There are no non-prime attributes, transitively dependent on a candidate key

 A candidate key is a minimal set of attributes such that there are no two distinct tuples with the same value for the candidate key attributes and there is no subset of the candidate key for which the preceding statement is true.

Although a 3NF table can be queried easily in many ways, there can be performance issues even when we use a highly normalized database, which is theoretically very well designed but is not practical to use and even worse, it can lead to poor performance.

We can apply denormalization even when creating materialized views with refresh on demand, and take advantage of normalization with no extra cost in OLTP performance.

Not 1NF structures

With Oracle databases we can have tables that don't follow the 1NF, also called 0NF. These tables use `nested tables` or `varray` fields to store information, which are multi-value attributes, for example, a table similar to the following:

```
CREATE OR REPLACE TYPE PHONE AS OBJECT (
PHONEKIND VARCHAR2(20),
AVAILABILITY VARCHAR2(30),
PHONENUMBER VARCHAR2(20));
/
CREATE OR REPLACE TYPE TAB_PHONES AS TABLE OF PHONE;
/
```

```
CREATE TABLE FRIEND_0NF (

ID NUMBER NOT NULL PRIMARY KEY,

FIRSTNAME VARCHAR2(30) NOT NULL,

LASTNAME VARCHAR2(30) NOT NULL,

PHONES TAB_PHONES)

NESTED TABLE PHONES STORE AS FRIEND_PHONES;
```

In this example, we have created a table which stores an unlimited number of phone numbers for every friend in the table. Structures like this are to be used only when we don't query details in the nested table alone. Otherwise, we will spend a lot of time in un-nesting and nesting the table, which isn't good from a performance point of view.

Avoiding dynamic SQL

The title of this recipe should be extended to say "... when you can do your stuff without using it". In this recipe, we will see when and how to use dynamic SQL.

Dynamic SQL is the only choice when:

- ▶ We want to execute DDL statements in our application.
- ▶ We have to code different queries depending on user input, for example, a search form with different search criteria that the user can choose from. This leads to different predicates in the WHERE clause.
- ▶ We want to code generic procedures, which can act on any table, for example, a generic "print" procedure, which shows the content of a table in a certain format.

For each of these situations, there are drawbacks to be taken care of.

How to do it...

To execute DDL statements in our application, we cannot use static SQL inside PL/SQL code. So, if we want to grant the RESOURCE role to the user SH, we have to do something similar to the following:

```
BEGIN

  EXECUTE IMMEDIATE 'GRANT RESOURCE TO SH'

END;
```

To search the EMPLOYEES table of the schema HR by FIRST_NAME or LAST_NAME field, we can write the following procedure:

```
CONNECT hr@TESTDB/hr
CREATE OR REPLACE PACKAGE DYNAMICSQL AS
  TYPE T_REFCURSOR IS REF CURSOR;
  PROCEDURE SEARCH_EMPLOYEES(
   FIRST_NAME IN EMPLOYEES.FIRST_NAME%TYPE,
   LAST_NAME IN EMPLOYEES.LAST_NAME%TYPE,
   SEARCH_CURSOR OUT T_REFCURSOR);
END;
/
CREATE OR REPLACE PACKAGE BODY DYNAMICSQL AS
 PROCEDURE SEARCH_EMPLOYEES(
  FIRST_NAME IN EMPLOYEES.FIRST_NAME%TYPE,
  LAST_NAME IN EMPLOYEES.LAST_NAME%TYPE,
  SEARCH_CURSOR OUT T_REFCURSOR) IS
    stmt VARCHAR2(4000);
    bindvar varchar2(100);
 BEGIN
   stmt := 'SELECT EMPLOYEE_ID, FIRST_NAME, LAST_NAME, SALARY
     FROM EMPLOYEES';
   bindvar := NULL;
   IF (FIRST_NAME IS NOT NULL) THEN
     stmt := stmt || ' WHERE FIRST_NAME LIKE :B ORDER BY
       FIRST_NAME';
   ELSIF (LAST_NAME IS NOT NULL) THEN
     stmt := stmt || ' WHERE LAST_NAME LIKE :B ORDER BY
       LAST_NAME';
   ELSE
     raise_application_error(-20001, 'No values for
       FirstName/LastName');
   END IF;
   bindvar := '%';
   OPEN SEARCH_CURSOR FOR stmt USING bindvar;
 END;
END;
/
```

How it works...

Static SQL is a common way in which SQL code is inserted in applications. The static SQL statements are hardcoded in application sources. Dynamic SQL, instead, is evaluated at runtime and then executed; this is the default behavior of many APIs, such as JDBC and ODBC. Static SQL is the natural choice for pre-compiler-based environments, such as PRO*COBOL and PRO*C.

In PL/SQL, we have both static and dynamic SQL. We are forced to use Dynamic SQL when we are in one of the situations listed in the previous section, because there isn't any feature to use with static SQL to meet those requirements.

In situations other than those listed earlier, the use of dynamic SQL can lead to unnecessary parsing and poor performance.

 In this recipe, we are discussing performance-related issues related to the use of dynamic SQL in Oracle databases. We aren't considering security flaws, such as SQL injection and others.

There's more...

Dynamic SQL is a powerful feature of the database but it should be used carefully.

When we execute Native Dynamic SQL (NDS), we are forcing a soft parse to occur, if the statement executed is equal to the previous statement, the parse phase is skipped. To avoid this drawback, we can use the DBMS_SQL package (its use is beyond the scope of this book), with which we can control which cursor we want to reuse to avoid reparsing the same statement over and over.

Even when we use dynamic SQL, we can use bind variables and we have to use them if we want to obtain good performance. Often developers, who write dynamic SQL, append the actual values within the query statement as literals. We have seen this in the *A working example* recipe in *Chapter 1*, not using bind variables led to poor performance, and we will investigate this further in *Using bind variables* in *Chapter 4*.

Obviously, there are elements that cannot bind, for example, table and column names cannot, as actual values have to be there when the parser analyses the statement to generate the execution plan. Besides parsing and the bind variables, there are other things to be cautious about when using dynamic SQL in PL/SQL:

- ▸ The code is more prone to bugs
- ▸ The database can't check dependencies for dynamic SQL
- ▸ Tuning a dynamic SQL procedure can be difficult

Let's explore these issues.

The code is more easily broken when we use dynamic SQL because the statements that our application will generate at runtime are unknown. There could be a case that we have not foreseen, which generates an error—often a syntactically wrong SQL statement to be exact. It could take long to test every SQL statement generated by our procedures.

When we submit a stored procedure to the database, there is a compilation phase that not only ensures that the syntax is correct and but also stores the dependencies of the stored procedure in the data dictionary. If we are referencing the table EMPLOYEES in the static SQL, the database knows it and stores this information to invalidate the procedure if there is a change made to the referenced object, for example, an ALTER TABLE, forcing the procedure to be recompiled the next time it's invoked.

The data dictionary is a read-only set of tables that provides administrative metadata about the database; it contains the definitions of every schema object, the amount of space allocated, the name of users and the privileges and roles granted to them. Auditing information is also stored in the data dictionary.

With dynamic SQL, the database engine cannot anticipate which objects will be referenced by the stored procedure, so these objects won't be stored in the data dictionary among the dependencies of the stored procedure. If there is a change affecting the object—even if it is a DROP TABLE—the database cannot force the procedure to be recompiled, because it doesn't know that there is a relationship between the object and the procedure.

Moreover, when we use dynamic SQL in a stored procedure, tuning the procedure can be a nightmare. If someone has coded a procedure similar to the example presented earlier, to search for the EMPLOYEES table, there may be situations where the search does not perform as expected, but by analyzing the code we cannot clearly point at the cause of slowdown, because the actual query is built at runtime.

See also

▶ *A working example* in Chapter 1, *Starting with Performance Tuning*
▶ *Using bind variables* in Chapter 4, *Optimizing SQL Code*

3
Optimizing Storage Structures

In this chapter, we will cover:

- ► Avoiding row chaining
- ► Avoiding row migration
- ► Using LOBs
- ► Using index clusters
- ► Using hash clusters
- ► Indexing the correct way
- ► Rebuilding index
- ► Compressing indexes
- ► Using reverse key indexes
- ► Using bitmap indexes
- ► Migrating to index organized tables
- ► Using partitioning

Introduction

In the previous chapter, we saw how to design an application which performs well (or has less chance to perform badly) by applying some simple rules of thumb, namely, connection management, reusable code, reducing requests to the database, schema denormalization, and the use of dynamic SQL.

In this chapter, we will look at some structures available in Oracle databases that store data and improve the access time—that is, the time needed to retrieve data—when the data is queried.

The first recipes relate to tables—the most used storage structure—with useful tips to avoid bottlenecks related to data stored in tables.

We will then move on to indexes (and inspect different index flavors). At the end of the chapter, we will finally see recipes related to index organized tables and partitioning options. Choosing the right structure to store data can drastically improve the performance of applications; using the right index can speed up our queries, as can introducing drawbacks in insert, update, and delete operations. As always, the performance tuning process aims to balance different needs to obtain the maximum average speed in the different operations involving the database.

Avoiding row chaining

We encounter row chaining when the size of the row data is larger than the size of the database block used to store it. In this situation, the row is split across more than one database block, so, to read it we need to access more than one database block, resulting in greater I/O.

Getting ready

Before we can start, we have to alter an initialization parameter of the test database (assuming the default block size is 8KB in the test database):

```
ALTER SYSTEM SET db_16k_cache_size = 16m scope=both;
```

We need to set this parameter to allocate a memory buffer dedicated to storing database blocks of a different size; in this recipe, we will create a tablespace using a 16KB block size, so we need the corresponding buffer allocated to use it.

How to do it...

In this recipe, we will examine how to detect row chaining issues, and how to avoid chaining in our tables. Follow these steps:

1. Connect to the HR schema:
   ```
   CONNECT hr@TESTDB/hr
   ```

2. Create the table BIG_ROWS:
   ```
   CREATE TABLE HR.BIG_ROWS (
       id number NOT NULL,
       field1 char(2000) DEFAULT 'A' NOT NULL,
       field2 char(2000) DEFAULT 'B' NOT NULL,
   ```

```
field3 char(2000) DEFAULT 'C' NOT NULL,
field4 char(2000) DEFAULT 'D' NOT NULL,
field5 char(2000) DEFAULT 'E' NOT NULL,
constraint PK_BIG_ROWS primary key (ID))
TABLESPACE EXAMPLE;
```

3. Populate the table:

```
INSERT INTO HR.BIG_ROWS (id)
select rownum from all_objects where rownum < 101;
```

4. Analyze the table to refresh the statistics:

```
ANALYZE TABLE HR.BIG_ROWS COMPUTE STATISTICS;
```

5. Verify if there are chained rows:

```
SELECT CHAIN_CNT FROM ALL_TABLES
WHERE OWNER = <HR> AND TABLE_NAME = <BIG_ROWS>;
```

6. In the next screenshot, we can see the results of these operations:

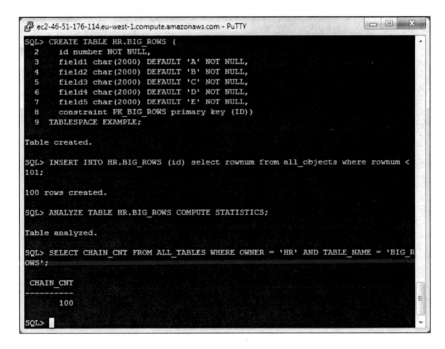

7. Create a tablespace with a different block size:

```
CREATE TABLESPACE TS_16K BLOCKSIZE 16K DATAFILE 'TS_16K.DBF'
SIZE 10M EXTENT MANAGEMENT LOCAL UNIFORM SIZE 1M;
```

8. Move the table `BIG_ROWS` to the tablespace just created:

   ALTER TABLE HR.BIG_ROWS MOVE TABLESPACE TS_16K;

9. Rebuild the indexes, as they are unusable after the move:

   ALTER INDEX HR.PK_BIG_ROWS REBUILD;

10. Analyze the table to refresh the statistics:

    ANALYZE TABLE HR.BIG_ROWS COMPUTE STATISTICS;

11. Verify if there are chained rows.

    SELECT CHAIN_CNT FROM ALL_TABLES

    WHERE OWNER = <HR> AND TABLE_NAME = <BIG_ROWS>;

12. In the next screenshot, we can see the results of these operations:

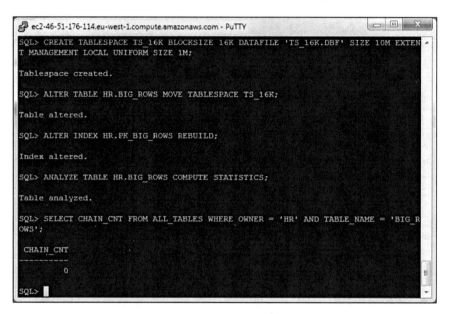

13. Drop the tablespace and the table:

    DROP TABLESPACE TS_16K INCLUDING CONTENTS AND DATAFILES;

How it works...

We have created the table BIG_ROWS in which row length is greater than 8 Kbytes, the DB block size value for the tablespace EXAMPLE of TESTDB.

We have populated this table with 100 rows, and after analyzing the table we know that there are 100 chained rows. A chained row is a row which cannot fit into one DB block, due to its size (when inserted or updated). So the database engine stores the initial part of the row in a DB block, which is chained to another DB block where the remaining part of the row content is stored.

To avoid chained rows, we can move the table to a tablespace with a greater DB block size; we have created the tablespace TS_16K with a block size of 16K, greater than the average row length of the BIG_ROWS table.

We have moved the BIG_ROWS table to the newly created tablespace and rebuilt the primary key index—which is marked unusable after the move. We then analyzed the table again to refresh the statistics.

After the move, the chained rows have disappeared from the BIG_ROWS table.

There's more...

We can use different block sizes in the Oracle database, but every tablespace can have only one block size. Before adding a tablespace with a different DB block size, we have to make room in the database buffer cache to store DB blocks of every size, as we have done in the *Getting ready* section of this recipe.

As stated earlier, row chaining occurs when the database block size isn't big enough to store a row entirely. In such cases, the only solution to avoid row chaining is to move the table to a tablespace with a bigger DB block size, as we have done.

After moving the table, we had to rebuild the index. Why?

The answer is simple. An index contains the ROWIDs of the table rows, and the ROWIDs identify the position of the row, madeup by the object, the datafile, the block number, and the slot (row) number. When we move a table, the datafile and the block number change, so the indexes have to be rebuilt.

There are some considerations to be taken care of, however; when having tablespaces with different DB block sizes in the database—as we have seen— we have to reserve space in the database buffer for a different DB block size, and the memory reserved to a particular block size cannot be used for caching database blocks of a different size. This situation led to a possible waste of memory. For example, we have 512 MB reserved for `db_16k_cache_size` unused, because we have few objects stored with this database block size, and the `db_8k_cache_size` is fully utilized. Tuning the buffer cache can become a nightmare in such an environment. Why? Because we need to identify the specific requirements for each database block size used in the database and to optimize the corresponding buffer size.

Row chaining causes poor performance because accessing a row in the database has to read more than one DB block, even when we access the table by an index lookup. When we plan to introduce different block sizes in the database, we have to keep in mind the pros and cons of a larger block size. The larger the block size, the more likely there will be contention issues on the database block.

There are also advantages in using multiple block sizes, which are as follows:

- **Contention reduction**: small rows in a large block perform worse under heavy DML than large rows in a small block size.

- **Reduced row chaining**: placing large object rows (BLOB, CLOB) into a tablespace with a larger block size can greatly reduce row chaining and improve I/O.

- **Faster updates**: heavy insert/update tables can see faster performance when segregated into another block size, which is mapped to a small data buffer cache. Smaller data buffer caches often see faster throughput performance.

- **Reduced Pinging**: RAC can perform far faster with a 2K block size, greatly reducing cache fusion overhead.

- **Less disk space waste**: when using Oracle 11g advanced compression, testing shows that a 32k block size is the best choice to maximize compression and minimize waste.

- **Less RAM waste**: moving random access small row tables to a smaller block size (with a corresponding small block size buffer) will reduce buffer waste and improve the chances of the other data blocks remaining in the cache.

- **Minimize redo generation**: some experts recommend a 2K block size for bitmap indexes, to minimize redo generation during bitmap index rebuilds.

- **Faster scans**: tables and indexes that require full scans can see faster performance when placed in a large block size.

See also

▶ The *Avoiding Full Table Scan* recipe in *Chapter 4, Optimizing SQL Code* and *Tuning the buffer cache* in *Chapter 9, Tuning Memory*

Avoiding row migration

When we update a row and it does not fit entirely within the original database block due to the corresponding growth in size, we have a row migration. In the original place (where the row was stored) we have placed a pointer to the new location of the row.

How to do it...

In this recipe, we will see how to detect row migration issues, and how to avoid migrating rows in our tables. Follow these steps:

1. Connect to HR schema:

    ```
    CONNECT hr@TESTDB/hr
    ```

2. Create the table `BIG_ROWS`:

    ```
    CREATE TABLE HR.BIG_ROWS (
        id number NOT NULL,
        field1 char(2000) DEFAULT 'A' NOT NULL,
        field2 char(2000),
        field3 char(2000),
        field4 char(1000),
        constraint PK_BIG_ROWS primary key (ID))
    TABLESPACE EXAMPLE PCTFREE 10;
    ```

3. Populate the table:

    ```
    INSERT INTO HR.BIG_ROWS (id)
    select rownum from all_objects where rownum < 101;
    ```

4. Analyze the table to refresh the statistics:

    ```
    ANALYZE TABLE HR.BIG_ROWS COMPUTE STATISTICS;
    ```

5. Verify if there are migrated rows:

    ```
    SELECT CHAIN_CNT FROM ALL_TABLES
    WHERE OWNER = <HR> AND TABLE_NAME = <BIG_ROWS>;3
    ```

6. In the next screenshot, we can see the results of these operations:

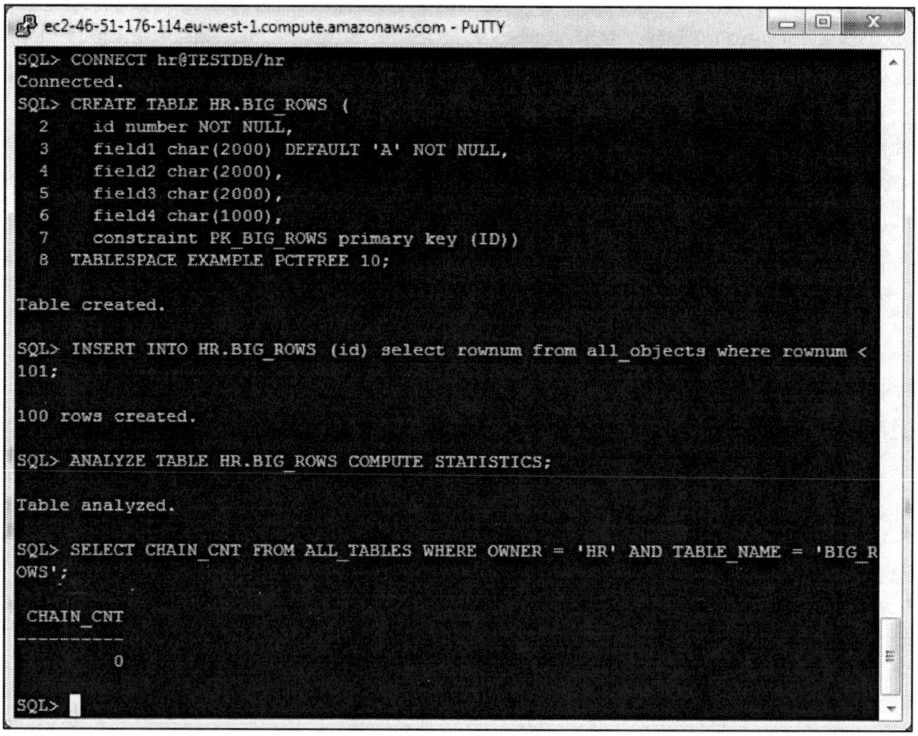

7. Update some data in the table:

```
UPDATE HR.BIG_ROWS SET field2 = 'B',
   field3 = <C>, field4 = <D>
WHERE MOD(id, 2) = 1;
```

8. Analyze the table to refresh the statistics:

```
ANALYZE TABLE HR.BIG_ROWS COMPUTE STATISTICS;
```

9. Verify if there are migrated rows:

```
SELECT CHAIN_CNT FROM ALL_TABLES
WHERE OWNER = <HR> AND TABLE_NAME = <BIG_ROWS>;
```

10. Create table `CHAINED_ROWS`:

```
create table HR.CHAINED_ROWS (
  owner_name           varchar2(30),
  table_name           varchar2(30),
  cluster_name         varchar2(30),
  partition_name       varchar2(30),
  subpartition_name    varchar2(30),
  head_rowid           rowid,
  analyze_timestamp    date
);
```

11. Analyze the table to list the migrated rows:

```
ANALYZE TABLE HR.BIG_ROWS LIST CHAINED ROWS
INTO HR.CHAINED_ROWS;
```

12. Count (or list) the migrated rows:

```
SELECT COUNT(*) FROM HR.CHAINED_ROWS;
```

13. In the next screenshot, we can see the results of these operations:

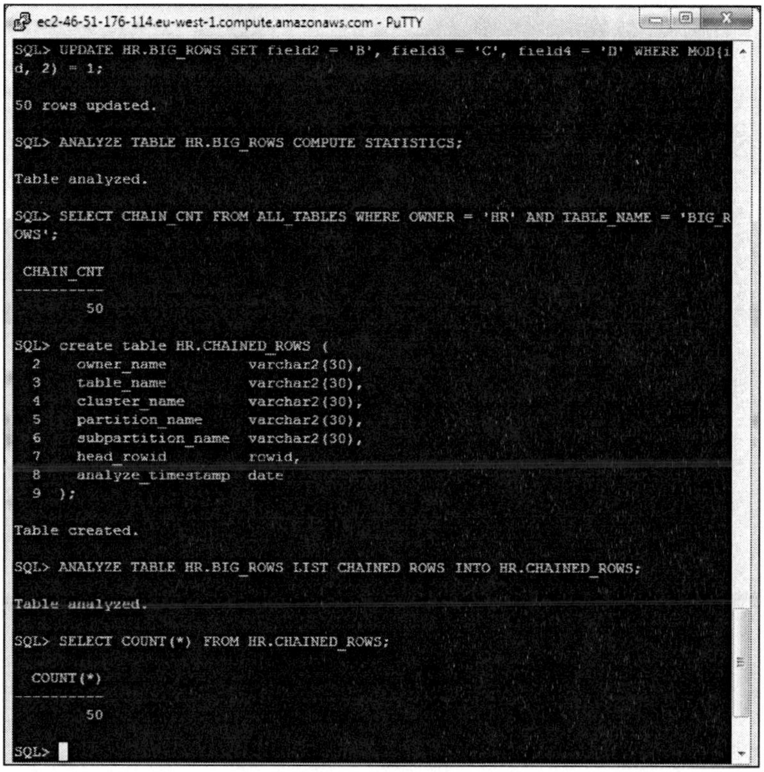

14. Create a temporary table, which is an empty copy of BIG_ROWS:

    ```
    CREATE.5* FROM HR.BIG_ROWS WHERE 1=0;
    ```

15. Copy the migrated rows to the temporary table:

    ```
    INSERT INTO TEMP_BIG_ROWS
      SELECT B.* FROM HR.BIG_ROWS B, HR.CHAINED_ROWS T
      WHERE T.OWNER_NAME = <HR> AND T.TABLE_NAME = <BIG_ROWS>
      AND T.HEAD_ROWID = B.ROWID;
    ```

16. Delete the migrated rows from the BIG_ROWS table:

    ```
    DELETE FROM HR.BIG_ROWS B WHERE EXISTS (
      SELECT T.ROWID FROM HR.CHAINED_ROWS T
      WHERE T.OWNER_NAME = <HR> AND T.TABLE_NAME = <BIG_ROWS>
      AND T.HEAD_ROWID = B.ROWID);
    ```

17. Copy the migrated rows from the temporary table back to the BIG_ROWS table:

    ```
    INSERT INTO HR.BIG_ROWS SELECT * FROM HR.TEMP_BIG_ROWS;
    ```

18. Analyze the table to refresh the statistics:

    ```
    ANALYZE TABLE HR.BIG_ROWS COMPUTE STATISTICS;
    ```

19. Verify if there are migrated rows:

    ```
    SELECT CHAIN_CNT FROM ALL_TABLES WHERE OWNER = 'HR'
    AND TABLE_NAME = <BIG_ROWS>;
    ```

20. In the next screenshot, we can see the results of these operations:

21. Drop the tables used for testing:

```
DROP TABLE HR.TEMP_BIG_ROWS;
DROP TABLE HR.CHAINED_ROWS;
DROP TABLE HR.BIG_ROWS;
```

How it works...

We have created the table BIG_ROWS in which row length is smaller than 8 KB, the DB block size value for the tablespace example of TESTDB, but whose length can grow from 2 to 7 KB depending on whether FIELD2, FIELD3, and FIELD4 are null or not.

 The size in the previous example is calculated for single-byte charactersets; if we use multi-byte charactersets the space needed by a single character is more than 1 byte.

We have populated this table with 100 rows keeping the latter fields null. After analyzing the table, we know that there aren't any chained/migrated rows.

A migrated row occurs when a row is updated but does not fit into the original DB block, due to its new size. Thus, the database engine stores a pointer in the original position of the row, which points to the new position of the row (hence "migrated").

Using the pointer allows us to avoid invalidating the indexes, because the original ROWID is kept. The database stores the row header in the original place, pointing to the new block where the row is entirely stored.

To prevent row migration, we have to set a higher value for the table PCTFREE storage parameters, to allow more space in the block, which is free for subsequent updates of the rows.

In the example, the table has a value of PCTFREE set to 10, meaning that the database will keep 10 percent of the DB block free to allow row growth due to subsequent updates.

To solve the migrated row issue once it's in place, we have to list the migrated rows in a (temporary) table, delete them from the original place, disable foreign key constraints and triggers if they exist, to avoid violating them, and insert them back from the temporary table to the original table. This is what we have done in the last part of the example, verifying that after such a move row migration has disappeared.

There's more...

Row migration, similar to row chaining, causes poor performance because the database engine must read more than one block in order to access to the row data.

The biggest difference between row chaining and row migration is that row chaining highlights a bad row design or a small DB block size, while row migration indicates that a very small PCTFREE parameter has been used for a table.

We have also seen how to list all migrated rows in a (temporary) table with the ANALYZE TABLE... LIST CHAINED ROWS INTO... command. The script to create a CHAINED_ROWS table is located at $ORACLE_HOME/rdbms/admin/utlchain.sql.

There are two other methods to resolve row migration: performing an ALTER TABLE MOVE, or using EXPORT/IMPORT procedures to dump and reload the data into the table.

Estimating table size with different PCTFREE parameter

Often the value of PCTFREE is set very low to avoid wasting space, this is not a wise strategy, unless we are talking about insert-only tables, for example, something similar to an audit trail, where we can use a PCTFREE 0 parameter.

To estimate the size of a table using different values for the PCTFREE parameter, we can use the CREATE_TABLE_COST of the DBMS_SPACE package:

```
SET SERVEROUTPUT ON
declare
  l_used_bytes number;
  l_alloc_bytes number;
begin
  dbms_space.create_table_cost (
    tablespace_name => 'EXAMPLE',
    avg_row_size => 4500,
    row_count => 100,
    pct_free => 10,
    used_bytes => l_used_bytes,
    alloc_bytes => l_alloc_bytes
  );
  dbms_output.put_line('Used Bytes: '||l_used_bytes);
  dbms_output.put_line('Allocated Bytes: '||l_alloc_bytes);
end;
/
```

In this procedure, we have set the tablespace to use the average row size and the row count, we can try different pct_free parameters to estimate the space needed by the table, both allocated and used.

In the next screenshot, we can see the calculated **Used** and **Allocated** bytes:

```
ec2-46-51-176-114.eu-west-1.compute.amazonaws.com - PuTTY
SQL> SET SERVEROUTPUT ON
SQL> declare
  2    l_used_bytes number;
  3    l_alloc_bytes number;
  4  begin
  5    dbms_space.create_table_cost (
  6      tablespace_name => 'EXAMPLE',
  7      avg_row_size => 4500,
  8      row_count => 100,
  9      pct_free => 10,
 10      used_bytes => l_used_bytes,
 11      alloc_bytes => l_alloc_bytes
 12    );
 13    dbms_output.put_line('Used: '||l_used_bytes);
 14    dbms_output.put_line('Allocated: '||l_alloc_bytes);
 15  end;
 16  /
Used: 819200
Allocated: 851968

PL/SQL procedure successfully completed.

SQL>
```

We can experiment with different input values for the previous procedure, obtaining what will be the wasted space in our table using a different PCT_FREE parameter in the storage options.

Using LOBs

LOBs (**Large OBjects**) are a particular data type, used to store large binary or character objects inside the database or outside the database when using BFILEs. In this recipe, we will see how to use LOB fields to avoid performance degradation and space wasting.

Getting ready

The following steps have to be performed initially;

1. Connect to the database as SYSDBA:

    CONNECT /@TESTDB AS SYSDBA

2. Grant the following permission to user SH:

    GRANT CREATE ANY DIRECTORY TO SH;

3. Create a tablespace for LOBs:

    CREATE TABLESPACE ASSM_TS DATAFILE 'ASSM_TS.DBF' SIZE 100M

    EXTENT MANAGEMENT LOCAL SEGMENT SPACE MANAGEMENT AUTO;

How to do it...

In this recipe, we will see how to use LOB felds to avoid performance degradation and space wasting. Follow these steps:

1. Connect to the database as user SH:

   ```
   CONNECT s.5h@TESTDB/sh
   ```

2. Create a table to do some tests copying the CUSTOMERS table and its contents:

   ```
   CREATE TABLE MyCustomers AS SELECT * FROM Customers;
   ```

3. Add a BLOB field to the table:

   ```
   ALTER TABLE MyCustomers ADD (c_file BLOB)
    LOB(c_file) STORE AS SECUREFILE (
      tablespace ASSM_TS
      enable storage in row
      nocache logging
   );
   ```

4. Create a reference to the $ORACLE_HOME/rdbms/admin folder (fill in the correct path for your Oracle Database installation):

   ```
   CREATE DIRECTORY TESTBLOB AS
   </u01/app/oracle/product/11.2.0/db_1/rdbms/admin>;
   ```

5. Load the blob field with some data:

   ```
   declare
     l_file bfile;
     l_blob blob;
     l_size number;
   begin
     l_file := bfilename(<TESTBLOB>, <catalog.sql>);
     dbms_lob.fileopen(l_file);
     l_size := dbms_lob.getlength(l_file);
     for J in 1 .. 100 loop
        update MyCustomers SET c_file = empty_blob() where CUST_ID = J
   returning c_file into l_blob;
        dbms_lob.loadfromfile(l_blob, l_file, l_size);
     end loop;
     commit;
     dbms_lob.close(l_file);
   end;
   ```

6. Test the space occupied by the BLOB data; the DBMS_SPACE.SPACE_USAGE procedure returns information about free data blocks in an object whose segment space management is AUTO:

```
SET SERVEROUTPUT ON
declare
  l_segment_name VARCHAR2(30);
  l_segment_size_blocks NUMBER;
  l_segment_size_bytes NUMBER;
  l_used_blocks NUMBER;
  l_used_bytes NUMBER;
  l_expired_blocks NUMBER;
  l_expired_bytes NUMBER;
  l_unexpired_blocks NUMBER;
  l_unexpired_bytes NUMBER;
begin
  select segment_name into l_segment_name from user_lobs where
table_name = 'MYCUSTOMERS';
  DBMS_OUTPUT.put_line('segment name: ' || l_segment_name);
  DBMS_SPACE.SPACE_USAGE(
    segment_owner       => USER,
    segment_name        => l_segment_name,
    segment_type        => 'LOB',
    segment_size_blocks => l_segment_size_blocks,
    segment_size_bytes  => l_segment_size_bytes,
    used_blocks         => l_used_blocks,
    used_bytes          => l_used_bytes,
    expired_blocks      => l_expired_blocks,
    expired_bytes       => l_expired_bytes,
    unexpired_blocks    => l_unexpired_blocks,
    unexpired_bytes     => l_unexpired_bytes);
  DBMS_OUTPUT.put_line('used_blocks ' || l_used_blocks);
  DBMS_OUTPUT.put_line('used_bytes ' || l_used_bytes);
end;
```

8. The results of this step are shown in the following screenshot:

```
ec2-46-51-176-114.eu-west-1.compute.amazonaws.com - PuTTY
SQL> SET SERVEROUTPUT ON
SQL> declare
  2      l_segment_name VARCHAR2(30);
  3      l_segment_size_blocks NUMBER;
  4      l_segment_size_bytes NUMBER;
  5      l_used_blocks NUMBER;
  6      l_used_bytes NUMBER;
  7      l_expired_blocks NUMBER;
  8      l_expired_bytes NUMBER;
  9      l_unexpired_blocks NUMBER;
 10      l_unexpired_bytes NUMBER;
 11  begin
 12      select segment_name into l_segment_name from user_lobs where table_name =
'MYCUSTOMERS';
 13      DBMS_OUTPUT.put_line('segment name: ' || l_segment_name);
 14      DBMS_SPACE.SPACE_USAGE(
 15        segment_owner        => USER,
 16        segment_name         => l_segment_name,
 17        segment_type         => 'LOB',
 18        segment_size_blocks  => l_segment_size_blocks,
 19        segment_size_bytes   => l_segment_size_bytes,
 20        used_blocks          => l_used_blocks,
 21        used_bytes           => l_used_bytes,
 22        expired_blocks       => l_expired_blocks,
 23        expired_bytes        => l_expired_bytes,
 24        unexpired_blocks     => l_unexpired_blocks,
 25        unexpired_bytes      => l_unexpired_bytes);
 26      DBMS_OUTPUT.put_line('used_blocks ' || l_used_blocks);
 27      DBMS_OUTPUT.put_line('used_bytes ' || l_used_bytes);
 28  end;
 29  /
segment name: SYS_LOB0000074673C00024$$
used_blocks 800
used_bytes 6553600

PL/SQL procedure successfully completed.

SQL>
```

9. Deduplicate the blob field:

```
ALTER TABLE MyCustomers MODIFY LOB (c_file) (deduplicate);
```

10. Test the space occupied by the BLOB data as in step 6.

11. The results of this step are shown in the following screenshot:

```
ec2-46-51-176-114.eu-west-1.compute.amazonaws.com - PuTTY
 22        expired_blocks        => l_expired_blocks,
 23        expired_bytes         => l_expired_bytes,
 24        unexpired_blocks      => l_unexpired_blocks,
 25        unexpired_bytes       => l_unexpired_bytes);
 26        DBMS_OUTPUT.put_line('used_blocks ' || l_used_blocks);
 27        DBMS_OUTPUT.put_line('used_bytes ' || l_used_bytes);
 28   end;
 29   /
segment name: SYS_LOB0000074673C00024$$
used_blocks 8
used_bytes 65536

PL/SQL procedure successfully completed.

SQL>
```

12. Compress the blob field:

```
ALTER TABLE MyCustomers MODIFY LOB (c_file) (compress high);
```

13. Test the space occupied by the BLOB data as in step 6.

14. The results of this step are shown in the next screenshot:

```
ec2-46-51-176-114.eu-west-1.compute.amazonaws.com - PuTTY
 22        expired_blocks        => l_expired_blocks,
 23        expired_bytes         => l_expired_bytes,
 24        unexpired_blocks      => l_unexpired_blocks,
 25        unexpired_bytes       => l_unexpired_bytes);
 26        DBMS_OUTPUT.put_line('used_blocks ' || l_used_blocks);
 27        DBMS_OUTPUT.put_line('used_bytes ' || l_used_bytes);
 28   end;
 29   /
segment name: SYS_LOB0000074673C00024$$
used_blocks 3
used_bytes 24576

PL/SQL procedure successfully completed.

SQL>
```

How it works...

BLOB fields are used to store binary unstructured data, such as multimedia data, that is, pictures, video, and audio. We have created a table MYCUSTOMERS with the data of the CUSTOMERS table in schema SH, adding a new BLOB field, c_file, to store a binary file with every customer.

We have instructed the database to store BLOB data *inline* with the row, in a newly created tablespace ASSM_TS whose segment space is set to automatic management.

We have chosen to store the BLOB data as SECUREFILE, an option available from Oracle Database 11gR1, which allows us to carry out subsequent steps to optimize BLOB storage.

To populate the BLOB field, we have defined a DIRECTORY called TESTBLOB to refer to the folder $ORACLE_HOME/rdbms/admin, and we have used a PL/SQL block to populate the c_file field for the first 100 customers in the table, loading the same file in it—the catalog.sql script, which is about 58 Kbytes.

To do so, we have used a simple sequence of operations: updating the row with an empty blob—returned by the function empty_blob()—and using the procedure DBMS_LOB. LOADFROMFILE to populate the newly created empty BLOB reference.

We have then used the procedure DBMS_SPACE.SPACE_USAGE to measure the used space —expressed in database blocks and in bytes—in the segment where the LOB data is stored.

We have then modified the definition of the c_file field, enabling deduplicating first—which means that Oracle stores only one copy for the same BLOB content—and then compression.

After each of these steps, we have again measured the space used by the BLOB storage, verifying a great decrease in occupation.

There's more...

In the example, there is an aspect related to the trivial nature of the test case: the content of the BLOB field is populated with the data of a text file; in real-life databases, we chose another data type to store text data, for example, VARCHAR, NVARCHAR, CLOB, and reserved BLOB fields to store binary data.

In creating the c_file BLOB field, we have the clause enable storage in row, which means "store the data in the same DB block in which other fields of the row are stored". We saw that the data are not actually stored in rows, because when the size of the BLOB field is greater than 4000 bytes it is always stored off-line. The same behavior occurs when the DB block size is large enough to accommodate the BLOB field.

We can even specify a CHUNK size when defining a BLOB field, which is an integer multiple of DB_BLOCK_SIZE: when the database engine reads BLOB fields, it accesses the data in pieces sized accordingly to the CHUNK parameter, and it's more efficient to read large chunks of data than small.

Here is an example of defining a BLOB field with a specified CHUNK size:

```
ALTER TABLE MyCustomers ADD (c_file BLOB)
 LOB(c_file) STORE AS SECUREFILE (
   tablespace ASSM_TS
   CHUNK 4096
   enable storage in row
   nocache
   logging
 );
```

The drawback of having a large CHUNK parameter occurs when we want to update the field, because the database engine writes CHUNK sized pieces of data in redo logs and in undo segments. The redo log files have block sizes equal to the physical sector size of the disk and since the release of 11gR2 we can specify a size of 512, 1024, or 4096 bytes. To write a chunk of 8192 bytes, for example, we need to write from 2 to 16 blocks in the redo log, so it's more efficient to have smaller CHUNK(s) in this situation.

We have specified the use of LOGGING for BLOB data. Sometimes we hear of using NOLOGGING for BLOB fields because it's faster; the counterpart of using NOLOGGING is in data availability. When we use LOGGING we are sure that data is recoverable in case of some database server failure or should the disk/tape or storage media fail. In using NOLOGGING we cannot recover changes from the redo log because the changes were never logged.

The use of SecureFile (s) allows us to apply some of the enhancements using BLOB fields; in fact we can deduplicate the field, compress, encrypt, manage caching, and log.

When we create a BLOB field in Oracle Database 11gR2, by default we are using BasicFile, that is, the standard BLOB definition that was in use before.

We can change this behavior with ALTER SYSTEM SET db_securefile = 'FORCE', to have any BLOB field created by default as SecureFile; other options are PERMITTED (the default), ALWAYS, NEVER, IGNORE.

Deduplication consists of storing one copy of a BLOB field when the same content is shared among different rows, thus reducing the space requirements. It's a good practice and useful in situations where the content of BLOB fields experience limited cardinality or a broad repetition of data.

The cardinality is the number of elements in a set; low cardinality refers to columns with few unique values, such as the gender column in a customer table, while high cardinality refers to columns with values which are (almost) unique, such as e-mail addresses or IDs.

The concept of data compression is easy to understand, compressing BLOB data reduces the size. The compression, obviously, will produce the best effect when the binary data is not initially compressed. In the example presented in this recipe, we have stored a text file, which is a very good candidate for data compression. If we are storing images compressed by a third party tool before being inserted into the DB in a BLOB field, compression will not offer great improvement because the original format is already compressed. In these situations, when we know that the content of a BLOB field will be a compressed format, it's better to disable the compression to save CPU time. However, from Oracle database 11gR2, the SecureFiles Compression feature automatically avoids compressing data that would not benefit from compression.

The encryption of BLOB data is an important feature that allows us to encrypt data stored in a particular BLOB field, for example, when we store an image diagnosis or digital documents that must remain confidential. To encrypt data we will use transparent database encryption, as for regular fields.

Caching LOB data in the database can be a nightmare, because this kind of data is usually very large in size, so caching a single field may prove costly in terms of the database buffers used to store the object. To accommodate enough space for a LOB—which ultimately won't be used anymore—there will be many database blocks which were once cached and have now been freed. For this reason, caching for LOB fields is often disabled, as we have done when defining the c_file field.

The last aspect to take care of when defining BLOB fields is logging. The default behavior is the same that is used for other data types, namely, full logging enabled. Due to the large size of BLOB data, we could choose to bypass the logging mechanism for this kind of information, using the NOLOGGING parameters. In this case, however, we are not able to rely on database read consistency, because the changes to the BLOB field were never logged.

With Oracle SecureFiles, we have a third choice for logging: we can use filesystem_like_logging, which will log the metadata information changes about the BLOB, but won't log the data itself, providing a comfortable alternative.

Using index clusters

A cluster is a group of tables that share common columns and are stored in the same data blocks; this organization is useful when we access this data using joins in queries.

How to do it...

In this recipe, we will see how and when to use index clusters, and some tricks to adopt when using this kind of storage. Follow these steps:

1. Connect to the HR schema of TESTDB database:

   ```
   CONNECT hr@TESTDB/hr
   ```

2. Create a cluster:

   ```
   CREATE CLUSTER LOC_ENTRIES (COUNTRY_ID CHAR(2)) SIZE 100;
   ```

3. Create the cluster index:

   ```
   CREATE INDEX IDX_LOC_ENTRIES ON CLUSTER LOC_ENTRIES;
   ```

4. Create and populate the first table:

   ```
   CREATE TABLE CL_COUNTRIES CLUSTER LOC_ENTRIES (COUNTRY_ID) AS
   SELECT * FROM COUNTRIES;
   ```

5. Create and populate the second table:

```
CREATE TABLE CL_LOCATIONS CLUSTER LOC_ENTRIES (COUNTRY_ID) AS
SELECT L.*, CAST(<*> AS CHAR(1000)) AS FOO_DATA
FROM LOCATIONS L;
```

6. Verify the database blocks where the data of the two tables is stored:

```
select
  cl_countries.country_id,
  dbms_rowid.rowid_block_number(cl_countries.rowid)
    as cou_blk,
  dbms_rowid.rowid_block_number(cl_locations.rowid) as loc_blk
from cl_countries, cl_locations
where cl_countries.country_id = cl_locations.country_id
order by 1;
```

7. In the following screenshot, we can see the results of the last query:

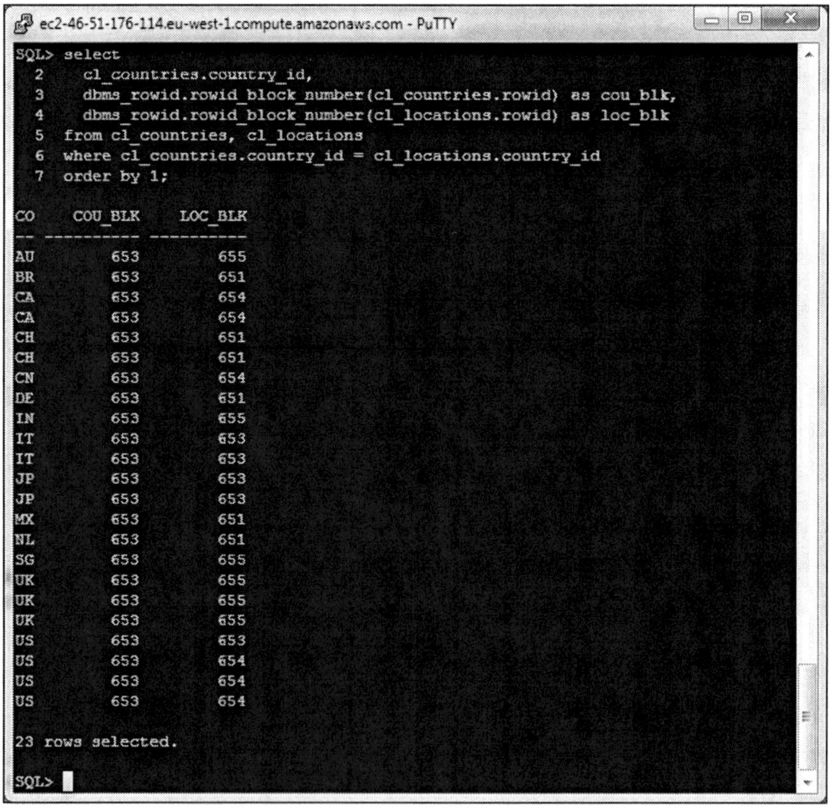

8. Clear the previous example:

```
DROP CLUSTER LOC_ENTRIES INCLUDING TABLES;
```

9. Recreate the cluster and index as before:

```
CREATE CLUSTER LOC_ENTRIES (COUNTRY_ID CHAR(2)) SIZE 100;

CREATE INDEX IDX_LOC_ENTRIES ON CLUSTER LOC_ENTRIES;
```

10. Create the first table without populating the data:

```
CREATE TABLE CL_COUNTRIES CLUSTER LOC_ENTRIES (COUNTRY_ID) AS
SELECT * FROM COUNTRIES WHERE 1=0;
```

11. Create the second table without populating the data:

```
CREATE TABLE CL_LOCATIONS CLUSTER LOC_ENTRIES (COUNTRY_ID) AS
SELECT L.*, CAST(<*> AS CHAR(1000)) AS FOO_DATA
FROM LOCATIONS L WHERE 1=0;
```

12. Populate the data in a "clustered" way using PL/SQL:

```
declare
   l_country_id char(2);
begin
   for c in (select * from countries)
   loop
     insert into CL_COUNTRIES
        (country_id, country_name, region_id) values
        (c.country_id, c.country_name, c.region_id);
     insert into CL_LOCATIONS select L.*, <*> from locations L
        where L.country_id = c.country_id;
   end loop;
end;
```

13. Verify the database blocks where the data of the two tables are stored:

```
select
   cl_countries.country_id,
   dbms_rowid.rowid_block_number(cl_countries.rowid)
     as cou_blk,
   dbms_rowid.rowid_block_number(cl_locations.rowid) as loc_blk
from cl_countries, cl_locations
where cl_countries.country_id = cl_locations.country_id
order by 1;
```

14. In the following screenshot, we can see the results of the last query:

```
SQL> select
  2    cl_countries.country_id,
  3    dbms_rowid.rowid_block_number(cl_countries.rowid) as cou_blk,
  4    dbms_rowid.rowid_block_number(cl_locations.rowid) as loc_blk
  5  from cl_countries, cl_locations
  6  where cl_countries.country_id = cl_locations.country_id
  7  order by 1;

CO      COU_BLK    LOC_BLK
---    --------   --------
AU          653        653
BR          653        653
CA          653        653
CA          653        653
CH          653        653
CH          653        653
CN          653        654
DE          654        654
IN          654        654
IT          654        654
IT          654        654
JP          654        654
JP          654        655
MX          655        655
NL          655        655
SG          655        655
UK          655        651
UK          655        655
UK          655        655
US          651        651
US          651        651
US          651        651
US          651        651

23 rows selected.

SQL>
```

How it works...

In the sample, we created the cluster LOC_ENTRIES to store information related to locations and countries, which share the common COUNTRY_ID attribute.

After defining the cluster, we created an index on it, which is a mandatory operation to do before the cluster can be used to store data.

We then created two tables, CL_COUNTRIES and CL_LOCATIONS, populating data from the corresponding tables COUNTRIES and LOCATIONS of the HR schema. We added a column FOO_DATA to the CL_LOCATIONS table to make the row size bigger emphasizing a particular behavior of clustered tables.

We then used the procedure dbms_rowid.rowid_block_number to identify the block number of the database blocks in which the rows of both tables are stored.

In step 7, we dropped the newly created cluster and tables, and recreated them without inserting data in the tables.

This time, the data—which in step 4 and step 5 was inserted one table at a time—was inserted in step 11 using a PL/SQL block to practice a particular trick, useful when loading data in a cluster (the first time). We load together the correlated data of both the CL_COUNTRIES and CL_LOCATIONS tables, proceeding "one country at a time".

In step 12, we executed the same query as in step 6, to compare the results of the two approaches.

There's more...

The major benefit of using clusters is in reduced I/O for accessing data from different tables joined together, reducing even the space occupied by the cluster key that is stored once for all the rows of all the tables participating in the cluster, which have the same key value.

This organization is called **Multi-Table Index Cluster Tables**; we can also create Single-Table Index Cluster Tables, where rows from a single table are stored in sequence, thus enhancing index range scan performance.

An index cluster works as an ordinary index, speeding up access to the rows with a specific cluster key value.

In the example presented in this recipe, we can see that by loading the cluster one table at a time, the rows which share the same cluster key value are stored in different database blocks, reducing the performance gain, which can be obtained by the introduction of clustered tables—we must read multiple database blocks to answer a query.

Loading the clustered tables involved inserting the rows which share the same cluster key value in all the tables; we try to pack the records of the clustered tables in the same database block. In our example, **CN**, **JP**, and **UK** countries are stored in different database blocks, thus reducing the I/O needed when accessing our tables.

The benefits of using clusters are reduced when we regularly access a single table of the cluster or when we perform more DML operations—insert, update, and delete—than select.

The reason for this performance delay is that storing rows from more than one table in the same database block, forces the engine to read a greater block than in the case of a standard table; full table scan performance is affected by the same issue, which causes poor performance in DML operations. This is because by updating an (eventually) small row in a table of the cluster, all the blocks containing the rows for the particular cluster key affected will be read and manipulated.

Introducing an index cluster must be a long-meditated decision: even if the rows for a cluster key value cannot be stored in few (1-2) database blocks, clusters are not a good choice.

If you are thinking that cluster tables are something exotic, probably not used in real world, take a look at the CLUSTER_NAME column of DBA_TABLES:

```
select table_name, cluster_name from dba_tables
where cluster_name is not null;
```

You will discover that some data dictionary tables are stored in clusters.

Consider introducing clusters in situations where data is almost static and you often query joined together tables.

Cluster size

When we have created the cluster, we have specified SIZE 100 in the CREATE CLUSTER statement.

This optional parameter specifies the estimated size—in bytes—required to store an average cluster key with related rows, which share the same cluster key value.

This value is used by the database to estimate the number of different cluster key values, which will be stored in a database block, to optimize the storage space for the cluster.

In our example, we have deliberately used a very small sized factor to force Oracle to store a lot of different key values in the same data block, for the sake of illustration.

Cluster index

We have built an index on the cluster key; this is a common index, except for two aspects:

- The cluster index stores only one entry for every key value, pointing to the database block that contains the rows with that particular key value.

- The cluster index stores an entry for the null key value too. This is a peculiar behavior, because the standard indexes don't store entries when the indexed fields contain all null values.

Clustering and truncating

Another circumstance when table clustering is not appropriate is when we have tables that need to be truncated. Due to the particular storage characteristics of a clustered table, we cannot perform a TRUNCATE TABLE statement, because the database blocks are shared among the tables in the cluster. The only way to eliminate the rows is with the DELETE command.

If we need to use the TRUNCATE TABLE statement on a table, clustering is not a choice.

Using hash clusters

In the previous recipe, we introduced index clusters and tested a particular way to load data in a cluster to optimize the storage of rows with the same cluster key value.

In this recipe, we introduce a different kind of cluster—hash clusters. The biggest difference between index clusters and hash clusters is in the way data is accessed given a particular cluster key value.

How to do it...

The following steps will demonstrate the use of hash clusters:

1. Connect to the HR schema of the TESTDB database:

   ```
   CONNECT hr@TESTDB/hr
   ```

2. Create the cluster:

   ```
   CREATE CLUSTER EMP_DEPT_CLUSTER (deptid NUMBER(4))
   SIZE 8192 HASHKEYS 100;
   ```

3. Create the first table and populate it with data:

   ```
   CREATE TABLE CL_DEPARTMENTS CLUSTER EMP_DEPT_CLUSTER
   (department_id) AS SELECT * FROM DEPARTMENTS;
   ```

4. Create the second table, populate it with data, and gather statistics:

   ```
   CREATE TABLE CL_EMPLOYEES CLUSTER EMP_DEPT_CLUSTER
   (department_id) AS SELECT * FROM EMPLOYEES;
   EXEC DBMS_STATS.GATHER_TABLE_STATS(<HR>, <CL_EMPLOYEES>,
      estimate_percent => 100,
      method_opt => <for all columns size 1>);
   ```

5. Verify the execution plan for the regular table:

   ```
   SET AUTOT TRACE EXP
   SELECT * FROM EMPLOYEES WHERE DEPARTMENT_ID = 20;
   ```

6. In the next screenshot, we can see the results of the previous statement:

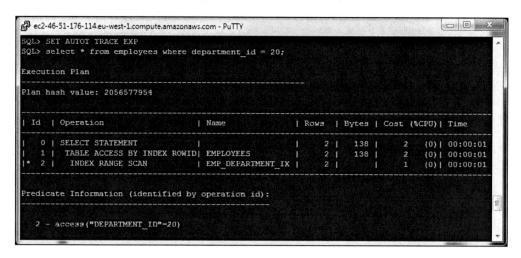

```
ec2-46-51-176-114.eu-west-1.compute.amazonaws.com - PuTTY

SQL> SET AUTOT TRACE EXP
SQL> select * from employees where department_id = 20;

Execution Plan
----------------------------------------------------------
Plan hash value: 2056577954

----------------------------------------------------------
| Id | Operation                   | Name            | Rows | Bytes | Cost (%CPU)| Time     |
----------------------------------------------------------
|  0 | SELECT STATEMENT            |                 |   2  |  138  |   2   (0)| 00:00:01 |
|  1 |  TABLE ACCESS BY INDEX ROWID| EMPLOYEES       |   2  |  138  |   2   (0)| 00:00:01 |
|* 2 |   INDEX RANGE SCAN          | EMP_DEPARTMENT_IX |  2 |       |   1   (0)| 00:00:01 |
----------------------------------------------------------

Predicate Information (identified by operation id):
----------------------------------------------------------

   2 - access("DEPARTMENT_ID"=20)
```

7. Verify the execution plan for the clustered table:

   SET AUTOT TRACE EXP

   SELECT * FROM CL_EMPLOYEES WHERE DEPARTMENT_ID = 20;

8. In the next screenshot, we can see the results of the query against the clustered table:

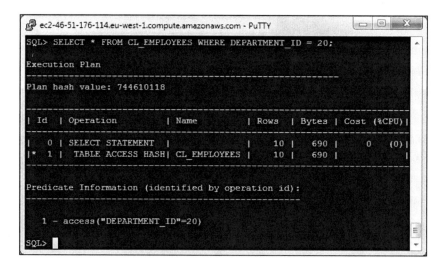

```
ec2-46-51-176-114.eu-west-1.compute.amazonaws.com - PuTTY

SQL> SELECT * FROM CL_EMPLOYEES WHERE DEPARTMENT_ID = 20;

Execution Plan
----------------------------------------------------------
Plan hash value: 744610118

----------------------------------------------------------
| Id | Operation           | Name         | Rows | Bytes | Cost (%CPU)|
----------------------------------------------------------
|  0 | SELECT STATEMENT    |              |  10  |  690  |   0   (0)|
|* 1 |  TABLE ACCESS HASH  | CL_EMPLOYEES |  10  |  690  |         |
----------------------------------------------------------

Predicate Information (identified by operation id):
----------------------------------------------------------

   1 - access("DEPARTMENT_ID"=20)
SQL>
```

9. Drop the cluster and the related tables:

   DROP CLUSTER EMP_DEPT_CLUSTER INCLUDING TABLES;

How it works...

The hash clusters use a hash function to identify the database block in which the rows with a particular cluster key value are stored, replacing the index functionalities of index clusters.

In this recipe, we have created the EMP_DEPT_CLUSTER cluster to store information related to DEPARTMENTS and EMPLOYEES, stored together using DEPARTMENT_ID as the cluster key.

We then created and populated the CL_DEPARTMENTS and CL_EMPLOYEES tables with the data of the DEPARTMENTS and EMPLOYEES tables of the HR schema.

In step 5 and step 6, we analyzed a simple query against the EMPLOYEES table and its hash-clustered counterpart CL_EMPLOYEES, to verify that. In the first query, we are using the EMP_DEPARTMENT_IX index to access the rows corresponding to the department identified by the ID 20. In the second query, we access only the clustered table segment with a TABLE ACCESS HASH operation.

The performance gain is clear we are not accessing two segments—the index and the table — to retrieve the queried data, but only the table segment.

There's more...

In hash-clustered tables, we have a greater saving in size, because we do not store any data outside the rows in the clustered tables—no indexes—and the cluster key values won't be duplicated as with index clusters.

The con is that we must know in advance the maximum cardinality of the tables, because in the cluster creating phase, we need to declare the maximum number of different keys with the HASHKEYS parameters. If the table grows over this value, we have to rebuild the cluster.

Someone could think of declaring a big HASHKEYS value, but this isn't a good idea. The space required to store HASHKEYS rows in the cluster will be allocated when the cluster is created. If we have oversized the hash cluster, there is a huge waste of space.

Hash clusters are useful when we know in advance—or can predict—the number of key values, and when we perform regular queries on clustered tables using the equality predicate on the cluster key.

Even for hash clusters, if we perform frequent full table scans, and we have to allocate a lot of space for our growing table, it's better to use regular (heap) tables.

Sorted hash clusters

Beginning with Oracle Database 10g, hash clusters can be sorted. We can decide the order in which the rows are sorted—within the same cluster key value—even on multiple fields.

The syntax to define sorted hash clusters is as follows:

```
CREATE CLUSTER ORDER_CLUSTER (orderid NUMBER(4))
SIZE 8192 HASHKEYS 100;

CREATE TABLE ORDERS(
  orderid NUMBER(4),
  date_placed DATE,
  customer_id NUMBER(4)
) CLUSTER ORDER_CLUSTER(orderid);

CREATE TABLE ORDER_DETAILS (
  orderid NUMBER(4),
  part_id NUMBER(4),
  price NUMBER(9,2) sort,
  description VARCHAR2(30)
) CLUSTER ORDER_CLUSTER(orderid);
```

In this example, we have created the hash cluster ORDER_CLUSTER to store order data with their details; these are sorted by the price column.

Custom hash function

By default, Oracle provides us with a hash function to generate the values to be used in hash clusters.

If we prefer, we can define our own hash function for a cluster, using the HASH IS clause in the CREATE CLUSTER statement. This capability is enabled only when the cluster key is made up by a single integer column.

Our hash function must evaluate to a positive value, needs to reference at least one field, and cannot reference PL/SQL functions. There are other restrictions, listed in the official Oracle documentation (http://docs.oracle.com/cd/E11882_01/server.112/e26088/toc.htm).

Single-table hash clusters

We can create a hash cluster consisting of a single table only, defining a so-called Single-table hash cluster.

This might seem an oxymoron: a cluster—which is to store more than one table in the same database block—made by a single table.

The reason for using such a cluster is simple: we can gain very fast performance in retrieving data from this kind of storage structure, when we access data by cluster key value; in this case, the I/O is better optimized than for regular hash clusters.

We have seen in the previous section that we can define a personalized hash function to use in a hash cluster. Commonly, with single-table hash clusters it is very simple to define a hash function based on the primary key value, which ensures that there will be no collisions at all.

Here follows an example of a single-table hash cluster:

```
CREATE CLUSTER SINGLE_CLUSTER (id NUMBER(6))
   SIZE 8192 HASHKEYS 100
   single table
   hash is id;
CREATE TABLE SCL_EMPLOYEES
   CLUSTER SINGLE_CLUSTER (employee_id) AS
   SELECT * FROM EMPLOYEES;
```

Indexing the correct way

When a table grows in size, it's very difficult and time-consuming to find the data we need by scanning the entire table data.

The well-known solution to this problem is indexing. We can build an index, which is a particular storage structure, to identify quickly where data is stored in the table. In the real world, indexes are often used, for example, in a book like this, so we are accustomed to using them.

In this recipe, we will see how indexes work and when to use them, and we'll also avoid over-indexing; we will introduce the B-tree indexes, and then look at other types of indexes and more details on their use.

How to do it...

In this recipe, we will use the CUSTOMERS table of SH schema. There are more than 55000 rows in the table. We will create several indexes on this table, and after the creation of each index we will execute the following queries (we will call them *TEST CASE* onwards):

```
SET AUTOT TRACE EXP
SELECT CUST_FIRST_NAME, CUST_LAST_NAME, CUST_YEAR_OF_BIRTH,
   CUST_EMAIL FROM CUSTOMERS WHERE CUST_LAST_NAME = 'WADE';
SELECT CUST_FIRST_NAME, CUST_LAST_NAME, CUST_YEAR_OF_BIRTH,
   CUST_EMAIL FROM CUSTOMERS WHERE CUST_LAST_NAME = 'Wade';
```

```
SELECT CUST_FIRST_NAME, CUST_LAST_NAME, CUST_YEAR_OF_BIRTH,
    CUST_EMAIL FROM CUSTOMERS
    WHERE UPPER(CUST_LAST_NAME) = 'WADE';
SELECT CUST_FIRST_NAME, CUST_LAST_NAME, CUST_YEAR_OF_BIRTH,
    CUST_EMAIL FROM CUSTOMERS WHERE CUST_FIRST_NAME = 'DARBY';
SELECT CUST_FIRST_NAME, CUST_LAST_NAME, CUST_YEAR_OF_BIRTH,
    CUST_EMAIL FROM CUSTOMERS WHERE CUST_FIRST_NAME = 'Darby';
SELECT CUST_FIRST_NAME, CUST_LAST_NAME, CUST_YEAR_OF_BIRTH,
    CUST_EMAIL FROM CUSTOMERS
    WHERE UPPER(CUST_FIRST_NAME) = 'DARBY';
```

1. Connect to SH schema:

   CONNECT sh@TESTDB/sh

2. Execute the TEST CASE:

3. In the following screenshot, we can see only the results of the first query in the test case; however, the results are also the same for other queries in the test case:

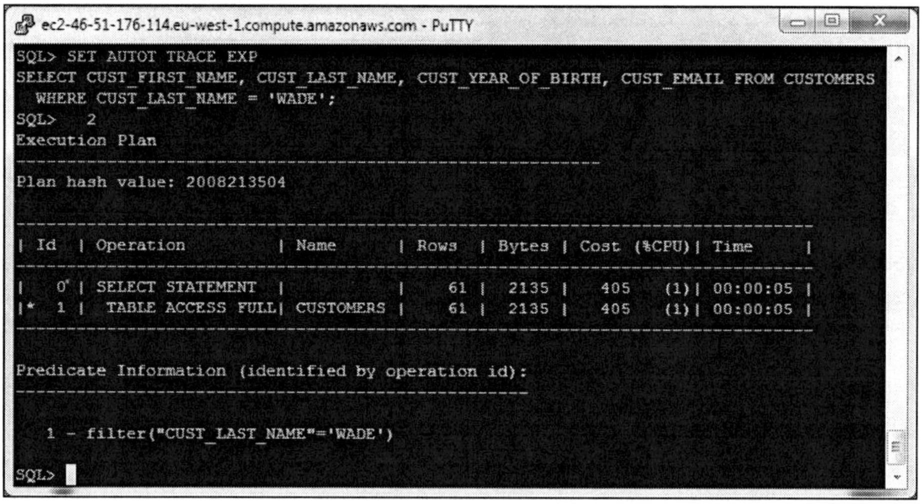

4. Create the index IX1_CUSTOMERS:

   CREATE INDEX IX1_CUSTOMERS ON
       CUSTOMERS (CUST_LAST_NAME, CUST_FIRST_NAME);

5. Execute the TEST CASE.

6. In the following screenshot, we can see the relevant part of the TEST CASE results after the index IX1_CUSTOMERS is in place:

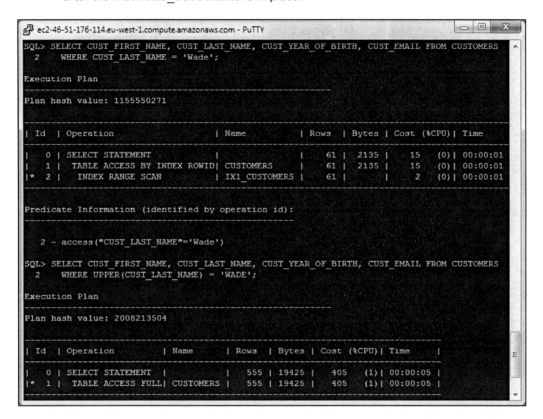

7. Create the index IX2_CUSTOMERS:

   CREATE INDEX IX2_CUSTOMERS ON
       CUSTOMERS (UPPER(CUST_LAST_NAME), UPPER(CUST_FIRST_NAME));

8. Execute the TEST CASE.

9. In the following screenshot, we can see the relevant part of the TEST CASE results after the index IX2_CUSTOMERS is in place:

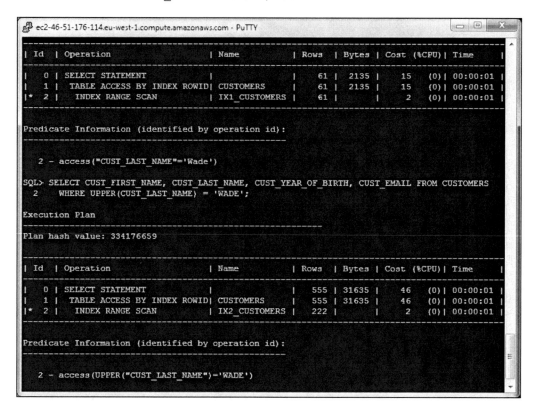

10. Create the index IX3_CUSTOMERS:

```
CREATE INDEX IX3_CUSTOMERS ON
    CUSTOMERS (CUST_LAST_NAME, CUST_YEAR_OF_BIRTH DESC);
```

11. Execute the following query to test the index just created:

```
SELECT CUST_LAST_NAME, CUST_YEAR_OF_BIRTH FROM CUSTOMERS
    WHERE CUST_LAST_NAME = <Wade>
ORDER BY CUST_LAST_NAME,  CUST_YEAR_OF_BIRTH DESC;
```

12. In the following screenshot, we can see the results of the last query:

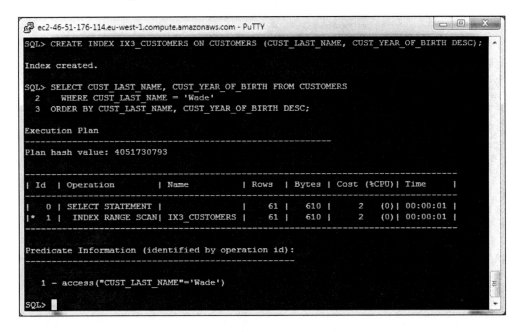

13. Execute the following queries to test the different uses of the same index:

```
SELECT
    CUST_FIRST_NAME, CUST_LAST_NAME
    FROM CUSTOMERS
    WHERE CUST_LAST_NAME = <Darby>;
SELECT
    CUST_FIRST_NAME, CUST_LAST_NAME
    FROM CUSTOMERS
    WHERE CUST_FIRST_NAME = <Darby>;
```

14. The following are the results of the previous two queries:

```
ec2-46-51-176-114.eu-west-1.compute.amazonaws.com - PuTTY

SQL> SELECT CUST_FIRST_NAME, CUST_LAST_NAME FROM CUSTOMERS WHERE CUST_LAST_NAME = 'Darby';

Execution Plan
----------------------------------------------------------
Plan hash value: 640095782

--------------------------------------------------------------------------------------
| Id  | Operation          | Name         | Rows  | Bytes | Cost (%CPU)| Time     |
--------------------------------------------------------------------------------------
|   0 | SELECT STATEMENT   |              |    61 |   793 |     2   (0)| 00:00:01 |
|*  1 |  INDEX RANGE SCAN  | IX1_CUSTOMERS |    61 |   793 |     2   (0)| 00:00:01 |
--------------------------------------------------------------------------------------

Predicate Information (identified by operation id):
---------------------------------------------------

   1 - access("CUST_LAST_NAME"='Darby')

SQL> SELECT CUST_FIRST_NAME, CUST_LAST_NAME FROM CUSTOMERS WHERE CUST_FIRST_NAME = 'Darby';

Execution Plan
----------------------------------------------------------
Plan hash value: 1463814208

--------------------------------------------------------------------------------------
| Id  | Operation             | Name         | Rows  | Bytes | Cost (%CPU)| Time     |
--------------------------------------------------------------------------------------
|   0 | SELECT STATEMENT      |              |    43 |   559 |    54   (0)| 00:00:01 |
|*  1 |  INDEX FAST FULL SCAN | IX1_CUSTOMERS |    43 |   559 |    54   (0)| 00:00:01 |
--------------------------------------------------------------------------------------
```

How it works...

When we execute the queries in the TEST CASE for the first time, there aren't indexes in place to help us, so every query ends in a FULL TABLE SCAN operation over the CUSTOMERS table. This means that we will scan all the database blocks of the CUSTOMERS table to retrieve the data we need, applying the different filters specified in our queries.

To solve this issue, we create the first index on the CUSTOMERS table—IX1_CUSTOMERS— made up by the columns CUST_LAST_NAME and CUST_FIRST_NAME.

When we execute the TEST CASE again, we have the following changes in place to retrieve the rows queried:

- ▸ We use the index IX1_CUSTOMERS to answer the first two queries. If we try to execute these queries, however, we will see that the first will answer "no rows selected", because the names in the CUSTOMERS table are stored with the first letter capitalized, so there is a "Wade" customer, but not a "WADE" one.

- To solve the issue represented by the possible different cases used in the CUST_LAST_NAME field, the third query makes use of the UPPER function to make a case-insensitive search. This query won't use the IX1_CUSTOMERS index, because of the function in place.

- The last three queries of the TEST CASE aren't affected by the new index; they will end in a full table scan operation as before.

To solve the issue of the case-insensitive search, we create a **function-based index**, IX2_CUSTOMERS, which uses the UPPER function in the definition of the indexed columns.

The new index affects the results for the third query of the TEST CASE, because it uses the index to retrieve the data, avoiding the full table scan operation needed before.

Even after the IX2_CUSTOMERS index creation, the last three queries are answered with a full table scan operation.

We create the IX3_CUSTOMERS index to show how we can create a **descending index**, that is, an index which stores the data for one or more fields in descending order. In our index, we have the CUST_LAST_NAME field in canonical order, and the CUST_YEAR_OF_BIRTH field in descending order. This kind of indexing lets us speed up the sorting operation when we execute a query with different ordering for the columns.

The query that we execute to test the new index will use it similarly to the other indexes we have created earlier. We avoid a SORT phase because using the index retrieves the rows in the correct order.

 We can also create a function-based descending index.

In our TEST CASE, the last three queries didn't use either of the indexes we have created.

This happens because we have an equality predicate on the CUST_FIRST_NAME, which is referenced in our indexes as the second field. In these situations, the indexes aren't used by the database. The last query, instead, will use the index even if we are filtering the table on the CUST_FIRST_NAME; this test allows us to dispel a myth. Oracle uses the indexes even if the leading columns are not referenced in the WHERE predicate of the query. We can see that in such a case, the operation will be an INDEX FAST FULL SCAN. Conversely, when we reference the leading column of the index, we will end up in an INDEX RANGE SCAN.

There's more...

In this recipe, we have used standard **B-tree Indexes**. A **B-tree Index** is a very common data structure in computer science, used to improve the performance of data access, when we are interested in retrieving only a small percentage of the overall data in the table.

A B-tree Index contains the data for the fields included in the index and the ROWIDs of the rows that contain the same values as for the indexed fields. These values are stored in **index entries**, packed together in the **leaf nodes** of the tree representing the index.

 When the indexed fields of a row are (all) NULL, the corresponding index entry is not stored in the index.

A peculiarity to this structure is in the way the leaf nodes are connected. They are linked to both the left and right adjacent leaf nodes, to allow the operation of range scan, which is useful when we have a predicate similar to WHERE FIELD BETWEEN A AND B. In this situation, we visit the tree structure to reach the leaf node related to the value A, and then we jump to the adjacent leaf node that contains the value B, without having to visit the entire tree structure again.

We have seen in this recipe how to build an index, a function-based index, and a descending index. The last type is useful when we want to use queries in which we want the data sorted in a mixed ascending/descending way on the fields indexed. If we use a regular index to access the data, Oracle is unable to do the sort in a mixed way, in a query like this:

```
SELECT FIELD1, FIELD2
FROM TABLE
WHERE FIELD1 BETWEEN A AND B
ORDER BY FIELD1 DESC, FIELD2
```

We have a regular (ascending) index in place on FIELD1, FIELD2.

If we create an index like this:

```
CREATE MIXED_INDEX ON TABLE (FIELD1 DESC, FIELD2)
```

Then, we can use the index to access the data and retrieve the rows sorted, that is, we don't have to do a SORT step after retrieving the rows.

In the last two queries, we have seen how the Oracle database uses an INDEX FAST FULL SCAN operation to retrieve the rows when there is a predicate, which involves the second field of the index (CUST_FIRST_NAME) but not the first (CUST_LAST_NAME).

This operation consists of visiting all the database blocks of the index, without any order or access path, to retrieve the data we are looking for. Why doesn't the fifth query of our TEST CASE use an index?

Let's try to answer this question. The following is the query from the TEST CASE:

```
SELECT CUST_FIRST_NAME, CUST_LAST_NAME,
  CUST_YEAR_OF_BIRTH, CUST_EMAIL
FROM CUSTOMERS WHERE CUST_FIRST_NAME = 'Darby';
```

The following is the last query of the recipe:

```
SELECT CUST_FIRST_NAME, CUST_LAST_NAME
FROM CUSTOMERS WHERE CUST_FIRST_NAME = 'Darby';
```

In the first case, we have a full table scan, because we cannot retrieve all the data from the index, so we have to do a `TABLE ACCESS BY ROWID` operation for each row, which satisfies the predicate. The latter query, instead, can be answered without accessing the table data, because we have asked only the indexed fields.

In the first query, if we use the `INDEX FAST FULL SCAN`, we have to visit every index block and, for each row with `CUST_FIRST_NAME` equaling `'Darby'`, we have to do a `TABLE ACCESS BY ROWID` to retrieve `CUST_YEAR_OF_BIRTH` and `CUST_EMAIL` field values. The optimizer has decided that this kind of access isn't as fast as a full table scan, hence the choice.

We can use the index even in the first query, using an optimizer hint (which will be discussed in depth in *Chapter 7*):

```
SELECT /*+ INDEX(CUSTOMERS IX3_CUSTOMERS) */
   CUST_FIRST_NAME, CUST_LAST_NAME,
   CUST_YEAR_OF_BIRTH, CUST_EMAIL
FROM CUSTOMERS WHERE CUST_FIRST_NAME = 'Darby';
```

In the next screenshot, we can see that Oracle knows (from the table statistics) that only 43 rows satisfy the `where` condition. If we use the index, we are going through 55500 potential row accesses (the first plan in the picture is from the previous query, the second one from the query shown in the screenshot itself):

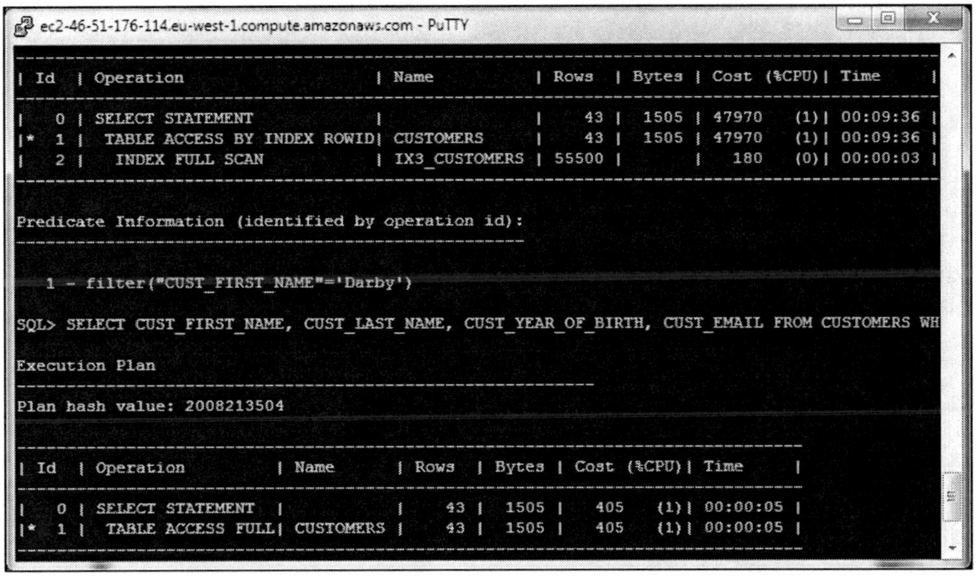

Last but not least, we have looked at various ways of indexing, without any consideration as to how indexes affect performance of operations other than as queries.

Surely, an index can improve query performance, reducing the number of I/O operations needed to retrieve the data. However, index maintenance has a cost in DML operations—on INSERTs and UPDATEs—when the database engine must update the index to reflect the changes to the data in the table.

The index, furthermore, requests space to store itself. This aspect, however, is less relevant due to inexpensive disks and memory on the market, but has to be considered when planning to add an index on a table.

What is the "small percentage" of the data which assures we can improve performances using B-tree indexes?

There isn't a rule of thumb to define what is the right percentage above which there is no improvement in the query using the index. We can however estimate the amount of data that has to be read to satisfy our inquiries.

Suppose that we have a table with an average row size of 200 bytes, and we create an index on some fields, which can be used to execute our query. The database block size is 8 KB, that is, 8192 bytes available. If we are using a PCTFREE of 20 for the table, we are allowed to insert about 30/32 rows in a database block—we are not considering row headers—we are interested in an estimated value, not a calculation of the real value. If the table contains 10000 rows, we are using more than 300 database blocks for the table.

Accessing the table using the index requires us to read the index block and access the data in the table by the ROWID. If the data we are retrieving with the index is 30 percent of the entire table (as per our example) we will access 3000 rows using an operation called TABLE ACCESS BY ROWID, reading 3000 blocks of data (many blocks will be read more than once). If we do a full table scan, in this situation, we will read all table data, which we have estimated to be slightly more than 300 blocks. Using the index, in this situation, won't be a good choice.

If the data we are interested in is one percent of the entire table, we will access 100 database blocks using the index, which is a considerable speed improvement when compared to the full table scan. Finally, if the average row size is 2000 bytes, we will have about three rows in a database block, so the table is made up of more than 3300 database blocks. In this situation, even the first query which accessed 30 percent of the entire table, would benefit from indexing.

As we have seen from this example, whether to use indexes depends upon various parameters, and there isn't a magic number to use for every situation.

▸ We will talk about full table scans in *Chapter 4* in the recipe *Avoiding full table scans*, and optimizer hints are explained in depth in *Chapter 7* in the recipe *Exploring the optimizer hints*.

Rebuilding index

In the previous recipe, we saw that using indexes leads to performance improvements; however, we need to take care that DML operations are slower due to the operations involved to keep the index synchronized with table data.

Rebuilding an index is an operation that can provide performance benefits because it reduces intra-block fragmentation.

Getting ready

The following steps have to be carried out initially:

1. Open a SQL*Plus session and connect to the SH schema:

   ```
   CONNECT sh@TESTDB/sh
   ```

2. Create a table to test:

   ```
   CREATE TABLE BIG_CUSTOMERS AS SELECT * FROM CUSTOMERS;
   ```

3. Insert more than 5 million records:

   ```
   BEGIN
       FOR j IN 1..100 LOOP
           INSERT INTO BIG_CUSTOMERS SELECT * FROM CUSTOMERS;
       END LOOP;
       COMMIT;
   END;
   ```

4. Instruct SQL*Plus to show the timings for the next operations:

   ```
   SET TIMING ON
   ```

5. Create an index on the table:

   ```
   CREATE INDEX IX1_BIG_CUSTOMERS
       ON BIG_CUSTOMERS (CUST_LAST_NAME, CUST_FIRST_NAME);
   ```

How to do it...

In this recipe, we will see how to rebuild an index minimizing the effects to the users who are using the database. Follow these steps:

1. Open another session of SQL*Plus and connect as user SH. The newly opened session is referred to as **SESSION B** from here on. The initial connection made in step 1 is **SESSION A**; set the timing in **SESSION B** too:

    ```
    CONNECT sh@TESTDB/sh

    SET TIMING ON
    ```

2. Start rebuilding the index in **SESSION A**:

    ```
    ALTER INDEX IX1_MYCUSTOMERS REBUILD ONLINE PARALLEL;
    ```

3. Insert a row in **SESSION B** while the operation in **SESSION A** is still in execution:

    ```
    DECLARE
      MAX_CUST NUMBER;
    BEGIN
      SELECT MAX(CUST_ID) INTO MAX_CUST FROM BIG_CUSTOMERS;
      INSERT INTO BIG_CUSTOMERS(
        CUST_ID, CUST_FIRST_NAME, CUST_LAST_NAME, CUST_GENDER,
    CUST_YEAR_OF_BIRTH,
        CUST_STREET_ADDRESS, CUST_POSTAL_CODE, CUST_CITY,
    CUST_CITY_ID, CUST_STATE_PROVINCE,
        CUST_STATE_PROVINCE_ID, COUNTRY_ID, CUST_MAIN_PHONE_NUMBER,
    CUST_TOTAL, CUST_TOTAL_ID)
      SELECT
        CUST_ID + MAX_CUST + 1, CUST_FIRST_NAME, CUST_LAST_NAME,
    CUST_GENDER, CUST_YEAR_OF_BIRTH,
        CUST_STREET_ADDRESS, CUST_POSTAL_CODE, CUST_CITY,
    CUST_CITY_ID, CUST_STATE_PROVINCE,
        CUST_STATE_PROVINCE_ID, COUNTRY_ID, CUST_MAIN_PHONE_NUMBER,
    CUST_TOTAL, CUST_TOTAL_ID
      FROM CUSTOMERS
      WHERE CUST_ID = 1;
      COMMIT;
    END;
    /
    ```

4. Wait until the operations in **SESSION A** and **SESSION B** are finished.

5. Rebuild the index in **SESSION A** with a different option:

    ```
    ALTER INDEX IX1_MYCUSTOMERS REBUILD PARALLEL;
    ```

6. Insert a row in **SESSION B** while the operation in **SESSION A** is still in execution with the same code in step 8.

7. Wait until the operations in **SESSION A** and **SESSION B** are finished.

8. In the next screenshot, we can see the results of **SESSION A**:

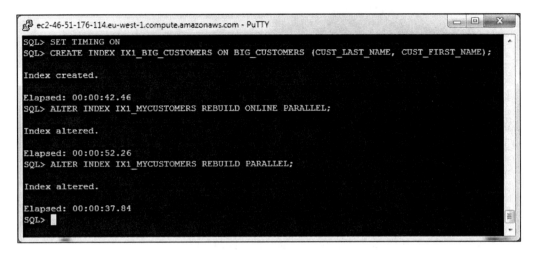

9. In the next screenshot, we can see the results of **SESSION B**:

10. Inspect the index status in the data dictionary:

```
SELECT
    TABLE_NAME, INDEX_NAME, STATUS
FROM USER_INDEXES
WHERE TABLE_NAME = <BIG_CUSTOMERS>
ORDER BY 1,2,3
```

11. Drop the table (and the index) to clean the objects created by this recipe (we will create the same table in the next recipe):

```
DROP TABLE BIG_CUSTOMERS;
```

How it works...

In this recipe, we have rebuilt an index in both online and offline mode.

In the first steps, we created a table with an index on it. We then used two simultaneous sessions to verify that an online index rebuild allows us to insert, update, and delete records in the table on which our index rebuilding is based. If we don't specify the ONLINE clause, the DML operations happen only at the end of the rebuild process.

This behavior is clear when we look at the screenshots with the timings. Looking at the picture from **Session A**, we can see that rebuilding an index is faster than creating the same index—and we will understand why later—while rebuilding an index online is slower than rebuilding the same index without this option in place.

The drawback of rebuilding an index offline is that while the rebuild is happening, DML commands are locked until the completion of the other operation. This can be verified looking at the screenshot in which **SESSION B** results are shown and comparing it with the screenshot for **SESSION A**. The second execution of the query—launched manually in another SQL*Plus session after the offline index rebuild—terminates *after* the rebuild operation, while when we are executing the ONLINE REBUILD the insert in **SESSION B** terminates before the rebuild operation.

There's more...

An index has to be rebuilt when its status is in an UNUSABLE/INVALID state. To inspect the status of an index we can use the statement in step 8.

An index becomes INVALID for various reasons, such as a direct path load operation and an ALTER TABLE MOVE command. Every time there is a change in the ROWIDs of a table, the indexes on that table have to be rebuilt.

The rebuild process is not like a DROP and CREATE sequence of operations. When an index is created, the table is completely scanned to build the index, while a REBUILD recalculates the ROWID for the index entries, which are already in the index, generating the new segments. At the end of the process, the old segments of the index are dropped and replaced by the new ones. The entries for the DML operations happened while the index was rebuilt, and are added/updated to the new index. These DML operations were recorded in a journal table, which is itself an index organized table. When all the operations are completed, information about the index on the data dictionary is updated, and only during dictionary updates is DML access blocked.

We have used the PARALLEL option too, to speed up the rebuild process.

As we have experimented, during an online index rebuild, we can execute DMLs on the base table, but take care as the operation will be slower than usual.

Normally, there is no need to rebuild an index if the status of the indexes is VALID. However, when we have a table on which there are many INSERTs and DELETEs, we could schedule an index rebuild, because when deleting an index entry, the space is not freed in the index leaf, but just marked as deleted. If we have massive DELETE and INSERT operations, we could have a skewed index structure, which could slow performance due to intra-block fragmentation.

In such cases, an index rebuild can be helpful, and the ONLINE options allow us to perform this operation without affecting the availability of the database.

We can check if an index needs to be rebuilt by executing the following statements:

```
ANALYZE INDEX index_name VALIDATE STRUCTURE;
SELECT HEIGHT, DEL_LF_ROWS, LF_ROWS, LF_BLKS FROM INDEX_STATS;
```

If the value for DEL_LF_ROWS/LF_ROWS is greater than 2, or LF_ROWS is lower than LF_BLKS, or HEIGHT is 4 then the index should be rebuilt.

Index rebuild and statistics

When we rebuild an index, we can add the COMPUTE STATISTICS option to the statement. With the index, even the statistics on it are rebuilt, with a minor effect on the performance of the operation.

See also

 ▶ We will talk about data loading and direct path load in *Chapter 8*, in the recipes *Direct path inserting* and *Loading data with SQL loader and Data Pump*

Compressing indexes

In this recipe, we will see another option we can use during index creation or rebuild—the COMPRESS parameter—and how it could affect the performance when using the index.

We will use the same table and index created in the previous recipe, *Index Rebuilding*.

How to do it...

If you have dropped the table, you have to recreate it as mentioned in the following steps:

1. Open a SQL*Plus session and connect to the SH schema:

   ```
   CONNECT sh@TESTDB/sh
   ```

2. Create a table to test:

   ```
   CREATE TABLE BIG_CUSTOMERS AS SELECT * FROM CUSTOMERS;
   ```

3. Insert more than 5 million records:

   ```
   BEGIN
     FOR j IN 1..100 LOOP
       INSERT INTO BIG_CUSTOMERS SELECT * FROM CUSTOMERS;
     END LOOP;
     COMMIT;
   END;
   ```

4. Create an index on the table:

   ```
   CREATE INDEX IX1_BIG_CUSTOMERS
     ON BIG_CUSTOMERS (CUST_LAST_NAME, CUST_FIRST_NAME);
   ```

5. Analyze the index to gather statistics:

   ```
   ANALYZE INDEX IX1_BIG_CUSTOMERS VALIDATE STRUCTURE;
   ```

6. Inspect statistics on the index:

   ```
   SELECT HEIGHT, BLOCKS, BTREE_SPACE, USED_SPACE,
   OPT_CMPR_COUNT, OPT_CMPR_PCTSAVE FROM INDEX_STATS
   WHERE NAME = <IX1_BIG_CUSTOMERS>;
   ```

7. Rebuild the index with the **COMPRESS** option, following the optimal parameter from the previous query (OPT_CMPR_COUNT):

   ```
   ALTER INDEX IX1_BIG_CUSTOMERS REBUILD ONLINE COMPRESS 2;
   ```

8. Analyze the index to refresh statistics:

   ```
   ANALYZE INDEX IX1_BIG_CUSTOMERS VALIDATE STRUCTURE;
   ```

9. Inspect statistics on the index:

```
SELECT HEIGHT, BLOCKS, BTREE_SPACE, USED_SPACE,
OPT_CMPR_COUNT, OPT_CMPR_PCTSAVE FROM INDEX_STATS
WHERE NAME = <IX1_BIG_CUSTOMERS>;
```

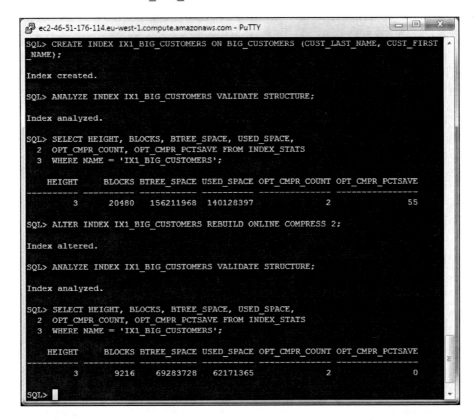

10. Drop the table and the index:

```
DROP TABLE BIG_CUSTOMERS;
```

How it works...

We have created a table with more than five million records and an index on it, based on the fields CUST_LAST_NAME and CUST_FIRST_NAME (which is not unique).

After creating the index, we have analyzed it to gather statistical information, using the data dictionary view INDEX_STATS.

We have seen the space occupied by the index expressed in database blocks (BLOCKS field) and in bytes (BTREE_SPACE and USED_SPACE).

There are two other fields on which we have to concentrate:

> ▶ OPT_CMPR_COUNT: It indicates how many fields can be compressed in the index to obtain the maximum benefit from index key compression

> ▶ OPT_CMPR_PCTSAVE: It indicates the percentage of saved space if the previous parameter is used in rebuilding the index

We have rebuilt the index with the recommended value for the COMPRESS parameter, reanalyzed the index, and compared the results. We have saved 55 percent of database blocks, as estimated previously. After the index was rebuilt, we have no further improvement in compressing the index, as shown by the results of the query on INDEX_STATS.

There's more...

Compressing an index allows us to store the index in fewer database blocks, as in the presented example, so we have fewer database blocks to read to navigate the index.

The value used when we execute a CREATE INDEX or ALTER INDEX REBUILD command with the COMPRESS parameter indicates how many fields of the key fields—in the order they are listed in the index creation statement—will be compressed.

We can compress any nonunique index with a value equal to the number of fields in the index, as in our example. If the index is unique (that is, no duplicate values can be stored in the key fields), we can use a value equal to the number of key fields minus one. By default, the **prefix length**—this is another way to name this value—is the number of key columns.

Prefix length limitation does not allow us to compress a unique index with only one field, but this isn't a problem. In this situation every key value is different—due to the uniqueness of the index—so there won't be any improvement in compressing index keys because there aren't duplicates.

From the performance point of view, when we use compressed indexes we make use of slightly more CPU to manage the compress/decompress work.

Using reverse key indexes

In this recipe, we will introduce reverse key indexes. We will look at when to use them and how they are related to performance.

How to do it...

The following steps will demonstrate reverse keys:

1. Connect to SQL*Plus as user SH:

   ```
   CONNECT sh@TESTDB/sh
   ```

2. Create a simple table:

   ```
   CREATE TABLE REVERSE_TEST (
     ID NUMBER NOT NULL,
     NAME VARCHAR(100)
   );
   ```

3. Create a sequence to generate the IDs for the table:

   ```
   CREATE SEQUENCE REV_SEQ
     START WITH 1 INCREMENT BY 1 CACHE 1000;
   ```

4. Create the trigger to insert sequence-generate values:

   ```
   CREATE OR REPLACE TRIGGER TR_REVERSE_TEST_INS
     BEFORE INSERT ON REVERSE_TEST FOR EACH ROW
     WHEN (NEW.ID IS NULL)
   BEGIN
     SELECT REV_SEQ.NEXTVAL INTO :NEW.ID FROM DUAL;
   END;
   ```

5. Create a UNIQUE INDEX on ID:

   ```
   CREATE UNIQUE INDEX PK_REVERSE_TEST ON REVERSE_TEST(ID);
   ```

6. Populate the table:

   ```
   INSERT INTO REVERSE_TEST (NAME)
     SELECT CUST_LAST_NAME || CUST_FIRST_NAME FROM CUSTOMERS;
   COMMIT;
   ```

7. Analyze the index:

   ```
   ANALYZE INDEX PK_REVERSE_TEST VALIDATE STRUCTURE;
   ```

8. Query the statistics on the index:

   ```
   SELECT
     BLOCKS, LF_BLKS, LF_ROWS_LEN,
     BTREE_SPACE, USED_SPACE, PCT_USED
   FROM INDEX_STATS WHERE NAME = <PK_REVERSE_TEST>;
   ```

9. In the next screenshot, we can see the results of the previous query:

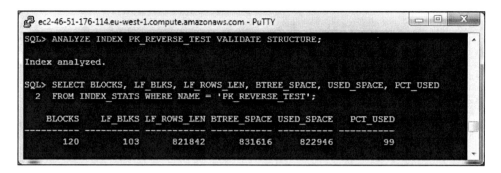

10. Drop the index:

```
DROP INDEX PK_REVERSE_TEST;
```

11. Empty the table:

```
TRUNCATE TABLE REVERSE_TEST;
```

12. Create a unique REVERSE KEY index on ID:

```
CREATE UNIQUE INDEX PK_REVERSE_TEST
   ON REVERSE_TEST(ID) REVERSE;
```

13. Populate the table:

```
INSERT INTO REVERSE_TEST (NAME)
   SELECT CUST_LAST_NAME || CUST_FIRST_NAME FROM CUSTOMERS;
COMMIT;
```

14. Analyze the index:

```
ANALYZE INDEX PK_REVERSE_TEST VALIDATE STRUCTURE;
```

15. Query the statistics on the REVERSE KEY index:

```
SELECT
   BLOCKS, LF_BLKS, LF_ROWS_LEN,
   BTREE_SPACE, USED_SPACE, PCT_USED
FROM INDEX_STATS WHERE NAME = <PK_REVERSE_TEST>;
```

16. In the next screenshot, we can see the results of the previous query:

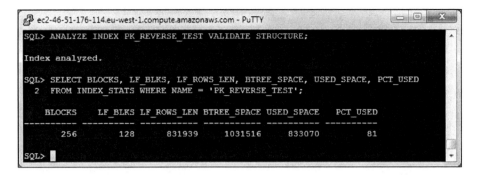

17. Execute a query with an equality predicate:

    SET AUTOT TRACE EXP

    SELECT NAME FROM REVERSE_TEST WHERE ID = 100;

18. Now, we can see the execution plan of the previous query:

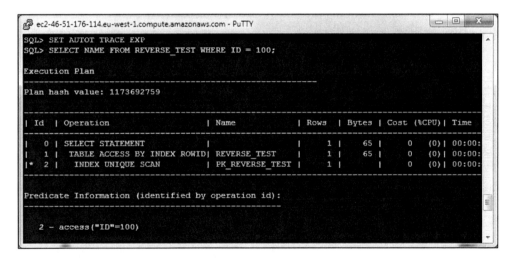

19. Execute a query with a range predicate:

    SET AUTOT TRACE EXP

    SELECT NAME FROM REVERSE_TEST WHERE ID BETWEEN 100 AND 110;

20. In the next screenshot, there is the execution plan of the previous query:

```
ec2-46-51-176-114.eu-west-1.compute.amazonaws.com - PuTTY

SQL> SELECT NAME FROM REVERSE_TEST WHERE ID BETWEEN 100 AND 110;

Execution Plan
----------------------------------------------------------
Plan hash value: 80098896

----------------------------------------------------------------------------------
| Id  | Operation          | Name         | Rows  | Bytes | Cost (%CPU)| Time     |
----------------------------------------------------------------------------------
|   0 | SELECT STATEMENT   |              |     3 |   195 |    68   (0)| 00:00:01 |
|*  1 |  TABLE ACCESS FULL | REVERSE_TEST |     3 |   195 |    68   (0)| 00:00:01 |
----------------------------------------------------------------------------------

Predicate Information (identified by operation id):
---------------------------------------------------

   1 - filter("ID">=100 AND "ID"<=110)

Note
-----
   - dynamic sampling used for this statement (level=2)

SQL>
```

21. Drop the table and the sequence:

```
DROP TABLE REVERSE_TEST;
DROP SEQUENCE REV_SEQ;
```

How it works...

In this recipe, we have created a small table, with a unique field ID populated using a sequence with a BEFORE INSERT trigger.

To ensure the uniqueness of the field, we have created a UNIQUE INDEX.

After populating the table with some data, we have analyzed the index and queried the statistics on it.

We have then dropped the index and deleted the data in the table, to return to the initial state. We have created a new UNIQUE INDEX with the REVERSE keyword, which creates the index, storing the key values reverse order. A **reverse key B-tree index** stores the value in the leaf nodes reversed (from right to left, instead of from left to right); for example, the value 123 will be stored in the index as 321.

We have analyzed the index again and queried the statistics, to compare with the data previously collected. We can see that by using the reverse key index, the index is spread across more database blocks, occupying more space on the disk. This is the exact behavior of this kind of index—distributing index key values in different database blocks.

This feature can improve performance, because where we have a table with a field populated by a sequence, massive inserts from multiple sessions could lead to contention issues on the index blocks. In fact, every session tries to insert new values in the table. Because the key values are produced by a sequence, the corresponding index entries will be adjacent in the leaf nodes of the B-tree index (for example, the values 123, 124, 125, and so on). Storing key values in reverse (for example, in the previous example the key values will be stored as 321, 421, 521, and so on) led to spreading the values in different leaf nodes of the index, reducing contention issues.

Before dropping the table, we have executed two queries — first with an equality predicate, the last with a range predicate, to analyze the execution plans generated by the database engine.

We can see that the first query—with an equality predicate—can use the index, resulting in an `INDEX UNIQUE SCAN` and a `TABLE ACCESS BY INDEX ROWID` operation to retrieve the data.

The last query, instead, has a range predicate. So, in the execution plan, the index is not used and the database will do a `TABLE ACCESS FULL` (full table scan) operation to answer our query.

The reason for this behavior is the particular way reversed key values are stored in the index. In a standard B-tree index, we will have the entries for 123, 124, 125 values in the same or in adjacent leaf nodes. In a reverse key index, the corresponding entries will be 321, 421, 521. So the index entries for these values aren't adjacent as the values themselves, hence, the `INDEX RANGE SCAN` cannot be used.

There's more...

We have stated that `INDEX RANGE SCAN` cannot be used. This is true when we are talking about a single column reverse key index.

When we have a reverse key index with two fields, for example, `CUST_LAST_NAME` and `CUST_FIRST_NAME` on the `CUSTOMERS` table of the `SH` schema, we could use the index range scan operation when we execute the following query:

```
SELECT CUST_FIRST_NAME, CUST_LAST_NAME, CUST_EMAIL
FROM CUSTOMERS
WHERE CUST_LAST_NAME = 'Rohrback'
AND CUST_FIRST_NAME BETWEEN 'Harry' AND 'Romney';
```

If, we have created an index similar to the following:

```
CREATE INDEX IXR_CUSTOMERS
   ON CUSTOMERS(CUST_LAST_NAME, CUST_FIRST_NAME) REVERSE;
```

We have talked about a performance gain obtained when we use reverse key indexes because they reduce contention on the index database blocks.

There is also another feature we can appreciate, related to the way the indexes grow.

When we add more rows in a table, the related index is updated. The index entries are stored in an ordered fashion in the B-tree index structure. So there will be a situation in which we have a full leaf block and we have to insert a new entry into that leaf.

When this occurs, the leaf block is split into two blocks, each one containing about 50 percent of the original block. The newly created block has to be added to the parent branch block, which in turn can be full, and the splitting process is iterated again.

When a row is deleted—or the index key field values are updated—the corresponding index entry is logically deleted, and the space will be reused only if we insert a new index entry with a value, which has to be inserted in that particular block, due to the sort constraint.

In situations similar to the one described in this recipe—a field populated with a growing value—when we delete an index entry, the space won't be claimed, ever, because the new values will always be greater than the old value. And if the block is full, new entries will always be in a new block.

Using reverse key indexes also solves this issue. For example, when the key 123—stored as 321—is deleted, the space could be reused by a key 723—stored as 327—so the empty space in index database blocks will be refilled when we insert new rows in the table.

Using bitmap indexes

In the last recipe, we looked at the use of B-tree indexes in depth.

In the Oracle database, there is also another type of index available, the bitmap index, presented in this recipe.

How to do it...

The following steps will demonstrate bitmap indexes:

1. Connect to SQL*Plus as user SH:

    `CONNECT sh@TESTDB/sh`

2. Create a table to do some tests:

    `CREATE TABLE MYCUSTOMERS AS SELECT * FROM CUSTOMERS;`

3. Execute the following queries to verify the execution plan adopted by the database:

```
SET AUTOT TRACE EXP STAT
SELECT COUNT(*) FROM MYCUSTOMERS
   WHERE CUST_GENDER = <F>;
SELECT COUNT(*) FROM MYCUSTOMERS
   WHERE CUST_MARITAL_STATUS = <single>;
SELECT COUNT(*) FROM MYCUSTOMERS
   WHERE CUST_MARITAL_STATUS = <married> AND CUST_GENDER = <F>;
SELECT COUNT(*) FROM MYCUSTOMERS
   WHERE CUST_MARITAL_STATUS = <single> AND CUST_GENDER = <M>
   AND CUST_YEAR_OF_BIRTH BETWEEN 1970 AND 1980;
SELECT COUNT(*) FROM MYCUSTOMERS
   WHERE CUST_MARITAL_STATUS = <single>
   AND CUST_YEAR_OF_BIRTH BETWEEN 1970 AND 1980;
SELECT COUNT(*) FROM MYCUSTOMERS
   WHERE CUST_YEAR_OF_BIRTH BETWEEN 1970 AND 1980;
```

4. In the next screenshot, we can see the results for the first query executed:

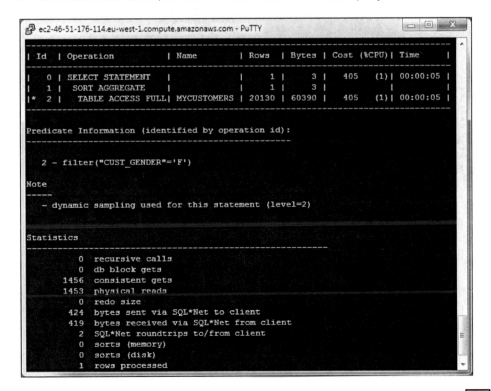

5. Create a `BITMAP INDEX` on some columns:

```
CREATE BITMAP INDEX BIX_GENDER_MARITAL_YOB
    ON MYCUSTOMERS
    (CUST_GENDER, CUST_MARITAL_STATUS, CUST_YEAR_OF_BIRTH);
```

6. Execute the same queries as in step 3 and compare the results.

7. In the next screenshot, we can see the results for the first query executed, after the bitmap index creation:

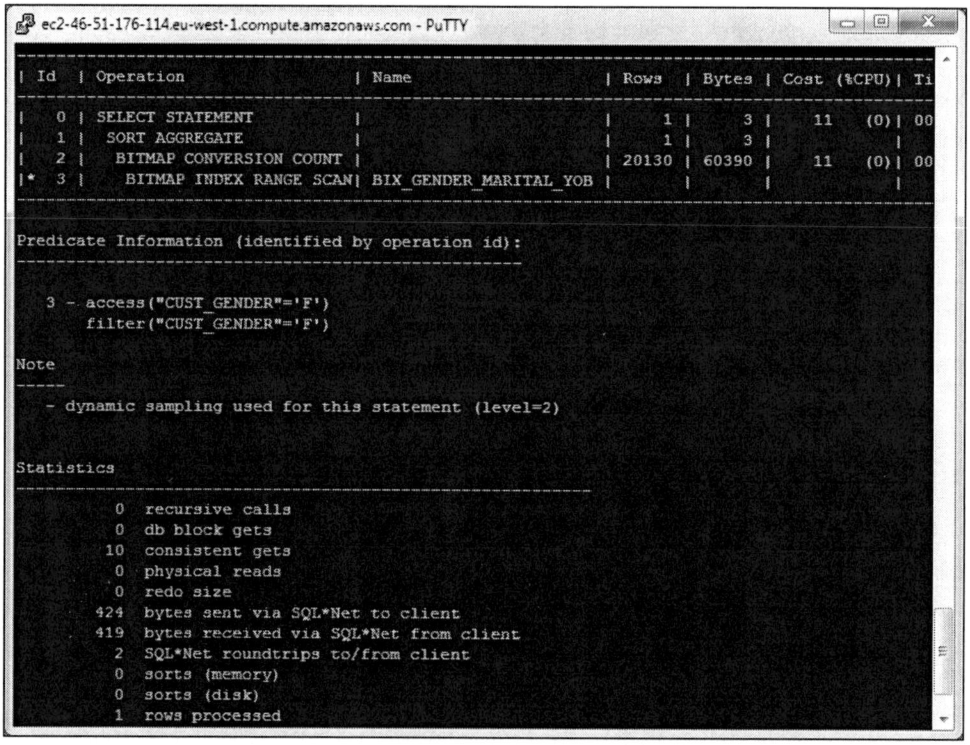

8. Drop the table:

```
DROP TABLE MYCUSTOMERS;
```

How it works...

We have created a table with some data in it. We have executed six queries in this table, using a different predicate combination on the fields CUST_MARITAL_STATUS, CUST_GENDER, and CUST_YEAR_OF_BIRTH, with equality and range conditions.

When we first execute this set of queries, the execution plan is always a FULL TABLE SCAN operation.

We have hence created a BITMAP INDEX on the table, choosing three fields as our key fields on which we are filtering the queries.

After index creation, we execute (once again) the same set of six queries. This time the execution plan uses the newly created bitmap index, with great enhancement in the number of database blocks processed, using the INDEX RANGE SCAN or INDEX FAST FULL SCAN operation, depending on whether we are filtering on the first key column of the index—CUST_GENDER—or not.

This result is obtained thanks to the particular structure of bitmap indexes. In this kind of index, the database stores few rows. These rows contain the different values in the key fields and a bitmap—which is a map of binary values—in which for every row there is a bit, which is "on" for value 1. For that row, the index key values correspond to those of the bitmap index row to which the bitmap belongs.

There's more...

Bitmap indexes offer very fast performance when we have a low cardinality field indexed on a table containing many rows. There isn't a fixed rule to define when field cardinality is "low": the CUST_GENDER column surely is, similar to a COUNTRY_ID field. BILL_ID will likely have very large cardinality, but we have to look at the table cardinality too. On a table containing 100 records, or 100 million records, a notion of low cardinality isn't the same.

When is it better to not use bitmap indexes? In OLTP environments.

When rows are frequently inserted, deleted, and updated, there is a performance bottleneck if we use a bitmap index. When the index is updated, all the bitmap segments are locked.

Indeed, the database cannot lock a single entry in the bitmap. So, when there are concurrent updates it will lead to poor performance.

The ideal environment where bitmap indexes fit very well is with Decision Support Systems, where data in tables is quite static by nature, read-only, with many rows in the table.

Another difference between bitmap and B-tree indexes is in how NULL values are managed. In bitmap indexes they are stored, in B-tree they are not.

There is also a big advantage in space when using bitmap indexes against B-Tree. Typically, a bitmap index uses between 2 percent and 10 percent the space of the corresponding B-Tree index on the same key fields. So even INDEX FAST FULL SCAN operations are faster with bitmap indexes (we have seen that B-Tree indexes are capable of FAST FULL SCAN of the values for key columns other than the first).

Bitmap join index

There is also another feature: starting with Oracle 9*i*, where we can have a particular kind of bitmap index, the **bitmap join index**. This is a bitmap index which represents the join between two tables, and can be used instead of a materialized view in certain conditions.

Before creating a bitmap join index, let's see the execution plan for the following query:

```
CONNECT sh@TESTDB/sh
SET AUTOT TRACE EXP
SELECT SUM(AMOUNT_SOLD) AS TOTAL
 FROM CUSTOMERS, SALES
 WHERE CUSTOMERS.CUST_ID = SALES.CUST_ID
 AND CUSTOMERS.CUST_POSTAL_CODE = '38083';
SET AUTOT OFF
```

In the next screenshot, we can see the execution plan needed to answer the simple question mentioned earlier: how much have we sold for a particular customer postal code?

```
SQL> SET AUTOT TRACE EXP
SQL> SELECT SUM(AMOUNT_SOLD) AS TOTAL
  2    FROM CUSTOMERS, SALES
  3    WHERE CUSTOMERS.CUST_ID = SALES.CUST_ID
  4    AND CUSTOMERS.CUST_POSTAL_CODE = '38083';

Execution Plan
----------------------------------------------------------
Plan hash value: 1198589537

--------------------------------------------------------------------------------
| Id  | Operation                          | Name           | Rows  | Bytes | Cost (%CPU)|
--------------------------------------------------------------------------------
|   0 | SELECT STATEMENT                   |                |     1 |    19 |  8847   (1)|
|   1 |  SORT AGGREGATE                    |                |     1 |    19 |            |
|   2 |   NESTED LOOPS                     |                |       |       |            |
|   3 |    NESTED LOOPS                    |                | 11596 |  215K |  8847   (1)|
|*  4 |     TABLE ACCESS FULL              | CUSTOMERS      |    89 |   801 |   405   (1)|
|   5 |     PARTITION RANGE ALL            |                |       |       |            |
|   6 |      BITMAP CONVERSION TO ROWIDS   |                |       |       |            |
|*  7 |       BITMAP INDEX SINGLE VALUE    | SALES_CUST_BIX |       |       |            |
|   8 |     TABLE ACCESS BY LOCAL INDEX ROWID| SALES        |   130 |  1300 |  8847   (1)|
--------------------------------------------------------------------------------

Predicate Information (identified by operation id):
---------------------------------------------------

   4 - filter("CUSTOMERS"."CUST_POSTAL_CODE"='38083')
   7 - access("CUSTOMERS"."CUST_ID"="SALES"."CUST_ID")

SQL>
```

Now, we can create a bitmap join index on the join between the tables CUSTOMERS and SALES. To do so, we will use the following statements:

```
ALTER TABLE CUSTOMERS ENABLE VALIDATE CONSTRAINT CUSTOMERS_PK;
CREATE BITMAP INDEX BJI_CUST_SALES
   ON SALES(CUSTOMERS.CUST_POSTAL_CODE)
   FROM SALES, CUSTOMERS
   WHERE SALES.CUST_ID = CUSTOMERS.CUST_ID LOCAL;
```

And we can execute the same query again; we will see the results displayed in the next screenshot:

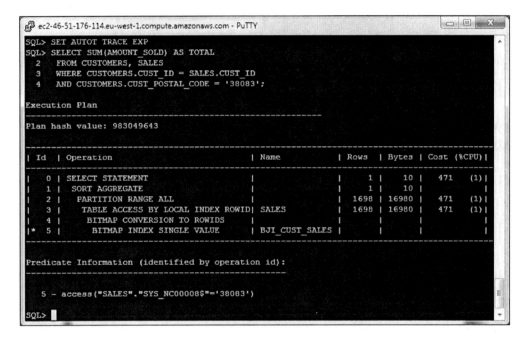

We will read less data, accessing only the SALES segment and the bitmap join index that we just created.

There are some clarifications needed:

- We have enabled and validated the primary key constraint on the CUSTOMERS table, because we can create a bitmap join index only on a key field (dimension) on which there is a unique constraint.

- We have used the LOCAL keyword when we built the bitmap join index because the SALES table is partitioned, so only LOCAL (to the partition) BITMAP INDEXES can be built on it.

A bitmap join index allows a denormalization without using materialized views, but in the index itself.

See also

▸ We have talked about denormalization in the receipe *Optimizing performance with schema denormalization* in *Chapter 2*.

Migrating to index organized tables

There are situations in which we access a table only—or mainly—using the primary key value. Situations such as a code lookup table, or a table containing inverted indexes, fit well in this definition.

In this recipe, we will see how to combine a heap table and a B-tree index in what is called an **index organized table**, and what benefits—and caveats—we have in performance when adopting this structure to store our data.

How to do it...

The following steps will demonstrate index organized tables:

1. Connect to the database as user SH:

   ```
   CONNECT sh@TESTDB/sh
   ```

2. Create an index organized table based on the COUNTRIES table of the SH schema:

   ```
   CREATE TABLE IOT_COUNTRIES (
     COUNTRY_ID NUMBER NOT NULL,
     COUNTRY_ISO_CODE CHAR(2) NOT NULL,
     COUNTRY_NAME VARCHAR2(40) NOT NULL,
     COUNTRY_SUBREGION VARCHAR2(30) NOT NULL,
     COUNTRY_SUBREGION_ID NUMBER NOT NULL,
     COUNTRY_REGION VARCHAR2(20) NOT NULL,
     COUNTRY_REGION_ID NUMBER NOT NULL,
     COUNTRY_TOTAL VARCHAR2(11) NOT NULL,
     COUNTRY_TOTAL_ID NUMBER NOT NULL,
     COUNTRY_NAME_HIST VARCHAR2(40),
     CONSTRAINT PK_IOT_COUNTRIES PRIMARY KEY (COUNTRY_ID))
   ORGANIZATION INDEX
   INCLUDING COUNTRY_NAME
   OVERFLOW TABLESPACE USERS;
   ```

3. Populate the table with data:

```
INSERT INTO IOT_COUNTRIES SELECT * FROM COUNTRIES;
```

4. Execute a query to the original (heap) table:

```
SET AUTOT TRACE EXP STAT
SELECT
    COUNTRY_ID, COUNTRY_NAME
FROM COUNTRIES
WHERE COUNTRY_ID = 52770;
```

5. In the next screenshot, we can see the execution plan and statistics for the query on the original table:

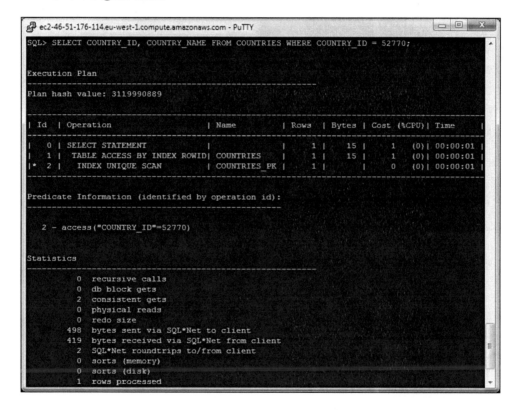

6. Execute the same query to the table (index organized) we just created:

```
SELECT
    COUNTRY_ID, COUNTRY_NAME
FROM IOT_COUNTRIES
WHERE COUNTRY_ID = 52770;
```

7. Now, we can see the execution plan and statistics for the query on the index organized table in the following screenshot:

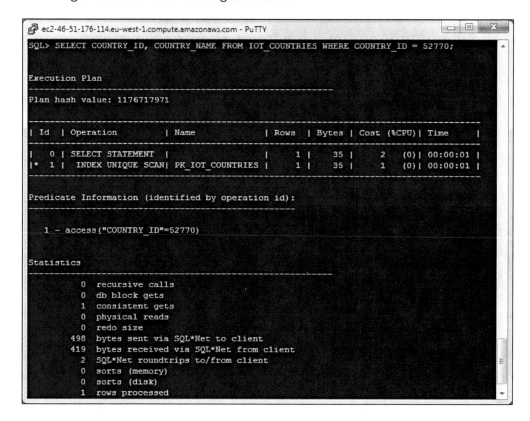

8. Drop the table:

```
DROP TABLE IOT_COUNTRIES;
```

How it works...

We have created a table with the same fields of the COUNTRIES table of the SH schema, specifying the ORGANIZATION INDEX clause in the CREATE TABLE statement. Hence, we have created an **Index Organized Table (IOT)**.

After populating the index organized table with the same data as the heap table, we have executed the same query against the two tables, collecting statistics and the execution plan. The query is a simple lookup of the country name based on the primary key value.

We can see that when we use the heap table, we look up on the INDEX segment, and then we access the row data using the ROWID. We have two consistent gets (on the INDEX and the TABLE segments) to access the data.

When we query the index organized table with the same query mentioned earlier, we have only one operation, namely the INDEX UNIQUE SCAN of the index, which retrieves (with 1 consistent get) the data we are asking for.

This behavior depends on the way data is organized in an index organized table. Similar to an index, there is a B-tree which stores the key values; instead of storing in the leaf nodes the ROWID of the table segment, an IOT stores the table data in the leaf nodes, so we have the table and the index in the same segment.

This solution allows space saving (the index key values are stored once) and performance is gained when accessing the table data by primary key values—or partial primary key values when the primary key is multi-field and we know the first value(s) of the key. The same benefits are in place when we access data using the primary key with an equality operation or with a range search.

On the other hand, if we want to scan the entire table, the operation reads more data on the IOT than on the heap table. This is because in the case of the IOT, it is the same segment of the table where we have also stored the index.

There's more...

In index organized tables, we have some unique properties due to the dual nature of this structure. One of these features is the use of COMPRESS and NOCOMPRESS options, to enable the key compression we have seen for indexes.

INCLUDING, OVERFLOW, PCTTHRESHOLD

When we have created the table IOT_COUNTRIES, we have used INCLUDING and OVERFLOW options.

These parameters—and the PCTTHRESHOLD, which we haven't used—are related to how much row data will be in the leaf nodes of the index.

These features enable us to decide whether to store only a part of the columns in the index. Because if we have many fields in the rows, we can store only a few index entries in each database block, reducing the performance of index searching.

The INCLUDING option lets us specify what fields (except primary key fields) are included in the index segment. In our example, we have included the COUNTRY_ID, COUNTRY_ISO_CODE, and COUNTRY_NAME fields in the index. The other fields are stored in a table segment, named OVERFLOW, which is stored in the USER tablespace, as requested, in our example.

The IOT can be stored in a different tablespace to the overflow segment.

The PCTTHRESHOLD parameter indicates the percentage of the leaf database block reserved for a row. If the row size exceeds the size indicated by this parameter, the fields not indicated by the INCLUDING option are stored in the OVERFLOW—if indicated, otherwise the row is not accepted.

Logical ROWID

Due to their nature, index organized tables don't have physical ROWIDs, because the rows are stored in the index and not in a regular table segment.

To avoid problems related to IOT not having ROWIDs, LOGICAL ROWIDs were introduced by Oracle. They give access to the rows in a IOT using two paths:

 ▶ A direct access to the file and block where the row is placed (this is a database engine guess)

 ▶ An access to the row made by the primary key values, if the guess of the preceding bullet fails

The guess in the first point is due to the fact that we have exact knowledge of the row position when we create the row in the index. Later, when the leaf block has been eventually split, our previous knowledge of the physical position is wrong, so the guess will fail.

We can use logical ROWIDs as if they were physical, so we can, for example, add secondary indexes to an index organized table.

See also

 ▶ In this chapter, see the recipe *Compressing indexes* for details about how to use the **COMPRESS** option

Using partitioning

Tables (and indexes) may become very large in a database, driving performance and maintenance problems.

Partitioning is the way to improve performance in large tables (Oracle suggests to partition tables with more than 2 GB of data), to ease the configuration and care of these objects and to reduce downtime in case of failures or scheduled maintenance such as move the tables or take some data offline.

In this recipe, we discuss partitioning a table using range partitioning. We will present hash, list, and composite partitioning as options.

How to do it...

We can create a table range partitioned adding the PARTITION BY RANGE clause to the CREATE TABLE statement:

```
CREATE TABLE SALES_RP (
 PROD_ID NUMBER NOT NULL,
 CUST_ID NUMBER NOT NULL,
 TIME_ID DATE NOT NULL,
 CHANNEL_ID NUMBER NOT NULL,
 PROMO_ID NUMBER NOT NULL,
 QUANTITY_SOLD NUMBER(10,2) NOT NULL,
 AMOUNT_SOLD NUMBER(10,2) NOT NULL)
PARTITION BY RANGE (TIME_ID)
(
   PARTITION SALES_BEFORE_2000 VALUES LESS THAN
      (TO_DATE('20000101','YYYYMMDD')) TABLESPACE EXAMPLE,
   PARTITION SALES_2000_2001_2002 VALUES LESS THAN
      (TO_DATE('20030101','YYYYMMDD')) TABLESPACE EXAMPLE,
   PARTITION SALES_2003 VALUES LESS THAN
      (TO_DATE('20040101','YYYYMMDD')) TABLESPACE EXAMPLE
);
```

Please note that we are connected to the SH schema, and the SALES_RP table logical structure is identical to the SALES table of this schema.

How it works...

We have created a table, indicating that we want to partition it BY RANGE.

The field TIME_ID, which is used to partition the table, is called the PARTITION KEY. We are partitioning the table in three parts, depending on the value of the partition key. We will store sales data before the year 2000 in the SALES_BEFORE_2000 partition, sales data between years 2000 and 2002 inclusive in the SALES_2000_2001_2002 partition, and sales data for the year 2003 in the SALES_2003 partition.

For simplicity, we have stored all the partitions in the same EXAMPLE tablespace. In real-life, you will probably spread the partitions in different tablespaces.

There's more...

Partitioning a table grants some advantages. When Oracle executes a query, there is an operation called **partition pruning**, which avoids having the database consider partitions not involved in the request. For example, if we execute the following query:

```
SELECT * FROM SALES_RP
  WHERE TIME_ID < TO_DATE('19990630','YYYYMMDD')
  AND CUST_ID = 1511;
```

Oracle will automatically use only the `SALES_BEFORE_2000` partition to retrieve the data needed. We could also put the tablespaces in which we store other partitions offline, without affecting the execution of the query.

Splitting the table into more partitions, lets us operate even on single partitions. For example, we can move the table to other tablespaces one partition at a time.

We can simply drop a partition instead of deleting rows related to certain partition key values. For example, when we only want to store data of the last period (a quarter, a year, a day) online, we can partition the table and drop the old partitions, instead of executing a long operation, such as `DELETE ... WHERE TIME < X`.

Partitioning is often used in OLAP systems, because it allows us to perform parallel DML operations, such as massive UPDATEs and INSERTs with a degree of parallelism equal to the number of partitions of the table.

In OLTP environments, there isn't a great performance gain—and if we implement a bad partitioning scheme we can have worse performance than without—but we will have easier maintenance tasks and increased availability, both as important as performance gains.

List partitioning

We have partitioned a table based on the range of values, which is the most common way to apply partitioning.

We can also partition a table based on a list of values. For example, the `COUNTRY` for a table of customers or the `CATEGORY` for a products table.

To create a list partitioned table, we can execute a statement similar to the following, in which we will partition the `SALES_LP` table based on `CHANNEL_ID` values:

```
CREATE TABLE SALES_LP (
 PROD_ID NUMBER NOT NULL,
 CUST_ID NUMBER NOT NULL,
 TIME_ID DATE NOT NULL,
 CHANNEL_ID NUMBER NOT NULL,
 PROMO_ID NUMBER NOT NULL,
```

```
 QUANTITY_SOLD NUMBER(10,2) NOT NULL,
 AMOUNT_SOLD NUMBER(10,2) NOT NULL)
PARTITION BY LIST (CHANNEL_ID)
(
  PARTITION DIRECT_SALES VALUES (3,9) TABLESPACE EXAMPLE,
  PARTITION INDIRECT_SALES VALUES (4,5) TABLESPACE EXAMPLE,
  PARTITION OTHER_SALES VALUES (DEFAULT) TABLESPACE EXAMPLE
);
```

We have defined two partitions to store direct and indirect sales, respectively and a default partition to store the rows whose partition key is not listed in the partitions mentioned earlier.

We can add partitions to a table, but if we have defined a default partition when applying list partitioning, we have to split the default partition instead of adding a new partition:

```
ALTER TABLE SALES_LP SPLIT PARTITION OTHER_SALES
   VALUES (2) INTO (PARTITION PARTNERS, PARTITION OTHER_SALES);
```

With the previous statement, we have split the OTHER_SALES partition, creating a new PARTNERS partition to store the sales made by partners, leaving the other kind of sales in the default OTHER_SALES partition. To test this assertion, we can insert two rows and query the single partition of the table to see if each row is in the correct partition, as follows:

```
INSERT INTO SALES_LP VALUES (1,2,SYSDATE,2,4,5,6);
INSERT INTO SALES_LP VALUES (1,2,SYSDATE,19,4,5,6);
SELECT * FROM SALES_LP PARTITION (PARTNERS);
SELECT * FROM SALES_LP PARTITION (OTHER_SALES);
```

Hash partitioning

We have seen list and range partitioning. The first fits well when we have a discrete number of values in the partition key, so we can easily split the table based on this criteria. The second one helps us when we have distinct range of values—for example, for historical data partitioned by a date, as in our example.

But can we partition a table when we aren't in the earlier mentioned situations? The answer is yes, using hash partitioning.

This time we divide our table based on a hash function computed over the partition key, to distribute table values without using a policy inherent in the data, ensuring only that the data will be distributed in partitions.

To obtain the best uniform data distribution, it's better to choose a number of partitions which is a power of 2, having a unique or near partition key.

The next statement creates a hash partitioned table:

```
CREATE TABLE SALES_HP (
 PROD_ID NUMBER NOT NULL,
 CUST_ID NUMBER NOT NULL,
 TIME_ID DATE NOT NULL,
 CHANNEL_ID NUMBER NOT NULL,
 PROMO_ID NUMBER NOT NULL,
 QUANTITY_SOLD NUMBER(10,2) NOT NULL,
 AMOUNT_SOLD NUMBER(10,2) NOT NULL)
PARTITION BY HASH (CHANNEL_ID)
(
  PARTITION P1 TABLESPACE EXAMPLE,
  PARTITION P2 TABLESPACE EXAMPLE,
  PARTITION P3 TABLESPACE EXAMPLE,
  PARTITION P4 TABLESPACE EXAMPLE
);
```

Please note that in creating a hash partitioned table, we don't specify the values for each partition.

Composite partitioning

We can adopt even a mixed partitioning schema, resulting in a **composite partitioned** table.

For example, we can partition a table by a range of dates and, within each partition, by a list of values, as follows:

```
CREATE TABLE SALES_CP (
 PROD_ID NUMBER NOT NULL,
 CUST_ID NUMBER NOT NULL,
 TIME_ID DATE NOT NULL,
 CHANNEL_ID NUMBER NOT NULL,
 PROMO_ID NUMBER NOT NULL,
 QUANTITY_SOLD NUMBER(10,2) NOT NULL,
 AMOUNT_SOLD NUMBER(10,2) NOT NULL)
PARTITION BY RANGE (TIME_ID)
 SUBPARTITION BY LIST (CHANNEL_ID)
(
 PARTITION SALES_BEFORE_2000
  VALUES LESS THAN (TO_DATE('20000101','YYYYMMDD'))
   (SUBPARTITION DIRECT_SALES_2000 VALUES (3,9)
      TABLESPACE EXAMPLE,
```

```
    SUBPARTITION INDIRECT_SALES_2000 VALUES (4,5)
      TABLESPACE EXAMPLE,
    SUBPARTITION OTHER_SALES_2000 VALUES (DEFAULT)
      TABLESPACE EXAMPLE
  ),
PARTITION SALES_2000_2001_2002
  VALUES LESS THAN (TO_DATE('20030101','YYYYMMDD'))
  (SUBPARTITION DIRECT_SALES_2000_2001_2002 VALUES (3,9)
      TABLESPACE EXAMPLE,
   SUBPARTITION INDIRECT_SALES_2000_2001_2002 VALUES (4,5)
      TABLESPACE EXAMPLE,
   SUBPARTITION OTHER_SALES_2000_2001_2002 VALUES (DEFAULT)
      TABLESPACE EXAMPLE
  ),
PARTITION SALES_2003
  VALUES LESS THAN (TO_DATE('20040101','YYYYMMDD'))
  (SUBPARTITION DIRECT_SALES_2003 VALUES (3,9)
      TABLESPACE EXAMPLE,
   SUBPARTITION INDIRECT_SALES_2003 VALUES (4,5)
      TABLESPACE EXAMPLE,
   SUBPARTITION OTHER_SALES_2003 VALUES (DEFAULT)
      TABLESPACE EXAMPLE
  )
);
```

When using composite partitioning, the subpartitions will have the corresponding physical segments in the tablespaces, while the partition will only have a logical meaning, because the rows of a partition will be stored in the segment of the subpartition to which they belong.

4
Optimizing SQL Code

In this chapter, we will cover the following topics:

- ▶ Using bind variables
- ▶ Avoiding full table scans
- ▶ Exploring index lookup
- ▶ Exploring index skip-scan and index range-scan
- ▶ Introducing arrays and bulk operations
- ▶ Optimizing joins
- ▶ Using subqueries
- ▶ Tracing SQL activity with SQL Trace and TKPROF

Introduction

In this chapter, we will see how to diagnose and solve typical performance problems caused by poorly written SQL code. We will inspect both queries and Data Manipulation Language (DML), starting with the correct use of bind variables in the first recipe.

This chapter will illustrate various aspects related to SQL code, providing solutions to the most common issues. We will see how to avoid full table scans, when possible,using indexes. For this, it is necessary to know the differences between index full scan, index skip-scan, and index range-scan operations.

We will also discuss arrays and bulk operations, revealing some tricks to increase performance in DML operations. Joins and subqueries will be discussed in the later part of the chapter.

The last recipe illustrates the use of SQL Trace and TKPROF, tools that help diagnose and correct problems. After reading this chapter, if you experience a problem in the SQL code of your database, you know how to start solving it using these tools.

Using bind variables

We have discussed bind variables in the *A working example* recipe in *Chapter 1, Starting with Performance Tuning*.

In this recipe, it is time to dig deeper into this topic, illustrating the benefits of using bind variables and testing the result of our efforts with simple examples. We will see examples on query statements, but the same methodologies and results apply to DML statements.

Getting ready

Follow these steps to prepare the database:

1. Create a package named `Chapter4` to test various aspects related to bind variables.

2. Connect to SQL*Plus using the `SH` schema:
   ```
   CONNECT sh@TESTDB/sh
   ```

3. Create the required package:
   ```
   CREATE OR REPLACE PACKAGE sh.CHAPTER4 AS
      PROCEDURE WORKLOAD_NOBIND;
      PROCEDURE WORKLOAD_BIND;
      PROCEDURE WORKLOAD_BIND_STATIC;
      PROCEDURE TEST_INJECTION(NAME IN
         sh.customers.cust_last_name%TYPE);
      PROCEDURE TEST_INJECTION2(NAME IN
         sh.customers.cust_last_name%TYPE);
   END;
   /

   CREATE OR REPLACE PACKAGE BODY sh.CHAPTER4 AS
      PROCEDURE TEST_NOBIND(CUSTID IN sh.customers.cust_id%TYPE)
      IS
      BEGIN
         DECLARE aRow sh.customers%ROWTYPE;
         l_stmt VARCHAR2(2000);
         BEGIN
            l_stmt := 'SELECT * FROM sh.customers s WHERE s.cust_id='
               || TO_CHAR (CUSTID);
   ```

```
      EXECUTE IMMEDIATE l_stmt INTO aRow;
    END;
  END TEST_NOBIND;


  PROCEDURE TEST_BIND(CUSTID IN sh.customers.cust_id%TYPE) IS
  BEGIN
    DECLARE aRow sh.customers%ROWTYPE;
    l_stmt VARCHAR2(2000);
    BEGIN
      l_stmt := 'SELECT * FROM sh.customers s WHERE s.cust_id =
        :p_cust_id';
      EXECUTE IMMEDIATE l_stmt INTO aRow USING CUSTID;
    END;
  END TEST_BIND;


  PROCEDURE TEST_BIND_STATIC(CUSTID IN
    sh.customers.cust_id%TYPE) IS
  BEGIN
    DECLARE aRow sh.customers%ROWTYPE;
    BEGIN
      SELECT * INTO aROW FROM sh.customers s WHERE s.cust_id =
        CUSTID;
      EXCEPTION
        WHEN NO_DATA_FOUND THEN
        NULL;
    END;
  END TEST_BIND_STATIC;


  PROCEDURE WORKLOAD_NOBIND IS
  BEGIN
    FOR i IN 1..50000
    LOOP
      TEST_NOBIND(i);
    END LOOP;
  END WORKLOAD_NOBIND;
```

```
PROCEDURE WORKLOAD_BIND IS
BEGIN
  FOR i IN 1..50000
  LOOP
    TEST_BIND(i);
  END LOOP;
END WORKLOAD_BIND;

PROCEDURE WORKLOAD_BIND_STATIC IS
BEGIN
  FOR i IN 1..50000
  LOOP
    TEST_BIND_STATIC(i);
  END LOOP;
END WORKLOAD_BIND_STATIC;

PROCEDURE TEST_INJECTION(NAME IN
  sh.customers.cust_last_name%TYPE) IS
BEGIN
  DECLARE l_stmt VARCHAR2(2000); res NUMBER;
  BEGIN
    l_stmt := 'SELECT COUNT(*) FROM sh.customers s WHERE
      s.cust_last_name = ''' || NAME || '''';
    EXECUTE IMMEDIATE l_stmt INTO res;
    DBMS_OUTPUT.PUT_LINE('Count: ' || TO_CHAR(res));
  END;
END TEST_INJECTION;

PROCEDURE TEST_INJECTION2(NAME IN
  sh.customers.cust_last_name%TYPE) IS
BEGIN
  DECLARE l_stmt VARCHAR2(2000);
  BEGIN
    l_stmt := 'BEGIN DBMS_OUTPUT.PUT_LINE (''You passed ' ||
      NAME || '''); END;';
```

```
    EXECUTE IMMEDIATE l_stmt;
  END;
 END TEST_INJECTION2;
END;
/
```

We are now ready to test bind variables.

How to do it...

We can test bind variables as follows:

1. Connect to the database as SYSDBA:

    ```
    CONNECT / AS SYSDBA
    ```

2. Flush the shared pool to be sure that previous statements don't influence current executions of the query:

    ```
    ALTER SYSTEM FLUSH SHARED_POOL;
    ```

3. Execute the WORKLOAD_NOBIND procedure, keeping track of the timing:

    ```
    SET TIMING ON
    exec sh.CHAPTER4.WORKLOAD_NOBIND;
    SET TIMING OFF
    ```

4. Execute the WORKLOAD_BIND procedure, keeping track of the timing, after flushing the cache from the previous statement's execution:

    ```
    ALTER SYSTEM FLUSH SHARED_POOL;
    SET TIMING ON
    exec sh.CHAPTER4.WORKLOAD_BIND;
    SET TIMING OFF
    ```

5. Execute the WORKLOAD_BIND_STATIC procedure; keep track of the execution time:

    ```
    ALTER SYSTEM FLUSH SHARED_POOL;
    SET TIMING ON
    exec sh.CHAPTER4.WORKLOAD_BIND_STATIC;
    SET TIMING OFF
    ```

    Review the results.

How it works...

We have created a package with five stored procedures available in it. There are three stored procedures in the package body that are not exposed to public execution—these are in the package body and are not listed in the package definition.

The first time we run the WORKLOAD_NOBIND procedure, it executes the stored procedure TEST_NOBIND 50,000 times, passing in a parameter between 1 and 50,000. The TEST_NOBIND procedure will look for a customer in the SH.CUSTOMERS table with the same customer ID as the input parameter. Here we use dynamic SQL statement execution, without using bind variables, but generating a new query for each parameter passed, concatenating the current value of the parameter to the query statement itself.

> A dynamic SQL statement is built dynamically at runtime and lets the developer create flexible applications because the full text of the SQL statement is unknown at compile time and it is defined only at runtime. A typical example of dynamic SQL statement use is in the software that lets the user type the query to execute—such as SQL*Plus or Oracle SQL Developer.

The output screen appears as follows:

```
ec2-46-51-176-114.eu-west-1.compute.amazonaws.com - PuTTY

SQL> CONNECT / AS SYSDBA
Connected.
SQL> ALTER SYSTEM FLUSH SHARED_POOL;

System altered.

SQL> SET TIMING ON
SQL> exec sh.CHAPTER4.WORKLOAD_NOBIND;

PL/SQL procedure successfully completed.

Elapsed: 00:01:25.56
SQL>
```

You can see that execution of the test case takes more than a minute and 25 seconds.

The second time we execute the WORKLOAD_BIND stored procedure, it will launch the stored procedure TEST_BIND, to do the same work as TEST_NOBIND, using bind variables to pass the current parameter (the customer ID) to the query.

The following is the output when the `WORKLOAD_BIND` stored procedure is executed:

Note that elapsed time, despite flushing of the shared pool, is slightly more than five seconds.

In the previous example, the `WORKLOAD_BIND_STATIC` procedure of the package was executed, which is functionally equivalent to the previous function's use. This example uses static SQL instead of dynamic SQL; the results obtained by this procedure are as follows:

This execution, on the test machine used, lasts for slightly more than four seconds.

There is better performance and reduced execution time in this example, when using bind variables to execute the query. This is due to the process involved in evaluating queries (and DML commands) by the parser. When using bind variables, the query is being hard parsed for the first time, and subsequent calls to the same statements—but with different parameters—will require only a soft parse, as illustrated in the example at the end of *Chapter 1*.

Another advantage of using static SQL to query the database instead of dynamic SQL, is minimizing parser overhead when executing the query. The results show that using bind variables is very important when evaluating database performance. However, this kind of behavior has to be pursued in the implementation phase of the application. In order to improve an application, which doesn't use bind variables, every query and DML command would have to be rewritten.

There's more...

A bind variable is a placeholder, used in our SQL statement, which can bind with actual values during execution. We can also obtain the statistics related to parses by selecting from the dynamic performance view `V$SYSSTAT`:

```
SELECT * FROM V$SYSSTAT WHERE NAME LIKE 'parse%';
```

In the following screenshot, you can see an example of the output:

```
ec2-46-51-176-114.eu-west-1.compute.amazonaws.com - PuTTY
SQL> SELECT * FROM V$SYSSTAT WHERE NAME LIKE 'parse%';

STATISTIC# NAME                                CLASS      VALUE    STAT_ID
---------- ------------------------------ ---------- ---------- ----------
       547 parse time cpu                         64         78  206905303
       548 parse time elapsed                     64        910 1431595225
       549 parse count (total)                    64       5110   63887964
       550 parse count (hard)                     64       1095  143509059
       551 parse count (failures)                 64          0 1118776443
       552 parse count (describe)                 64          0  469016317

6 rows selected.

SQL>
```

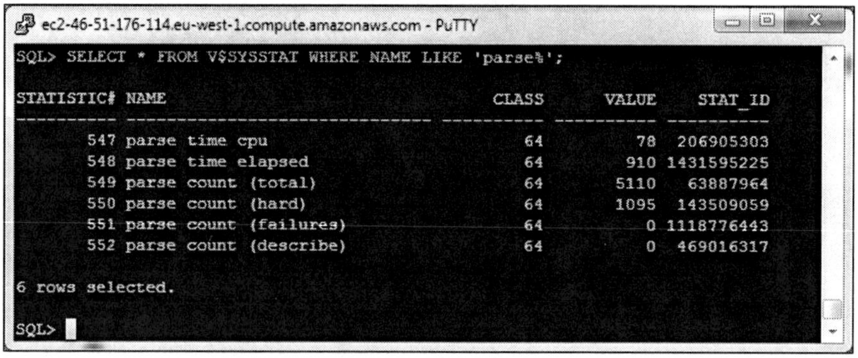

In this example, 1095 out of 5110 are hard parses.

Concurrency and scalability

We have seen that using bind variables improves performance, due to the hard/soft parse of the statements; there is a huge improvement in latch contention as well. When the database is parsing a statement, it acquires a latch on the structures involved (shared SQL area and library cache), and this is a huge limitation on concurrency and scalability. If there are many users using the same application—without bind variables—the contention for these shared latches will increase, and there will be many wait events as many users try to acquire the same resource.

If there is an application that doesn't use bind variables, the entire database, and other applications that use them, will suffer a drop in performance. The "bad" application (the one that doesn't use bind variables) will insert many statements in the library cache. This is because it doesn't reuse them, and every statement is different from the previous execution. In most cases, the statements of the "good" applications are flushed from the library cache because there isn't enough space.

Security issues

We have seen that there are many reasons to restrict the use of bind variables, from a performance point of view. Security is also one of the reasons to use bind variables in database applications.

Let's try to execute the stored procedure `TEST_INJECTION` in our package. This simple procedure has a string parameter `NAME` and shows the number of customers with the last name passed as a parameter:

```
SET SERVEROUTPUT ON
exec sh.CHAPTER4.TEST_INJECTION('Hanson');
exec sh.CHAPTER4.TEST_INJECTION(''' or 1=1--');
```

The output screen is as follows:

In the second execution, we have passed a tricky parameter value, so the query executed from the procedure will be as follows:

```
SELECT COUNT(*) FROM sh.customers s
WHERE s.cust_last_name = '' or 1=1--'
```

This statement, due to the `1=1` condition ORed, will count every customer in the table. We have modified the behavior of the program. Think about the consequences if a similar procedure can access sensible data, and the name parameter is bound to a field the user can modify in the interface. If we use bind variables, this would not happen.

In the next sample, we will use the `TEST_INJECTION2` procedure to illustrate how a malicious user can use our application to make unwanted changes to the database.

Create a table `TEST_INJ` and fill it with some data:

```
CREATE TABLE sh.TEST_INJ (ID INT, NAME VARCHAR2(100));
INSERT INTO sh.TEST_INJ
  SELECT cust_id, cust_first_name
  FROM sh.customers WHERE ROWNUM < 101;
```

Let's see the result after executing the `TEST_INJECTION2` procedure:

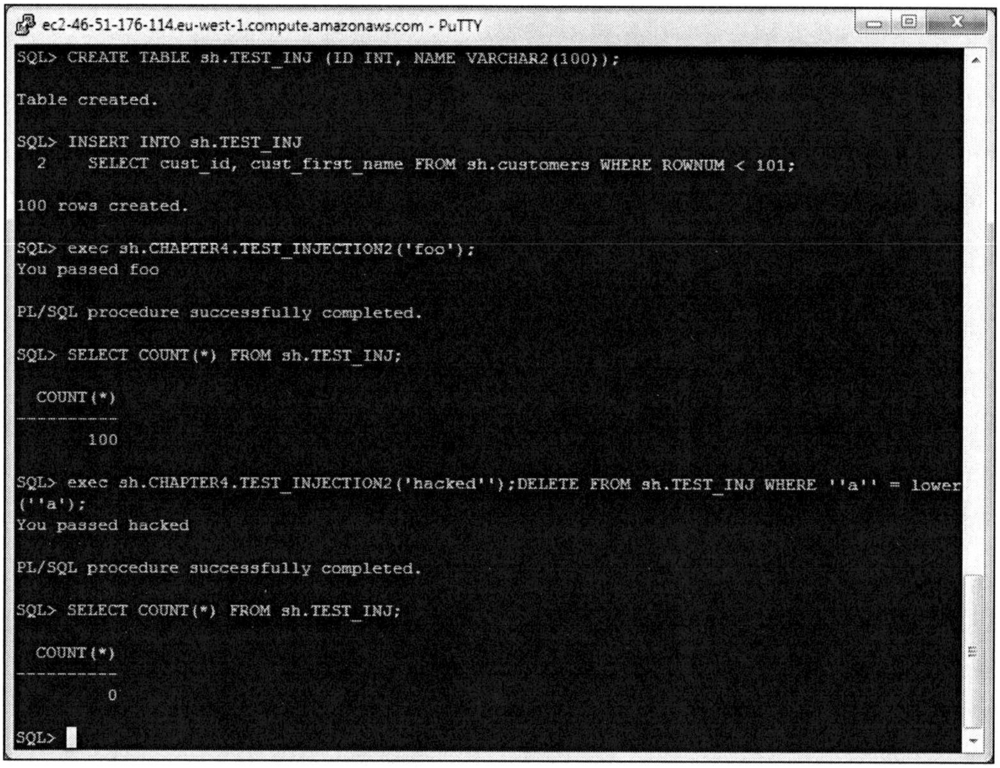

The procedure that is being called simply shows information on the screen and requires a string parameter. With a certain parameter value, we can delete data from the database, emptying the `TEST_INJ` table.

In such cases, the use of bind variables would have avoided the problems described.

Implementing the previously mentioned functions using bind variables would be done as follows:

```
PROCEDURE TEST_INJECTION(
  NAME IN sh.customers.cust_last_name%TYPE) IS
BEGIN
  DECLARE
    l_stmt VARCHAR2(2000);
    res NUMBER;
  BEGIN
    l_stmt := 'SELECT COUNT(*) FROM sh.customers s WHERE
      s.cust_last_name = :p_name';
    EXECUTE IMMEDIATE l_stmt INTO res USING NAME;
    DBMS_OUTPUT.PUT_LINE('Count: ' || TO_CHAR(res));
  END;
END TEST_INJECTION;

PROCEDURE TEST_INJECTION2(
  NAME IN sh.customers.cust_last_name%TYPE) IS
BEGIN
  DECLARE
    l_stmt VARCHAR2(2000);
  BEGIN
    l_stmt := 'BEGIN DBMS_OUTPUT.PUT_LINE (''You passed '' ||
      :p_name); END;';
    EXECUTE IMMEDIATE l_stmt USING NAME;
  END;
END TEST_INJECTION2;
```

See also

▸ We will see more about latches in the recipe *Minimizing latches using bind variables* in *Chapter 11, Tuning Contention*

▸ To know more about dynamic SQL refer to *Avoiding dynamic SQL* in *Chapter 2, Optimizing Application Design* and *Introduce Adaptive Cursor Sharing for bind variable peeking* in *Chapter 7, Improving the Oracle Optimizer*

Avoiding full table scans

In this recipe, we will see what a full table scan is, how to avoid it, and when to choose a full table scan over other methods.

How to do it...

Let's start by creating two tables from the data in the SALES table of the SH schema:

1. Connect to the SH schema:

   ```
   CONNECT sh@TESTDB/sh
   ```

2. Create the MY_SALES_ALL table:

   ```
   CREATE TABLE sh.MY_SALES_ALL AS
     SELECT ROWNUM AS ID, X.* FROM sh.SALES X;
   ```

3. Create the MY_SALES_2 table:

   ```
   CREATE TABLE sh.MY_SALES_2 AS
     SELECT * FROM sh.MY_SALES_ALL NOLOGGING;
   ```

4. Compute statistics on the tables we just created:

   ```
   EXEC DBMS_STATS.GATHER_TABLE_STATS('SH', 'MY_SALES_ALL',
     estimate_percent => 100,
     method_opt => 'for all columns size 1');
   EXEC DBMS_STATS.GATHER_TABLE_STATS('SH', 'MY_SALES_2',
     estimate_percent => 100,
     method_opt => 'for all columns size 1');
   ```

5. Verify the database blocks used by the two tables:

   ```
   SELECT BLOCKS FROM DBA_TABLES
     WHERE TABLE_NAME IN ('MY_SALES_ALL', 'MY_SALES_2');
   ```

6. Delete some rows from MY_SALES_2, resulting in a table with about 1/100 rows of the original SALES table:

   ```
   DELETE FROM sh.MY_SALES_2 WHERE MOD(ID,100) <> 0;
   COMMIT;
   ```

7. Re-compute statistics on the `MY_SALES_2` table:

```
EXEC DBMS_STATS.GATHER_TABLE_STATS('SH', 'MY_SALES_2',
   estimate_percent => 100,
   method_opt => 'for all columns size 1');
```

8. Count the database blocks used by `MY_SALES_ALL` and `MY_SALES_2` tables:

```
SELECT BLOCKS FROM DBA_TABLES
   WHERE TABLE_NAME IN ('MY_SALES_ALL', 'MY_SALES_2');
```

9. Select some rows from the `MY_SALES_ALL` table, showing the execution plan with statistics:

```
SET LINESIZE 120
SET AUTOT TRACE EXP STAT
SELECT * FROM sh.MY_SALES_ALL
   WHERE TIME_ID > TO_DATE('20011220', 'YYYYMMDD');
```

10. Flush the buffer cache:

```
CONNECT / AS SYSDBA
ALTER SYSTEM FLUSH BUFFER_CACHE;
```

11. Select some rows using the same query from `MY_SALES_2` table, showing the execution plan with statistics:

```
CONNECT sh@TESTDB/sh
SET LINESIZE 120
SET AUTOT TRACE EXP STAT
SELECT * FROM sh.MY_SALES_2
   WHERE TIME_ID > TO_DATE('20011220', 'YYYYMMDD');
SET AUTOT OFF
```

12. Shrink space on the `MY_SALES_2` table:

```
ALTER TABLE sh.MY_SALES_2 ENABLE ROW MOVEMENT;
ALTER TABLE sh.MY_SALES_2 SHRINK SPACE;
EXEC DBMS_STATS.GATHER_TABLE_STATS('SH', 'MY_SALES_2',
   estimate_percent => 100,
   method_opt => 'for all columns size 1');
```

13. Count the used database blocks by `MY_SALES_ALL` and `MY_SALES_2` tables after space shrinking:

```
SELECT BLOCKS FROM DBA_TABLES
    WHERE TABLE_NAME IN ('MY_SALES_ALL', 'MY_SALES_2');
```

14. View some statistics on full table scans:

```
SELECT NAME, VALUE FROM V$SYSSTAT
    WHERE NAME LIKE '%table scan%';
```

15. Drop the tables created earlier:

```
DROP TABLE sh.MY_SALES_ALL;
DROP TABLE sh.MY_SALES_2;
```

How it works...

We have created two tables, `MY_SALES_ALL` and `MY_SALES_2`; they are equal and take up 5157 database blocks, as shown in the following screenshot:

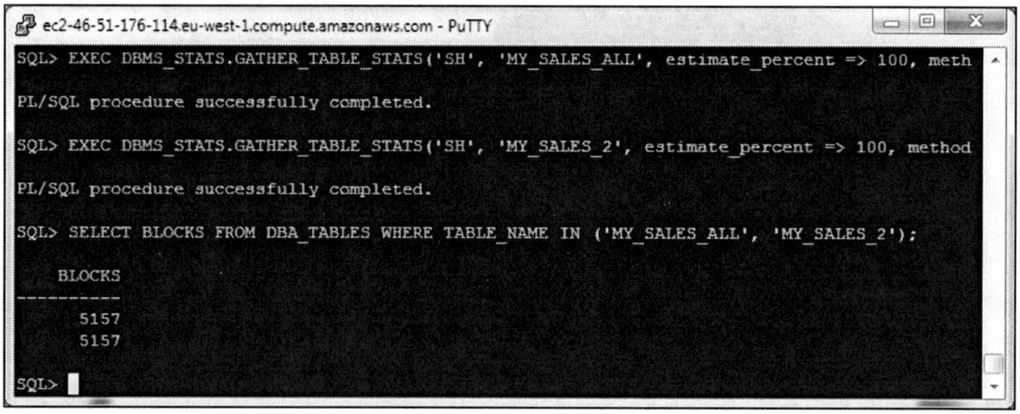

We have deleted more than 900,000 records from `MY_SALES_2`, which are about 90 percent of the original records in the table. After re-analyzing the table, we execute the same `SELECT` statement, and the results are the same, as shown in the following screenshot:

We have the same number of used blocks for both tables, even if one of these is 10 percent the size of the other.

If we execute a query on the first table, we obtain the following results:

We can see that there are **5068 physical reads** to answer the query, because the database is scanning the entire table—so each database block of the table—to find the data we have asked for.

If we execute the same query on the `MY_SALES_2` table, we obtain the following results:

```
ec2-46-51-176-114.eu-west-1.compute.amazonaws.com - PuTTY

-------------------------------------------------------------
Plan hash value: 3083133199

-------------------------------------------------------------
| Id  | Operation          | Name      | Rows | Bytes | Cost (%CPU)| Time     |
-------------------------------------------------------------
|   0 | SELECT STATEMENT   |           |   69 |  1932 |  1399   (1)| 00:00:17 |
|*  1 |  TABLE ACCESS FULL| MY_SALES_2 |   69 |  1932 |  1399   (1)| 00:00:17 |
-------------------------------------------------------------

Predicate Information (identified by operation id):
-------------------------------------------------------------

   1 - filter("TIME_ID">TO_DATE(' 2001-12-20 00:00:00', 'syyyy-mm-dd
               hh24:mi:ss'))

Statistics
-------------------------------------------------------------
          1  recursive calls
          0  db block gets
       5077  consistent gets
       5068  physical reads
          0  redo size
       4192  bytes sent via SQL*Net to client
        474  bytes received via SQL*Net from client
          7  SQL*Net roundtrips to/from client
          0  sorts (memory)
          0  sorts (disk)
         89  rows processed

SQL>
```

Comparing the previous two screenshots, we can observe that the number of physical reads haven't changed between the execution. So, even if the `MY_SALES_2` table contains only 10 percent of the rows, the number of database blocks scanned to answer the query will not vary, because the number of blocks used by the table is the same.

We try to shrink the space used by the table, executing the `ALTER TABLE SHRINK SPACE` command. After getting the updated stats, you can see that the number of blocks have changed.

```
ec2-46-51-176-114.eu-west-1.compute.amazonaws.com - PuTTY

SQL> ALTER TABLE sh.MY_SALES_2 ENABLE ROW MOVEMENT;

Table altered.

SQL> ALTER TABLE sh.MY_SALES_2 SHRINK SPACE;

Table altered.

SQL> EXEC DBMS_STATS.GATHER_TABLE_STATS('SH', 'MY_SALES_2', estimate_percent => 100, method_

PL/SQL procedure successfully completed.

SQL> SELECT BLOCKS, EMPTY_BLOCKS FROM DBA_TABLES
  2    WHERE TABLE_NAME IN ('MY_SALES_ALL', 'MY_SALES_2');

    BLOCKS EMPTY_BLOCKS
---------- ------------
      5157            0
        50            0

SQL>
```

Execute the same query and you will notice that the statistics of the query execution have changed accordingly, as shown in the following screenshot:

```
ec2-46-51-176-114.eu-west-1.compute.amazonaws.com - PuTTY

Execution Plan
----------------------------------------------------------
Plan hash value: 3083133199

-------------------------------------------------------------------------
| Id | Operation          | Name       | Rows | Bytes | Cost (%CPU)| Time     |
-------------------------------------------------------------------------
|  0 | SELECT STATEMENT   |            |   69 |  2277 |   15   (0)| 00:00:01 |
|* 1 |  TABLE ACCESS FULL| MY_SALES_2 |   69 |  2277 |   15   (0)| 00:00:01 |
-------------------------------------------------------------------------

Predicate Information (identified by operation id):
---------------------------------------------------

   1 - filter("TIME_ID">TO_DATE(' 2001-12-20 00:00:00', 'syyyy-mm-dd
             hh24:mi:ss'))


Statistics
----------------------------------------------------------
          0  recursive calls
          0  db block gets
         59  consistent gets
         51  physical reads
          0  redo size
       4202  bytes sent via SQL*Net to client
        474  bytes received via SQL*Net from client
          7  SQL*Net roundtrips to/from client
          0  sorts (memory)
          0  sorts (disk)
         89  rows processed
SQL>
```

In step 14, we query some data from the database dynamic performance views for full table scans executed on the database, obtaining the following result:

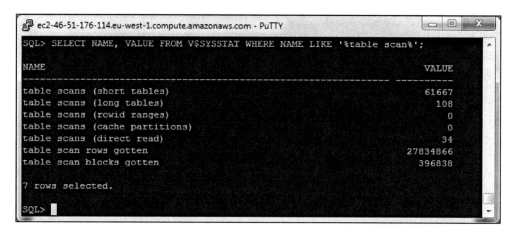

You can see from the results that they are divided between table scans on short tables and table scans on long tables; let's see why.

When the database executes a Full Table Scan (FTS) operation, it reads all the database blocks of a table to retrieve the data needed. This operation is often undesirable in OLTP databases, because if we have to scan a very large table to retrieve the desired data, there is most often something wrong with the access paths of data in the database.

It's better to use a Full Table Scan when we have small tables. You should follow this advice because it may be more expensive to read an index entry and the corresponding data instead of reading the full table. The first operation (index + data) reads a minimum of two database blocks, one for the index and one for the data. Reading the full table, instead, is done by reading only the table data, which could be only one database block in size. Hence, there is a difference in the dynamic performance view between short tables and long tables.

The Full Table Scan operation has two problems related to performance; the first one is obvious, many I/O operations are needed to perform the FTS to retrieve the blocks. The second flaw is related to the buffer cache; if we have a well-tuned application, when we execute a query it is better to find the data we need in the buffer cache, avoiding I/O operations. If we do an FTS, database buffers are used to read all the table data, and this situation may lead to flushing the buffer cache data to make room for the FTS data. To avoid this situation and to limit the consequences on the database buffer cache, the database blocks from FTS operations are put on the top of the LRU (Least Recently Used) list. This list is used to keep track of the database buffers, deciding if they are good candidates to be flushed. These candidates will be flushed before the database blocks the ones in use by other kinds of operations in the database.

However, in data warehouse environments, the use of FTS operations is often preferable. This is because when we have a larger database block, we can read many rows in a block and even subsequent database blocks—in one operation—by setting the parameter `DB_FILE_MULTIBLOCK_READ_COUNT` (at the instance or session level). This parameter controls the number of database blocks read in one I/O operation. Obviously, there is a limit—imposed by the operating system—to the maximum size of bytes (or number of OS blocks) that can be read with a single I/O operation. The use of this parameter influences even the optimizer—if it's less expensive to read all the rows in a table than using an index, the optimizer will use an FTS even if there are usable indexes in place.

There's more...

We need to understand how database rows are stored in database blocks, and some storage parameters used when creating a table that affects this conduct.

The High-Water Mark

The High-Water Mark (HWM) is recorded in the segment header block, which indicates the last used block in the segment.

You need to differentiate between unused blocks above and below the HWM. If we think of the segments as a tank, we start filling the segments from the bottom up; if we draw a line when the level increases, then that is the HWM, representing the highest level reached by water. If we empty the tank a bit, the HWM will remain at the same level.

When applied to tables, there is unused space (empty blocks) above the HWM; this space of the segment is never used.

In our example, in step 6 we have deleted many rows from the `MY_SALES_2` table, resulting in a lot of unused space below the HWM. We have deleted the rows at many different points in the blocks, so there are many unused rows in a block, but there aren't empty blocks at all. We can inspect the situation with the following queries:

```
SELECT BLOCKS, EMPTY_BLOCKS
FROM DBA_TABLES
WHERE TABLE_NAME IN ('MY_SALES_ALL', 'MY_SALES_2');
```

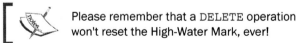 Please remember that a `DELETE` operation won't reset the High-Water Mark, ever!

The HWM is very important in FTS operations—the database will read every single block in the table segments, which are below the HWM, even if they are not used. So keep the HWM as low as possible, to avoid the unnecessary scan of unused database blocks.

The only ways to reset the HWM are:

▶ `TRUNCATE`: Truncating the table will reset the HWM, but all the data in the table will be lost. There is an option to de-allocate the space—`REUSE STORAGE`—this is useful when we want to unload all the data and reload it keeping the same segments, resulting in a faster loading process.

▶ `ALTER TABLE MOVE`: The table can be moved, but all indexes will be marked unusable and must be rebuilt.

▶ `EXPORT + DROP + IMPORT`: You can export the table data, drop the table, and import the data back in the database.

Please note that the `ALTER TABLE ... DEALLOCATE UNUSED` command de-allocates database blocks above the High-Water Mark.

PctFree, PctUsed, and FREELISTs

When we create a table, `PCTFREE` and `PCTUSED` are two parameters of the `STORAGE` clause— they are useful in specifying the behavior of the database blocks in the segment.

`PCTFREE` defines the minimum percentage of a database block to be reserved for future updates on the rows in the data block. If we define a `PCTFREE` of 10, then the database will fill the data block with new rows until the data block is filled up to 90 percent of its size; then the data block is removed from the `FREELIST`, so it's not used for new inserts.

`PCTUSED` sets the minimum percentage of a database block above which a database block can return on the `FREELIST`. In the previous example, after we have reached the `PCTFREE`, the database block is removed from the `FREELIST`. We have set a `PCTUSED` of 45 on table creation, so when we delete rows from the table and when the database block reaches a percentage of usage space less than 45 percent, the database block is put in the `FREELIST`. Now the subsequent inserts will put rows in the data block, until the free space reaches the `PCTFREE`, and so on.

Having a table with a small `PCTFREE` parameter will lead to blocks with more data in it, so FTS operations will benefit from this situation, accessing the same number of rows reading fewer database blocks. Please note that setting small values to the `PCTFREE` parameter could lead to `ROW MIGRATION` problems during subsequent updates to the rows. `PCTUSED` has no meaning, when using Automatic Segment Space Management (ASSM).

See also

▶ Recipes in *Chapter 3, Optimizing Storage Structures* about indexing to avoid Full Table Scans

▶ In *Chapter 8, Other Optimizations* the *Loading data with SQL Loader and Data Pump recipe* explains the EXPORT/IMPORT process and data loading in more depth

▶ For row chaining refer to the *Avoiding row migration* recipe in *Chapter 3*

Exploring index lookup

In the previous recipe, we have seen some issues related to FTS operations and when it's better to avoid them.

One of the methods to avoid FTS is indexing. In this recipe, several issues related to index lookup and index scan will be presented along with an illustration of the counterpart for indexes of FTS operation—Index Full Scan.

Getting ready

The examples given are based on a copy of the CUSTOMERS table in the SH schema; we will use SQL*Plus to execute our tests.

How to do it...

The following steps will demonstrate index lookup:

1. Connect to SH schema:

   ```
   CONNECT sh@TESTDB/sh
   ```

2. Create the MY_CUSTOMERS table as a copy of CUSTOMERS:

   ```
   CREATE TABLE sh.MY_CUSTOMERS AS
       SELECT * FROM sh.CUSTOMERS NOLOGGING;
   ```

3. Update the CUST_VALID field to obtain a skewed distribution of values:

   ```
   UPDATE sh.MY_CUSTOMERS SET
       CUST_VALID = 'I'
       WHERE CUST_VALID = 'A' AND MOD(CUST_ID,100) <> 0;
   SELECT CUST_VALID, COUNT(*)
       FROM sh.MY_CUSTOMERS
       GROUP BY CUST_VALID;
   ```

4. Create an index on the MY_CUSTOMERS table to test different execution plans:

   ```
   CREATE INDEX sh.MY_CUSTOMERS_IXVALID
       ON sh.MY_CUSTOMERS (CUST_VALID);
   ```

5. Test a query on the table, looking for the most common value:

   ```
   SET AUTOT TRACE EXP STAT
   SELECT * FROM sh.MY_CUSTOMERS WHERE CUST_VALID = 'I';
   ```

6. Test the same query from the previous step but with the less common value:

```
SET AUTOT TRACE EXP STAT

SELECT * FROM sh.MY_CUSTOMERS WHERE CUST_VALID = 'A';
```

7. Execute a slightly different query, and replace the previous predicate with a not equal condition (resulting in the same data):

```
SET AUTOT TRACE EXP STAT

SELECT * FROM sh.MY_CUSTOMERS WHERE CUST_VALID <> 'I';
```

8. Finally, drop the table created for testing:

```
DROP TABLE sh.MY_CUSTOMERS;
```

How it works...

After following step 1 to step 3, we will reach the following situation:

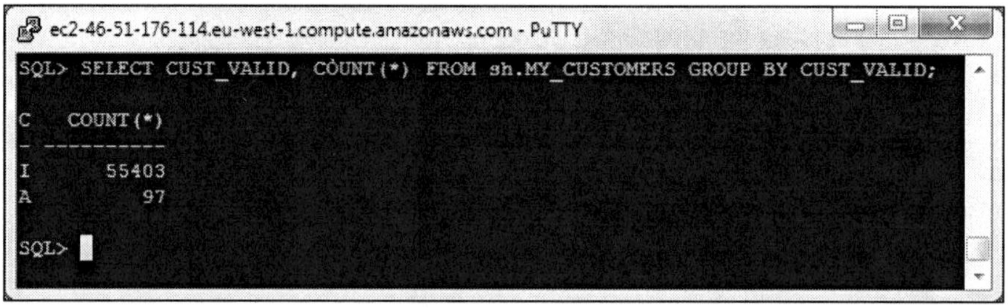

We have a table where the values in CUST_VALID column are largely skewed—we define a column as skewed where the values in the column are not equi-distributed, resulting in less than 0.2 percent of rows with a value of "A" in this field.

In the same column, create an index and execute a query with the same column in the predicate.

In the first query (step 5), it will ask for the rows with the most common value for the CUST_VALID field, resulting in the execution plan illustrated in the following screenshot:

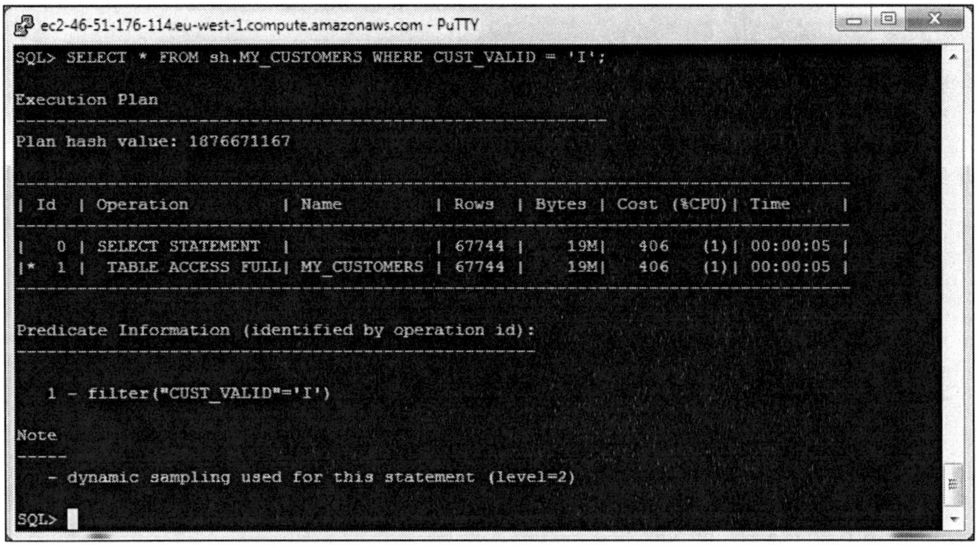

We can see that the database will perform an FTS operation. Using the index to access rows in the table will use more resources, because most of the data in the table satisfies the where condition.

Execute the same query, in step 6, but ask for the least common value "A" in CUST_VALID field. The execution plan of the query changes, as shown in the following screenshot:

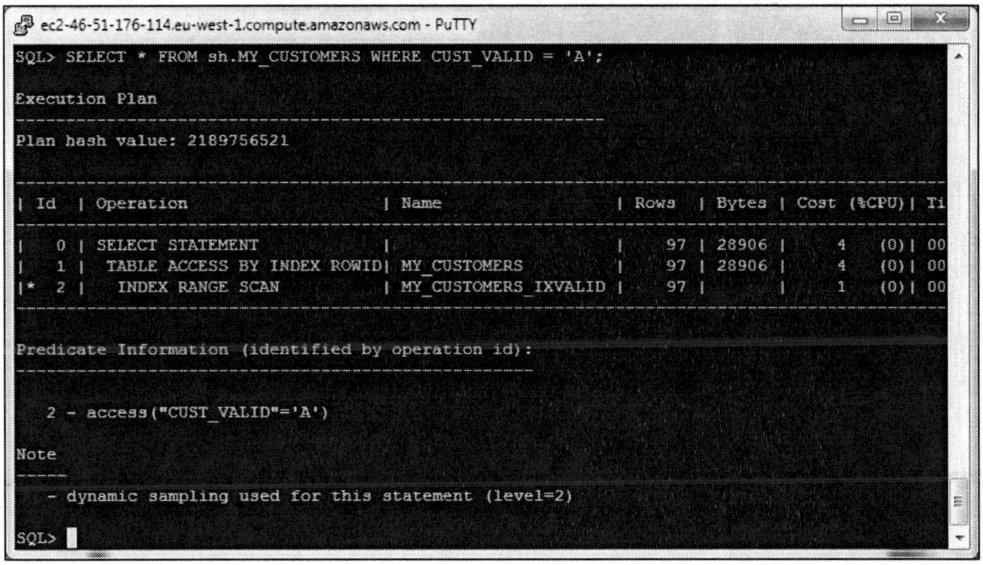

Due to the **selectivity** of the new value used in the predicate (less than 0.2 percent of the rows in the table will satisfy the predicate), the database switches the execution plan to an **Index Range Scan** operation. The index is scanned (only in the range related to "A" values for the CUST_VALID attribute) to find the rows which satisfy the WHERE clause; this is a very efficient way to access a table (when the returned rows are few when compared to the total number of rows in the table).

> The effectiveness of an index depends on the number of rows selected out of the total number of rows in the table. This is the selectivity of an index. In an ideal index, there is only one row for each index value. In the real world, an index with a selectivity of less than 10 percent is considered suitable enough.

The last query will ask for the same result-set, but changing the way in which the predicate is expressed. There are only "A" and "I" values in the column CUST_VALID, so the condition expressed as not equal is equivalent to that of the previous query, expressed with an equal comparison.

Again, there is a change in the execution plan, as shown in the following screenshot:

```
ec2-46-51-176-114.eu-west-1.compute.amazonaws.com - PuTTY

SQL> SELECT * FROM sh.MY_CUSTOMERS WHERE CUST_VALID <> 'I';

Execution Plan
----------------------------------------------------------
Plan hash value: 1876671167

----------------------------------------------------------
| Id  | Operation          | Name        | Rows  | Bytes | Cost (%CPU)| Time     |
----------------------------------------------------------
|   0 | SELECT STATEMENT   |             |    71 | 21158 |   406   (1)| 00:00:05 |
|*  1 |  TABLE ACCESS FULL | MY_CUSTOMERS |   71 | 21158 |   406   (1)| 00:00:05 |
----------------------------------------------------------

Predicate Information (identified by operation id):
---------------------------------------------------

   1 - filter("CUST_VALID"<>'I')

Note
-----
   - dynamic sampling used for this statement (level=2)

SQL>
```

Why did the database optimizer switch back to a long-running FTS operation, instead of the previous Index Range Scan? The answer is simple—indexes cannot be used when we compare values with a not equal operator.

There's more...

We have seen how using a not equal comparison in the WHERE clause of a query, doesn't allow us to use an index to select the values.

There are other situations which prevent an index from being used:

- ▸ **Using a function**: A function is often used as a predicate. In such cases, it's better to express the function on the constant side of the comparison and not on the field side. For example, we want to know the orders less than 1000 including the shipping fee of 5.25 percent. Suppose we have the TOTAL column of the ORDERS table in which the value is stored without the shipping fee and this column is indexed, if we query for (TOTAL * (1 + 5.25 / 100.00)) < 1000.00, it will not use the index.

  If we express the same condition as TOTAL < 1000.00 / (1+5.25 / 100.00), the index on the TOTAL field will be used—if it's convenient to use it instead of a Full Table Scan.

- ▸ **Searching for NULL values**: NULL values are not stored in indexes, so when we query for the records with a NULL value in a field X, even if the X column is indexed, the index will not be used.

  The index will be used, instead, if we query for NOT NULL elements, but only if the resulting operation (accessing the index plus accessing the table) is less expensive than an FTS. In this case, a **Fast Full Scan** operation will be performed on the index, that is, a complete scan of the entire index.

See also

- ▸ See the *Indexing the correct way* recipe in *Chapter 3, Optimizing Storage Structures* for more info about using indexes

Exploring index skip-scan and index range-scan

In this recipe, we will see how to use composite indexes and also the difference between index skip-scan and index range-scan operations.

Getting ready

For this recipe, we will use a copy of the CUSTOMERS table in the SH schema and SQL*Plus to execute our tests.

How to do it...

The following steps will demonstrate index skip-scan and index range-scan:

1. Connect to SH schema:

   ```
   CONNECT sh@TESTDB/sh
   ```

2. Create MY_CUSTOMERS table as a copy of CUSTOMERS:

   ```
   CREATE TABLE sh.MY_CUSTOMERS AS
       SELECT * FROM sh.CUSTOMERS NOLOGGING;
   ```

3. Create an index on the MY_CUSTOMERS table based on multiple fields:

   ```
   CREATE INDEX sh.CUSTOMERS_IXMULTI ON sh.MY_CUSTOMERS
       (CUST_GENDER, CUST_YEAR_OF_BIRTH, CUST_FIRST_NAME);
   ```

4. Compute statistics on the table:

   ```
   EXEC DBMS_STATS.GATHER_TABLE_STATS('SH', 'MY_CUSTOMERS',
       estimate_percent => 100,
       method_opt => 'for all columns size 1');
   ```

5. Execute a query on the table, using the first two fields of the CUSTOMERS_IXMULTI index in the predicate:

   ```
   SET AUTOT TRACE EXP
   SELECT CUST_ID FROM sh.MY_CUSTOMERS
       WHERE CUST_GENDER = 'M' AND CUST_YEAR_OF_BIRTH = 1945;
   ```

6. Execute a query using the first and the last fields of the index in the predicate:

   ```
   SELECT CUST_ID FROM sh.MY_CUSTOMERS
       WHERE CUST_GENDER = 'F' AND CUST_FIRST_NAME = 'Yvette';
   ```

7. Execute a query using the second and the last fields of the index in the predicate:

   ```
   SELECT * FROM sh.MY_CUSTOMERS
       WHERE CUST_YEAR_OF_BIRTH = 1951
       AND CUST_FIRST_NAME = 'Yvette';
   ```

8. Drop the table used for testing:

   ```
   SET AUTOT OFF
   DROP TABLE sh.MY_CUSTOMERS;
   ```

How it works...

When we query the table using the first fields of a multi-column index, the optimizer can choose to use an Index Range Scan operation. This is what happens in step 5, as shown in the following screenshot:

When running an Index Range Scan operation, the database finds the first block of the index containing values that satisfy the predicate (in our example CUST_GENDER = "M" and CUST_YEAR_OF_BIRTH = 1945) and scans the index data block to find all the entries that satisfy the conditions—examining the leaf blocks of the index using the link between the leaves. This operation is very fast.

In step 6 we use the first and the third field of the index in our predicate in this case the execution plan will change as shown in the following screenshot:

The Index Skip Scan operation is a compromise between the Index Range Scan and Fast Full Scan. In our example, the database looks up the first leaf in the index in which entries have CUST_GENDER = "F", then scans all the possible values for CUST_YEAR_OF_BIRTH and, for each value, scans the index for CUST_FIRST_NAME = "Yvette".

See the Oracle Database Concepts 11gR2 documentation for a complete description of how B-tree indexes work and what B-tree branch and leaf nodes are, available online at:

http://download.oracle.com/docs/cd/E14072_01/
server.112/e10713/indexiot.htm#CNCPT811

This operation is slower than an Index Range Scan, but faster than a Fast Full Scan because less data blocks have to be read.

In step 7, we query rows with a predicate not involving the first field of the CUSTOMERS_IXMULTI index, the results are as follows:

```
ec2-46-51-176-114.eu-west-1.compute.amazonaws.com - PuTTY

SQL> SELECT * FROM sh.MY_CUSTOMERS
  2  WHERE CUST_YEAR_OF_BIRTH = 1951 AND CUST_FIRST_NAME = 'Yvette';

Execution Plan
----------------------------------------------------------
Plan hash value: 2090538446

-----------------------------------------------------------------------------
| Id  | Operation                    | Name             | Rows | Bytes | Cost (%CPU)| Time
-----------------------------------------------------------------------------
|   0 | SELECT STATEMENT             |                  |    1 |   167 |     5   (0)| 00:0
|   1 |  TABLE ACCESS BY INDEX ROWID | MY_CUSTOMERS     |    1 |   167 |     5   (0)| 00:0
|*  2 |   INDEX SKIP SCAN            | CUSTOMERS_IXMULTI |    1 |       |     3   (0)| 00:0
-----------------------------------------------------------------------------

Predicate Information (identified by operation id):
---------------------------------------------------

   2 - access("CUST_YEAR_OF_BIRTH"=1951 AND "CUST_FIRST_NAME"='Yvette')
       filter("CUST_FIRST_NAME"='Yvette' AND "CUST_YEAR_OF_BIRTH"=1951)

SQL>
```

We can see that even in this case the Index Skip Scan is chosen by the optimizer, and the behavior in executing this plan will be similar to the previous one.

There's more...

In this recipe, we have seen that we can use multi-column indexes to access our data faster. When creating such an index, keep in mind that if the first column of the index is more selective, operations like Index Range Scans will benefit. If we perform Index Skip Scan operations, instead, performance will benefit more with a less selective column in the first place of the index.

Try to create multi-column indexes on the attributes of a table you use together in the predicate. If the index contains fields of the projection, the database could use the index only to answer the query, without accessing table data.

If the leading columns of the index have low cardinality (that is, the number of distinct values in the column is very small compared to the number of rows in the table), using compression will lead to performance improvement in Index Range Scanning operations.

See also

- ▶ See the *Indexing the correct way* recipe in *Chapter 3, Optimizing Storage Structures* for more information on using indexes

Introducing arrays and bulk operations

In this recipe, we will see different ways to insert data in our tables and we will make some considerations about the `INSERT` statement's performance.

We will see how arrays can be used to speed up insert and select statements, and why it may be better to use a single statement to achieve certain goals than using a procedural approach.

How to do it...

The following steps will demonstrate the use of arrays to insert data into the tables:

1. Connect to the SH schema:

   ```
   CONNECT sh@TESTDB/sh
   ```

2. Create an empty table called MY_SALES with the same structure as the SALES table:

   ```
   CREATE TABLE sh.MY_SALES AS
     SELECT cust_id, prod_id FROM sh.sales WHERE 1=0;
   ```

3. Enable timing:

```
SET TIMING ON
```

4. Create a PL/SQL block to insert the sales of the second half of year 2001 from the
SALES table to the new table using a cursor to scroll the SALES table:

```
DECLARE
  CURSOR curs_c1 IS
    SELECT cust_id, prod_id FROM sh.sales
    WHERE time_id between TO_DATE('20010701', 'YYYYMMDD')
      AND TO_DATE('20011231', 'YYYYMMDD');
BEGIN
  FOR x IN curs_c1
  LOOP
    INSERT INTO sh.MY_SALES (cust_id, prod_id)
    VALUES (x.cust_id, x.prod_id);
  END LOOP;
END;
```

5. Create a PL/SQL block to insert the sales of the second half of 2001 from the
SALES table to the new table using ARRAYS to collect and insert data:

```
DECLARE
  TYPE t_products_list IS TABLE OF
    sh.sales.prod_id%TYPE INDEX BY BINARY_INTEGER;
  TYPE t_customers_list IS TABLE OF
    sh.customers.cust_id%TYPE INDEX BY BINARY_INTEGER;

  products_list t_products_list;
  customers_list t_customers_list;
BEGIN
  SELECT cust_id, prod_id
    BULK COLLECT INTO customers_list, products_list
  FROM sh.sales
  WHERE time_id between TO_DATE('20010701', 'YYYYMMDD')
    AND TO_DATE('20011231', 'YYYYMMDD');

  FORALL j IN 1 .. customers_list.COUNT
    INSERT INTO sh.MY_SALES (cust_id, prod_id)
      VALUES (customers_list(j), products_list(j));
END;
```

6. Insert the data using a simple SQL statement:

```
INSERT /*+ APPEND */ INTO sh.MY_SALES (cust_id, prod_id)
  SELECT cust_id, prod_id
  FROM sh.sales
  WHERE time_id between TO_DATE('20010701', 'YYYYMMDD')
    AND TO_DATE('20011231', 'YYYYMMDD');
```

7. After our tests, drop the used table:

```
SET TIMING OFF
DROP TABLE sh.MY_SALES;
```

How it works...

In the first steps, we have created an empty table called MY_SALES to test different methods to insert data.

The first example, in step 4, uses a procedural approach. We open the curs_c1 cursor to loop through the SALES table, selecting the rows we want to insert in the MY_SALES table; the insert is done using a row-by-row loop.

The results obtained are shown in the following screenshot:

```
SQL> DECLARE
  2      CURSOR curs_c1 IS SELECT cust_id, prod_id
  3        FROM sh.sales WHERE time_id between
  4          TO_DATE('20010701', 'YYYYMMDD')
  5            AND TO_DATE('20011231', 'YYYYMMDD');
  6  BEGIN
  7    FOR x IN curs_c1
  8    LOOP
  9      INSERT INTO sh.MY_SALES (cust_id, prod_id) VALUES (x.cust_id, x.prod_id);
 10    END LOOP;
 11  END;
 12  /

PL/SQL procedure successfully completed.

Elapsed: 00:00:10.38
SQL>
```

The second example, in step 5, again uses a PL/SQL block. This time we use two arrays, customers_list and products_list, to store data temporarily; one is used for the cust_id and the other for the prod_id, as defined in the DECLARE section of the code.

These arrays are used to BULK COLLECT the data from the SALES table and then to insert the data in the MY_SALES table using a FORALL instruction. A common mistake is to think that the FORALL statement is a loop—this statement is executed only once, for passing the arrays as arguments to the INSERT.

We can see the results of this example in the following screenshot:

```
SQL> DECLARE
  2     TYPE t_products_list IS TABLE
  3       OF sh.sales.prod_id%TYPE INDEX BY BINARY_INTEGER;
  4     TYPE t_customers_list IS TABLE
  5       OF sh.customers.cust_id%TYPE INDEX BY BINARY_INTEGER;
  6
  7     products_list t_products_list;
  8     customers_list t_customers_list;
  9  BEGIN
 10     SELECT cust_id, prod_id
 11       BULK COLLECT INTO customers_list, products_list
 12     FROM sh.sales WHERE time_id between
 13       TO_DATE('20010701', 'YYYYMMDD')
 14     AND TO_DATE('20011231', 'YYYYMMDD');
 15
 16     FORALL j IN 1 .. customers_list.COUNT
 17       INSERT INTO sh.MY_SALES (cust_id, prod_id)
 18         VALUES (customers_list(j), products_list(j));
 19  END;
 20  /

PL/SQL procedure successfully completed.

Elapsed: 00:00:00.64
SQL>
```

We can see a huge improvement in performance using the latter approach, instead of the cursor-for-loop used in the first example, because the latter approach is more than 10 orders of magnitude faster.

In the last example, all of the work is done in a single INSERT statement, selecting from the SALES table to insert directly into the MY_SALES table. We use the hint /*+ APPEND */ (see *Exploring the optimizer hints* in *Chapter 7, Improving the Oracle Optimizer* for more details about hints) to instruct the database to load the data in the table using a **direct path load**, that is, bypassing the buffer cache and writing directly to the disk.

We can see the results for this example in the following screenshot:

The timing for the operation is slightly better in this case than in the example in which we used the arrays. However, there are some considerations to be taken care of, when using direct path load, explained later in this recipe.

In the last step, we drop the table to clear the schema from our tests.

There's more...

Looking at the examples in this recipe, there are two lessons to be learned. The first is "never write procedural code when you can perform the same task in a single SQL instruction" — let the optimizer do the work it's designed for.

The second lesson is "use arrays and set operations when you can". The Oracle database works better when the operations are expressed in sets, so the engine can use all the resources available to satisfy the requests optimally.

When to use direct path load

In step 6, we used a direct path load to insert data in the MY_SALES table using the APPEND hint. However, there are some considerations to be taken care of when using direct path load, to understand when to use and when not to use this type of operation. If direct path load would be the fastest method to insert data in tables, without constraints, the optimizer would use it by default.

The first consideration is what happens when the database engine "moves" data blocks to the disk, without using the buffer cache. When we have to move small datasets, direct path load would be slower than conventional path load, which uses the buffer cache.

Another issue is serialization, there can be only one direct path load on a table, with no other concurrent updates, deletes, or inserts. This is a scalability issue in a concurrent environment. The table cannot be queried when the load operation is in progress, until a commit (or a rollback) is executed.

The last peculiarity of direct path load is related to the High-Water Mark. It loads data above the High-Water Mark, even if there is room in the blocks below it. We have analyzed the effects of the High-Water Mark on performance in this chapter in *Avoiding full table scans*.

Now that we have a better comprehension of the direct path load, you will know when to use it best—in data loading batches, populating staging, data warehouses, and so on. But also when not to use it—in transaction processing and concurrent environments.

However, the considerations made when commenting our example are still valid. We can use the single SQL statement without the APPEND hint, as follows:

```
INSERT INTO sh.MY_SALES (cust_id, prod_id)
  SELECT cust_id, prod_id FROM sh.sales
  WHERE time_id between
    TO_DATE('20010701', 'YYYYMMDD')
    AND TO_DATE('20011231', 'YYYYMMDD');
```

In this case, we obtain results similar to the previous execution with the APPEND hint, as shown in the following screenshot:

See also

- There's more on arrays and BULK COLLECT in *Array processing and bulk collect* in *Chapter 6, Optimizing PL/SQL Code*

- You can find more details on optimizer hints in *Exploring the optimizer hints* in *Chapter 7, Improving the Oracle Optimizer*

- *Using create table as select* in *Chapter 8, Other Optimizations* shows more information on this kind of operation

- Direct path load from external files is explored in more detail in *Chapter 9, Tuning memory* in the *Direct path inserting* recipe

Optimizing joins

One of the most time-consuming operations in a database is the JOIN. We use this when we need to join two or more tables due to the normalized structure of the database. There are many types of joins (equi-join, self-join, outer join, anti-join, and so on).

In this recipe, we will see some join algorithms the database can use to answer our queries, performance related to every type of join, and some tricks to avoid joins (when possible).

How to do it...

The following steps will demonstrate some common types of joins:

1. Connect to the SH schema:

   ```
   CONNECT sh@TESTDB/sh
   ```

2. Create a table called MY_CUSTOMERS as a copy of the CUSTOMERS table:

   ```
   CREATE TABLE sh.MY_CUSTOMERS AS SELECT * FROM sh.CUSTOMERS;
   ALTER TABLE sh.MY_CUSTOMERS
      ADD CONSTRAINT PK_MY_CUSTOMERS PRIMARY KEY (CUST_ID);
   ```

3. Create a table called MY_COUNTRIES as a copy of the COUNTRIES table:

   ```
   CREATE TABLE sh.MY_COUNTRIES AS SELECT * FROM sh.COUNTRIES;
   ALTER TABLE sh.MY_COUNTRIES
      ADD CONSTRAINT PK_MY_COUNTRIES PRIMARY KEY (COUNTRY_ID);
   ```

4. Execute a first join between the table MY_CUSTOMERS and the original CUSTOMERS table:

   ```
   SET AUTOT TRACE EXP STAT
   SELECT COUNT(*)
      FROM sh.MY_CUSTOMERS M, sh.CUSTOMERS C
      WHERE M.CUST_ID = C.CUST_ID;
   ```

5. Execute a join between the two tables:

   ```
   SET AUTOT TRACE EXP STAT
   SELECT C.CUST_FIRST_NAME, C.CUST_LAST_NAME, N.COUNTRY_NAME
      FROM sh.MY_CUSTOMERS C, sh.MY_COUNTRIES N
      WHERE C.COUNTRY_ID = N.COUNTRY_ID;
   ```

6. Execute the same join between the two tables with a different condition:

```
SET AUTOT TRACE EXP STAT
SELECT C.CUST_FIRST_NAME, C.CUST_LAST_NAME, N.COUNTRY_NAME
   FROM sh.MY_CUSTOMERS C, sh.MY_COUNTRIES N
   WHERE N.COUNTRY_ID BETWEEN C.COUNTRY_ID
      AND C.COUNTRY_ID + 10;
```

7. Clean the SH schema:

```
DROP TABLE sh.MY_COUNTRIES;
DROP TABLE sh.MY_CUSTOMERS;
```

How it works...

We have created two tables, MY_CUSTOMERS and MY_COUNTRIES, to experiment with some of the different types of joins.

In the query in step 4, the MY_CUSTOMERS table is joined with CUSTOMERS, using an equi-join on the primary key (the field CUST_ID).

We can see the execution plan and statistics for this query in the following screenshot:

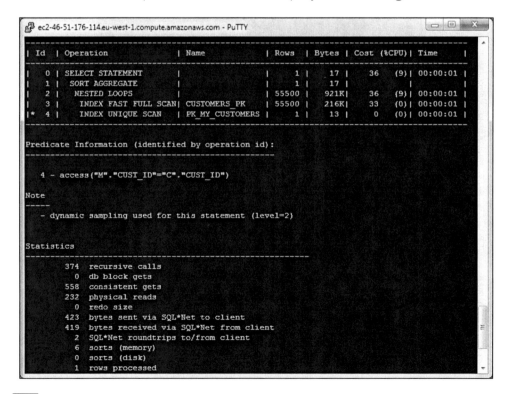

In this operation, the database used **NESTED LOOPS** to fulfill the query. This algorithm works as follows:

1. Read a row from the first dataset (the CUSTOMERS_PK index, in our example, using an **INDEX FAST FULL SCAN** to scroll all index leaf nodes).

2. For each row of the first dataset query the second dataset (the PK_MY_CUSTOMERS index in our example, using an **INDEX UNIQUE SCAN** to locate the record that matches the join condition).

3. Repeat from step 1 until the end of the first dataset is reached.

In the execution plan shown earlier, the last operation **SORT AGGREGATE**, calculates the requested COUNT(*) value.

The use of a **NESTED LOOP** could be a problem if we need to access the major part of the inner table and there isn't an index to speedup this operation.

In step 5, we query MY_CUSTOMERS and MY_COUNTRIES tables joined together on COUNTRY_ID field, using an equi-join. We can see the execution plan in the following screenshot:

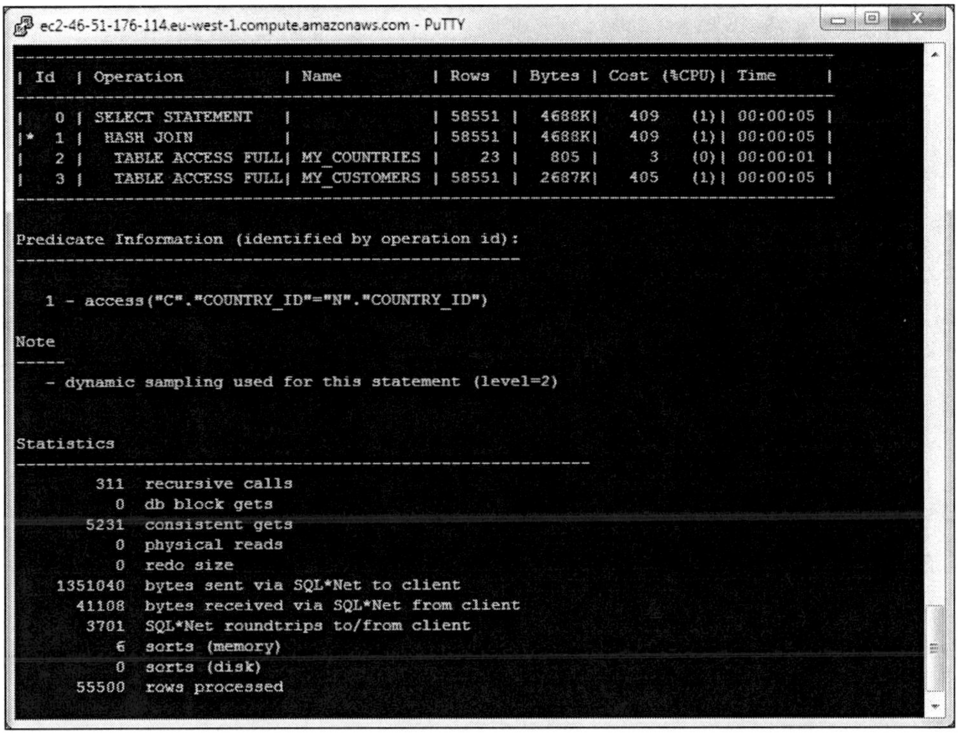

In this operation, the algorithm selected by the database engine is the Hash Join.

To execute the join, the database first creates a hash table based on the join fields of the inner table. It then executes the query for nested loops, locating the rows which satisfy the join condition using the hash function.

In our example, we can see the full table scan of the MY_COUNTRIES table, used to build the hash table, and the full table scan of MY_CUSTOMERS—scrolling the last table. The hash sort is executed using the hash function to locate the corresponding values of the MY_CUSTOMERS table.

The hash join is quickly executed, but it can be used only when we have an equi-join condition, because we cannot perform a range operation on the hash table, to satisfy for example, a "greater than" condition.

In step 6, we can see a slightly modified version of the previous example. Here the equi-join condition is replaced by a range match criteria (this makes no sense in the real world, but is useful to explain the matter).

We can see the execution plan for this query in the following screenshot:

```
ec2-46-51-176-114.eu-west-1.compute.amazonaws.com - PuTTY

| Id  | Operation                          | Name            | Rows  | Bytes |TempSpc| Cost (%CPU
|   0 | SELECT STATEMENT                   |                 |  3367 |  269K|       | 1097    (1
|   1 |  MERGE JOIN                        |                 |  3367 |  269K|       | 1097    (1
|   2 |   SORT JOIN                        |                 |    23 |  805 |       |    2    (0
|   3 |    TABLE ACCESS BY INDEX ROWID|     MY_COUNTRIES  |    23 |  805 |       |    2    (0
|   4 |     INDEX FULL SCAN                | PK_MY_COUNTRIES |    23 |      |       |    1    (0
|*  5 |   FILTER                           |                 |       |      |       |         
|*  6 |    SORT JOIN                       |                 | 58551 | 2687K| 6904K| 1095    (1
|   7 |     TABLE ACCESS FULL              | MY_CUSTOMERS    | 58551 | 2687K|       |  405    (1

Predicate Information (identified by operation id):
---------------------------------------------------

   5 - filter("N"."COUNTRY_ID"<="C"."COUNTRY_ID"+10)
   6 - access(INTERNAL_FUNCTION("N"."COUNTRY_ID")>=INTERNAL_FUNCTION("C"."COUNTRY_ID"))
       filter(INTERNAL_FUNCTION("N"."COUNTRY_ID")>=INTERNAL_FUNCTION("C"."COUNTRY_ID"))

Note
-----
   - dynamic sampling used for this statement (level=2)
```

In the following screenshot, you can see statistics for the same query:

```
ec2-46-51-176-114.eu-west-1.compute.amazonaws.com - PuTTY

Statistics
----------------------------------------------------------
          0   recursive calls
          0   db block gets
       1460   consistent gets
          0   physical reads
          0   redo size
    7228588   bytes sent via SQL*Net to client
     276332   bytes received via SQL*Net from client
      25085   SQL*Net roundtrips to/from client
          2   sorts (memory)
          0   sorts (disk)
     376257   rows processed

SQL>
```

In the previous example, we have seen a Sort-Merge Join in action. This algorithm works as follows:

1. The first table is sorted by join fields.
2. The second table is sorted by join fields.
3. A merge operation between the two sorted datasets is executed.

The Sort-Merge Join is more efficient than the **NESTED LOOPS** and doesn't need indexes to quickly access the inner table. It's slower than the Hash Join, but can be used for nonequi-join queries, as the one in our example.

There's more...

There are some considerations to be kept in mind when choosing the join method that best fits your needs.

For example, Sort-Merge Joins joins are based upon two sort operations, which uses memory and CPU, while Hash joins use memory to generate the hash table.

Generally speaking, nested loops are used only when there is an index on the inner table—the table which is scanned for every row in the outer table—and the rows of the inner table intersected by the join are a small subset (so scanning the entire table to merge-sort or to build the hash table isn't efficient); otherwise the hash join method is preferred.

There are also some tricks to avoid the join operation—denormalization, clusters, and materialized views.

The first trick is denormalization. If we denormalize some tables, we don't need to join them while executing our queries on these tables, because all the required data is in a single table.

We can also use clusters to speed our join queries (when the cluster key contains our join keys); by reading clusters we get the data from both the tables, and hence can avoid joins.

The last trick is to use materialized views, enabling query rewrite, so we can find the answer for our join queries in the materialized view.

See also

- ▶ We have seen denormalization in *Chapter 2, Optimizing Application Design* in the *Optimizing performance with schema denormalization* recipe
- ▶ We have talked about index clusters in the *Using index clusters* recipe in *Chapter 3, Optimizing Storage Structures*
- ▶ For more information on materialized views, see the *Reducing the number of requests to the database using materialized views* recipe also in *Chapter 2*

Using subqueries

We often use subqueries in our SQL statements to nest more queries in one statement, using the results from an "inner" query to calculate other values.

In this recipe, we will see the use of subqueries for getting only a subset of records, demonstrating the constructs (NOT) EXISTS and (NOT) IN, highlighting the semantic difference between them (and when to choose one type of statement or the other).

How to do it...

The following steps will demonstrate the use of subqueries:

1. Connect to the SH schema:

```
CONNECT sh@TESTDB/sh
SET AUTOT TRACE EXP STAT
```

2. Select a table using the IN operator:

```
SET AUTOT TRACE EXP STAT
SELECT AMOUNT_SOLD FROM sh.SALES S
WHERE S.CUST_ID IN (
   SELECT C.CUST_ID FROM sh.CUSTOMERS C
   WHERE C.CUST_CREDIT_LIMIT IN (10000, 11000, 15000)
);
```

3. Rewrite the same query using the `EXISTS` construct:

```
SELECT AMOUNT_SOLD FROM sh.SALES S
WHERE EXISTS (
    SELECT NULL FROM sh.CUSTOMERS C
    WHERE S.CUST_ID = C.CUST_ID
    AND C.CUST_CREDIT_LIMIT IN (10000, 11000, 15000)
);
```

4. Select a table using the `NOT EXISTS` operator:

```
SELECT AMOUNT_SOLD FROM sh.SALES S
WHERE NOT EXISTS (
    SELECT NULL FROM sh.CUSTOMERS C
    WHERE S.CUST_ID = C.CUST_ID
    AND C.CUST_CREDIT_LIMIT IN (10000, 11000, 15000)
);
```

5. Rewrite the same query using the `NOT IN` construct:

```
SELECT AMOUNT_SOLD FROM sh.SALES S
WHERE S.CUST_ID NOT EXISTS (
    SELECT C.CUST_ID FROM sh.CUSTOMERS C
    WHERE C.CUST_CREDIT_LIMIT IN (10000, 11000, 15000)
);
```

6. The following is a different (algebraic) way to express the same query:

```
SELECT AMOUNT_SOLD FROM sh.SALES S
    LEFT OUTER JOIN sh.CUSTOMERS C
        ON S.CUST_ID = C.CUST_ID
        AND C.CUST_CREDIT_LIMIT IN (10000, 11000, 15000)
WHERE C.CUST_ID IS NULL;
```

How it works...

The query in step 2 selects the amount sold for the sales regarding customers who have a credit limit which is either `10000`, `11000`, or `15000`.

We have expressed the query using a subquery to identify the customers with the appropriate credit limit and the `IN` operator to filter only the sales related to those customers. We have used the `IN` operator to correlate the subquery to the main query:

```
SELECT C.CUST_ID FROM sh.CUSTOMERS C WHERE C.CUST_CREDIT_LIMIT
```

When we have a subquery, we can try to optimize the subquery and the main query separately.

The execution plan for this query and the statistics are shown in the following screenshot:

```
ec2-46-51-176-114.eu-west-1.compute.amazonaws.com - PuTTY

| Id | Operation              | Name      | Rows  | Bytes | Cost (%CPU)| Time     | Pstart| P
|  0 | SELECT STATEMENT       |           | 918K|   14M| 11860   (1)| 00:02:23 |       |
|* 1 |  HASH JOIN             |           | 918K|   14M| 11860   (1)| 00:02:23 |       |
|* 2 |   TABLE ACCESS FULL    | CUSTOMERS | 20813 |  142K|   405   (1)| 00:00:05 |       |
|  3 |   PARTITION RANGE ALL|           | 918K| 8973K| 11451   (1)| 00:02:18 |     1 |
|  4 |    TABLE ACCESS FULL   | SALES     | 918K| 8973K| 11451   (1)| 00:02:18 |     1 |

Predicate Information (identified by operation id):

   1 - access("S"."CUST_ID"="C"."CUST_ID")
   2 - filter("C"."CUST_CREDIT_LIMIT"=10000 OR "C"."CUST_CREDIT_LIMIT"=11000 OR
       "C"."CUST_CREDIT_LIMIT"=15000)

Statistics

         0  recursive calls
         0  db block gets
     53817  consistent gets
     41351  physical reads
         0  redo size
   2344156  bytes sent via SQL*Net to client
    118735  bytes received via SQL*Net from client
     10758  SQL*Net roundtrips to/from client
         0  sorts (memory)
         0  sorts (disk)
    161354  rows processed

SQL>
```

In step 3, we execute a query—similar to the previous one—changing the way in which selection is made on the SALES table. We use the EXISTS operator to verify that for every SALES row we are examining, there is at least one related row in the CUSTOMERS table with one of the specified credit limits.

In the subquery we select NULL, but we can select every field or scalar value, even * (star). We use NULL to explicitly clarify that we are "not selecting" anything from the CUSTOMERS table, but we are using the subquery only to filter the outer query on SALES.

In the following screenshot you can see the execution plan and statistics generated when the query is executed:

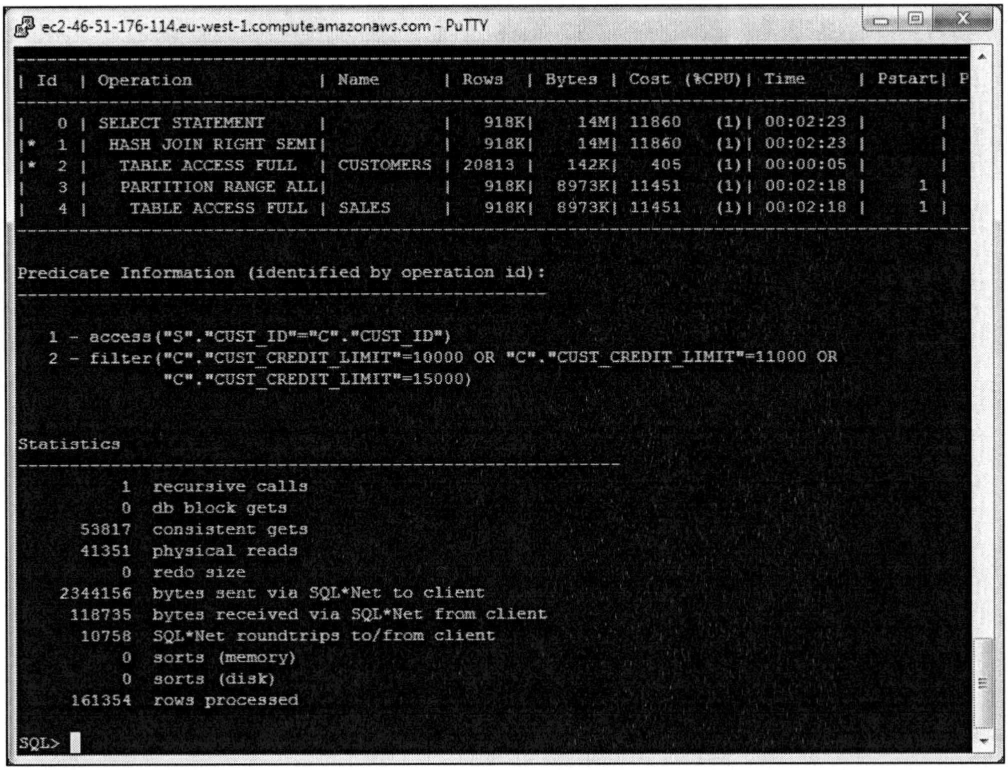

Comparing the results of the two queries, we can see that the same execution plan is chosen by the optimizer, and the same gets/reads are made to satisfy our request. They end up in the same execution plan, so the same work is done in the same execution time.

In step 4, we execute an **anti-join** query to obtain the opposite result of the query executed in the previous step. We want the amount of SALES made by a customer with a credit limit different from the values used earlier.

In our outer query, we use the NOT EXISTS clause to consider the records that are not related to the customers with the undesired credit limit values.

The execution plan and statistics for this query are shown in the following screenshot:

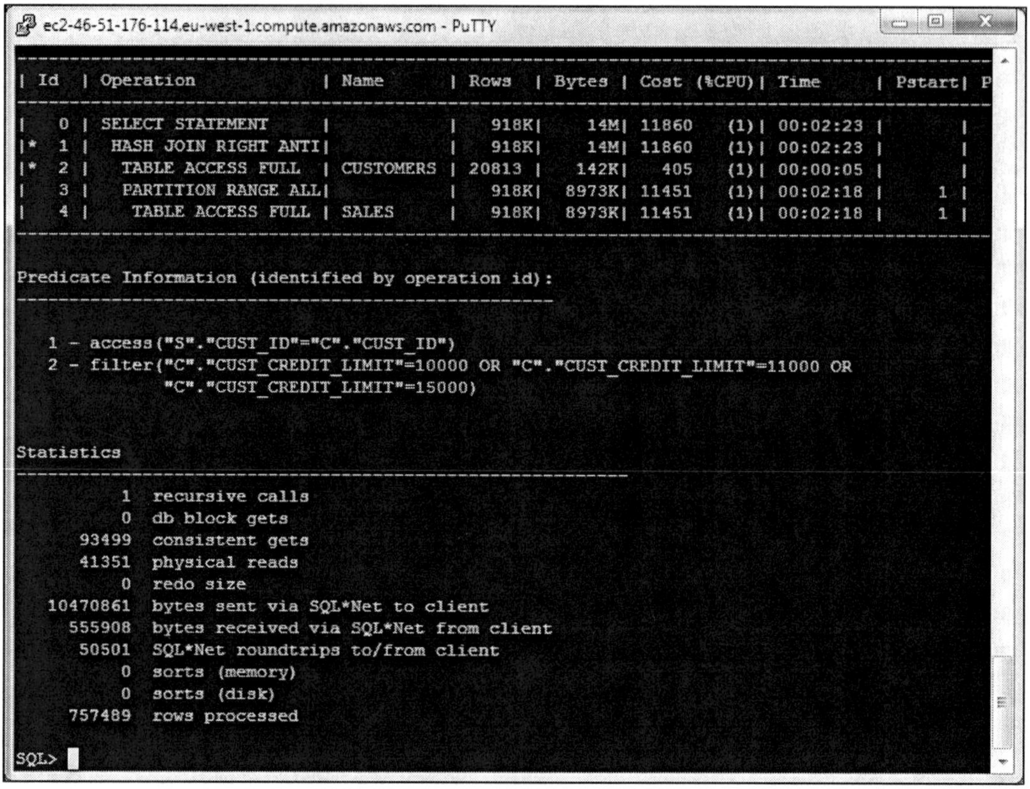

In step 5, we rewrite the previous query using the NOT IN operator; in the next screenshot we can see the results of this execution:

```
ec2-46-51-176-114.eu-west-1.compute.amazonaws.com - PuTTY

| Id  | Operation               | Name       | Rows   | Bytes  | Cost (%CPU)| Time     | Pstart| P

|   0 | SELECT STATEMENT        |            |   918K |   14M| 11860   (1)| 00:02:23 |       |
|*  1 |  HASH JOIN RIGHT ANTI|            |   918K |   14M| 11860   (1)| 00:02:23 |       |
|*  2 |   TABLE ACCESS FULL  | CUSTOMERS  | 20813  |  142K|   405   (1)| 00:00:05 |       |
|   3 |   PARTITION RANGE ALL|            |   918K | 8973K| 11451   (1)| 00:02:18 |     1 |
|   4 |    TABLE ACCESS FULL | SALES      |   918K | 8973K| 11451   (1)| 00:02:18 |     1 |

Predicate Information (identified by operation id):
-----------------------------------------------------

   1 - access("S"."CUST_ID"="C"."CUST_ID")
   2 - filter("C"."CUST_CREDIT_LIMIT"=10000 OR "C"."CUST_CREDIT_LIMIT"=11000 OR
             "C"."CUST_CREDIT_LIMIT"=15000)


Statistics
-----------------------------------------------------
          0  recursive calls
          0  db block gets
      93499  consistent gets
      41351  physical reads
          0  redo size
   10470861  bytes sent via SQL*Net to client
     555908  bytes received via SQL*Net from client
      50501  SQL*Net roundtrips to/from client
          0  sorts (memory)
          0  sorts (disk)
     757489  rows processed

SQL>
```

Even in the previous case we can see the substantial equivalence of the NOT IN and NOT EXISTS operations, related to gets/reads.

In step 6, we do a transformation to the query, using an algebraic expression equivalent to the intersection of two sets:

A ∩ B = A – (A – B)

So we have:

A – B = A – (A ∩ B)

In our query, we select all records in SALES (A) minus (NOT EXISTS) records in CUSTOMERS (B). So we can use the equivalent **A – (A ∩ B)** form, using a LEFT OUTER JOIN:

```
SELECT AMOUNT_SOLD FROM sh.SALES S
  LEFT OUTER JOIN sh.CUSTOMERS C
    ON S.CUST_ID = C.CUST_ID
    AND C.CUST_CREDIT_LIMIT IN (10000, 11000, 15000)
  WHERE C.CUST_ID IS NULL;
```

The result of the execution of this query is in the next screenshot:

Even if we have the same statistics and almost the same execution plan, the meaning of the last query isn't as intuitive as in the previous case. So, it's better to avoid using such transformation in our code, and we have seen that there is no performance improvement (or detriment) in doing so.

There's more...

We have seen that there is no performance improvement in using IN or EXISTS in our queries. However, we cannot use one of them without considering the expected result.

Let's perform a small experiment:

1. Connect to the HR schema:

   ```
   CONNECT hr@TESTDB/hr
   ```

2. Query for employees who are not managers using NOT IN:

   ```
   SELECT COUNT(*) FROM hr.EMPLOYEES E
     WHERE E.EMPLOYEE_ID NOT IN (
       SELECT E2.MANAGER_ID FROM hr.EMPLOYEES E2
   );
   ```

   The result for this statement is as shown in the following screenshot:

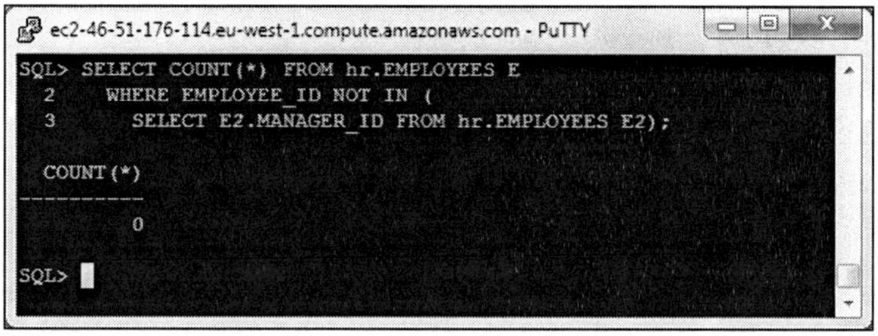

   The query replies that there are no employees (zero) who aren't managers.

3. Query for employees who are not managers using NOT EXISTS:

   ```
   SELECT COUNT(*) FROM hr.EMPLOYEES E
     WHERE NOT EXISTS (
       SELECT NULL FROM hr.EMPLOYEES E2
       WHERE E2.MANAGER_ID = E.EMPLOYEE_ID
   );
   ```

The result is as shown in the following screenshot:

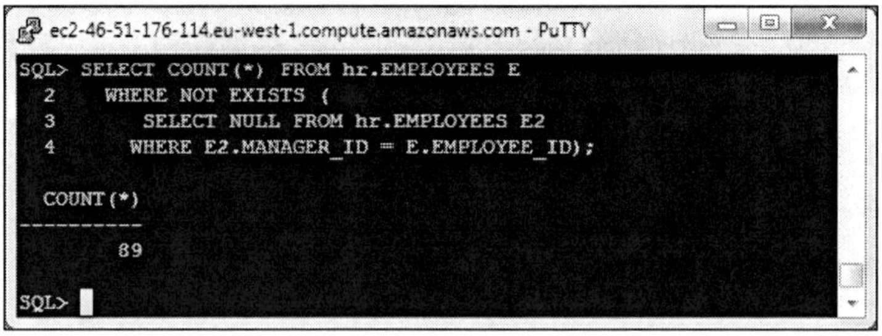

The query shows that there are 89 employees who aren't managers.

What happens now? We have two equivalent queries showing different results?

No errors: simply the `IN` and `EXISTS` behave differently when we consider `NULL` values. Let's modify the query in step 2.

4. A modified version of the query in step 2 would look similar to the following:

```
SELECT COUNT(*) FROM hr.EMPLOYEES E
  WHERE E.EMPLOYEE_ID NOT IN (
    SELECT E2.MANAGER_ID FROM hr.EMPLOYEES E2
    WHERE E2.MANAGER_ID IS NOT NULL
);
```

We have added the condition that `MANAGER_ID` is not null in our subquery. The results of the modified query are shown in the following screenshot:

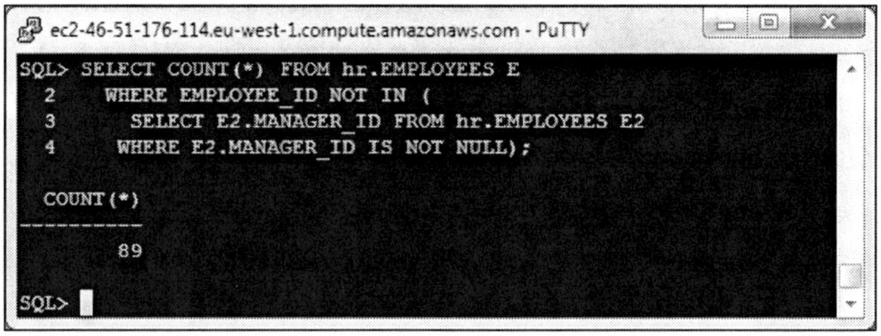

The result is now equivalent (and correct); it replies that there are 89 employees who aren't managers in our table.

It's very important to remember this difference when using `(NOT) IN` queries instead of `(NOT) EXISTS`, which isn't affected by the same problem.

Tracing SQL activity with SQL Trace and TKPROF

In this recipe, we will see how to use SQL Trace and TKPROF to trace SQL statements in a session.

There could be situations when we have to diagnose and tune a database, on which an application is running for which we don't have the source code, so we don't know which SQL statements are executed. In these situations, or when we want to investigate deeper than the AUTOTRACE feature we have used until now, the use of these tools is invaluable.

Getting ready

To trace SQL in our session, we have to make some modifications to the database parameters (if not set according to our needs).

The first parameter to set is TIMED_STATISTICS=TRUE, it can be set at the system or session level, to allow the database to trace the timing of the operations. It adds a very little overhead to the operations, so it can be left in place forever.

```
ALTER SYSTEM SET TIMED_STATISTICS=TRUE;
```

We have to set the destination for our trace files also. When using dedicated servers, the parameter is USER_DUMP_DEST. In the multi-threaded server environment the parameter is BACKGROUND_DUMP_DEST, and it will be a nightmare to trace the SQL statements with the session hopping from one shared server to another shared server.

For example, we can also set the maximum size of our trace file to 100 MB:

```
ALTER SYSTEM SET MAX_DUMP_FILE_SIZE='100M';
```

 You can use the following statement to change the name of the generated trace file:
```
ALTER SESSION SET TRACEFILE_IDENTIFIER = SYSDUMP_SESSION;
```

How to do it...

The following steps will show how to trace SQL activity:

1. Connect to the database as SYSDBA:

    ```
    CONNECT / AS SYSDBA
    ```

2. Start tracing by issuing the following command:

    ```
    ALTER SESSION SET SQL_TRACE=TRUE;
    ```

3. Execute some work:

    ```
    SELECT AMOUNT_SOLD
      FROM sh.SALES S
      WHERE S.CUST_ID IN (
        SELECT C.CUST_ID
        FROM sh.CUSTOMERS C
        WHERE C.CUST_CREDIT_LIMIT IN (10000, 11000, 15000)
    );
    ```

4. Stop tracing by using the following command:

    ```
    ALTER SESSION SET SQL_TRACE=FALSE;
    ```

5. Identify the session:

    ```
    SELECT s.sid, s.serial#, s.process, p.spid
      FROM v$session s, v$process p
      WHERE s.audsid = userenv('sessionid')
      AND s.paddr = p.addr;
    ```

6. Run TKPROF (replacing 22801 in the example with the SPID value returned from the previous query):

    ```
    SQL>HOST
    $ TKPROF TESTDB_ora_22801.trc 22801.txt
    ```

7. Review the generated report file (22801.txt in our example).

How it works...

To enable SQL tracing in our session, we can simply set the parameter SQL_TRACE to TRUE.

In step 3, we have executed a simple query, but we could perform many queries, procedures, jobs, and so on.

In step 4, we have stopped the trace by setting the SQL_TRACE parameter to FALSE.

To identify the trace file to use with TKPROF, we can query the database as in step 5. The SPID field represents the server process ID used to name the trace file, while the process field is the PID of our process in the operating system (as shown by PS).

In the following screenshot, we can see the results of the query and the PS command in the test environment:

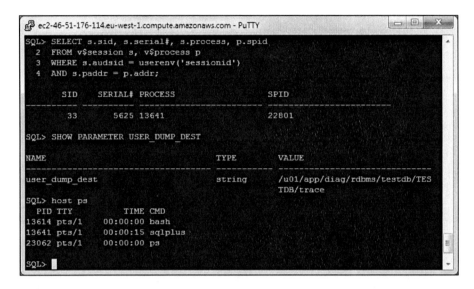

We can go to the directory set in the USER_DUMP_DEST parameter and launch TKPROF to format the trace file to a human-readable form, as shown in the following screenshot:

In the following screenshot, we can see an excerpt of the report generated by TKPROF:

```
SQL ID: fd4q9jyhsjfh4
Plan Hash: 3549450340
SELECT AMOUNT_SOLD
FROM
 sh.SALES S WHERE S.CUST_ID IN (SELECT C.CUST_ID FROM sh.CUSTOMERS C WHERE
  C.CUST_CREDIT_LIMIT IN (10000, 11000, 15000))


call     count       cpu    elapsed       disk      query    current        rows
------- ------  -------- ---------- ---------- ---------- ---------- ----------
Parse        2      0.00       0.00          0          0          0           0
Execute      2      0.00       0.00          0          0          0           0
Fetch    12540      0.84       2.39      44458      57373          0      188070
------- ------  -------- ---------- ---------- ---------- ---------- ----------
total    12544      0.84       2.39      44458      57373          0      188070

Misses in library cache during parse: 0
Optimizer mode: ALL_ROWS
Parsing user id: SYS


Rows     Row Source Operation
------- ---------------------------------------------------
  26716  HASH JOIN  (cr=3556 pr=1454 pw=0 time=103392 us cost=11860 size=15619957 card=918821)
  10740   TABLE ACCESS FULL CUSTOMERS (cr=1457 pr=1454 pw=0 time=15724 us cost=405 size=145691
 163647   PARTITION RANGE ALL PARTITION: 1 28 (cr=2099 pr=0 pw=0 time=279786 us cost=11451 size
 163647    TABLE ACCESS FULL SALES PARTITION: 1 28 (cr=2099 pr=0 pw=0 time=122636 us cost=11451
```

In the results you can see a table showing different information related to the query.

The three phases required to execute the statement are reported in rows—**Parse**, **Execute**, and **Fetch**. The parse step includes syntax and permission checks, and transforms the statement into an execution plan. The execute step is the execution of the statement, and the fetch step is the iteration over the returned rows.

For each phase, there are seven columns. They are as follows:

- **count**: The number of times the operation on the row (**Parse**, **Execute**, and **Fetch**) is executed
- **cpu**: The total CPU time in seconds
- **elapsed**: The total elapsed time in seconds
- **disk**: The number of physical disk reads (from the datafiles)
- **query**: The number of buffers retrieved
- **current**: The number of buffers retrieved in current mode (for DML statements UPDATE, INSERT, DELETE)
- **rows**: The number of rows returned

There's more...

We have seen how simple it is to trace SQL statements executed in our session.

However, if we want to set up tracing in a different session, we cannot use the `SQL_TRACE` parameter as shown in our example. We have to execute the procedure `SYS.DBMS_SYSTEM.SET_SQL_TRACE_IN_SESSION`, giving the `SID` and `SERIAL#` of the session to be traced as parameters to the procedure.

The `SID` and `SERIAL#` of the sessions can be queried from the `V$SESSION` dynamic performance view, as shown in the following query:

```
SELECT
    SID, SERIAL#, AUDSID, PADDR, USERNAME,
    COMMAND, SERVER, OSUSER, PROCESS, MACHINE,
    PORT, TERMINAL, PROGRAM
FROM V$SESSION
```

See also

- ▸ In *Appendix A, Dynamic Performance Views* there is a summary of useful Dynamic Performance Views used in the book
- ▸ *Appendix B, A Summary of Oracle Packages Used for Performance Tuning* shows Oracle Tools and Packages used for performance tuning

5
Optimizing Sort Operations

In this chapter, we will cover:

- ▶ Sorting—in-memory and on-disk
- ▶ Sorting and indexing
- ▶ Writing top *n* queries and ranking
- ▶ Using count, min/max, and group-by
- ▶ Avoiding sorting in set operations: union, minus, and intersect
- ▶ Troubleshooting temporary tablespaces

Introduction

In this chapter, we analyze some performance issues related to the most time-consuming operation in the database—sort operations.

In the next few recipes, you will see that sorting is related not only to the order-by clause in an SQL query, but also to other type of statements, such as group by and distinct, set operations, ranking, certain kinds of joins and subqueries, as well as index creation.

In the first recipe, we will see the difference between in-memory and on-disk sort operations, and the differences between optimal, one pass, and multi-pass sort operations.

The second recipe is about sorting and indexing. In this recipe, observe how an index can change the execution plan of a query, hence improving the performance by reducing or avoiding sort operations altogether.

In the third recipe, we will investigate what happens when we perform the top *n* queries, queries which return the first *n* elements of a sorted set—and how to tune such statements.

In the fourth recipe, we will see the use of aggregate functions—with or without the group-by clause, and some tips on improving them.

The fifth recipe is about set operations and their equivalent join and anti-join queries. The last recipe is about troubleshooting temporary tablespace performance issues.

Sorting—in-memory and on-disk

In this recipe, we will see how to diagnose in-memory and on-disk sort, and the differences between optimal, one-pass, and multi-pass sort.

Getting ready

We will use a SQL script from SQL*Plus environment to test in-memory and on-disk sort (without displaying tons of data on the screen).

Open a text editor (for example, vi on UNIX systems or notepad for Windows) and save the following script as 2602_05_TestSort.sql in a directory of your choice (the home directory, for example):

```
CONNECT sh@TESTDB/sh
SET LINESIZE 120
SELECT * FROM v$sysstat WHERE name like '%sorts%';
-- Setting small sort area
ALTER SESSION SET WORKAREA_SIZE_POLICY = 'MANUAL';
ALTER SESSION SET SORT_AREA_SIZE = 1000;
ALTER SESSION SET SORT_AREA_RETAINED_SIZE = 1000;
SET TERMOUT OFF
SPOOL /dev/null
SELECT prod_id, cust_id, time_id FROM sales ORDER BY amount_sold desc;
SPOOL OFF
SET TERMOUT ON
SELECT * FROM v$sysstat WHERE name like '%sorts%';
-- Automatic sort area
ALTER SESSION SET WORKAREA_SIZE_POLICY = 'AUTO';
SET TERMOUT OFF
SPOOL /dev/null
SELECT prod_id, cust_id, time_id FROM sales ORDER BY amount_sold desc;
SPOOL OFF
SET TERMOUT ON
SELECT * FROM v$sysstat WHERE name like '%sorts%';
```

How to do it...

Let's start by opening a SQL*Plus session and executing the following commands:

1. Connect to the SH schema:

   ```
   CONNECT sh@TESTDB/sh
   ```

2. Query a dynamic performance view to know the kind of sorts executed from instance start-up:

   ```
   SELECT * FROM v$sysstat WHERE name like '%sorts%';
   ```

3. Read the memory required for a sort operation in a query:

   ```
   SET AUTOT TRACE EXP
   SELECT prod_id, cust_id, time_id FROM sales ORDER BY time_id;
   SET AUTOT OFF
   ```

4. Connect as SYSDBA and reset the dynamic performance views by restarting the database instance:

   ```
   CONNECT / AS SYSDBA
   SHUTDOWN IMMEDIATE
   STARTUP OPEN
   ```

5. Launch the script prepared before (prefix the filename with the folder in which the script is located):

   ```
   @2602_05_TestSort.sql
   ```

6. Show optimal, one-pass, and multi-pass sorts:

   ```
   SELECT
       (low_optimal_size / 1024) as Low_KB,
       ((high_optimal_size + 1) / 1024) as High_KB,
       (optimal_executions * 100 / total_executions)
         as Pct_Optimal,
       (onepass_executions * 100 / total_executions)
         as Pct_OnePass,
       (multipasses_executions * 100 / total_executions)
         as Pct_MultiPasses
   FROM v$sql_workarea_histogram
   WHERE total_executions <> 0
   order by 1;
   ```

7. Investigate the optimal PGA size:

```
SELECT
    round(PGA_TARGET_FOR_ESTIMATE / 1024 / 1024)
      AS PGA_Target_MB,
    ESTD_PGA_CACHE_HIT_PERCENTAGE,
    ESTD_OVERALLOC_COUNT
FROM V$PGA_TARGET_ADVICE
ORDER BY 1;
```

How it works...

Let's explain the steps of this recipe.

The query in step 2 shows the statistics collected in the database after sorting. You can see an example of the output in the following screenshot:

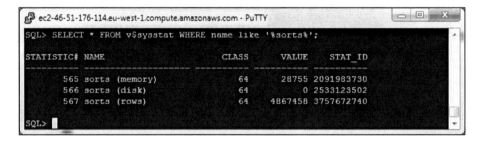

The output is divided between in-memory (the first row) and on-disk (the second row) sorts, while the number of rows sorted is displayed in the last row. To obtain better performance, we need to perform sorts in memory and not on disk.

In step 3, the execution plan of a simple query—involving an ORDER BY clause—is elaborated, and the output can be seen in the following screenshot:

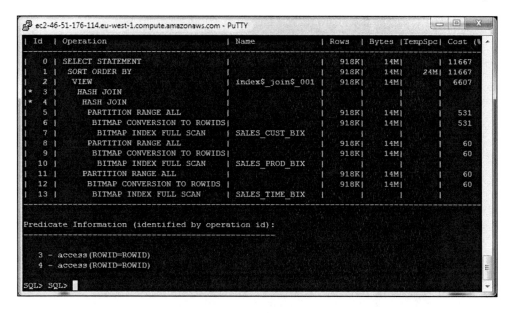

We can use this method to estimate memory requirements to execute the sort in the memory. The value in the `TempSpc` column of our example is **24 MB**, which is the memory required to execute the sort in memory.

In step 4, we restart the database to reset the values collected in dynamic performance views; we can perform this operation because we are in a test environment and we want to compare the statistic values generated by two different executions in a fast way for the sake of brevity.

In step 5, the script is shorter; in this script the same query on dynamic performance view as in step 2 is executed, before and after a query on the `SALES` table with an order by clause.

The same group of queries is executed using the `AUTOMATIC` policy for memory management and using a `MANUAL` policy, which allocates some space for the work, so it's executed on-disk.

> We can use the recommended parameter `PGA_AGGREGATE_TARGET` to set the PGA memory available to all server processes attached to the instance. This parameter can be set to a value expressed in `KB`, `MB`, or `GB`, and when this value is nonzero, the `WORKAREA_SIZE_POLICY` is automatically set to `AUTO`. Setting `PGA_AGGREGATE_TARGET` to `0` automatically sets `WORKAREA_SIZE_POLICY` to `MANUAL`.

The output can be seen in the following screenshot:

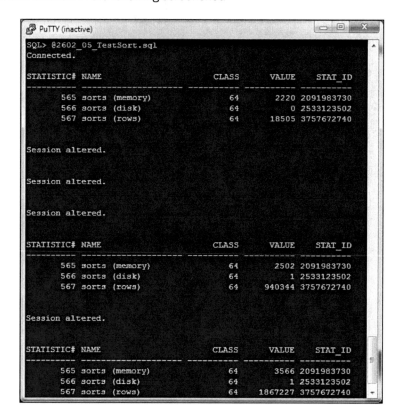

We can see that before the first execution we have **2220** sorts in-memory and **0** sorts on-disk.

We then set a MANUAL policy, reserving the size of 1000 database blocks of memory for sorting, with the following statements:

```
ALTER SESSION SET WORKAREA_SIZE_POLICY = 'MANUAL';

ALTER SESSION SET SORT_AREA_SIZE = 1000;

ALTER SESSION SET SORT_AREA_RETAINED_SIZE = 1000;
```

After this change in the session configuration, observe that the number of on-disk sorts changes from zero to one, because the sort cannot execute in-memory.

In fact, the `DB_BLOCK_SIZE` for our database is 8 KB, which reserves 8192 KB of memory for sort operations, but actually needs 24 MB of memory to complete the sort in-memory. When we restore the `WORKAREA_SIZE_POLICY` to `AUTO`, the sorts occur in memory and not on-disk.

The query in step 6 indicates the percentage of **optimal, single-pass**, and **multi-pass sorts** depending on the memory used for the `WORKAREA`. The output of this operation is as shown in the following screenshot:

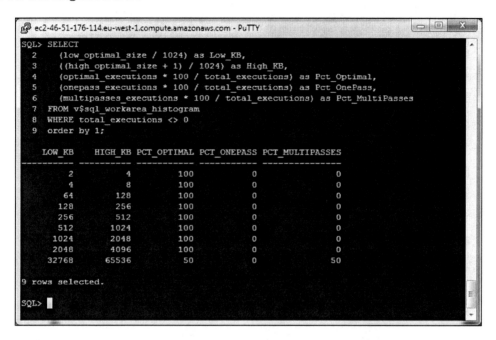

The first two columns show the range in KB that is used to evaluate the optimal `WORKAREA` size. The last three columns show the percentage of optimal executions (that is the sort operations occurred totally in memory), the percentage of one-pass sorts (that is the sort operations with a final merge completely in memory), and the percentage of multi-pass sorts respectively, when the merge operation is executed using more steps with partial results stored on-disk.

In the last step, we execute a query which returns three columns: `PGA Target`, `Estimated PGA Cache Hit Percentage`, and `Estimated Overallocation Count`.

The output of this query is as follows:

```
ec2-46-51-176-114.eu-west-1.compute.amazonaws.com - PuTTY
SQL> SELECT
  2     round(PGA_TARGET_FOR_ESTIMATE / 1024 / 1024) AS PGA_Target_MB,
  3     ESTD_PGA_CACHE_HIT_PERCENTAGE,
  4     ESTD_OVERALLOC_COUNT
  5  FROM V$PGA_TARGET_ADVICE
  6  ORDER BY 1;

PGA_TARGET_MB ESTD_PGA_CACHE_HIT_PERCENTAGE ESTD_OVERALLOC_COUNT
------------- ----------------------------- --------------------
          30                            63                      2
          59                            87                      0
         118                            87                      0
         177                            87                      0
         236                           100                      0
         283                           100                      0
         330                           100                      0
         378                           100                      0
         425                           100                      0
         472                           100                      0
         708                           100                      0
         944                           100                      0
        1416                           100                      0
        1888                           100                      0

14 rows selected.

SQL>
```

With the help of this query we can find the optimal size for the PGA, because for multiple PGA Target sizes (in MB) there is an estimated over-allocation (which we want to avoid, so we'll consider only those rows with a value of zero in this field) and an estimated percentage of cache hit for PGA. We will choose the last value after which the increase in the value of the second field is very small. In our example, values of more than 236 MB are useless, because there is no increase in the ESTD_PGA_CACHE_HIT_PERCENTAGE field even if we increase the PGA size (we have already reached 100 percent, so using more memory won't get a further performance increase).

In our example, a value of 59 MB is the optimal value, because there is more than 85 percent in cache hit (exactly 87 percent), and to increase this percentage we need to multiply the memory usage by 4 up to 236 MB to obtain an increase of 13 percent in the cache hit value.

There's more...

For a better understanding of the concepts introduced in this recipe, let's see how the database manages sort operations. We will also look at some concepts of database memory architecture.

The sort operation can be done in memory if there is enough space in the sort area, which is a part of the User Global Area; in this case we have an **optimal** sort.

If we are using a dedicated server connection, the User Global Area is located inside the Program Global Area (PGA). If we use an Oracle Shared Server Connection, the User Global Area is not inside the PGA, but it's in the Shared Pool. Hence, an application which often performs sorting should not use Oracle Shared Server Connections.

If the space needed for sorting is greater than the space reserved for the sort area, the data to be sorted is split into smaller pieces, called sort runs. The sort occurs on every single byte, which is stored in temporary segments on-disk.

The data of sort runs are finally merged together to obtain the final result. If there is enough space for this merge operation in the sort area, we have a **single-pass** (on-disk) sort, otherwise the merge operation is executed in more steps, merging two subsets of sort runs in each step; in this case, we have a **multi-pass** (on-disk) sort.

When the I/O operation from and to disk is involved, an optimal sort cannot take place, so it is better to have a single-pass sort than the multi-pass.

> The initialization parameter STATISTICS_LEVEL should be set to TYPICAL (the default value) or ALL; setting this parameter to BASIC turns off the generation of PGA advice performance views. The data in these views is reset at instance start-up or when the value of the PGA_AGGREGATE_TARGET parameter is altered.
>
> Please note that the PGA_AGGREGATE_TARGET parameter value can change automatically over time, starting with Oracle Database 11*g* as part of the Automatic Memory Management enhancements available at 11*g*. For more details check the note **443746.1** at the following URL:
>
> https://support.oracle.com/CSP/main/article?
> cmd=show&type=NOT&id=443746.1

See also

▶ More information on memory management in *Chapter 9, Tuning Memory* in the recipe *Tuning the Program Global Area and the User Global Area*

▶ In this chapter, the recipe *Troubleshooting temporary tablespace* gives more information about temporary segments and temporary tablespaces

Sorting and indexing

We have seen various aspects of indexing in *Chapter 3, Optimizing Storage Structures.* In this recipe, we will focus on how to use indexes to avoid sort operations.

How to do it...

The following steps will demonstrate how to use indexes and avoid sorts:

1. Connect to the SH schema:

   ```
   CONNECT sh@TESTDB/sh
   ```

2. Execute an ORDER BY query:

   ```
   SET AUTOT TRACE EXP STAT
   SELECT CUST_FIRST_NAME, CUST_LAST_NAME, CUST_CITY
   FROM CUSTOMERS
   ORDER BY CUST_CITY;
   ```

3. Execute a SELECT DISTINCT query:

   ```
   SET AUTOT TRACE EXP STAT
   SELECT DISTINCT CUST_CITY FROM CUSTOMERS;
   ```

4. Execute a GROUP BY query:

   ```
   SET AUTOT TRACE EXP STAT
   SELECT CUST_CITY, COUNT(*)
   FROM CUSTOMERS
   GROUP BY CUST_CITY;
   ```

5. Add an index on the CUSTOMERS table:

   ```
   CREATE INDEX IX_CUST_CITY ON CUSTOMERS(
      CUST_CITY, CUST_LAST_NAME, CUST_FIRST_NAME);
   ```

6. Execute an ORDER BY query (the same query as in step 2):

   ```
   SET AUTOT TRACE EXP STAT
   SELECT CUST_FIRST_NAME, CUST_LAST_NAME, CUST_CITY
   FROM CUSTOMERS
   ORDER BY CUST_CITY;
   ```

7. Execute a SELECT DISTINCT query (the same query as in step 3):

   ```
   SET AUTOT TRACE EXP STAT
   SELECT DISTINCT CUST_CITY FROM CUSTOMERS;
   ```

8. Execute a GROUP BY query (the same query as in step 4):

```
SET AUTOT TRACE EXP STAT
SELECT CUST_CITY, COUNT(*)
FROM CUSTOMERS
GROUP BY CUST_CITY;
```

9. Drop the index:

```
SET AUTOT OFF
DROP INDEX IX_CUST_CITY;
```

How it works...

In this recipe, we use the CUSTOMERS table of the SH schema to perform our experiments.

We execute three different queries on this table. The first query (in step 2) uses an ORDER BY clause. We can see the execution plan of this query in the following screenshot; it requires a SORT ORDER BY step to be evaluated:

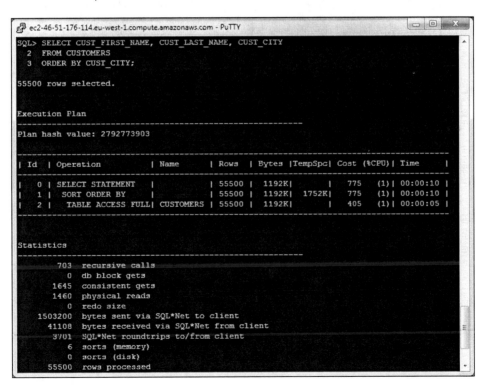

The second query, in step 3, uses a `SELECT DISTINCT` statement, and the corresponding execution plan is shown in the next screenshot. We can see that no sort operation occurs, except for a single `HASH UNIQUE` step after a Full Table Scan operation.

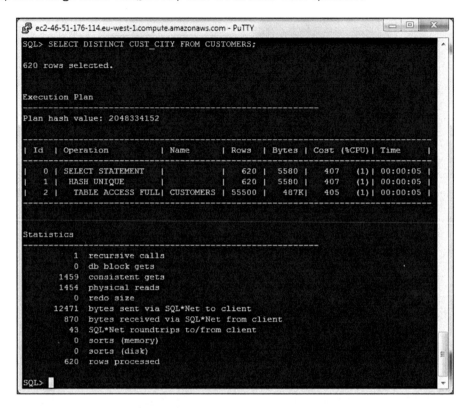

The last query, in step 4, executes a `GROUP BY` operation and an aggregate function `COUNT(*)` to show the number of customers for each city.

In the next screenshot, you can see the execution plan for this query. Even in this case, the operations required are a FULL TABLE SCAN and a HASH GROUP BY.

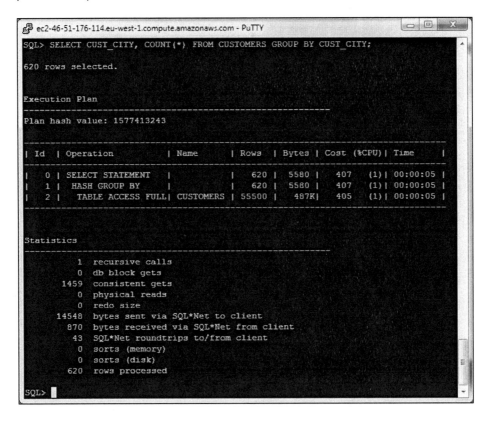

In step 5, we create an index on the CUSTOMERS table on the columns CUST_CITY, CUST_LAST_NAME, and CUST_FIRST_NAME.

In the later steps, we execute the same queries as in step 2, step 3, and step 4 with the index in place. The corresponding execution plan is as follows:

```
ec2-46-51-176-114.eu-west-1.compute.amazonaws.com - PuTTY

SQL> SELECT CUST_FIRST_NAME, CUST_LAST_NAME, CUST_CITY
  2  FROM CUSTOMERS
  3  ORDER BY CUST_CITY;

55500 rows selected.


Execution Plan
----------------------------------------------------------
Plan hash value: 2382468486

--------------------------------------------------------------------------
| Id  | Operation        | Name        | Rows  | Bytes | Cost (%CPU)| Time     |
--------------------------------------------------------------------------
|   0 | SELECT STATEMENT |             | 55500 | 1192K|   270   (0)| 00:00:04 |
|   1 |  INDEX FULL SCAN | IX_CUST_CITY | 55500 | 1192K|   270   (0)| 00:00:04 |
--------------------------------------------------------------------------

Statistics
----------------------------------------------------------
          1  recursive calls
          0  db block gets
       3950  consistent gets
        269  physical reads
          0  redo size
    1499400  bytes sent via SQL*Net to client
      41108  bytes received via SQL*Net from client
       3701  SQL*Net roundtrips to/from client
          0  sorts (memory)
          0  sorts (disk)
      55500  rows processed
```

In the first query, the presence of the index is very important, because the sort operation is avoided. To obtain the results (in the same order of the index) a simple INDEX FULL SCAN is required, because all the columns we select in the query are part of the index, so the optimizer goes for index full scan.

The second query, in step 7, requires a FTS and a HASH UNIQUE operation. It uses the index instead of the table, so the FTS is avoided in favor of an Index Fast Full Scan and is faster (there are fewer blocks to read).

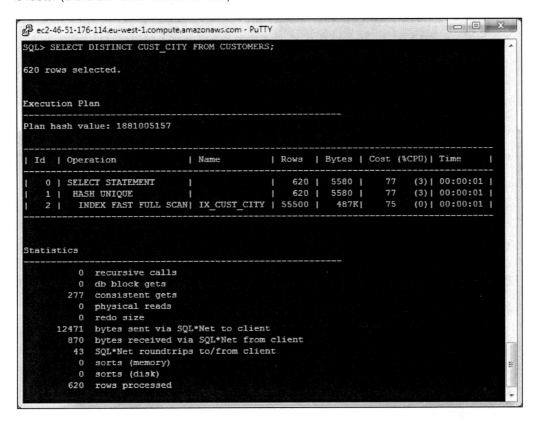

```
SQL> SELECT DISTINCT CUST_CITY FROM CUSTOMERS;

620 rows selected.


Execution Plan
----------------------------------------------------------
Plan hash value: 1881005157

---------------------------------------------------------------------------------
| Id | Operation            | Name        | Rows  | Bytes | Cost (%CPU)| Time     |
---------------------------------------------------------------------------------
|  0 | SELECT STATEMENT     |             |   620 |  5580 |    77   (3)| 00:00:01 |
|  1 |  HASH UNIQUE         |             |   620 |  5580 |    77   (3)| 00:00:01 |
|  2 |   INDEX FAST FULL SCAN| IX_CUST_CITY | 55500 |  487K |    75   (0)| 00:00:01 |
---------------------------------------------------------------------------------


Statistics
----------------------------------------------------------
          0  recursive calls
          0  db block gets
        277  consistent gets
          0  physical reads
          0  redo size
      12471  bytes sent via SQL*Net to client
        870  bytes received via SQL*Net from client
         43  SQL*Net roundtrips to/from client
          0  sorts (memory)
          0  sorts (disk)
        620  rows processed
```

In the last query, in step 8, you can observe a similar behavior. The FTS operation is replaced by an Index Fast Full Scan. The output is as follows:

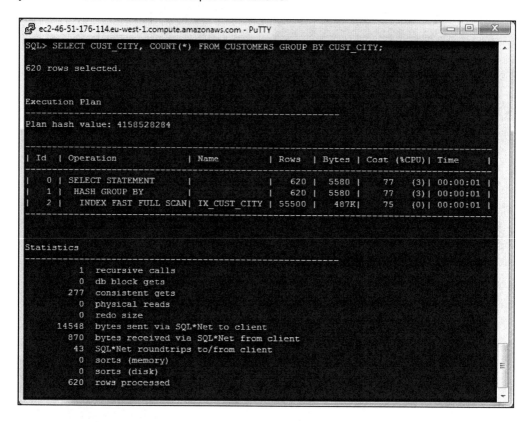

There's more...

If we add an ORDER BY clause in the DISTINCT and GROUP BY queries, there is a change in the execution plans. The queries will change as follows:

```
SELECT
  DISTINCT CUST_CITY
FROM CUSTOMERS
ORDER BY CUST_CITY;


SELECT CUST_CITY, COUNT(*)
FROM CUSTOMERS
GROUP BY CUST_CITY
ORDER BY CUST_CITY;
```

With this change in the query, the execution plan uses a SORT operation. This can be observed in the following screenshot:

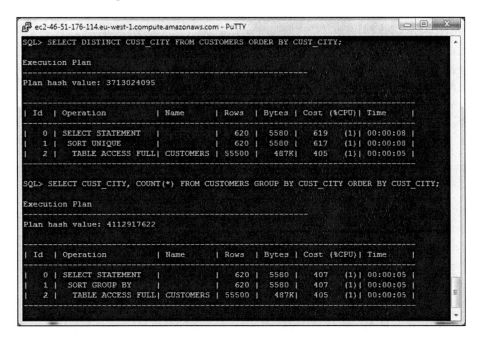

If we have the index in place, the execution plan changes as follows:

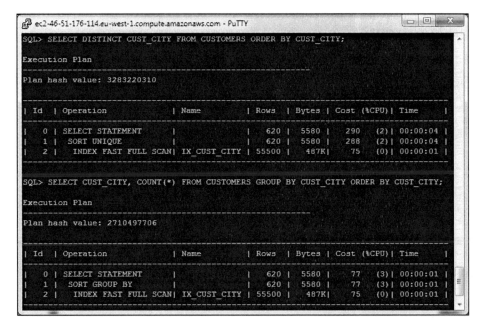

We can see that the SORT UNIQUE and SORT GROUP BY operations are performed in both situations against the corresponding HASH UNIQUE and HASH GROUP BY. The previous operations don't return the rows ordered, so a subsequent SORT pass would be required, using SORT UNIQUE and SORT GROUP BY. The SORT operation is executed to obtain the unique and group-by functions, so the rows are already ordered.

Here, we can also see that the index IX_CUST_CITY will be used to avoid the full table scan operation on the table, but it won't be useful in avoiding the sort operation.

Some developers overuse the DISTINCT keyword to ensure a unique set of results. We can avoid this situation by using the correct JOINS operations and FOREIGN KEY constraints, resulting in an optimal execution plan.

See also

▶ See *Chapter 3, Optimizing Storage Structures* for recipes on indexing
▶ Full Table Scan operation was explained in *Chapter 4, Optimizing SQL Code* in the *Avoiding Full Table Scans* recipe

Writing top n queries and ranking

One common problem when developing database applications is to show the first *n* rows of a set, ordering the data in a specific manner. For example, if we want to see the last 10 articles submitted in a web application.

In this recipe, we will see how to obtain this scope and how to obtain it faster.

How to do it...

The following steps will demonstrate how to get the top *n* queries and their ranking:

1. Connect to the SH schema:

    ```
    CONNECT sh@TESTDB/sh
    ```

2. Select the first 10 customers, ordered by their age, from youngest to oldest:

    ```
    SELECT CUST_ID, CUST_FIRST_NAME, CUST_LAST_NAME,
        CUST_YEAR_OF_BIRTH
    FROM CUSTOMERS
    WHERE ROWNUM < 11
    ORDER BY CUST_YEAR_OF_BIRTH DESC;
    ```

3. The correct way to express the previously selected statement is:

```
SELECT * FROM (

  SELECT CUST_ID, CUST_FIRST_NAME, CUST_LAST_NAME,
        CUST_YEAR_OF_BIRTH

  FROM CUSTOMERS

  ORDER BY CUST_YEAR_OF_BIRTH DESC

)

WHERE ROWNUM < 11;
```

4. Using the RANK() function may lead to different results:

```
SELECT * FROM (

  SELECT CUST_ID, CUST_FIRST_NAME, CUST_LAST_NAME,
        CUST_YEAR_OF_BIRTH,

  RANK() OVER (ORDER BY CUST_YEAR_OF_BIRTH DESC) AS RANKING

  FROM CUSTOMERS

)

WHERE RANKING < 11;
```

5. The DENSE_RANK() function is different (again):

```
SELECT * FROM (

  SELECT CUST_ID, CUST_FIRST_NAME, CUST_LAST_NAME,
        CUST_YEAR_OF_BIRTH,

  DENSE_RANK() OVER (ORDER BY CUST_YEAR_OF_BIRTH DESC) AS RANKING

  FROM CUSTOMERS

)

WHERE RANKING < 11;
```

6. Activate the explain plan option:

```
SET AUTOT TRACE EXP STAT
```

7. Execute the query in step 3:

```
SELECT * FROM (

  SELECT CUST_ID, CUST_FIRST_NAME, CUST_LAST_NAME,
        CUST_YEAR_OF_BIRTH

  FROM CUSTOMERS

  ORDER BY CUST_YEAR_OF_BIRTH DESC

)

WHERE ROWNUM < 11;
```

8. Execute the query in step 4:

```
SELECT * FROM (
    SELECT CUST_ID, CUST_FIRST_NAME, CUST_LAST_NAME,
        CUST_YEAR_OF_BIRTH,
    RANK() OVER (ORDER BY CUST_YEAR_OF_BIRTH DESC) AS RANKING
    FROM CUSTOMERS
)
WHERE RANKING < 11;
```

9. Execute the query in step 5:

```
SELECT * FROM (
    SELECT CUST_ID, CUST_FIRST_NAME, CUST_LAST_NAME,
        CUST_YEAR_OF_BIRTH,
    DENSE_RANK() OVER (ORDER BY CUST_YEAR_OF_BIRTH DESC) AS RANKING
    FROM CUSTOMERS
)
WHERE RANKING < 11;
```

How it works...

We want to retrieve the 10 youngest customers in our CUSTOMERS table.

The query in step 2 *is wrong*, because the filter—the WHERE condition—is evaluated *before* the ORDER BY clause. The output displayed in this case shows the first 10 rows in the CUSTOMERS table (retrieved without any particular ordering) ordered in descending order by the CUST_YEAR_OF_BIRTH field.

You can see the results of this query in the next screenshot:

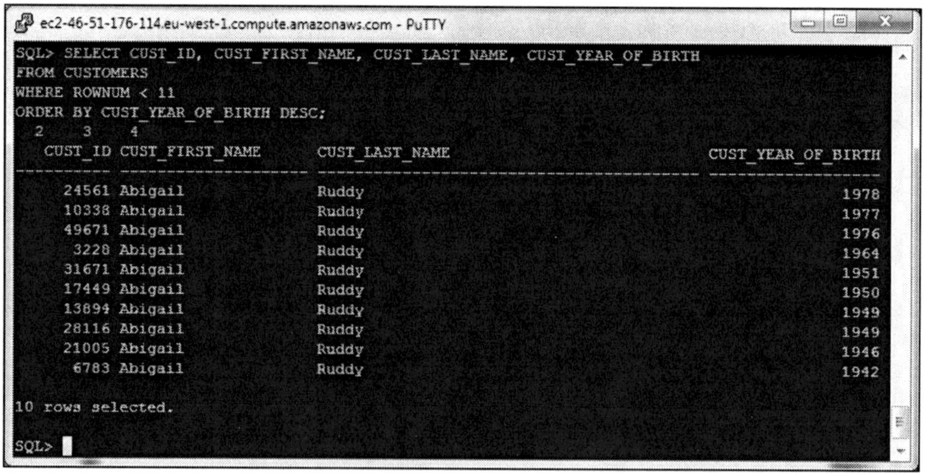

The query in step 3 is the right one for our goal, and you can see the correct results in the next screenshot:

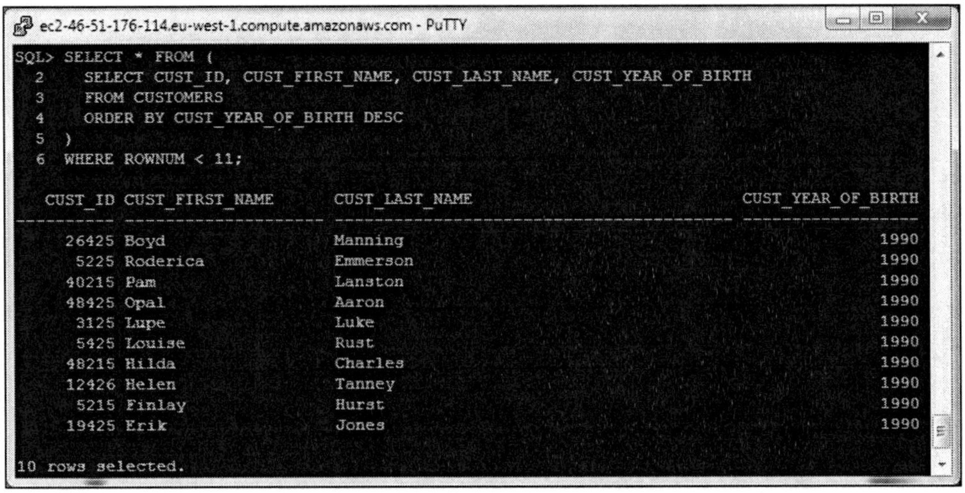

In step 4, we use another query to obtain the same result, using the RANK() analytical function. In the following screenshot, you can see the output (an excerpt) of this query:

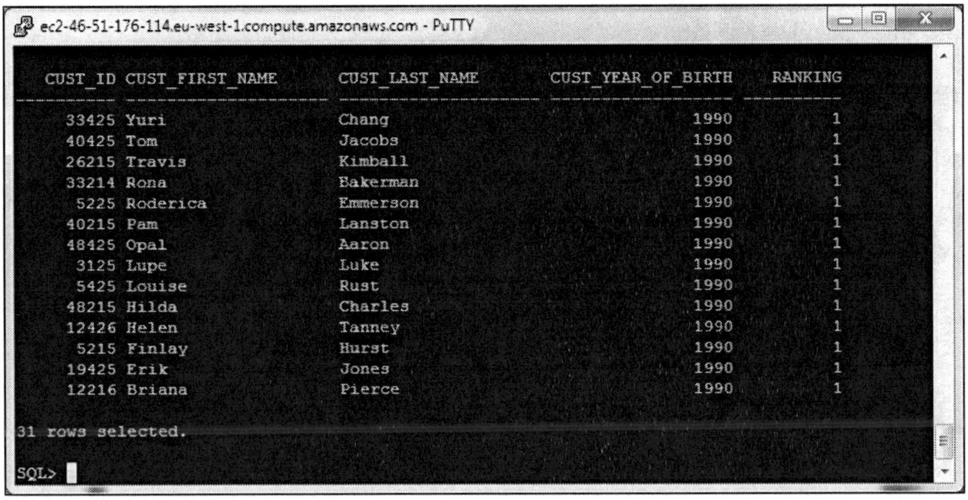

As we can see, in this case **31** rows are returned. The RANK() function assigns the same rank to each row with the same value in the field of the ORDER BY ranking clause. To obtain the same result as earlier, we have to change the WHERE condition to the following:

```
WHERE ROWNUM < 11
```

We can also use the DENSE_RANK() function, as in step 5. You can see the output (an excerpt) in the following screenshot:

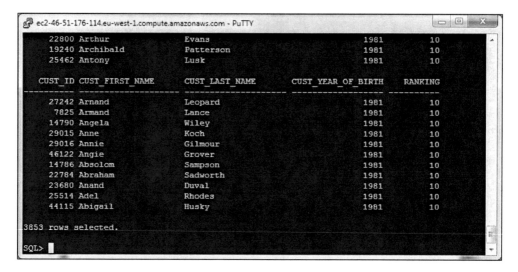

In this case, it returns **3853** rows that satisfy the WHERE condition. This example is useful to understand the difference between the RANK() and DENSE_RANK() functions. Both the functions assign a ranking to each row based on the ORDER BY clause; they assign the same rank if the rows have the same value—in our example on the CUST_YEAR_OF_BIRTH field. But when doing so, the DENSE_RANK() function doesn't increment the counter used to assign the rank. So after 100 rows with the same rank, the next rank assigned will be the previous rank + 1, while the RANK() function will assign—under the same conditions—the previous rank + 100.

In step 7, step 8, and step 9, we execute the same queries, as mentioned earlier, to view the execution plan.

In the following screenshot, you can see the execution plan of the query after executing step 7:

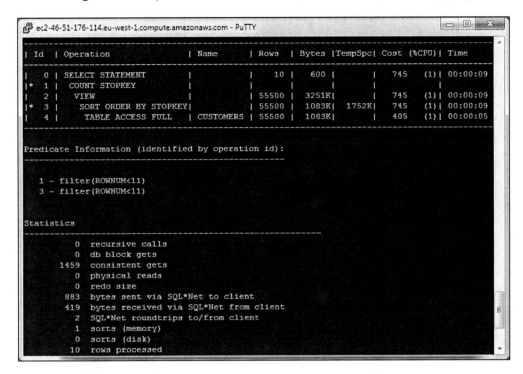

We can see a FULL TABLE ACCESS on the CUSTOMERS table, followed by a SORT ORDER BY STOPKEY. The next step is to execute COUNT STOPKEY over the VIEW created in the previous steps, so we have a SORT operation inside the subquery.

When we use the RANK() function, in step 8, the execution plan changes, as shown in the following screenshot:

```
ec2-46-51-176-114.eu-west-1.compute.amazonaws.com - PuTTY

|   0 |  SELECT STATEMENT       |           |  55500 |  3956K|       |   745   (1)| 00:00:09
|*  1 |   VIEW                  |           |  55500 |  3956K|       |   745   (1)| 00:00:09
|*  2 |    WINDOW SORT PUSHED RANK|         |  55500 |  1083K| 1752K|   745   (1)| 00:00:09
|   3 |     TABLE ACCESS FULL   | CUSTOMERS |  55500 |  1083K|       |   405   (1)| 00:00:05


Predicate Information (identified by operation id):
---------------------------------------------------

   1 - filter("RANKING"<11)
   2 - filter(RANK() OVER ( ORDER BY INTERNAL_FUNCTION("CUST_YEAR_OF_BIRTH") DESC
             )<11)


Statistics
----------------------------------------------------------
          0  recursive calls
          0  db block gets
       1459  consistent gets
          0  physical reads
          0  redo size
       1653  bytes sent via SQL*Net to client
        441  bytes received via SQL*Net from client
          4  SQL*Net roundtrips to/from client
          1  sorts (memory)
          0  sorts (disk)
         31  rows processed
```

We also have a SORT operation, namely WINDOW SORT PUSHED RANK, in this query, after the full table scan of the CUSTOMERS table.

If we use the DENSE_RANK() function, the execution plan is the same, as when we have used the RANK() function, the only difference is that the FILTER predicate is applied.

There's more...

Please note that execution time for the last two queries—those using analytical functions—is longer than the time required to execute the query in step 3 and step 7. This is not noticed in the example because the CUSTOMERS table is very small.

If we execute the following script on the SALES table (about 1 million rows), you will observe that the second query executes in about 175 percent of the time needed by the first query:

```
SET TIMING ON
SELECT * FROM (
  SELECT * FROM sh.SALES ORDER BY AMOUNT_SOLD DESC
) WHERE ROWNUM < 11;
```

```
SELECT * FROM (
  SELECT S.*,
    DENSE_RANK() OVER (ORDER BY AMOUNT_SOLD DESC) AS RANKING
    FROM sh.SALES S
) WHERE ROWNUM < 11;
SET TIMING OFF
```

The output is as follows:

```
ec2-46-51-176-114.eu-west-1.compute.amazonaws.com - PuTTY
   PROD_ID    CUST_ID TIME_ID   CHANNEL_ID   PROMO_ID QUANTITY_SOLD AMOUNT_SOLD
---------- ---------- --------- ---------- ---------- ------------- -----------
        18        510 03-JAN-99          3        999             1     1782.72
        18       9238 20-JAN-99          3        999             1     1782.72
        18       7204 20-JAN-99          3        999             1     1782.72
        18       6930 20-JAN-99          3        999             1     1782.72
        18       6897 20-JAN-99          3        999             1     1782.72
        18       5796 20-JAN-99          3        999             1     1782.72
        18       1064 20-JAN-99          3        999             1     1782.72
        18         27 20-JAN-99          3        999             1     1782.72
        18       4200 03-JAN-99          3        999             1     1782.72
        18       2420 03-JAN-99          3        999             1     1782.72

10 rows selected.

Elapsed: 00:00:01.79

   PROD_ID    CUST_ID TIME_ID   CHANNEL_ID   PROMO_ID QUANTITY_SOLD AMOUNT_SOLD   RANKING
---------- ---------- --------- ---------- ---------- ------------- ----------- ---------
        18        520 14-JUN-99          3        999             1     1782.72         1
        18       1280 14-JUN-99          3        999             1     1782.72         1
        18       1908 14-JUN-99          3        999             1     1782.72         1
        18       3587 14-JUN-99          3        999             1     1782.72         1
        18       3638 14-JUN-99          3        999             1     1782.72         1
        18       4108 14-JUN-99          3        999             1     1782.72         1
        18       4882 14-JUN-99          3        999             1     1782.72         1
        18       5918 14-JUN-99          3        999             1     1782.72         1
        18       6060 14-JUN-99          3        999             1     1782.72         1
        18       6922 14-JUN-99          3        999             1     1782.72         1

10 rows selected.

Elapsed: 00:00:03.57
```

See also

▶ There's more on subqueries in *Chapter 4*, *Optimizing SQL Code* in the *Using subqueries* recipe

Using count, min/max, and group-by

In this recipe, we will see how to count rows, compute min/max aggregates, and use filters in group-by queries.

How to do it...

The following steps will demonstrate the use of count, min/max, and group-by:

1. Connect to the SH schema:

   ```
   CONNECT sh@TESTDB/sh
   ```

2. Show the execution plan for a MIN/MAX query:

   ```
   SET AUTOT TRACE EXP
   SELECT MAX(CUST_CREDIT_LIMIT) FROM CUSTOMERS;
   SELECT MIN(CUST_CREDIT_LIMIT) FROM CUSTOMERS;
   ```

3. Show the execution plan for a query which returns the MIN and the MAX:

   ```
   SELECT MAX(CUST_CREDIT_LIMIT), MIN(CUST_CREDIT_LIMIT)
   FROM CUSTOMERS;
   ```

4. Create an index on CUSTOMERS in the column in which we need to aggregate:

   ```
   CREATE INDEX IX_CUST_CREDIT_LIMIT
      ON CUSTOMERS (CUST_CREDIT_LIMIT);
   ```

5. Execute the query in step 2:

   ```
   SET AUTOT TRACE EXP STAT
   SELECT MAX(CUST_CREDIT_LIMIT) FROM CUSTOMERS;
   SELECT MIN(CUST_CREDIT_LIMIT) FROM CUSTOMERS;
   ```

6. Execute the query in step 3:

   ```
   SELECT MAX(CUST_CREDIT_LIMIT), MIN(CUST_CREDIT_LIMIT)
   FROM CUSTOMERS;
   ```

7. Use different ways to count the rows in a table:

   ```
   SELECT COUNT(*) FROM CUSTOMERS;
   SELECT COUNT(1) FROM CUSTOMERS;
   ```

8. Execute a group-by query with a filter (using the `HAVING` clause):

    ```
    SELECT CUST_CREDIT_LIMIT, MAX(CUST_YEAR_OF_BIRTH) AS DATAMAX
    FROM CUSTOMERS
    GROUP BY CUST_CREDIT_LIMIT
    HAVING CUST_CREDIT_LIMIT > 10000
    ORDER BY CUST_CREDIT_LIMIT;
    ```

9. Execute a group-by query with the same filter above applied in the `WHERE` clause:

    ```
    SELECT CUST_CREDIT_LIMIT, MAX(CUST_YEAR_OF_BIRTH) AS DATAMAX
    FROM CUSTOMERS
    WHERE CUST_CREDIT_LIMIT > 10000
    GROUP BY CUST_CREDIT_LIMIT
    ORDER BY CUST_CREDIT_LIMIT;
    ```

10. Drop the index created in step 4:

    ```
    SET AUTOT OFF
    DROP INDEX IX_CUST_CREDIT_LIMIT;
    ```

How it works...

After connecting to the `SH` schema, we execute two queries to retrieve the `MIN` and `MAX` value in the `CUST_CREDIT_LIMIT` field of the `CUSTOMERS` table. The execution plan for these two queries is the same, and is as shown in the following screenshot:

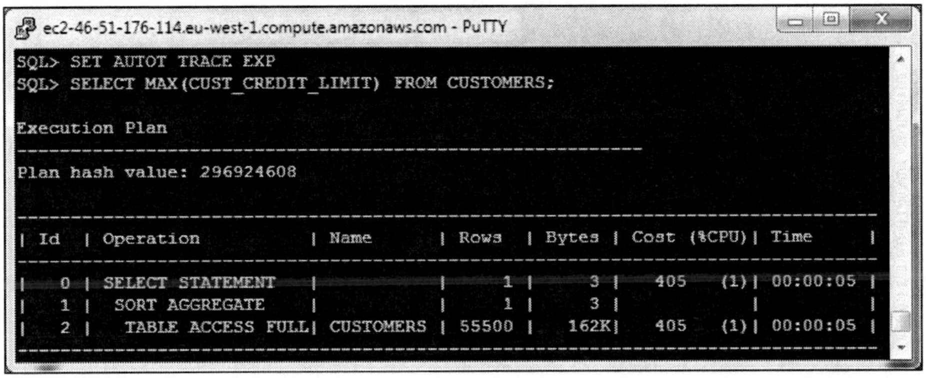

We can see that there is a Full Table Scan of the `CUSTOMERS` table followed by a `SORT AGGREGATE` to retrieve the `MIN` (or `MAX`) value as requested.

The same execution plan is used by the database if we execute a query that retrieves both the MIN and MAX values for the CUST_CREDIT_LIMIT field in step 3, as shown in the next screenshot:

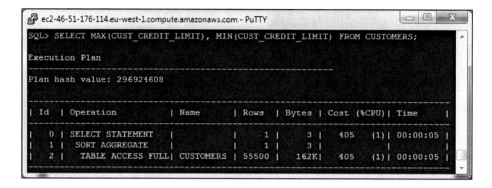

In step 4, we create an index on the field (CUST_CREDIT_LIMIT) where we execute the aggregate function. This allows us to use the index instead of the full table scan operation, resulting in a very fast execution of the query. The corresponding execution plan is as shown in the following screenshot:

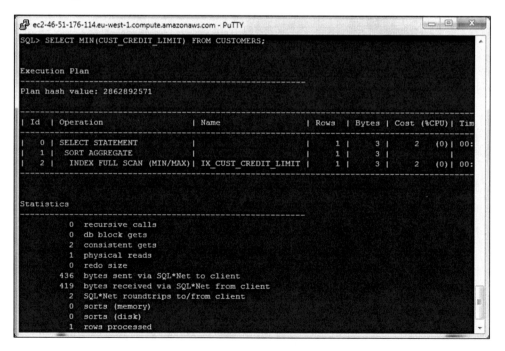

We can see that there are only two consistent gets to answer the query, with reduced I/O operations. If we ask for both the MIN and MAX values of the field, as in the query in step 6, the execution plan will be as follows:

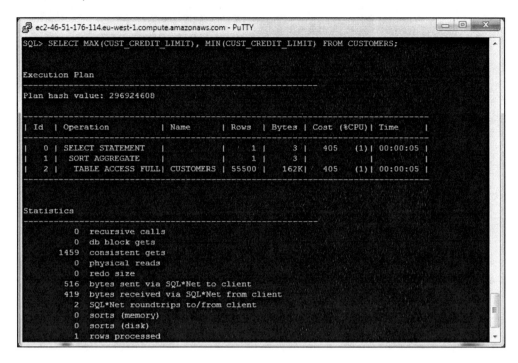

You can see that the index is not used and we return to the full table scan of the CUSTOMERS table, with 1459 consistent gets (and more I/O).

If we want both the values, it's better to split the query into two separate queries, as in the following statement:

```
SELECT
  MIN(CUST_CREDIT_LIMIT) AS MIN_VALUE,
  0 AS MAX_VALUE
FROM CUSTOMERS
UNION ALL
SELECT
  0,
  MAX(CUST_CREDIT_LIMIT)
FROM CUSTOMERS;
```

You can see the corresponding execution plan in the following screenshot:

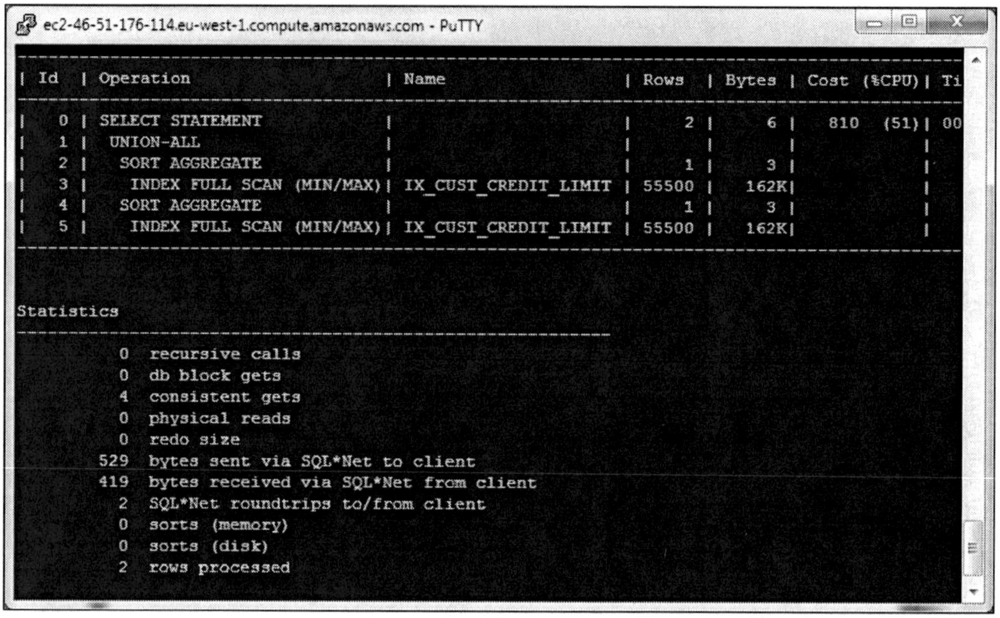

We can see that only four consistent gets are required to answer this query.

In step 7, we execute two different queries to count the number of rows in the CUSTOMERS table, using * and 1 respectively, as the argument of the COUNT() function. We have used these values because it is a common practice, and there is a myth about which performs better.

Let's observe the execution plan in the next screenshot.

When counting using COUNT(*), we have only seven consistent gets, because the optimizer chooses to use the bitmap index CUSTOMERS_GENDER_BIX on the CUST_GENDER field to count rows. In the BITMAP CONVERSION COUNT step, the engine computes the number of rows in the table by counting the used bit in the bitmap, as we can see in the following screenshot:

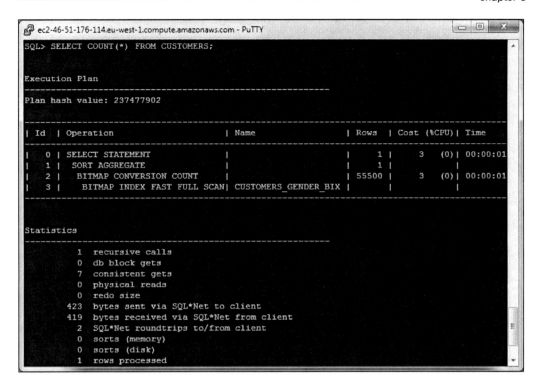

```
ec2-46-51-176-114.eu-west-1.compute.amazonaws.com - PuTTY

SQL> SELECT COUNT(*) FROM CUSTOMERS;


Execution Plan
----------------------------------------------------------
Plan hash value: 237477902

----------------------------------------------------------------------------------------
| Id  | Operation                   | Name                 | Rows  | Cost (%CPU)| Time     |
----------------------------------------------------------------------------------------
|   0 | SELECT STATEMENT            |                      |     1 |     3   (0)| 00:00:01 |
|   1 |  SORT AGGREGATE             |                      |     1 |            |          |
|   2 |   BITMAP CONVERSION COUNT   |                      | 55500 |     3   (0)| 00:00:01 |
|   3 |    BITMAP INDEX FAST FULL SCAN| CUSTOMERS_GENDER_BIX |       |            |          |
----------------------------------------------------------------------------------------


Statistics
----------------------------------------------------------
          1  recursive calls
          0  db block gets
          7  consistent gets
          0  physical reads
          0  redo size
        423  bytes sent via SQL*Net to client
        419  bytes received via SQL*Net from client
          2  SQL*Net roundtrips to/from client
          0  sorts (memory)
          0  sorts (disk)
          1  rows processed
```

When we execute the query using the SELECT COUNT(1) statement, we obtain the same execution plan—there is no difference in execution plans, as the database does the same work to answer both queries. Hence, they are equivalent—the myth SELECT(1) is faster than SELECT(*) is wrong—**they are the same query**.

In step 8, we execute a query to retrieve, for each distinct credit limit value, the maximum year of birth of the corresponding customers; we want to retrieve only customers with a credit limit of more than 10000.

The execution plan of this query is shown in the following screenshot:

We can see that there is a SORT GROUP BY operation after the full table scan of the CUSTOMERS table.

The query in step 9 executes the same request, but this time the predicate is in the WHERE condition and not in the HAVING clause. This is correct, because we want to filter the values before grouping. The HAVING clause is used when we want to impose a condition on the aggregated values.

If the HAVING clause is misused, the database engine has to elaborate the GROUP BY operation on a wider data set. We have seen that a SORT GROUP BY operation is required, and the less the data is elaborated by the sort the better the performance will be.

In the following screenshot, we can see the execution plan for this query, which endorses this reasoning—we have only 32 consistent gets (instead of 1459) and we can use the bitmap index instead of a full table scan of the CUSTOMERS table.

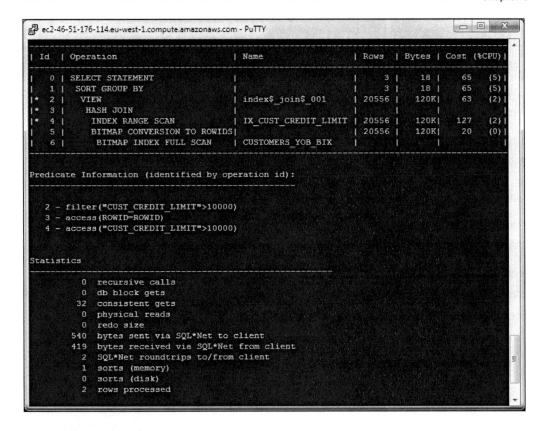

```
ec2-46-51-176-114.eu-west-1.compute.amazonaws.com - PuTTY

| Id  | Operation                    | Name                | Rows  | Bytes | Cost (%CPU)|

|   0 | SELECT STATEMENT             |                     |     3 |    18 |    65   (5)|
|   1 |  SORT GROUP BY               |                     |     3 |    18 |    65   (5)|
|*  2 |   VIEW                       | index$_join$_001    | 20556 |  120K |    63   (2)|
|*  3 |    HASH JOIN                 |                     |       |       |            |
|*  4 |     INDEX RANGE SCAN         | IX_CUST_CREDIT_LIMIT| 20556 |  120K |   127   (2)|
|   5 |     BITMAP CONVERSION TO ROWIDS|                   | 20556 |  120K |    20   (0)|
|   6 |      BITMAP INDEX FULL SCAN  | CUSTOMERS_YOB_BIX   |       |       |            |


Predicate Information (identified by operation id):


   2 - filter("CUST_CREDIT_LIMIT">10000)
   3 - access(ROWID=ROWID)
   4 - access("CUST_CREDIT_LIMIT">10000)


Statistics

         0  recursive calls
         0  db block gets
        32  consistent gets
         0  physical reads
         0  redo size
       540  bytes sent via SQL*Net to client
       419  bytes received via SQL*Net from client
         2  SQL*Net roundtrips to/from client
         1  sorts (memory)
         0  sorts (disk)
         2  rows processed
```

There's more...

In this recipe, we have seen different problems related to aggregate functions and sorting.

See also

▶ The *Using Bitmap Indexes* recipe in *Chapter 3, Optimizing Storage Structures*
▶ *Avoiding Full Table Scans* recipe in *Chapter 4, Optimizing SQL Code*

Avoiding sorting in set operations: union, minus, and intersect

In this recipe, we will investigate performance-related issues when using set operations, such as UNION, INTERSECT, and MINUS.

Getting ready

We will use the SH schema and a copy of the EMPLOYEES table from the HR schema to do our test. To create the MY_EMPLOYEES table in the SH schema, we will use the following script:

```
CONNECT / AS SYSDBA
CREATE TABLE sh.MY_EMPLOYEES AS SELECT * FROM hr.EMPLOYEES;
```

How to do it...

The following steps will demonstrate how to avoid sorting:

1. Connect to the SH schema and enable tracing:

   ```
   CONNECT sh@TESTDB/sh
   SET AUTOT TRACE EXP STAT
   ```

2. Execute a query using the UNION operator to show the customers with a credit limit higher than 13000 and the employees with a salary greater than 10000:

   ```
   SELECT
     CUST_LAST_NAME AS LastName, CUST_FIRST_NAME AS FirstName
    FROM sh.CUSTOMERS
    WHERE CUST_CREDIT_LIMIT > 13000
   UNION
   SELECT
     LAST_NAME, FIRST_NAME
    FROM sh.MY_EMPLOYEES
    WHERE SALARY > 10000;
   ```

3. Execute the same query, as mentioned earlier, using the `UNION ALL` operator:

```
SELECT
    CUST_LAST_NAME AS LastName, CUST_FIRST_NAME AS FirstName
 FROM sh.CUSTOMERS
 WHERE CUST_CREDIT_LIMIT > 13000
UNION ALL
SELECT
    LAST_NAME, FIRST_NAME
 FROM sh.MY_EMPLOYEES
 WHERE SALARY > 10000;
```

4. Use the `INTERSECT` operator to retrieve the last names in common between customers and employees:

```
SELECT CUST_LAST_NAME AS LastName FROM sh.CUSTOMERS
INTERSECT
SELECT LAST_NAME FROM sh.MY_EMPLOYEES;
```

5. Write a query which returns the same results of the previous query using a `JOIN` instead of the `INTERSECT` operator:

```
SELECT DISTINCT
    C.CUST_LAST_NAME AS LastName
FROM sh.CUSTOMERS C
    INNER JOIN sh.MY_EMPLOYEES E
        ON C.CUST_LAST_NAME = E.LAST_NAME;
```

6. Use the `MINUS` operator to retrieve the last name of the customers that are not present in the `EMPLOYEES` table:

```
SELECT C.CUST_LAST_NAME AS LastName FROM sh.CUSTOMERS C
MINUS
SELECT E.LAST_NAME FROM sh.MY_EMPLOYEES E;
```

7. Write a query that returns the same result of the previous query using an `ANTI-JOIN` instead of the `MINUS` operator:

```
SELECT DISTINCT
    C.CUST_LAST_NAME AS LastName
FROM sh.CUSTOMERS C
WHERE C.CUST_LAST_NAME NOT IN (
    SELECT E.LAST_NAME FROM sh.MY_EMPLOYEES E);
```

How it works...

In step 2, we execute a query using the UNION operator, which retrieves the **distinct** rows that are returned by one or both the queries. The execution plan for this query is as shown in the following screenshot:

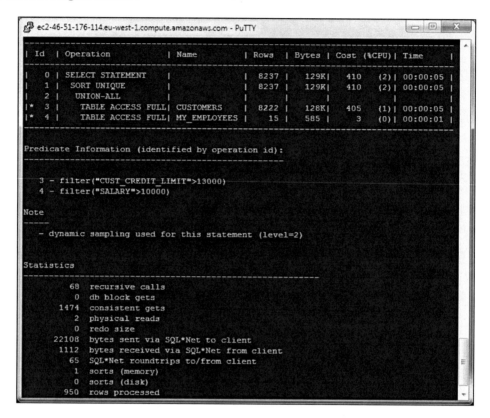

We can see that there is a full table access of both tables and a UNION-ALL operation followed by a SORT UNIQUE operation.

In step 3, we execute the same query mentioned earlier, but using the `UNION ALL` operator, resulting in the following execution plan:

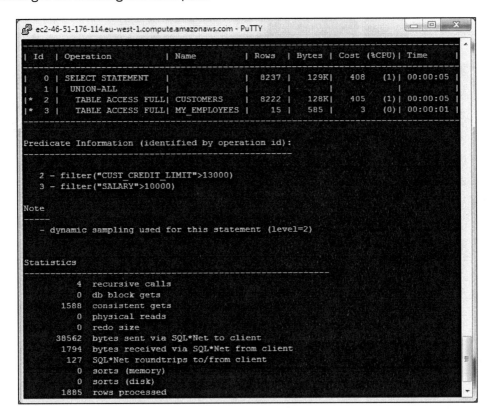

We can see that if we use `UNION ALL` instead of the `UNION` operator, the `SORT UNIQUE` operation is not required. Remember that the two operations are similar, but the `UNION ALL` returns duplicate records, and the `UNION` operator doesn't. When we don't have to worry about the duplicates (or they are not required by the design), it's better to use the `UNION ALL` operator to improve performance.

In step 4, we use the INTERSECT operator to retrieve the last names which are in both CUSTOMERS and MY_EMPLOYEES tables. The corresponding execution plan is shown in the following screenshot:

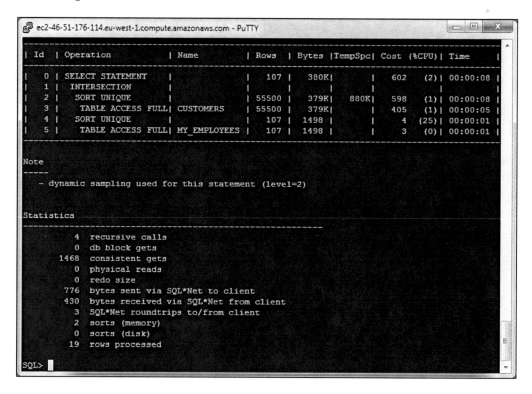

We can see that there are two full table scans of the CUSTOMERS and the MY_EMPLOYEES tables, followed by two SORT UNIQUE operations required to compute the INTERSECTION between the two tables.

The same query can be expressed using a JOIN, as in step 5, using a SELECT DISTINCT to mimic the behavior of the INTERSECT operator, and this removes duplicates.

In the following screenshot, we can see the execution plan and statistics for this query:

```
ec2-46-51-176-114.eu-west-1.compute.amazonaws.com - PuTTY

| 0 | SELECT STATEMENT        |              |     1 |    21 |  409  | (1)| 00:00:05 |
| 1 |  HASH UNIQUE            |              |     1 |    21 |  409  | (1)| 00:00:05 |
|* 2 |   HASH JOIN            |              |  6540 |  134K |  408  | (1)| 00:00:05 |
| 3 |    TABLE ACCESS FULL| MY_EMPLOYEES    |   107 |  1498 |    3  | (0)| 00:00:01 |
| 4 |    TABLE ACCESS FULL| CUSTOMERS       | 55500 |  379K |  405  | (1)| 00:00:05 |

Predicate Information (identified by operation id):
---------------------------------------------------

   2 - access("C"."CUST_LAST_NAME"="E"."LAST_NAME")

Note
-----
   - dynamic sampling used for this statement (level=2)


Statistics
---------------------------------------------------------------
          0  recursive calls
          0  db block gets
       1463  consistent gets
          0  physical reads
          0  redo size
        776  bytes sent via SQL*Net to client
        430  bytes received via SQL*Net from client
          3  SQL*Net roundtrips to/from client
          0  sorts (memory)
          0  sorts (disk)
         19  rows processed
```

Using a JOIN, we have avoided the two SORT operations required in the previous query (but the Full Table Scans are always there), obtaining better performance for the same query.

In step 6, we execute a query using the MINUS operator to retrieve all the last names of the CUSTOMERS except the last names that are also in the MY_EMPLOYEES table.

The execution plan also shows that in this case two full table scans and two SORT UNIQUE operations are required. The execution plan and statistics for this query are shown in the following screenshot:

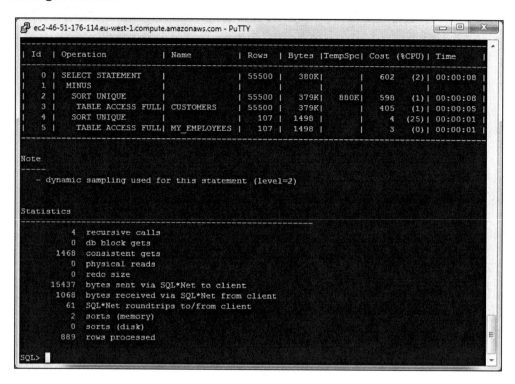

However, in this case, we can translate the MINUS operation in a different query using the ANTI-JOIN (the NOT IN clause) and SELECT DISTINCT statements, obtaining the query in step 7. The execution plan and statistics for this are shown in the following screenshot:

```
ec2-46-51-176-114.eu-west-1.compute.amazonaws.com - PuTTY

| Id  | Operation                | Name         | Rows  | Bytes | Cost (%CPU)| Time     |

|   0 | SELECT STATEMENT         |              |     1 |    21 |   411   (1)| 00:00:05 |
|   1 |  HASH UNIQUE             |              |     1 |    21 |   411   (1)| 00:00:05 |
|*  2 |   HASH JOIN RIGHT ANTI|              | 55500 | 1138K|   408   (1)| 00:00:05 |
|   3 |    TABLE ACCESS FULL     | MY_EMPLOYEES |   107 | 1498 |     3   (0)| 00:00:01 |
|   4 |    TABLE ACCESS FULL     | CUSTOMERS    | 55500 |  379K|   405   (1)| 00:00:05 |


Predicate Information (identified by operation id):
---------------------------------------------------

   2 - access("C"."CUST_LAST_NAME"="E"."LAST_NAME")

Note
-----

   - dynamic sampling used for this statement (level=2)


Statistics
----------------------------------------------------------
          4  recursive calls
          0  db block gets
       1468  consistent gets
          0  physical reads
          0  redo size
      15437  bytes sent via SQL*Net to client
       1068  bytes received via SQL*Net from client
         61  SQL*Net roundtrips to/from client
          1  sorts (memory)
          0  sorts (disk)
        889  rows processed
```

We can see that there is only one sort operation (instead of the two required earlier). In *Chapter 4, Optimizing SQL Code the Using subqueries* recipe, we have seen the performance improvements related to the HASH JOIN RIGHT ANTI operation, so we can use this modified query instead of the original one using the MINUS operator.

There's more...

Set operators are very intuitive, because they are related to the **Set Theory**. However, it's better to substitute the queries which use MINUS and INTERSECT with their corresponding counterparts as we have seen in this recipe (ANTI-JOIN and SELECT DISTINCT statements, respectively), because the optimizer can execute them better, in terms of sort operations required.

In the examples provided in this recipe, we are not demonstrating indexes, but even if some useful indexes were used, the execution plans (SORT operations) wouldn't change. The only difference would be that the FTS operation is replaced by another data access operation using the indexes.

 Many developers use UNION instead of UNION ALL without understanding the difference in execution time. An additional condition to the WHERE clauses can often avoid the use of the costly UNION operation.

See also

▶ In *Chapter 4, Optimizing SQL Code* the *Using Subqueries* and *Optimizing joins* recipes

Troubleshooting temporary tablespaces

At the beginning of this chapter, we saw that sorts may occur in memory or on disk, and that in-memory sorts are faster than on-disk ones because fewer I/O operations are involved.

However, system memory is finite and cannot expand the sort area above the limits of the physical memory available. If sorts exceed the sort area, it's better to use on-disk sort than over allocating memory—ending in very slow pagination (swap to disk managed by the host Operating System).

On-disk sort operations require space to save sort runs, which cannot be stored in memory. Oracle uses sort segments to store this type of information on disk.

In this recipe, we will see how to configure temporary tablespaces to speed up on-disk sort operations and some diagnostic queries to be used when we want to retrieve information about them.

How to do it...

The following steps will demonstrate how to configure temporary tablespaces:

1. Connect as SYSDBA to the database:

   ```
   CONNECT / AS SYSDBA
   ```

2. Examine the number of sorts in the system (from instance startup):

   ```
   SELECT NAME, VALUE FROM V$SYSSTAT WHERE NAME LIKE '%sorts%';
   ```

3. Examine statistics about temporary tablespace blocks:

```
COL TABLESPACE_NAME FOR A16
SELECT
  TABLESPACE_NAME, CURRENT_USERS,
  TOTAL_BLOCKS, USED_BLOCKS, FREE_BLOCKS,
  MAX_BLOCKS, MAX_USED_BLOCKS, MAX_SORT_BLOCKS
FROM V$SORT_SEGMENT
ORDER BY TABLESPACE_NAME;
```

4. Examine statistics about temporary tablespace extents:

```
SELECT
  TABLESPACE_NAME, CURRENT_USERS, EXTENT_SIZE,
  TOTAL_EXTENTS, USED_EXTENTS, FREE_EXTENTS,
  EXTENT_HITS
FROM V$SORT_SEGMENT
ORDER BY TABLESPACE_NAME;
```

5. Execute a query to retrieve the temporary files:

```
COL NAME FOR A32
SELECT
  NAME, STATUS, ENABLED,
  BYTES, BLOCKS, BLOCK_SIZE
FROM V$TEMPFILE;
```

6. Create a temporary tablespace TEMP_TEST:

```
CREATE TEMPORARY TABLESPACE TEMP_TEST
  TEMPFILE '/u01/oradata/TESTDB/temp_test.dbf' SIZE 160M
  EXTENT MANAGEMENT LOCAL UNIFORM SIZE 16M;
```

7. Assign a temporary tablespace TEMP_TEST to a user:

```
ALTER USER sh TEMPORARY TABLESPACE TEMP_TEST;
```

8. Drop temporary tablespace TEMP_TEST and clean up the database:

```
ALTER USER sh TEMPORARY TABLESPACE TEMP;
DROP TABLESPACE TEMP_TEST INCLUDING CONTENTS AND DATAFILES;
```

How it works...

In step 2, we retrieve information about the sorts executed on the database from instance startup, from the dynamic performance views. The results are differentiated between in-memory and on-disk sorts. An example of the execution of this query is shown in the next screenshot:

In step 3, we retrieve information on temporary tablespaces, showing used and free database blocks, while in step 4 we retrieve the same information expressed in extents instead of database blocks. In the next screenshot, we can see the results for both:

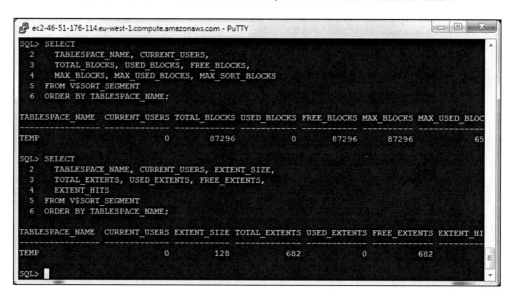

In step 5, we retrieve information about temporary datafiles; the results of this query are shown in the next screenshot:

In step 6, we create a temporary tablespace, which we assign to the user SH in step 7. We create it with the extent management local to obtain better performance than using the dictionary managed tablespaces. Locally managed tablespaces keep track of the free extents in a bitmap stored in the header of the first datafile of the tablespace, where each bit is mapped to a free block in the tablespace.

The results of these operations are as follows:

In the last step, restore the TEMP tablespace as the default temporary tablespace for the user SH and drop the temporary tablespace created in step 6.

There's more...

For each user of the database, there is a default temporary tablespace to be used to sort the data when required. If we haven't defined a default temporary tablespace for a user, the SYSTEM tablespace is used to store SORT SEGMENTS.

This situation is very critical, because the space in SORT SEGMENTS is frequently allocated and deallocated. When doing so, the operations become serialized as space management autoallocates new extents when needed.

If we define the default temporary tablespace for a user, this pre-allocates a SORT SEGMENT, which is never deallocated. When there is the need for a sort operation, no sequential space management actions (allocations) are executed to satisfy the request, resulting in a great improvement in performance.

In fact, temporary space segments are created when the first sort occurs. They are extended when there is a need for a greater sort area in memory, and they shrink to leave enough place for other sort operations when these operations occur.

Optimal storage parameters for temporary tablespaces

We can use INITIAL and NEXT values as integer multiples of SORT_AREA_SIZE parameter and PCTINCREASE set to zero to obtain optimal performance when not using locally managed tablespaces. However, Oracle recommends (http://download. oracle.com/docs/cd/B28359_01/server.111/b28274/memory.htm) we use the PGA_AGGREGATE_TARGET parameter and to set WORKAREA_SIZE_POLICY to AUTO in order to obtain the best performance.

The PCTINCREASE parameter cannot be specified when we use the AUTOALLOCATE option for the tablespace. We can have different tablespaces for each database user and we can query the dynamic performance view V$SORT_USAGE to retrieve the details about the active disk sorts occurring in the instance.

We can obtain better performance by striping the temporary tablespace using multiple disks. Please note that—due to their nature—temporary tablespaces are not affected by backup and restore operations.

See also

▶ There's more information on Dynamic Performance Views in *Appendix A, Dynamic Performance Views* and in *Chapter 9, Tuning Memory* the *Tuning the Program Global Area and the User Global Area* recipe

6
Optimizing PL/SQL Code

In this chapter, we will cover:

- ▸ Using bind variables and parsing
- ▸ Array processing and bulk-collect
- ▸ Passing values with NOCOPY (or not)
- ▸ Using short-circuit IF statements
- ▸ Avoiding recursion
- ▸ Using native compilation
- ▸ Taking advantage of the function result cache
- ▸ Inlining PL/SQL code
- ▸ Using triggers and virtual columns

Introduction

In this chapter, we will focus on PL/SQL code, such as stored procedures, functions, and triggers.

The topics explained in this chapter are easier to apply than those in *Chapter 4, Optimizing SQL Code* because you can make changes to PL/SQL code without having to rebuild the entire application—and they can be just as easily reversed if something doesn't work as expected.

It is relatively easy to obtain great performance improvements by tuning PL/SQL code with very little effort. As always, we have to measure the results before and after our changes, using the process introduced in *Chapter 1, Starting with Performance Tuning* in the recipe *The performance tuning process*.

Using bind variables and parsing

We have already discussed bind variables and parsing in the *Using bind variables* recipe in *Chapter 4*, *Optimizing SQL Code*. In this recipe, we will see another example, using the same principles applied to a PL/SQL procedure.

How to do it...

The following steps will demonstrate the bind variables using PL/SQL:

1. Connect to the database as user `SH`:

   ```
   CONNECT sh@TESTDB/sh
   ```

2. Create a function to calculate the maximum length of data stored in an arbitrary field with a variable condition on another field:

   ```
   CREATE FUNCTION CONDITIONAL_COLUMN_LEN(TABLE_NAME IN VARCHAR2,
    COLUMN_NAME IN VARCHAR2, COND_FIELD IN VARCHAR2,
    COND_VALUE IN VARCHAR2) RETURN NUMBER
   IS
     L_RESULT NUMBER := 0;
     L_STMT VARCHAR2(2000);
   BEGIN
     L_STMT := 'SELECT MAX(LENGTH(' || COLUMN_NAME ||
      ')) FROM ' || TABLE_NAME ||
      ' WHERE ' || COND_FIELD || ' = ' || COND_VALUE;
     EXECUTE IMMEDIATE L_STMT INTO L_RESULT;
     RETURN L_RESULT;
   END;
   /
   ```

3. Calculate using the function created in the previous step for the records in the table CUSTOMERS with an ID between 1 and 10000:

   ```
   SET TIMING ON
   DECLARE X NUMBER := 0;
   BEGIN
     FOR J IN 1..10000 LOOP
       X := X + CONDITIONAL_COLUMN_LEN ('CUSTOMERS',
         'CUST_FIRST_NAME', 'CUST_ID', J);
   ```

```
      END LOOP;
   END;
   /
   SET TIMING OFF
```

4. Create a function that acts as the one in step 2, making use of bind variables:

```
CREATE FUNCTION CONDITIONAL_COLUMN_LEN_BIND(
 TABLE_NAME IN VARCHAR2, COLUMN_NAME IN VARCHAR2,
 COND_FIELD IN VARCHAR2, COND_VALUE IN VARCHAR2) RETURN NUMBER
IS
  L_RESULT NUMBER := 0;
  L_STMT VARCHAR2(2000);
BEGIN
  L_STMT := 'SELECT MAX(LENGTH(' || COLUMN_NAME ||
   ')) FROM ' || TABLE_NAME || ' WHERE ' || COND_FIELD ||
   ' = :COND_VALUE';
  EXECUTE IMMEDIATE L_STMT INTO L_RESULT USING COND_VALUE;
  RETURN L_RESULT;
END;
/
```

5. Recalculate the same values as in step 3 to compare the results:

```
SET TIMING ON
DECLARE X NUMBER := 0;
BEGIN
  FOR J IN 1..10000 LOOP
    X := X + CONDITIONAL_COLUMN_LEN_BIND ('CUSTOMERS',
      'CUST_FIRST_NAME', 'CUST_ID', J);
  END LOOP;
END;
/
SET TIMING OFF
```

6. Clear the functions created:

```
DROP FUNCTION CONDITIONAL_COLUMN_LEN;
DROP FUNCTION CONDITIONAL_COLUMN_LEN_BIND;
```

How it works...

In step 2, we created a function CONDITIONAL_COLUMN_LEN, that calculates the maximum length of data contained in the COLUMN_NAME field of TABLE_NAME, when the COND_FIELD is equal to COND_VALUE.

In step 3, the function is tested by calculating the maximum length of the data contained in the CUST_FIRST_NAME field of the CUSTOMERS table for the records that have a CUST_ID between 1 and 10000.

In the following screenshot, you can see the execution output and the execution time:

In step 4, we have created the function CONDITIONAL_COLUMN_LEN_BIND, which is equivalent to the one in step 3—except for the use of binding variables. In step 5, we have executed this function using the same benchmark of step 3, obtaining the following output:

Hence, there is a huge performance improvement in our function when we use bind variables.

There's more...

In PL/SQL procedures and functions, the use of bind variables is automatic—we can use the variables declared in the function/procedure directly in the SQL code, without worrying about assigning values to the placeholders, as in **JDBC** (**Java DataBase Coectivity**) programming.

The only exception to this behavior is when we use dynamic SQL statements, as in the function used in this recipe. We have seen that in such situations bind variables can be adopted with the USING clause of the EXECUTE statement.

In our example function, we cannot use bind variables for TABLE_NAME, COLUMN_NAME, and COND_FIELD parameters, because they are not parameters of our query. Field and table names in a query cannot be passed as bind parameters, because the parser needs to know all the objects involved in the query before the binding phase.

See also

▶ We have discussed bind variables in depth in _Chapter 4, Optimizing SQL Code_ in the recipe _Using bind variables_

Array processing and bulk-collect

In this recipe, we will see how to use the BULK COLLECT and FORALL statements to speed up the processing of huge amounts of data in a single statement.

We will also see how to limit the amount of memory used for these statements, to avoid a decrease in performance due to reduced available memory for other processes.

How to do it...

The following steps will demonstrate array processing:

1. Connect to the SH schema:

    ```
    CONNECT sh@TESTDB/sh
    ```

2. Create a MY_CUSTOMERS table to store the ID and FIRST_NAME of the customers:

    ```
    CREATE TABLE sh.MY_CUSTOMERS (
      CUST_ID NUMBER,
      CUST_FIRST_NAME VARCHAR2(20));
    ```

3. Populate the `MY_CUSTOMERS` table using an `INSERT` statement inside a `FOR` loop:

```
SET TIMING ON
BEGIN
  FOR aRow IN (SELECT CUST_ID, CUST_FIRST_NAME FROM CUSTOMERS)
  LOOP
    INSERT INTO sh.MY_CUSTOMERS (CUST_ID, CUST_FIRST_NAME)
      VALUES (aRow.CUST_ID, aRow.CUST_FIRST_NAME);
  END LOOP;
END;
/
SET TIMING OFF
```

4. Truncate the `MY_CUSTOMERS` table to empty it:

```
TRUNCATE TABLE sh.MY_CUSTOMERS;
```

5. Create a custom datatype `T_ID` to store a table of numbers:

```
CREATE OR REPLACE TYPE sh.T_ID AS TABLE OF NUMBER;
```

6. Create a custom datatype `T_NAME` to store a table of `varchars`:

```
CREATE OR REPLACE TYPE sh.T_NAME AS TABLE OF VARCHAR2(20);
```

7. Populate the `MY_CUSTOMERS` table by retrieving the data from the `CUSTOMERS` table with a `BULK COLLECT` statement and using a `FORALL` statement to insert the records as a whole:

```
SET TIMING ON
DECLARE
  TAB_ID T_ID;
  TAB_NAME T_NAME;
BEGIN
  SELECT CUST_ID, CUST_FIRST_NAME
  BULK COLLECT INTO TAB_ID, TAB_NAME
  FROM CUSTOMERS;

  FORALL J IN TAB_ID.FIRST..TAB_ID.LAST
    INSERT INTO sh.MY_CUSTOMERS (CUST_ID, CUST_FIRST_NAME)
      VALUES (TAB_ID(J), TAB_NAME(J));
END;
/
SET TIMING OFF
```

8. Truncate the MY_CUSTOMERS table to empty it:

    ```
    TRUNCATE TABLE sh.MY_CUSTOMERS;
    ```

9. Populate the MY_CUSTOMERS table by retrieving the data from the CUSTOMERS table with a BULK COLLECT statement and using a FORALL statement to insert the records in batches of 200:

    ```
    SET TIMING ON
    DECLARE
      TAB_ID T_ID;
      TAB_NAME T_NAME;
      CURSOR MY_CURSOR IS SELECT CUST_ID, CUST_FIRST_NAME FROM
    CUSTOMERS;
    BEGIN
      OPEN MY_CURSOR;
      LOOP
        FETCH MY_CURSOR BULK COLLECT INTO TAB_ID, TAB_NAME LIMIT 200;
        EXIT WHEN TAB_ID.COUNT = 0;

        FORALL J IN TAB_ID.FIRST..TAB_ID.LAST
          INSERT INTO sh.MY_CUSTOMERS (CUST_ID, CUST_FIRST_NAME)
            VALUES (TAB_ID(J), TAB_NAME(J));
      END LOOP;
      CLOSE MY_CURSOR;
    END;
    /
    SET TIMING OFF
    ```

10. Clean the schema by dropping the objects used in this recipe:

    ```
    DROP TABLE sh.MY_CUSTOMERS;
    DROP TYPE sh.T_ID;
    DROP TYPE sh.T_NAME;
    ```

How it works...

In this recipe, we have used three methods to insert records (huge amounts of data) in the MY_CUSTOMERS table, by selecting rows from the CUSTOMERS table.

In step 3, we have used a simple FOR loop that reads records from CUSTOMERS and inserts them in MY_CUSTOMERS, one row at a time.

The timed result of this execution can be seen in the following screenshot:

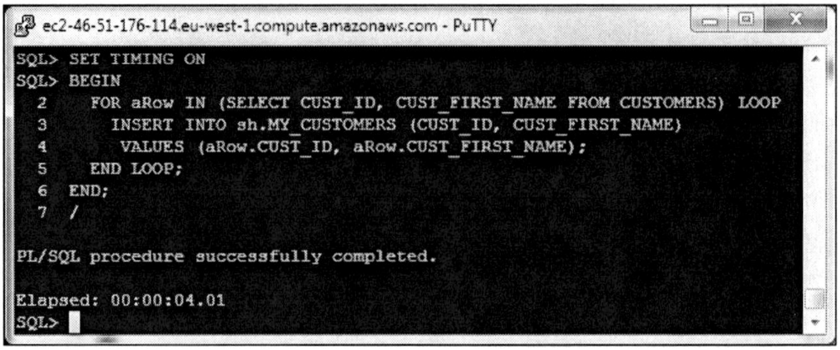

```
ec2-46-51-176-114.eu-west-1.compute.amazonaws.com - PuTTY
SQL> SET TIMING ON
SQL> BEGIN
  2     FOR aRow IN (SELECT CUST_ID, CUST_FIRST_NAME FROM CUSTOMERS) LOOP
  3        INSERT INTO sh.MY_CUSTOMERS (CUST_ID, CUST_FIRST_NAME)
  4          VALUES (aRow.CUST_ID, aRow.CUST_FIRST_NAME);
  5     END LOOP;
  6  END;
  7  /

PL/SQL procedure successfully completed.

Elapsed: 00:00:04.01
SQL>
```

In step 5 and step 6, we created two custom datatypes to store the CUST_ID and CUST_FIRST_NAME. In step 7, we used these datatypes to define two corresponding variables, TAB_ID and TAB_NAME, used to retrieve all the required values from the CUSTOMERS TABLE, using the BULK COLLECT statement.

We can then use TAB_ID and TAB_NAME in a FORALL loop to insert the values in the MY_CUSTOMERS table in a single statement execution.

The output of this execution is as follows:

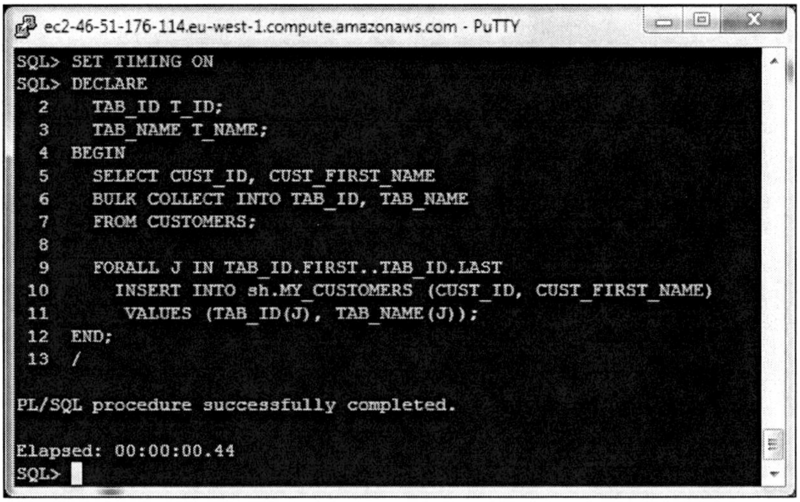

```
ec2-46-51-176-114.eu-west-1.compute.amazonaws.com - PuTTY
SQL> SET TIMING ON
SQL> DECLARE
  2     TAB_ID T_ID;
  3     TAB_NAME T_NAME;
  4  BEGIN
  5     SELECT CUST_ID, CUST_FIRST_NAME
  6     BULK COLLECT INTO TAB_ID, TAB_NAME
  7     FROM CUSTOMERS;
  8
  9     FORALL J IN TAB_ID.FIRST..TAB_ID.LAST
 10        INSERT INTO sh.MY_CUSTOMERS (CUST_ID, CUST_FIRST_NAME)
 11          VALUES (TAB_ID(J), TAB_NAME(J));
 12  END;
 13  /

PL/SQL procedure successfully completed.

Elapsed: 00:00:00.44
SQL>
```

In step 9, we use a slightly modified version of the script, thanks to the LIMIT CLAUSE of the BULK COLLECT statement. We divide the job in batches of 200 records each; for every batch of records we use the same BULK COLLECT and FORALL statements used in step 7.

In the following screenshot, we can see the output of this execution:

In step 10, we drop the table and custom datatypes used for this recipe.

There's more...

We are aware that BULK COLLECT and FORALL statements complete the process faster than the *one row at a time* approach of the FOR statement in step 3.

Using the LIMIT clause, we can see a slight decline in performance, so why use it?

The reason is to conserve memory—when we BULK COLLECT a large amount of data in our user-defined datatype arrays, it is storing them in memory, using a resource that is also being used for other purposes (sorts, joins, buffers, and so on). Limiting the number of rows retrieved in every single batch execution, allows us to see a performance benefit using array processing, without impacting the need for memory for other processes.

Beginning with Oracle Database 10g, automatic array fetching is applied by default, with a limit of 100 rows for each loop iteration. Find out more details here:

```
http://www.oracle.com/technetwork/
database/focus-areas/performance/designing-
applications-for-performa-131870.pdf
```

Also, refer to the following link for more information on this:

```
http://www.oracle.com/technetwork/issue-
archive/2011/11-may/o31asktom-354139.html
```

The FORALL statements allow us to use array processing for INSERT operations also. Despite the appearance suggesting an iterative way of executing the statements inside the FORALL loop, the operation is not really a loop, and it's executed once for all the values in the arrays used.

There is no automatic application of FORALL for insert-loop statements.

See also

> ▸ See the *Introducing array and bulk operations* recipe in *Chapter 4, Optimizing SQL Code*

Passing values with NOCOPY (or not)

In programming languages, we can pass parameters by reference and by value to a function. In this recipe, we will see how to make out this difference in PL/SQL functions and procedures.

How to do it...

The following steps will demonstrate passing parameters to functions:

1. Connect to the SH schema:
   ```
   CONNECT sh@TESTDB/sh
   ```

2. Create the type TAB_NUMBERS, which is a table of numbers:
   ```
   CREATE OR REPLACE TYPE sh.TAB_NUMBERS AS TABLE OF NUMBER;
   ```

3. Create a function called `MY_VALUE`, which returns an element of an array:

```
CREATE OR REPLACE FUNCTION MY_VALUE(ATABLE IN OUT TAB_NUMBERS,
 AIND IN NUMBER) RETURN NUMBER
IS
  L_VALUE NUMBER := 0;
BEGIN
  L_VALUE := ATABLE(AIND);
  RETURN L_VALUE;
END;
/
```

4. Create the function `MY_VALUE_NOCOPY`, which acts as the previous one, but the array parameter is defined as `NOCOPY`:

```
CREATE OR REPLACE FUNCTION MY_VALUE_NOCOPY(
 ATABLE IN OUT NOCOPY TAB_NUMBERS,
 AIND IN NUMBER) RETURN NUMBER
IS
  L_VALUE NUMBER := 0;
BEGIN
  L_VALUE := ATABLE(AIND);
  RETURN L_VALUE;
END;
/
```

5. Compare the performance of the solutions:

```
SET SERVEROUTPUT ON
DECLARE
  MY_IDS TAB_NUMBERS := TAB_NUMBERS(NULL);
  L_VALUE NUMBER := 0;
  t1 NUMBER;
  t2 NUMBER;

  PROCEDURE get_time (t OUT NUMBER) IS
  BEGIN
    t := DBMS_UTILITY.get_time;
  END;
```

```
BEGIN
  SELECT CUST_ID INTO MY_IDS(1) FROM CUSTOMERS
   WHERE ROWNUM < 2;
  MY_IDS.EXTEND(9999999, 1);

  get_time(t1);
  FOR J IN 1..9999999 LOOP
    L_VALUE := L_VALUE + MY_VALUE(MY_IDS, J);
  END LOOP;
  get_time(t2);
  DBMS_OUTPUT.PUT_LINE('RESULT ' || TO_CHAR(L_VALUE));
  DBMS_OUTPUT.PUT_LINE('TIME (CALL BY VALUE): ' || (t2 - t1));

  L_VALUE := 0;
  get_time(t1);
  FOR J IN 1..9999999 LOOP
    L_VALUE := L_VALUE + MY_VALUE_NOCOPY(MY_IDS, J);
  END LOOP;
  get_time(t2);
  DBMS_OUTPUT.PUT_LINE('RESULT ' || TO_CHAR(L_VALUE));
  DBMS_OUTPUT.PUT_LINE('TIME (NOCOPY - CALL BY REF): ' ||
    (t2 - t1));
END;
/
SET SERVEROUTPUT OFF
```

6. Clean the database:

```
DROP TYPE TAB_NUMBERS;
DROP FUNCTION MY_VALUE;
DROP FUNCTION MY_VALUE_NOCOPY;
```

How it works...

In step 3, we have created a simple function that accepts an array as the first parameter with the IN OUT clause. This parameter is then passed by value to the function. When a parameter is passed by value, the actual value of the parameter is copied in memory before launching the function, and this copy is used by the function during execution.

In step 4, the same function as in the previous step is created, declaring the array parameter with the IN OUT NOCOPY clause. The parameter is then passed by reference—a pointer to the actual data is passed to the function—so the function directly manipulates the original array and its copy.

In step 5, we populate an array with 10 million records, and we loop through these elements to calculate their sum—using the functions in step 3 and step 4—measuring the time required to perform the operations. The output is as follows:

```
 9       t := DBMS_UTILITY.get_time;
10    END;
11
12  BEGIN
13    SELECT CUST_ID INTO MY_IDS(1) FROM CUSTOMERS WHERE ROWNUM < 2;
14    MY_IDS.EXTEND(9999999, 1);
15
16    get_time(t1);
17    FOR J IN 1..9999999 LOOP
18      L_VALUE := L_VALUE + MY_VALUE(MY_IDS, J);
19    END LOOP;
20    get_time(t2);
21    DBMS_OUTPUT.PUT_LINE('RESULT ' || TO_CHAR(L_VALUE));
22    DBMS_OUTPUT.PUT_LINE('TIME (CALL BY VALUE): ' || (t2 - t1));
23
24    L_VALUE := 0;
25    get_time(t1);
26    FOR J IN 1..9999999 LOOP
27      L_VALUE := L_VALUE + MY_VALUE_NOCOPY(MY_IDS, J);
28    END LOOP;
29    get_time(t2);
30    DBMS_OUTPUT.PUT_LINE('RESULT ' || TO_CHAR(L_VALUE));
31    DBMS_OUTPUT.PUT_LINE('TIME (NOCOPY - CALL BY REF): ' || (t2 - t1));
32  END;
33  /
RESULT 9999999
TIME (CALL BY VALUE): 2053
RESULT 9999999
TIME (NOCOPY - CALL BY REF): 2066

PL/SQL procedure successfully completed.

SQL>
```

Finally, in step 6, we drop the objects created in this recipe.

In this recipe, we have used the DBMS_OUTPUT package to send messages from our stored procedure, using the PUT_LINE procedure. You can find more on this package in the documentation:

http://download.oracle.com/docs/cd/E14072_01/appdev.112/e10577/d_output.htm

There's more...

Many DBAs recommend the use of NOCOPY when passing large objects to functions/ procedures, to obtain a performance gain, when there is no need to copy the value in and out from the function. In our test, the results indicated a small dip in performance (13ms after 10 million executions, the number of loop iterations), and executing the same script many times leads to an average value that tends to zero (so there are no improvements nor worsening).

Even the example used in the Oracle documentation, about the use of NOCOPY, shows the same timing with or without the use of NOCOPY.

The reason is that NOCOPY is a hint to the PL/SQL engine, that "suggests" the use of the call by-reference for the parameter. This can lead to a theoretical performance gain, but not in all situations.

There are two issues associated with the use of NOCOPY:

> ▶ When we pass a parameter by reference, if we make changes to the value of the parameter inside the function, the changes are made to the copy only, leading to possible side-effects.
>
> We say that a function has side-effects when some state—for example, a variable—external to the function is changed by the function itself; the behavior of the function in these cases depends on history, so the order of evaluation matters.

> ▶ The other issue is related to exceptions. If the function fails, the value of the original parameter can be in an inconsistent state, as the function was interrupted but the changes already made to the parameter would not be reverted.

Due to these considerations, the NOCOPY hint should be used with extreme care after analyzing if there would be performance gain for each particular situation.

Using short-circuit IF statements

In this recipe, we will see how the order in which we evaluate a compound IF statement of more than one condition, may affect performance.

How to do it...

The following steps will demonstrate compound IF statements:

1. Connect to the SH schema:

```
CONNECT sh@TESTDB/sh
```

2. Retrieve the records in the `SALES` table and loop through them to count the number of sales that took place before June 28, 1998 with a quantity greater than 1:

```
SET TIMING ON
DECLARE
   TAB_QTY DBMS_SQL.NUMBER_TABLE;
   TAB_TIME DBMS_SQL.DATE_TABLE;
   CNT NUMBER := 0;
BEGIN
   SELECT AMOUNT_SOLD, TIME_ID
     BULK COLLECT INTO TAB_QTY, TAB_TIME FROM SALES;
   FOR J IN TAB_QTY.FIRST..TAB_QTY.LAST LOOP
     IF TAB_QTY(J) > 1 AND TAB_TIME(J) < '27-JUN-98' THEN
       CNT := CNT + 1;
     END IF;
   END LOOP;
END;
/
SET TIMING OFF
```

3. In the previous script, we change the order in which the two conditions are expressed in the `IF` statement:

```
SET TIMING ON
DECLARE
   TAB_QTY DBMS_SQL.NUMBER_TABLE;
   TAB_TIME DBMS_SQL.DATE_TABLE;
   CNT NUMBER := 0;
BEGIN
   SELECT AMOUNT_SOLD, TIME_ID
    BULK COLLECT INTO TAB_QTY, TAB_TIME FROM SALES;
   FOR J IN TAB_QTY.FIRST..TAB_QTY.LAST LOOP
     IF TAB_TIME(J) < '27-JUN-98' AND TAB_QTY(J) > 1 THEN
       CNT := CNT + 1;
     END IF;
   END LOOP;
END;
/
SET TIMING OFF
```

How it works...

In step 2, we collect the quantity sold and the date from the SALES table in two arrays and then we loop through this array to count the records that satisfy these two conditions:

1. The quantity is greater than 1.

2. The sale took place before June 28, 1998.

We test these two conditions in the same order, obtaining the following output:

```
ec2-46-51-176-114.eu-west-1.compute.amazonaws.com - PuTTY
SQL> SET TIMING ON
SQL> DECLARE
  2    TAB_QTY DBMS_SQL.NUMBER_TABLE;
  3    TAB_TIME DBMS_SQL.DATE_TABLE;
  4    CNT NUMBER := 0;
  5  BEGIN
  6    SELECT AMOUNT_SOLD, TIME_ID BULK COLLECT INTO TAB_QTY, TAB_TIME FROM SALES;
  7    FOR J IN TAB_QTY.FIRST..TAB_QTY.LAST LOOP
  8      IF TAB_QTY(J) > 1 AND TAB_TIME(J) < '27-JUN-98' THEN
  9        CNT := CNT + 1;
 10      END IF;
 11    END LOOP;
 12  END;
 13  /

PL/SQL procedure successfully completed.

Elapsed: 00:00:15.25
SQL>
```

In step 3, the only difference in our script is the order in which the conditions are tested using the IF statement, which is reversed as follows:

```
IF TAB_TIME(J) < '27-JUN-98' AND TAB_QTY(J) > 1 THEN
```

When we test the changed script again, we obtain the following output:

```
ec2-46-51-176-114.eu-west-1.compute.amazonaws.com - PuTTY
SQL> SET TIMING ON
SQL> DECLARE
  2    TAB_QTY DBMS_SQL.NUMBER_TABLE;
  3    TAB_TIME DBMS_SQL.DATE_TABLE;
  4    CNT NUMBER := 0;
  5  BEGIN
  6    SELECT AMOUNT_SOLD, TIME_ID BULK COLLECT INTO TAB_QTY, TAB_TIME FROM SALES;
  7    FOR J IN TAB_QTY.FIRST..TAB_QTY.LAST LOOP
  8      IF TAB_TIME(J) < '27-JUN-98' AND TAB_QTY(J) > 1 THEN
  9        CNT := CNT + 1;
 10      END IF;
 11    END LOOP;
 12  END;
 13  /

PL/SQL procedure successfully completed.

Elapsed: 00:00:03.54
SQL>
```

There's more...

The performance gain obtained in the example is huge, as we are testing against a condition that is true for all records in the table. The quantity sold is always greater than 1; this can be verified with a simple command:

```
SELECT COUNT(*) FROM SALES WHERE AMOUNT_SOLD > 1
```

In this situation, it's better to first test the condition which is true less often. If this condition is false (and the conditions are related with a logical AND to each other), the whole predicate (compound by adding more conditions) is false, hence, the remaining conditions are not checked.

This behavior is called **short-circuit IF**, because the execution flow takes the shortest route to the destination. A similar behavior also occurs in logical ORed conditions, but in this case, the short circuit shows when the first condition is true and hence the predicate.

Avoiding recursion

In this recipe, we will investigate the use of recursive PL/SQL functions and their impact on performance.

How to do it...

The following steps demonstrate recursive functions:

1. Connect to the SH schema:

    ```
    CONNECT sh@TESTDB/sh
    ```

2. Create the FACTORIAL_RECURSIVE function to calculate the factorial of a given number (which is the product of all positive integers less than or equal to the given number) using the well-known recursive algorithm, as follows:

    ```
    CREATE OR REPLACE FUNCTION FACTORIAL_RECURSIVE (ANUM NUMBER)
    RETURN NUMBER IS
      AVALUE NUMBER;
    BEGIN
      IF ANUM <= 1 THEN
        AVALUE := 1;
      ELSE
        AVALUE := ANUM * FACTORIAL_RECURSIVE(ANUM - 1);
      END IF;
      RETURN AVALUE;
    END;
    ```

3. Create the function FACTORIAL_ITERATIVE to calculate the factorial of a given number using an iterative algorithm:

```
CREATE OR REPLACE FUNCTION FACTORIAL_ITERATIVE (ANUM NUMBER)
RETURN NUMBER IS
  AVALUE NUMBER := 1;
BEGIN
  FOR J IN 2..ANUM LOOP
    AVALUE := AVALUE * J;
  END LOOP;
  RETURN AVALUE;
END;
```

4. Compare the execution speed of the functions, while calculating the factorial of a big number:

```
SET TIMING ON
SELECT FACTORIAL_RECURSIVE(1000000) FROM DUAL;
SELECT FACTORIAL_ITERATIVE(1000000) FROM DUAL;
SET TIMING OFF
```

5. Drop the functions created in this recipe:

```
DROP FUNCTION FACTORIAL_RECURSIVE;
DROP FUNCTION FACTORIAL_ITERATIVE;
```

How it works...

In step 2, we created a function to calculate the factorial of a number—denoted by **n!** in mathematics—using a recursive function, that is, a function that calls itself to calculate the result.

In step 3, we implement the same function, using an iterative algorithm to calculate the same value.

In step 4, we execute these two functions with the same number to verify the speed of the two implementations. The result of the execution is as follows:

In step 5, we finally drop the functions created to clean the database.

There's more...

We have seen how using iterative functions led to better performance, even if the recursive form of the algorithms is always more elegant and often less complicated.

We need to avoid recursive PL/SQL functions for one more reason—invoking recursive functions consumes more memory in the PGA than its iterative counterpart. This is because for each recursion, the state of the function (the copy of each parameter and variable and the pointer to the current instruction) has to be stored in memory, and retrieved when the execution flow returns to that recursion.

See also

> ▸ The *Tuning the Program Global Area and the User Global Area* recipe in *Chapter 9, Tuning Memory*

Using native compilation

In this recipe, we will see how to instruct the database to compile our stored procedures in native form—rather than interpreted—to speed up the execution time.

Getting ready

To be sure that our database is not using native compilation by default, we can execute the following command from a SQL*Plus Session:

```
SHOW PARAMETER PLSQL_CODE_TYPE
```

If the result is NATIVE, we can execute the following statement to return to the original default value:

```
ALTER SYSTEM SET PLSQL_CODE_TYPE = INTERPRETED;
```

How to do it...

The following steps will demonstrate how to use native compilation:

1. Connect to the SH schema:

    ```
    CONNECT sh@TESTDB/sh
    ```

2. Create the function C_N_K, which calculates the number of *k-combinations* in a set of *n* elements:

    ```
    CREATE OR REPLACE FUNCTION C_N_K (N IN NUMBER, K IN NUMBER)
       RETURN NUMBER
    IS
      N_FAT NUMBER := 1;
      K_FAT NUMBER := 1;
      N_K_FAT NUMBER := 1;
    BEGIN
      FOR J IN 1..N LOOP
        N_FAT := N_FAT * J;
      END LOOP;
      FOR J IN 1..K LOOP
        K_FAT := K_FAT * J;
      END LOOP;
      FOR J IN 1..(N - K) LOOP
        N_K_FAT := N_K_FAT * J;
      END LOOP;
      RETURN (N_FAT / (N_K_FAT * K_FAT));
    END;
    /
    ```

3. Create a procedure by the name STRESS to test the function in a loop:

```
CREATE OR REPLACE PROCEDURE STRESS(ANUM NUMBER)
IS
  AVAL NUMBER;
BEGIN
  FOR J IN 1..ANUM LOOP
    AVAL := C_N_K (50,10);
  END LOOP;
END;
/
```

4. Execute the STRESS procedure measuring the time needed:

```
SET TIMING ON
BEGIN
  STRESS(100000);
END;
/
SET TIMING OFF
```

5. Alter the session to enable native compilation as the default:

```
ALTER SESSION SET PLSQL_CODE_TYPE = NATIVE;
```

6. Re-create the function C_N_K:

```
CREATE OR REPLACE FUNCTION C_N_K (N IN NUMBER, K IN NUMBER)
  RETURN NUMBER
IS
  N_FAT NUMBER := 1;
  K_FAT NUMBER := 1;
  N_K_FAT NUMBER := 1;
BEGIN
  FOR J IN 1..N LOOP
    N_FAT := N_FAT * J;
  END LOOP;
  FOR J IN 1..K LOOP
    K_FAT := K_FAT * J;
  END LOOP;
  FOR J IN 1..(N - K) LOOP
    N_K_FAT := N_K_FAT * J;
  END LOOP;
  RETURN (N_FAT / (N_K_FAT * K_FAT));
END;
/
```

7. Re-create the STRESS procedure:

```
CREATE OR REPLACE PROCEDURE STRESS(ANUM NUMBER)
IS
  AVAL NUMBER;
BEGIN
  FOR J IN 1..ANUM LOOP
    AVAL := C_N_K (50,10);
  END LOOP;
END;
/
```

8. Execute the STRESS procedure measuring the time needed:

```
SET TIMING ON
BEGIN
  STRESS(100000);
END;
/
SET TIMING OFF
```

9. Reset the parameter and clean the database:

```
ALTER SESSION SET PLSQL_CODE_TYPE = INTERPRETED;
DROP FUNCTION C_N_K;
DROP PROCEDURE STRESS;
```

How it works...

In step 2, we create a function C_N_K to calculate the number of *k-combinations* in a set of *n* elements—the binomial coefficient *n choose k*. We use the iterative form to calculate the factorial values required.

In step 3, we create a procedure STRESS, which calculates the C_N_K function for 50 choose 10, the number of times equal to its parameter ANUM.

In step 4, we execute the STRESS procedure with a value of 100000 for its ANUM parameter, obtaining the results shown in the following screenshot:

In step 5, we change a parameter in the current session—the same statement can be executed, with the necessary grants, to change the parameter in the whole system—to enable the native compilation of PL/SQL.

In step 6, we create the function C_N_K again—with the native compilation enabled—and in step 7 we create the procedure STRESS.

In step 8, we execute the STRESS procedure as in step 4, obtaining the following result:

In step 9, we alter our session parameter PLSQL_CODE_TYPE again to reset the default behavior and drop the C_N_K function and STRESS procedure.

There's more...

In this recipe, we have seen that the `PLSQL_CODE_TYPE` parameter controls the compilation of the PL/SQL code. It can assume two values—`INTERPRETED` (the default) and `NATIVE`.

 When a native compilation occurs, the source code (PL/SQL in our examples) is translated to a binary form that can be directly executed by the CPU. If there is no native compile phase, the source code is interpreted (translated in a binary form as mentioned earlier) at runtime when the code needs to be executed.

After changing the parameter to `NATIVE`, we have created a function and a procedure, obtaining a significant performance gain.

 If we use mathematical functions, such as `SQRT`, `SIN`, and so on, in our compiled procedure, `NATIVE`, then the performance gain is less evident, because those functions are already native-compiled in the Oracle libraries. The best performance gain is obtained by compiling user-defined PL/SQL functions.

Performance of SQL statements is not affected by native compilation.

See also

> ▸ See the *Taking advantage of function result cache, Avoiding recursion*, and *In-lining PL/SQL code* recipes in this chapter

Taking advantage of function result cache

In this recipe, we will see how to use the function result cache feature, available from Oracle 11*g* upwards, to enhance our function's performance.

How to do it...

The following steps will demonstrate the use of the functions result cache:

1. Connect to the `SH` schema:

   ```
   CONNECT sh@TESTDB/sh
   ```

2. Create the function C_N_K, which calculates the number of *k-combinations* in a set of *n* elements:

```
CREATE OR REPLACE FUNCTION C_N_K (N IN NUMBER, K IN NUMBER)
  RETURN NUMBER
IS
  N_FAT NUMBER := 1;
  K_FAT NUMBER := 1;
  N_K_FAT NUMBER := 1;
BEGIN
  FOR J IN 1..N LOOP
    N_FAT := N_FAT * J;
  END LOOP;
  FOR J IN 1..K LOOP
    K_FAT := K_FAT * J;
  END LOOP;
  FOR J IN 1..(N - K) LOOP
    N_K_FAT := N_K_FAT * J;
  END LOOP;
  RETURN (N_FAT / (N_K_FAT * K_FAT));
END;
/
```

3. Create a procedure with the name STRESS to test the function in a loop:

```
CREATE OR REPLACE PROCEDURE STRESS(ANUM NUMBER)
IS
  AVAL NUMBER;
BEGIN
  FOR J IN 1..ANUM LOOP
    AVAL := C_N_K (50,10);
  END LOOP;
END;
/
```

4. Create the function C_N_K_CACHE with the RESULT_CACHE option:

```
CREATE OR REPLACE FUNCTION C_N_K_CACHE (N IN NUMBER,
  K IN NUMBER) RETURN NUMBER RESULT_CACHE
IS
  N_FAT NUMBER := 1;
  K_FAT NUMBER := 1;
  N_K_FAT NUMBER := 1;
BEGIN
  FOR J IN 1..N LOOP
    N_FAT := N_FAT * J;
  END LOOP;
  FOR J IN 1..K LOOP
    K_FAT := K_FAT * J;
  END LOOP;
  FOR J IN 1..(N - K) LOOP
    N_K_FAT := N_K_FAT * J;
  END LOOP;
  RETURN (N_FAT / (N_K_FAT * K_FAT));
END;
/
```

5. Create the STRESS_CACHE procedure to test the C_N_K_CACHE function:

```
CREATE OR REPLACE PROCEDURE STRESS_CACHE(ANUM NUMBER)
IS
  AVAL NUMBER;
BEGIN
  FOR J IN 1..ANUM LOOP
    AVAL := C_N_K_CACHE (50,10);
  END LOOP;
END;
/
```

6. Execute the STRESS procedure measuring the time needed:

```
SET TIMING ON
BEGIN
  STRESS(100000);
END;
/
```

7. Execute the STRESS_CACHE procedure measuring the time needed:

```
BEGIN
  STRESS_CACHE(100000);
END;
/
```

8. Clean the database:

```
SET TIMING OFF
DROP FUNCTION C_N_K;
DROP PROCEDURE STRESS;
DROP FUNCTION C_N_K_CACHE;
DROP PROCEDURE STRESS_CACHE;
```

How it works...

In step 2 and step 3, we create the function C_N_K and the procedure STRESS as in the *Using native compilation* recipe in this chapter.

In step 4, we create a function C_N_K_CACHE, equivalent to the function C_N_K except for the RESULT_CACHE option in its heading:

```
CREATE OR REPLACE FUNCTION C_N_K_CACHE (N IN NUMBER,
  K IN NUMBER) RETURN NUMBER
  RESULT_CACHE
```

In step 5, we create the procedure STRESS_CACHE, which is the same as STRESS but invokes the C_N_K_CACHE function instead of the original C_N_K function.

In step 6 and step 7 we execute the `STRESS` and `STRESS_CACHE` procedures, obtaining an output as shown in the following screenshot:

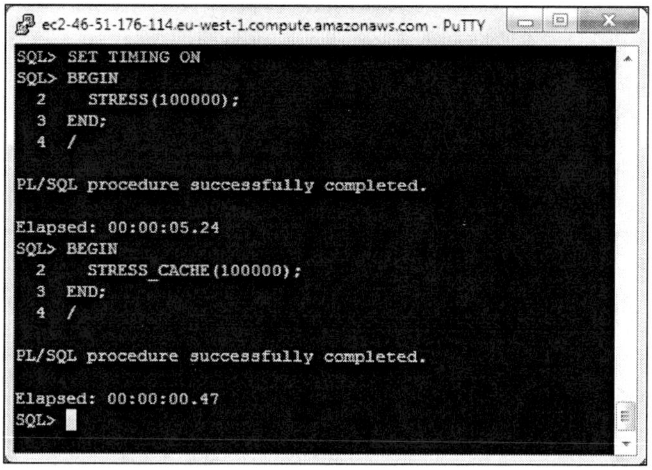

ec2-46-51-176-114.eu-west-1.compute.amazonaws.com - PuTTY
SQL> SET TIMING ON
SQL> BEGIN
2 STRESS(100000);
3 END;
4 /
PL/SQL procedure successfully completed.
Elapsed: 00:00:05.24
SQL> BEGIN
2 STRESS_CACHE(100000);
3 END;
4 /
PL/SQL procedure successfully completed.
Elapsed: 00:00:00.47
SQL>

In step 8, we clean the database by dropping the procedures and functions created in this recipe.

We can see a large performance improvement by executing the function defined with the `RESULT_CACHE` option enabled.

There's more...

Using the result cache can lead to a huge performance gain when we have a deterministic function—a function which always returns the same result for the same parameters—often invoked with the same parameters.

The introduction of this change in our PL/SQL code doesn't require a lot of work; it's just a matter of adding a parameter in the function definition, and there aren't warnings in the use of this feature.

The result cache can also be used for functions with a result based on the contents of infrequently updated tables. In this case, when we define a function we add the `RELIES ON` clause to indicate the table to which the function is related, as in the following example, where the function `FOO` relies on the table `EMPLOYEES`:

```
CREATE OR REPLACE FUNCTION FOO (APARAMETER NUMBER, ...)
  RETURN NUMBER RESULT_CACHE
  RELIES ON (EMPLOYEES)
IS...
```

See also

See the *Using native compilation*, *Avoiding recursion*, and *Inlining PL/SQL code* recipes in this chapter

Inlining PL/SQL code

In this recipe, we will see the benefits of inlining the PL/SQL code in our functions and procedures.

How to do it...

The following steps will demonstrate how to make PL/SQL functions inline:

1. Connect to the SH schema:

```
CONNECT sh@TESTDB/sh
```

2. Create a SIMPLE_FUNCTION function, which returns the area of a triangle given the length of the base and the height:

```
CREATE OR REPLACE FUNCTION SIMPLE_FUNCTION (N IN NUMBER,
 K IN NUMBER) RETURN NUMBER
IS
BEGIN
  RETURN (N * K / 2);
END;
/
```

3. Create a STRESS procedure, which calculates the area for a number of triangles using the SIMPLE_FUNCTION function created in step 2:

```
CREATE OR REPLACE PROCEDURE STRESS(ANUM NUMBER)
IS
  AVAL NUMBER;
  T1 NUMBER;
BEGIN
  T1 := DBMS_UTILITY.get_time;
  FOR J IN 1..ANUM LOOP
    AVAL := SIMPLE_FUNCTION (50,ANUM);
  END LOOP;
  DBMS_OUTPUT.PUT_LINE('TIME: ' ||
    (DBMS_UTILITY.get_time - T1));
END;
/
```

4. Create the same procedure as in the previous step, inlining the `SIMPLE_FUNCTION` by adding a `PRAGMA INLINE` statement, naming it `STRESS_INLINING`:

```
CREATE OR REPLACE PROCEDURE STRESS_INLINING(ANUM NUMBER)
IS
   AVAL NUMBER;
   T1 NUMBER;
BEGIN
   T1 := DBMS_UTILITY.get_time;
   FOR J IN 1..ANUM LOOP
     PRAGMA INLINE (SIMPLE_FUNCTION, 'YES');
     AVAL := SIMPLE_FUNCTION (50,ANUM);
   END LOOP;
   DBMS_OUTPUT.PUT_LINE('TIME (INLINE): ' ||
     (DBMS_UTILITY.get_time - T1));
END;
/
```

5. Execute the `STRESS` procedure:

```
SET SERVEROUTPUT ON
BEGIN
   STRESS(9999999);
END;
/
```

6. Execute the `STRESS_INLINING` procedure:

```
SET SERVEROUTPUT ON
BEGIN
   STRESS_INLINING(9999999);
END;
/
```

7. Clean the database:

```
SET SERVEROUTPUT OFF
DROP PROCEDURE STRESS_INLINING;
DROP PROCEDURE STRESS;
DROP FUNCTION SIMPLE_FUNCTION;
```

How it works...

In the next screenshot, we can see the output obtained after the execution of step 5 and step 6:

In the previous example, we are using a function many times. Every time we call `SIMPLE_FUNCTION`, there is an overhead due to subprogram calling, which can be significant when the called procedure is small and is called many times, so the procedure execution time is negligible compared to the subprogram calling overhead.

The **function inlining** technique is very common in compilers—together with loop unrolling and other tricks—and its implementation is very simple. The compiler inserts the body (the entire source code) of the called subprogram into the caller body instead of the calling code (the function call) avoiding the subprogram calls and their overhead, at the expense of longer code.

Starting from Oracle Database 11*g*, there is a new feature that allows us to make our procedures and functions inline—`PRAGMA INLINE`. With this simple statement, we have instructed the database to inline (the parameter `YES`) the `SIMPLE_FUNCTION` implementation inside our `STRESS_INLINING` procedure. The statement is as follows:

```
PRAGMA INLINE (SIMPLE_FUNCTION, 'YES');
```

Using this feature, we can see a performance improvement in terms of our code execution time, without losing the modularity and isolation of the code.

There's more...

In this recipe, we have used manual inlining, because we have written the `PRAGMA INLINE` directive by ourselves to inform the database about the function call that has to be inlined.

There is another option to avoid manual inlining, which works without changing our code. We can set the parameter `PLSQL_OPTIMIZE_LEVEL` to the value 3, with the following statement:

```
ALTER SYSTEM SET PLSQL_OPTIMIZE_LEVEL = 3;
```

Even if we change the value of this parameter, we can still use the `PRAGMA INLINE` directive. This parameter lets the database choose if it's a good idea to inline function calls at compile time, while with the `PRAGMA INLINE` directive, we ask the database to use inlining (it's not a hint).

 We can also use `ALTER SESSION` to modify the `PLSQL_OPTIMIZE_LEVEL` only in the current user session. The default value for the `PLSQL_OPTIMIZE_LEVEL` parameter is 2 in Oracle Database 11g.

Please note that the use of value 3 for `PLSQL_OPTIMIZE_LEVEL` can increase compile time, and also affects other optimizations.

See also

▸ Other recipes related to functions and procedures in this chapter are *Avoiding recursion*, *Using native compilation*, and *Taking advantage of function result cache*

Using triggers and virtual columns

In this recipe, we will see how to use **virtual columns**, a new feature in Oracle Database 11g, to avoid the use of DML triggers, resulting in a performance gain in our applications.

 Virtual columns can also be used in referential integrity, tables can be partitioned by them, and statistics can be gathered on them.

How to do it...

The following steps will demonstrate the use of virtual columns:

1. Connect to the SH schema:

    ```
    CONNECT sh@TESTDB/sh
    ```

2. Create a table and call it LOANS:

```
CREATE TABLE sh.LOANS (
   LOAN_ID INT NOT NULL,
   PAYMENT NUMBER,
   NUMBER_PAYMENTS NUMBER,
   GROSS_CAPITAL NUMBER);
```

3. Create a trigger on the LOANS table to calculate the GROSS_CAPITAL field, giving the number of payments and the amount of every single payment:

```
CREATE OR REPLACE TRIGGER TR_LOANS_INS
   BEFORE UPDATE OR INSERT ON sh.LOANS
   FOR EACH ROW
BEGIN
   :new.GROSS_CAPITAL := :new.PAYMENT * :new.NUMBER_PAYMENTS;
END;
/
```

4. Insert several rows in the LOANS table and query against it, measuring the execution time:

```
SET TIMING ON
INSERT INTO sh.LOANS (LOAN_ID, PAYMENT, NUMBER_PAYMENTS)
   SELECT
      ROWNUM, AMOUNT_SOLD, QUANTITY_SOLD
   FROM SALES;
SELECT COUNT(*)
   FROM sh.LOANS
   WHERE GROSS_CAPITAL < 10000;
SET TIMING OFF
```

5. Create a table LOANS_VC with a virtual column for the GROSS_CAPITAL:

```
CREATE TABLE sh.LOANS_VC (
   LOAN_ID INT NOT NULL,
   PAYMENT NUMBER,
   NUMBER_PAYMENTS NUMBER,
   GROSS_CAPITAL AS (PAYMENT * NUMBER_PAYMENTS));
```

6. Insert several rows in the LOANS_VC table and query against it, measuring the execution time:

```
SET TIMING ON
INSERT INTO sh.LOANS_VC (LOAN_ID, PAYMENT, NUMBER_PAYMENTS)
  SELECT
    ROWNUM, AMOUNT_SOLD, QUANTITY_SOLD
  FROM SALES;
SELECT COUNT(*)
  FROM sh.LOANS_VC
  WHERE GROSS_CAPITAL < 10000;
SET TIMING OFF
```

7. Clean the database:

```
DROP TABLE sh.LOANS;
DROP TABLE sh.LOANS_VC;
```

How it works...

In step 2, we create a table to store loan data; the GROSS_CAPITAL field can be computed as PAYMENT * NUMBER_PAYMENTS. In step 3, we create a trigger to calculate this value for each insert/update on the LOANS table.

In step 4, we insert about 1 million rows into the LOANS table, using dummy data from the SALES table, and we obtain the timing in the following screenshot:

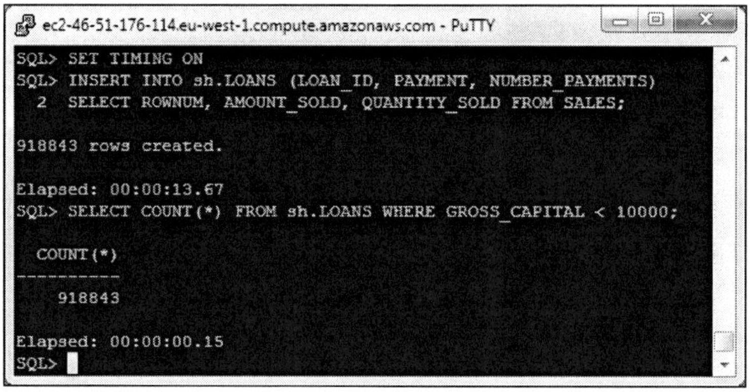

In step 5, we create a similar table, named LOANS_VC, to store loan data. In this table, the GROSS_CAPITAL field is not stored in the table, but it's a virtual column, for which we provide the expression to calculate.

By executing the tests that we executed in step 4 on the LOANS table, on the table LOANS_VC in step 6 we obtain the results shown in the following screenshot:

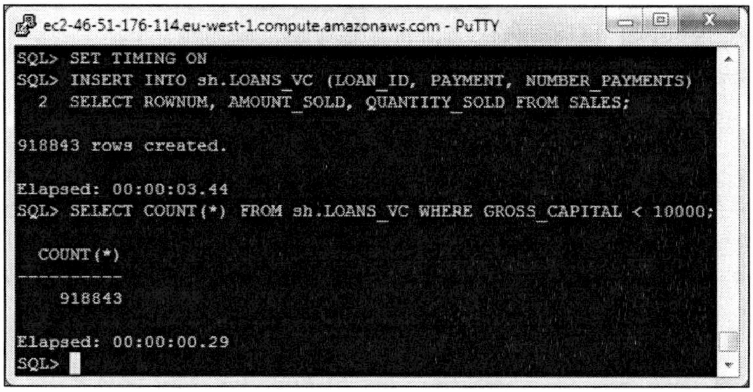

In step 7, we drop the tables created in this recipe to clean up the database.

There's more...

In this recipe, we have seen virtual columns in action, a feature useful in many situations, which allows us to have calculated fields whose values aren't stored in the database.

Our test has shown that using virtual columns leads to performance gain over a solution based on a regular field populated with a trigger.

Also, there are some other considerations for triggers that relate to performance improvement.

Using WHEN and OF in trigger definition

We have defined our trigger using the following definition:

```
CREATE OR REPLACE TRIGGER TR_LOANS_INS
  BEFORE UPDATE OR INSERT ON sh.LOANS
  FOR EACH ROW
```

When we define a trigger, it is better to avoid execution when not needed. In our example, the trigger has to be executed only when the fields PAYMENT and NUMBER_PAYMENTS are updated. So, we can define the trigger using an OF clause to identify the updated columns, which fire the trigger execution, as shown in the following code:

```
CREATE OR REPLACE TRIGGER TR_LOANS_INS
    BEFORE UPDATE OR INSERT
    OF PAYMENT, NUMBER_PAYMENTS
    ON sh.LOANS
    FOR EACH ROW
```

Using the highlighted OF clause, we have declared that the trigger needs to be executed only if the fields PAYMENT and NUMBER_PAYMENTS are updated, avoiding unnecessary code execution when updating other fields (in our LOANS table, there are few fields to provide a simple test environment; in real world scenarios a similar table would contain a lot more information).

Another improvement in this direction is the use of the WHEN clause, which limits the execution of the trigger only when certain conditions are met. For example, we can write a trigger as follows:

```
CREATE OR REPLACE TRIGGER TR_LOANS_INS
    BEFORE UPDATE OR INSERT
    OF PAYMENT, NUMBER_PAYMENTS
    ON sh.LOANS
    FOR EACH ROW
    WHEN ((new.PAYMENT > 0) AND (new.NUMBER_PAYMENTS > 0))
```

In the WHEN clause (the last line in the previous code excerpt), we have defined two conditions to be met to fire the trigger, namely, the new values for the fields PAYMENT and NUMBER_PAYMENTS have to be greater than zero.

If we use the WHEN clause in trigger declaration, the specified conditions are tested for each row and the trigger body is executed only for the rows that match these conditions.

Avoid FOR EACH ROW in triggers, when possible

Our trigger is declared with the clause FOR EACH ROW, because it has to be executed once for each row inserted or updated in the LOANS table.

There are situations where it's enough to execute the trigger once for each insert or update operation, regardless of the rows affected.

In such situations, it's better to declare the trigger without the FOR EACH ROW clause, avoiding unnecessary execution of the trigger for each row interested in the operation, reducing the execution time.

See also

▶ See the recipe *Reducing the number of requests to the database using materialized views* in *Chapter 2, Optimizing Application Design*

7
Improving the Oracle Optimizer

In this chapter, we will cover:

- ▸ Exploring optimizer hints
- ▸ Collecting statistics
- ▸ Using histograms
- ▸ Managing stored outlines
- ▸ Introducing Adaptive Cursor Sharing for bind variable peeking
- ▸ Creating SQL Tuning Sets
- ▸ Using the SQL Tuning Advisor
- ▸ Configuring and using SQL Baselines

Introduction

In this chapter, we discuss the query optimizer, which is a built-in component of the Oracle database. The optimizer chooses the most efficient way to execute a SQL statement, using three steps:

1. Query transformation.
2. Estimation.
3. Plan generation.

The query transformation step accepts the parsed statement, divides it into query blocks (for example, identifying a subquery), and determines if it's better to transform the query blocks into a different SQL statement—semantically equivalent—that can be processed in a more efficient way.

The estimator determines the overall cost of an execution plan, based on selectivity, cardinality, and the cost of each operation involved in the plan. If statistics are available, the estimator uses them for computation, improving the accuracy of the result.

The plan generator explores various plans for each query block, due to various factors: different access paths, joins, and/or join order. We can follow many paths to answer a query; the plan generator chooses the plan with the minimal cost.

Even though the Oracle optimizer does a great job without user intervention, in this chapter, we will see how to tweak the query optimizer to obtain the best performance from each query. We will suggest to the optimizer the best strategy to obtain the answer to our queries, use statistics and histograms to provide more information about our data to the estimator, create stored outlines for plan stability, and use some tools to tune our queries.

Exploring optimizer hints

In this recipe, we will see how to suggest (to the optimizer) the strategy to adopt for choosing the best execution plan, using optimizer hints.

> The use of optimizer hints is a trick and should be considered only when no solution seems to work. The query optimizer is designed to choose the best execution plan, based on many different considerations, so it's very important to keep updated statistics to help the query optimizer in doing its work.

How to do it...

The following steps will explore optimizer hints:

1. Connect the database to the SH schema:

   ```
   CONNECT sh@TESTDB/sh
   ```

2. Set the auto-trace functionality in SQL*Plus to see only the execution plan without executing the queries:

   ```
   SET AUTOT TRACE EXP
   ```

3. Select some records from the CUSTOMERS table (say, all customers born in 1949):

```
SELECT
    C.CUST_FIRST_NAME, C.CUST_LAST_NAME
FROM sh.CUSTOMERS C
WHERE C.CUST_YEAR_OF_BIRTH = 1949;
```

4. Execute the same query suggesting that it's better to full-scan the CUSTOMERS table in order to answer the same query we just saw:

```
SELECT /*+ FULL(C) */
    C.CUST_FIRST_NAME, C.CUST_LAST_NAME
FROM sh.CUSTOMERS C
WHERE C.CUST_YEAR_OF_BIRTH = 1949;
```

5. Inform the optimizer that we are only interested in the first 10 rows of the result:

```
SELECT /*+ FIRST_ROWS(10) */
    C.CUST_FIRST_NAME, C.CUST_LAST_NAME
FROM sh.CUSTOMERS C
WHERE C.CUST_YEAR_OF_BIRTH = 1949;
```

6. Tell the optimizer to use indexes on the CUSTOMERS table:

```
SELECT /*+ INDEX(C) */
    C.CUST_FIRST_NAME, C.CUST_LAST_NAME
FROM sh.CUSTOMERS C
WHERE C.CUST_YEAR_OF_BIRTH = 1949;
```

7. Disable the auto-trace functionality:

```
SET AUTOT OFF
```

How it works...

In this recipe, there is a query to extract the customers who were born in 1949; we want to retrieve their first and last names.

In step 3, we execute a simple query in order to satisfy our requirements, obtaining the following execution plan:

```
ec2-46-51-176-114.eu-west-1.compute.amazonaws.com - PuTTY

SQL> SET AUTOT TRACE EXP
SQL> SELECT
  2    C.CUST_FIRST_NAME, C.CUST_LAST_NAME
  3  FROM sh.CUSTOMERS C
  4  WHERE C.CUST_YEAR_OF_BIRTH = 1949;

Execution Plan
----------------------------------------------------------
Plan hash value: 3460183038

-------------------------------------------------------------------------------
| Id | Operation                    | Name              | Rows | Bytes | Cost (%CPU)| Time
-------------------------------------------------------------------------------
|  0 | SELECT STATEMENT             |                   |  740 | 11840 |  146    (0)| 00:0
|  1 |  TABLE ACCESS BY INDEX ROWID | CUSTOMERS         |  740 | 11840 |  146    (0)| 00:0
|  2 |   BITMAP CONVERSION TO ROWIDS|                   |      |       |            |
|* 3 |    BITMAP INDEX SINGLE VALUE | CUSTOMERS_YOB_BIX |      |       |            |
-------------------------------------------------------------------------------

Predicate Information (identified by operation id):
----------------------------------------------------

   3 - access("C"."CUST_YEAR_OF_BIRTH"=1949)

SQL>
```

We can see that the optimizer has chosen to use the CUSTOMERS_YOB_BIX bitmap index (on field CUST_YEAR_OF_BIRTH) to access the data in the CUSTOMERS table.

In step 4, we execute the same query, adding a hint to the optimizer, suggesting the use of a full table scan operation, resulting in the following execution plan:

```
ec2-46-51-176-114.eu-west-1.compute.amazonaws.com - PuTTY

SQL> SET AUTOT TRACE EXP
SQL> SELECT /*+ FULL(C) */
  2    C.CUST_FIRST_NAME, C.CUST_LAST_NAME
  3  FROM sh.CUSTOMERS C
  4  WHERE C.CUST_YEAR_OF_BIRTH = 1949;

Execution Plan
----------------------------------------------------------
Plan hash value: 2008213504

-----------------------------------------------------------------------------
| Id | Operation          | Name      | Rows | Bytes | Cost (%CPU)| Time     |
-----------------------------------------------------------------------------
|  0 | SELECT STATEMENT   |           |  740 | 11840 |  405    (1)| 00:00:05 |
|* 1 |  TABLE ACCESS FULL | CUSTOMERS |  740 | 11840 |  405    (1)| 00:00:05 |
-----------------------------------------------------------------------------

Predicate Information (identified by operation id):
----------------------------------------------------

   1 - filter("C"."CUST_YEAR_OF_BIRTH"=1949)

SQL>
```

We can see that, using the /*+ FULL(C) */ hint in our query, the execution plan changes, and the access to the CUSTOMERS table is made through a full table scan instead of using indexes, as before.

In step 5, we changed our hint, informing the optimizer that we are not interested in the complete dataset, but only in the first 10 rows, using the hint /*+ FIRST_ROWS (10) */. The execution plan changes again; we can see the result in the following screenshot:

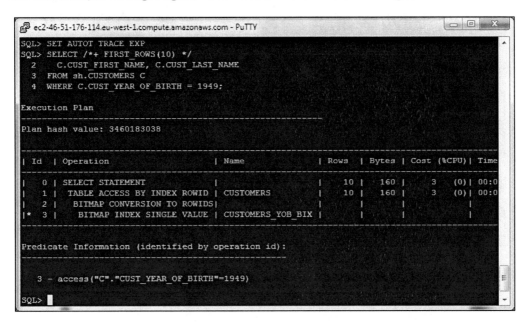

We can see that the optimizer has chosen to use the CUSTOMERS_YOB_BIX index to answer our query, as in step 3.

In step 6, we change the hint again, asking the optimizer to use indexes to access data on the CUSTOMERS table, with the /*+ INDEX(C) */ hint. The corresponding execution plan is shown in the following screenshot. We can see that the optimizer has chosen the primary key index CUSTOMERS_PK to answer our query, instead of the bitmap index used before.

In step 7, we disable the auto-trace functionality of SQL*Plus.

There's more...

We have seen how simple it is to hint the optimizer by inserting our hint in a comment starting with a plus sign /*+ our_hint */.

Hints are used because we may know information about data that is unknown to the Oracle optimizer. With the hint mechanism, we can provide this information to achieve a better execution plan.

There are many different hints we can use, and here is a list of the ones most commonly used:

- ALL_ROWS: Informs the optimizer that we want to retrieve **all** the rows of the query
- FIRST_ROWS (n): Informs the optimizer that we are interested only in the first **n** rows of the query
- FULL (table_name): Asks for full table access to the table table_name
- CLUSTER (table_name): Instructs the optimizer to use a cluster scan when accessing the specified table
- HASH (table_name): Allows access to a table in the hash cluster using a hash scan

- ▶ INDEX (table_name index_name): Specifies to access the table_name using an index (using index_name if specified)

- ▶ NO_INDEX (table_name index_name): Specifies not to use an index (a specific index, if index_name specified, otherwise any index) when accessing table_name

- ▶ LEADING (table_name1 table_name2 ...): Asks the optimizer to join table_name1 and table_name2 in the given order

- ▶ ORDERED: Asks the optimizer to join the tables in the order in which they appear in the FROM clause

- ▶ USE_NL (table_name1 table_name2 ...): Instructs the optimizer to use nested loops join when joining table_name1 (and table_name2) to another row source

- ▶ USE_MERGE (table_name1 table_name2 ...): Instructs the optimizer to use a sort-merge join when joining table_name1 (and table_name2) to another row source

- ▶ USE_HASH (table_name1 table_name2 ...): Instructs the optimizer to use a hash join when joining table_name1 (and table_name2) to another row source

- ▶ PARALLEL (DEFAULT | AUTO | MANUAL | n): Instructs the optimizer to use the specified number of concurrent servers for a parallel operation

- ▶ STAR_TRANSFORMATION: The optimizer will chose the best execution plan obtained through a star transformation

- ▶ REWRITE (materialized_view): Instructs the optimizer to rewrite the query using materialized views (if materialized_view is specified); the optimizer won't take care of the costs involved in using the materialized view

- ▶ APPEND: Instructs the optimizer to use direct-path INSERT (data is appended to the end of the table, regardless of whether there is free space in blocks below the high watermark)

- ▶ CACHE (table_name): Instructs the optimizer to place the blocks retrieved from table_name at the top of the least recently-used list in the buffer cache when a full table scan is performed; this hint is useful with a small lookup table

When specifying a hint related to a table (for example, the FULL hint used in step 4), if we have used an alias in our query, we must use the alias in the hint too. This rule doesn't apply to the schema. Even if we have specified the schema in our query, for example, SH.CUSTOMERS, we must use only the table name (or the alias) in the hint. In the preceding example, we used only CUSTOMERS.

The hint is, in effect, a suggestion, so if the optimizer is able to follow the suggestion, it will generate a plan that follows the suggestion, even if performance is poor!

> There are certain hints—such as, LEADING and ORDERER—that the optimizer will always follow. The optimizer will ignore a hint when there is a typo or when an incorrect hint is supplied.

Errors in hints

If there are errors in our hints, the optimizer will simply treat them as remarks. After adding a hint, always compare the execution plans to check for the expected change, because there will be no errors or exceptions to inform us of this situation.

Common errors, in addition to typos, are missing the plus sign or using the table name instead of the table alias, when the latter was used in the query.

See also

▸ The *Managing stored outlines* recipe in this chapter

Collecting statistics

To work well, the optimizer relies on information about both—the data structures involved in the query and the data contained in them; the latter information is provided by statistics.

In this recipe, we will see how to collect statistics on database objects and see its effects on the optimizer's performance.

How to do it...

The following steps will show how to collect statistics on database objects:

1. Connect to SH schema:

```
CONNECT sh@TESTDB/sh
```

2. Collect statistics on the CUSTOMERS table:

```
EXEC DBMS_STATS.GATHER_TABLE_STATS (OWNNAME => 'SH', -
   TABNAME => 'CUSTOMERS', -
   ESTIMATE_PERCENT => 20, BLOCK_SAMPLE => TRUE, -
   CASCADE => TRUE, DEGREE => 4);
```

3. Query for some statistic data collected in the previous step:

```
SET PAGESIZE 100
SET LINESIZE 90
SELECT
   NUM_ROWS, BLOCKS, EMPTY_BLOCKS, AVG_SPACE, CHAIN_CNT,
   AVG_ROW_LEN, AVG_SPACE_FREELIST_BLOCKS, NUM_FREELIST_BLOCKS,
   SAMPLE_SIZE, GLOBAL_STATS, USER_STATS, LAST_ANALYZED
FROM DBA_TABLES
WHERE TABLE_NAME = 'CUSTOMERS' AND OWNER = 'SH';
```

4. Create a regular table (MYSTATS) to store the statistics:

    ```
    EXEC DBMS_STATS.CREATE_STAT_TABLE (OWNNAME => 'SH', -
        STATTAB => 'MYSTATS', TBLSPACE => 'EXAMPLE');
    ```

5. Export the statistics collected in the data dictionary about SH schema to the MYSTATS table created in the previous step:

    ```
    EXEC DBMS_STATS.EXPORT_SCHEMA_STATS (OWNNAME => 'SH', -
        STATTAB => 'MYSTATS');
    ```

6. Inspect the execution plan for a simple query (with the statistics in place):

    ```
    SET AUTOT TRACE EXP
    SELECT
        C.CUST_FIRST_NAME, C.CUST_LAST_NAME
    FROM sh.CUSTOMERS C
    WHERE C.CUST_YEAR_OF_BIRTH = 1949;
    ```

7. Delete the statistics on SH schema:

    ```
    EXEC DBMS_STATS.DELETE_SCHEMA_STATS (OWNNAME => 'SH');
    ```

8. Execute the query in step 6, again (without the statistics in place):

    ```
    SELECT
        C.CUST_FIRST_NAME, C.CUST_LAST_NAME
    FROM sh.CUSTOMERS C
    WHERE C.CUST_YEAR_OF_BIRTH = 1949;
    ```

9. Import the statistics from the MYSTATS table:

    ```
    EXEC DBMS_STATS.IMPORT_SCHEMA_STATS (OWNNAME => 'SH', -
        STATTAB => 'MYSTATS');
    ```

10. Execute the query in step 6, again (with the statistics again in place):

    ```
    SELECT
        C.CUST_FIRST_NAME, C.CUST_LAST_NAME
    FROM sh.CUSTOMERS C
    WHERE C.CUST_YEAR_OF_BIRTH = 1949;
    ```

11. Drop the MYSTATS table:

    ```
    SET AUTOT OFF
    EXEC DBMS_STATS.DROP_STAT_TABLE ('SH','MYSTATS');
    ```

12. Set up automatic statistics gathering for schema SH:

    ```
    EXEC DBMS_STATS.GATHER_SCHEMA_STATS (OWNNAME => 'SH', -
        OPTIONS => 'GATHER AUTO');
    ```

13. Use automatic sampling size when collecting statistics:

    ```
    EXEC DBMS_STATS.GATHER_SCHEMA_STATS (OWNNAME => 'SH', -
        ESTIMATE_PERCENT => DBMS_STATS.AUTO_SAMPLE_SIZE, -
        METHOD_OPT => 'FOR ALL COLUMNS SIZE AUTO');
    ```

How it works...

In step 2, we collect statistics over the CUSTOMERS table, using the GATHER_TABLE_STATS procedure of the DBMS_STATS package, identifying the table to collect statistics over and other parameters for this operation.

In step 3, we query the DBA_TABLES dictionary view to see some results of the previous operation. Observe some parameters of the table—such as, number of rows, blocks, and average row length—and some information about the previous statistics collection phase—such as, the sample size used and the last analyzed timestamp—if we have global or user stats.

We can see these operations in the following screenshot:

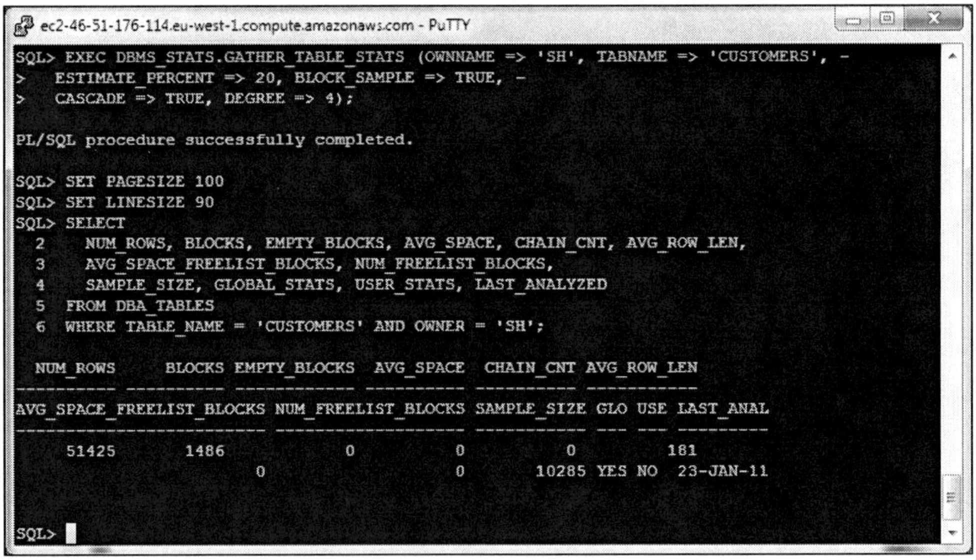

In step 4, we create a table MYSTATS on the tablespace EXAMPLE, to store statistics data in a regular table. In step 5, we copy SH schema statistics from the data dictionary to the MYSTATS table. This operation is useful when we want to transfer statistics among different databases, to avoid recollecting them, which can be a time consuming task.

In the following screenshot, observe the output of these operations, using the DBMS_STATS package and the CREATE_STAT_TABLE and EXPORT_SCHEMA_STATS procedures:

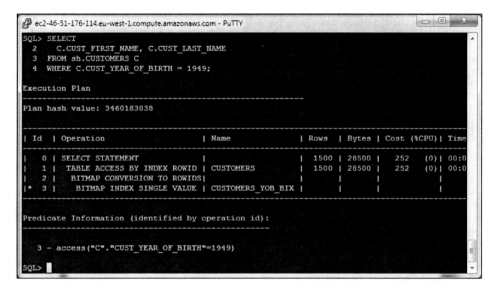

We are now ready to test how statistics affect the execution plan of the queries. Let's create a baseline, executing a simple query on the CUSTOMERS table, as in step 6. The execution plan of this query is as follows:

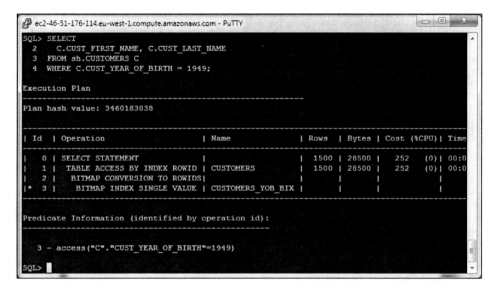

We can see that, to answer our query, the optimizer choice is to use the CUSTOMERS_YOB_BIX bitmap index to access the required data.

In step 7, we execute the DELETE_SCHEMA_STATS procedure of the DBMS_STATS package, to delete statistics from the SH schema. We execute the same query again in step 8, and then we can see the effects of working without statistics. The execution plan can change, but in our example—thanks to dynamic sampling, a feature we will discuss in the next section—the execution plan remains the same.

In the following screenshot, we can see the result of these operations, and we can see in the NOTE section that dynamic sampling was used for this statement:

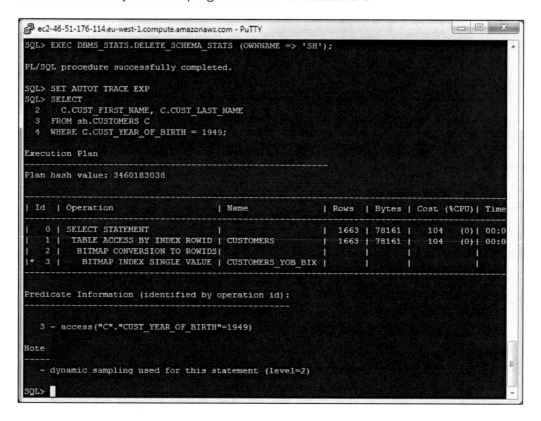

In step 9, we use the DBMS_STATS.IMPORT_SCHEMA_STATS procedure to import the statistics data from the MYSTATS table in the data dictionary. This operation can be carried out when we transfer statistics among different databases—export them from one database, as in step 4 and step 5, and then we can use the export utility to transfer the MYSTATS table to the other database and IMPORT it. After these operations, we execute the procedure in this step to populate the data dictionary tables with our statistics.

In step 10, we execute the same query again. In the following screenshot, you can observe that we have the same execution plan as in step 6, without the use of dynamic sampling as in step 8:

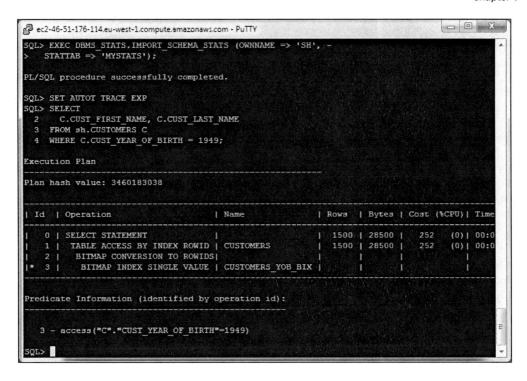

In step 11, we drop the MYSTATS table using the proper stored procedure of the DBMS_STATS package.

In step 12, we instruct the database to automatically collect statistics on schema SH. This option is turned on by default in Oracle databases from 10g onward, thanks to the job GATHER_STATS_JOB.

Statistics computation on a large table is a long job and requires both a scan and a sort on the tables. To reduce the execution time, we can gather statistics using only some of the data. We can decide the amount of data to be processed by setting the ESTIMATE_PERCENT parameter in the DBMS_STATS.GATHER_SCHEMA_STATS procedure.

From Oracle Database 9i onward, we can assign a DBMS_STATS.AUTO_SAMPLE_SIZE value to this parameter. By doing so, the database decides the value to be used to balance performance and statistics accuracy, as in step 13.

There's more...

Oracle optimizer needs up-to-date statistics to choose the best execution plan for our queries.

From Oracle Database 9*i*R2 onward, **Dynamic Sampling** was introduced. But, from 11*g*R2, the optimizer automatically detects whether dynamic sampling should be used and determines the appropriate sampling level. This allows us to have a better execution plan than in previous database releases, even if we don't have statistics on the objects interested in our query, as in our example.

However, relying on Dynamic Sampling in production databases is not a good idea. We can use Dynamic Sampling when we have out-of-date statistics, and we can also use a hint to inform the optimizer that we want to use this feature, as follows:

```
SELECT /*+ DYNAMIC_SAMPLING (CUSTOMERS 8) */ …
```

In this example, we have asked the optimizer to use Dynamic Sampling on the CUSTOMERS table, using a parameter of 8—the scale ranges from 0 (don't use) to 10 (use "aggressive" sampling).

> The greatest drawback to using Dynamic Sampling is that it is only an estimate of the table contents based on a random selected sample block of rows; computed statistics are much more precise, resulting in an optimal execution plan.

The default level for Dynamic Sampling is set by the OPTIMIZER_DYNAMIC_SAMPLING parameter, which defaults to 2, as we can see in the screenshot for step 8 in the Note section (level = 2). With this level, the optimizer will use Dynamic Sampling to analyze a small number of blocks, only for tables without statistics.

Lock table statistics for load or highly volatile tables

We have seen that, with Oracle Database 10*g*, the automatic statistics gathering feature was introduced; however, we may prefer not to collect statistics on some tables, due to the highly volatile data stored in them, or because they are load tables. For example, in a table used to load data, we could collect statistics when the table is almost empty or when only one specific kind of data is present in the table.

In such situations, we can inform the database to lock statistics on the table, using the following DMBS_STATS procedure to lock the TABLE_NAME table of schema SH:

```
DBMS_STATS.LOCK_TABLE_STATS('SH', 'TABLE_NAME');
```

Other procedures in DBMS_STATS

In this recipe, we have used some stored procedures of the DBMS_STATS package. The following are some other useful procedures, to collect statistics at database, schema, table, or index level:

```
EXEC DBMS_STATS.GATHER_DATABASE_STATS;
EXEC DBMS_STATS.GATHER_SCHEMA_STATS;
EXEC DBMS_STATS.GATHER_TABLE_STATS('SH', 'CUSTOMERS');
EXEC DBMS_STATS.GATHER_INDEX_STATS('SH', 'CUSTOMERS_YOB_BIX');
```

We can also use the corresponding procedures when we want to delete the statistics:

```
EXEC DBMS_STATS.DELETE_DATABASE_STATS;
EXEC DBMS_STATS.DELETE_SCHEMA_STATS;
EXEC DBMS_STATS.DELETE_TABLE_STATS('SH', 'CUSTOMERS');
EXEC DBMS_STATS.DELETE_INDEX_STATS('SH', 'CUSTOMERS_YOB_BIX');
```

From Oracle 10g onward, old versions of statistics are automatically saved, and we can use the DBA_OPTSTAT_OPERATIONS dictionary view to explore the history of statistics operations performed at the schema and database level. The DBMS_STATS.RESTORE procedure lets us restore the statistics as they were at the timestamp used as a parameter when invoking the procedure.

 Older versions of statistics are not automatically saved when we use the (old) ANALYZE statement to collect statistics.

See also

▶ See *Chapter 3*, *Optimizing Storage Structures*, the *Avoiding row chaining* and *Avoiding row migration* recipes

▶ The *Exploring the optimizer hints*, *Using histogram*, and *Managing stored outlines* recipes in this chapter

Using histograms

In this recipe, we will see how to use histograms on tables to provide a detailed estimate of value distribution inside a column.

How to do it...

The following steps will show how to represent our data in the form of histograms:

1. Connect to SH schema:

   ```
   CONNECT sh@TESTDB/sh
   ```

2. Create the table TEST_HIST with some data from ALL_OBJECTS:

   ```
   CREATE TABLE sh.TEST_HIST AS
     SELECT
        ROWNUM AS ID,
        OBJECT_NAME AS NAME,
        MOD(ROWNUM, 10) AS FIELD1,
        TRUNC(MOD(ROWNUM, 10)/9) AS FIELD2
     FROM ALL_OBJECTS;
   ```

3. Query for FIELD1 and FIELD2 values grouped to see the data distribution:

   ```
   SELECT FIELD1, COUNT(*)
   FROM TEST_HIST
   GROUP BY FIELD1 ORDER BY 1;

   SELECT FIELD2, COUNT(*)
   FROM TEST_HIST
   GROUP BY FIELD2 ORDER BY 1;
   ```

4. Create histograms for column FIELD1 of the table TEST_HIST:

   ```
   EXEC DBMS_STATS.GATHER_TABLE_STATS (OWNNAME => 'SH', -
      TABNAME => 'TEST_HIST', -
      METHOD_OPT => 'FOR COLUMNS SIZE 10 FIELD1');
   ```

5. Query USER_TAB_HISTOGRAMS to see the values stored in the histogram for FIELD1:

   ```
   SELECT ENDPOINT_NUMBER, ENDPOINT_VALUE
   FROM USER_TAB_HISTOGRAMS
   WHERE TABLE_NAME = 'TEST_HIST' AND COLUMN_NAME = 'FIELD1'
   ORDER BY 2;
   ```

6. Create histograms for column `FIELD2` of the table `TEST_HIST`:

```
EXEC DBMS_STATS.GATHER_TABLE_STATS (OWNNAME => 'SH', -
  TABNAME => 'TEST_HIST', -
  METHOD_OPT => 'FOR COLUMNS SIZE 10 FIELD2');
```

7. Query `USER_TAB_HISTOGRAMS` to see the values stored in the histogram for `FIELD2`:

```
SELECT ENDPOINT_NUMBER, ENDPOINT_VALUE
FROM USER_TAB_HISTOGRAMS
WHERE TABLE_NAME = 'TEST_HIST' AND COLUMN_NAME = 'FIELD2'
ORDER BY 2;
```

8. Drop the table `TEST_HIST`:

```
DROP TABLE TEST_HIST;
```

How it works...

In step 2, we created the table `TEST_HIST`, in which `FIELD1` is populated with values ranging from 0 to 9 and `FIELD2` contains only the values 0 and 1, with a 9:1 ratio.

We confirm the data distribution we just saw with the queries in step 3. The output can be seen in the following screenshot:

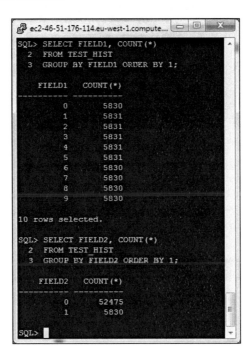

A histogram is an object in which values from a column are put in a limited number of buckets, 75 by default, with a distribution based on ranges—the column values within the same range are put in the same bucket.

Using the data in histograms, the optimizer can estimate the data distribution better in a column, so it can choose a better execution plan, due to a greater knowledge of the data.

In step 4, we create a histogram for `FIELD1`, using a size of 10 as the number of buckets used for the histogram. In our example, this is equivalent to the different values stored in `FIELD1`, so in every bucket there is only one distinct value, as shown by the query in step 5. In the following screenshot, we can see the results of this query:

```
ec2-46-51-176-114.eu-west-1.compute.amazonaws.com - PuTTY

SQL> EXEC DBMS_STATS.GATHER_TABLE_STATS (OWNNAME => 'SH', TABNAME => 'TEST_HIST', -
>    METHOD_OPT => 'FOR COLUMNS SIZE 10 FIELD1');

PL/SQL procedure successfully completed.

SQL> SELECT ENDPOINT_NUMBER, ENDPOINT_VALUE
  2  FROM USER_TAB_HISTOGRAMS
  3  WHERE TABLE_NAME = 'TEST_HIST' AND COLUMN_NAME = 'FIELD1'
  4  ORDER BY 2;

ENDPOINT_NUMBER ENDPOINT_VALUE
--------------- --------------
            538              0
           1094              1
           1706              2
           2251              3
           2798              4
           3329              5
           3874              6
           4406              7
           4936              8
           5475              9

10 rows selected.

SQL>
```

The `ENDPOINT_VALUE` shows us the value stored for each bucket, while the meaning of `ENDPOINT_NUMBER` changes due to the kind of histogram. In this example, we have the number of buckets equal to the number of distinct values, so `ENDPOINT_NUMBER` represents the cumulative frequency (in the first bucket, the value 0 appears 538 times, in the second 1094-538 = 556 times, and so on).

In step 6, we create a histogram on `FIELD2`, and the query on this histogram gives the following output:

```
                                                                          _  □  X
  ec2-46-51-176-114.eu-west-1.compute.amazonaws.com - PuTTY
SQL> EXEC DBMS_STATS.GATHER_TABLE_STATS (OWNNAME => 'SH', TABNAME => 'TEST_HIST', -
>    METHOD_OPT => 'FOR COLUMNS SIZE 10 FIELD2');

PL/SQL procedure successfully completed.

SQL> SELECT ENDPOINT_NUMBER, ENDPOINT_VALUE
  2  FROM USER_TAB_HISTOGRAMS
  3  WHERE TABLE_NAME = 'TEST_HIST' AND COLUMN_NAME = 'FIELD2'
  4  ORDER BY 2;

ENDPOINT_NUMBER ENDPOINT_VALUE
--------------- --------------
           4837              0
           5414              1

SQL>
```

In this case, the number of buckets (10) is more than the number of distinct values (2) in the `FIELD2` column, and `ENDPOINT_NUMBER` represents the cumulative frequency as shown earlier.

There's more...

In this recipe, we have seen how to create histograms to represent our data to help the optimizer choose the right execution plan for our queries.

We might think that having histograms on all the columns of all the tables is a better solution, to help the optimizer in choosing the best execution plan, but that's not the case.

Histograms are useful only on **indexed** columns containing **skewed values**, because they help the optimizer to choose whether to use the index or not to access values. Obviously, if the frequency for a specific value is very high, using the index won't be the best choice. If a column with these characteristics is also used often in the `WHERE` clause, it's a very good candidate for a histogram.

Don't use histograms in situations where:

- ▶ The column is not used in the `WHERE` clauses of queries
- ▶ The data in the column is uniformly distributed (like `FIELD1`, in our example)
- ▶ Bind variables are used when comparing against the column (we will see more on this in the *Introducing Adaptive Cursor Sharing for bind variable peeking* recipe, later in this chapter)

Another issue with using histograms is that they need to be updated manually to reflect changes in column data, using the statements presented in this recipe.

Height-based and value-based (frequency) histograms

There are two types of histograms—**height-based** and **value-based**:

▶ In height-based histograms, the same number of values are placed in each bucket approximately, so we can have multiple buckets ending at the same ENDPOINT_ VALUE. In this situation the ENDPOINT_NUMBER represents the cumulative number of rows.

▶ In value-based histograms, also known as **frequency histograms**, we have a number of buckets greater than or equal to the number of distinct value in the field, as in our previous example.

> According to Oracle documentation, the histogram will be created as value-based—also known as frequency histograms— by default, when the number of distinct values is less than or equal to the number of histogram buckets specified.

See also

▶ The *Introducing Adaptive Cursor Sharing for bind variables peeking* recipe in this chapter, for a more detailed description of possible problems related to the use of bind variables

▶ The *Collecting statistics* recipe in this chapter, to see how to collect and transport statistics between different databases

Managing stored outlines

In production environments, there is a very simple golden rule about database performance—it's better to have a database that always performs quite well than a database that performs even 10 times faster but not always; that is, a database whose performance sometimes dips.

Execution plan stability is a must for ensuring performance that persists over time; in production environments, we need an optimal and predictable performance.

In this recipe, we will see how to create stored outlines to achieve execution plan stability and how to manage these stored outlines.

Getting ready

To create stored outlines, we need an appropriate grant. Connect to the database as SYSDBA, and grant the user SH permission to create stored outlines:

```
CONNECT / AS SYSDBA
GRANT CREATE ANY OUTLINE TO sh;
```

How to do it...

The following steps will demonstrate stored outlines, their creation, and management:

1. Connect to SH schema:

   ```
   CONNECT sh@TESTDB/sh
   ```

2. Execute a query on the CUSTOMERS and COUNTRIES tables, analyzing the execution plan:

   ```
   SET AUTOT TRACE EXP
   SELECT C.CUST_ID, C.CUST_FIRST_NAME, C.CUST_LAST_NAME,
     C.CUST_STREET_ADDRESS, C.CUST_POSTAL_CODE, C.CUST_CITY,
     C.CUST_STATE_PROVINCE, CN.COUNTRY_NAME
   FROM sh.CUSTOMERS C, sh.COUNTRIES CN
   WHERE C.COUNTRY_ID = CN.COUNTRY_ID;
   ```

3. Execute the same query using the primary key index COUNTRIES_PK to analyze the execution plan:

   ```
   SELECT /*+ INDEX (CN COUNTRIES_PK) */
     C.CUST_ID, C.CUST_FIRST_NAME, C.CUST_LAST_NAME,
     C.CUST_STREET_ADDRESS, C.CUST_POSTAL_CODE, C.CUST_CITY,
     C.CUST_STATE_PROVINCE, CN.COUNTRY_NAME
   FROM sh.CUSTOMERS C, sh.COUNTRIES CN
   WHERE C.COUNTRY_ID = CN.COUNTRY_ID;
   SET AUTOT OFF
   ```

4. Create an outline, named CUST_LIST_OUTLINE, to store the execution plan, obtained in step 3, in the APP_LISTS category:

   ```
   CREATE OR REPLACE OUTLINE CUST_LIST_OUTLINE FOR CATEGORY
   APP_LISTS ON
   SELECT /*+ INDEX (CN COUNTRIES_PK) */
     C.CUST_ID, C.CUST_FIRST_NAME, C.CUST_LAST_NAME,
     C.CUST_STREET_ADDRESS, C.CUST_POSTAL_CODE, C.CUST_CITY,
     C.CUST_STATE_PROVINCE, CN.COUNTRY_NAME
   FROM sh.CUSTOMERS C, sh.COUNTRIES CN
   WHERE C.COUNTRY_ID = CN.COUNTRY_ID;
   ```

5. Alter the session to use the stored outlines of the APP_LISTS category:

   ```
   ALTER SESSION SET USE_STORED_OUTLINES = APP_LISTS;
   ```

6. Execute the query in step 3 again:

```
SET AUTOT TRACE EXP
SELECT /*+ INDEX (CN COUNTRIES_PK) */
   C.CUST_ID, C.CUST_FIRST_NAME, C.CUST_LAST_NAME,
   C.CUST_STREET_ADDRESS, C.CUST_POSTAL_CODE, C.CUST_CITY,
   C.CUST_STATE_PROVINCE, CN.COUNTRY_NAME
FROM sh.CUSTOMERS C, sh.COUNTRIES CN
WHERE C.COUNTRY_ID = CN.COUNTRY_ID;
SET AUTOT OFF
```

7. Clean the session state, drop the outline, and revoke the grant:

```
ALTER SESSION SET USE_STORED_OUTLINES = FALSE;

CONNECT / AS SYSDBA
DROP OUTLINE CUST_LIST_OUTLINE;
REVOKE CREATE ANY OUTLINE FROM sh;
```

How it works...

The execution plan for the same statement may change due to different reasons, such as changes to the schema objects, different parameters, changes in data, accuracy of statistics, presence of histograms, and so on. Another big issue can be the upgrade to a newer database release.

> Over time, different techniques were used to manage SQL Plan's stability in the Oracle database. In Oracle 10g, SQL Profiles and SQL Tuning Sets were launched, and, starting with Oracle 11g, Oracle SQL Plan Management was introduced.
>
> We can migrate stored outlines to SQL Plan Management using the DBMS_SPM.MIGRATE_STORED_OUTLINE procedure.

If we want to avoid changes to the execution plans, we can store them in stored outlines—the plans in the stored outlines don't change, and the optimizer uses them to generate equivalent execution plans.

In step 2, we execute a query, and the corresponding execution plan provides the full table scan of the CUSTOMERS and COUNTRIES tables. We can see the execution plan generated by the optimizer in the following screenshot:

We decide to add an index hint to the query in step 3, so that the optimizer changes the execution plan and uses the primary key, as suggested. The corresponding execution plan is as follows:

We are now satisfied with the execution plan obtained, and we want it to be the access path for this query from now onwards. For this, we create a stored outline in step 4. Stored outlines can be grouped together in categories, so we define CUST_LIST_OUTLINE to be part of the APP_LISTS category, where we will store all the outlines related to lists in our application. There is no need to create a category before creating the outline—the category APP_LISTS doesn't already exist in our database, so it's created along with the stored outline, with a single statement.

In step 5, we instruct the optimizer to use, for our session, the stored outlines of the APP_LISTS category. We can carry out the same operation also at a database level, affecting all the users connected to the database instance. In the following screenshot, you can see the execution of these statements:

```
SQL> CREATE OR REPLACE OUTLINE CUST_LIST_OUTLINE FOR CATEGORY APP_LISTS ON
  2  SELECT /*+ INDEX (CN COUNTRIES_PK) */
  3    C.CUST_ID, C.CUST_FIRST_NAME, C.CUST_LAST_NAME,
  4    C.CUST_STREET_ADDRESS, C.CUST_POSTAL_CODE, C.CUST_CITY,
  5    C.CUST_STATE_PROVINCE, CN.COUNTRY_NAME
  6  FROM sh.CUSTOMERS C, sh.COUNTRIES CN
  7  WHERE C.COUNTRY_ID = CN.COUNTRY_ID;

Outline created.

SQL> ALTER SESSION SET USE_STORED_OUTLINES = APP_LISTS;

Session altered.

SQL>
```

In step 6, we execute the same query as in step 3, obtaining the same execution plan. The execution plan will be the same even if we alter database parameters and/or the schema, for example, adding an index. Our aim of plan stability is reached, as we can see in the following screenshot (in the **Note** section):

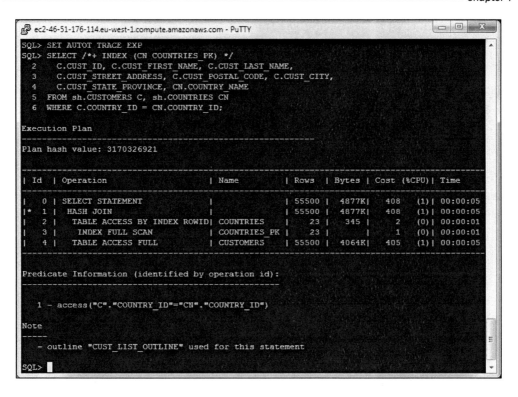

In step 7, we clean the database of our test objects, dropping the stored outline and revoking the grant from SH user.

There's more...

The most important thing to keep in mind about stored outlines is that they are used only if the statement executed **exactly** matches the one stored in the outline (case sensitive and included blanks). This is not an issue when the SQL statements come from an application where the statement is stored in a fixed form, but it's inapplicable when the statements are the result of user input.

We have also seen that we can create stored outlines for a single statement. We can also collect outlines for all the statements executed, using the following statement:

```
ALTER SYSTEM SET CREATE_STORED_OUTLINES = our_category_name;
```

Hereafter, we collect the outlines for all the executed statements in `our_category_name`. The outlines will have system-generated names, of course, and we can stop collecting outlines with the following statement:

```
ALTER SYSTEM SET CREATE_STORED_OUTLINES = FALSE;
```

We can use the `ALTER OUTLINE` statement to rename stored outlines, to change their category, or to change the corresponding SQL statement and execution plan. The `OUTLN_PKG` package helps us in massive operations, such as:

▶ Drop outlines of a specified category, using the `DROP_BY_CAT` procedure

▶ Drop outlines that will never be used, using the `DROP_UNUSED` procedure

▶ Changing the category of outlines to a new category, using the `UPDATE_BY_CAT` procedure

> If we are using the `FOO` category in the session, and if there is no matching outline for our statement, but there is one in the `DEFAULT` category, the outline from the `DEFAULT` category will be used.

Private and public stored outlines

We can have private and public stored outlines; in this recipe, we have seen how to create public stored outlines and how to use them.

When we have a public stored outline in place, we may want to test another stored outline for the same query, without affecting the performance of other users who are using the same statement.

In this situation, we can create a private stored outline, test it, and—if the results are satisfactory—publish the outline to let other users access it.

To do so, we need to:

1. Create the outline tables in our schema:

   ```
   EXEC DBMS_OUTLN_EDIT.CREATE_EDIT_TABLES;
   ```

2. Copy a public stored outline in our schema tables:

   ```
   CREATE PRIVATE OUTLINE PVT_CUST_LIST_OUTLINE
     FROM CUST_LIST_OUTLINE;
   ```

3. Edit the private outline and update it:
   ```
   EXEC DBMS_OUTLN_EDIT.REFRESH_PRIVATE_OUTLINE(
     'PVT_CUST_LIST_OUTLINE');
   ```

4. Use the private outline and test it:
   ```
   ALTER SESSION SET USE_PRIVATE_OUTLINES = TRUE;
   ```

5. Publish the modified outline back to the public stored outlines:
   ```
   CREATE OR REPLACE OUTLINE CUST_LIST_OUTLINE
       FROM PRIVATE PVT_CUST_LIST_OUTLINE;
   ```

6. Disable private outlines and drop the corresponding tables:
   ```
   ALTER SESSION SET USE_PRIVATE_OUTLINES = FALSE;
   EXEC DBMS_OUTLN_EDIT.DROP_EDIT_TABLES;
   ```

See also

▸ The *Exploring the optimizer hints* and *Configuring and using SQL Baselines* recipes in this chapter

Introducing Adaptive Cursor Sharing for bind variable peeking

In the previous chapter, we have explored the (recommended) use of bind variables.

In this recipe, we will see how using bind variables can be disadvantageous in certain situations and learn about a feature of Oracle Database 11*g* that helps us with this.

How to do it...

The following steps will demonstrate Adaptive Cursor Sharing:

1. Connect to SH schema:
   ```
   CONNECT sh@TESTDB/sh
   ```

2. Create a table for testing with a field ID that equals 1:
   ```
   CREATE TABLE sh.MY_TEST AS SELECT
     OBJECT_NAME AS NAME, 1 AS ID
   FROM ALL_OBJECTS NOLOGGING;
   ```

3. Insert eight records with different values for the `ID` field:

```
INSERT INTO sh.MY_TEST (ID, NAME)
   VALUES (2, 'ONLY THIS RECORD HAS ID=2');
INSERT INTO sh.MY_TEST (ID, NAME)
   VALUES (3, 'ONLY THIS RECORD HAS ID=3');
INSERT INTO sh.MY_TEST (ID, NAME)
   VALUES (4, 'ONLY THIS RECORD HAS ID=4');
INSERT INTO sh.MY_TEST (ID, NAME)
   VALUES (5, 'ONLY THIS RECORD HAS ID=5');
INSERT INTO sh.MY_TEST (ID, NAME)
   VALUES (6, 'ONLY THIS RECORD HAS ID=6');
INSERT INTO sh.MY_TEST (ID, NAME)
   VALUES (7, 'ONLY THIS RECORD HAS ID=7');
INSERT INTO sh.MY_TEST (ID, NAME)
   VALUES (8, 'ONLY THIS RECORD HAS ID=8');
INSERT INTO sh.MY_TEST (ID, NAME)
   VALUES (9, 'ONLY THIS RECORD HAS ID=9');
COMMIT;
```

4. Create an index on the `ID` field:

```
CREATE INDEX X1_MY_TEST ON MY_TEST (ID);
```

5. Query the `MY_TEST` table, to see the skewed data in the `ID` field:

```
SELECT ID, COUNT(*)
FROM sh.MY_TEST
GROUP BY ID ORDER BY 1;
```

6. Collect statistics and histograms on the `MY_TEST` table and the `ID` field:

```
EXEC DBMS_STATS.GATHER_TABLE_STATS (OWNNAME => 'SH', -
   TABNAME => 'MY_TEST', -
   ESTIMATE_PERCENT => 100, -
   METHOD_OPT => 'FOR COLUMNS SIZE 10 ID');
```

7. Query the histogram values to confirm that they reflect data distribution:

```
SELECT ENDPOINT_NUMBER, ENDPOINT_VALUE
FROM USER_TAB_HISTOGRAMS
WHERE TABLE_NAME = 'MY_TEST' AND COLUMN_NAME = 'ID'
ORDER BY 2;
```

8. Set the auto-trace feature and define a variable for binding:

```
SET AUTOT TRACE EXP
var aid number;
```

9. Query for records in MY_TEST where the value for ID equals 2, using bind variables:

```
exec :aid := 2;
SELECT * FROM sh.MY_TEST WHERE ID = :aid;
```

10. Query for records in MY_TEST where the value for ID equals 1, using bind variables:

```
exec :aid := 1;
SELECT * FROM sh.MY_TEST WHERE ID = :aid;
```

11. Query for records in MY_TEST where the value for ID equals 2, without bind variables:

```
SELECT * FROM sh.MY_TEST WHERE ID = 2;
```

12. Query for records in MY_TEST where the value for ID equals 1, without bind variables:

```
SELECT * FROM sh.MY_TEST WHERE ID = 1;
```

13. Stop the auto-trace:

```
SET AUTOT OFF
```

14. Connect as SYSDBA:

```
CONNECT / AS SYSDBA
```

15. Prepare the session for tracing:

```
ALTER SYSTEM SET TIMED_STATISTICS = TRUE;
ALTER SYSTEM SET MAX_DUMP_FILE_SIZE='100M';
ALTER SESSION SET SQL_TRACE=TRUE;
```

16. Execute the query in step 9:

```
var aid number;
exec :aid := 2;
SELECT * FROM sh.MY_TEST WHERE ID = :aid;
```

17. Execute the query in step 10:

```
exec :aid := 1;
SELECT * FROM sh.MY_TEST WHERE ID = :aid;
```

18. Stop tracing:

```
ALTER SESSION SET SQL_TRACE=FALSE;
```

19. Query for `SPID` to identify the generated trace file:

    ```
    SELECT s.sid, s.serial#, s.process, p.spid
    FROM v$session s, v$process p
    WHERE s.audsid = userenv('sessionid')
    AND s.paddr = p.addr;
    ```

20. Use `TKPROF` to format the trace file generated earlier in a text file:

    ```
    HOST
    cd /u01/app/diag/rdbms/testdb/TESTDB/trace/
    tkprof TESTDB_ora_2324.trc 2324.txt
    ```

21. Show the `TKPROF` report:

    ```
    vi 2324.txt
    ```

22. Clean the database:

    ```
    DROP TABLE sh.MY_TEST;
    ```

How it works...

In this recipe, from step 1 to step 3, we create a `MY_TEST` table containing more than 50000 rows. The values in the `ID` field are skewed, and the query executed in step 5 confirms this situation. The results are shown in the following screenshot:

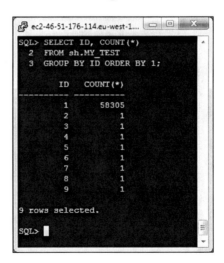

In step 4, we create an index on the `ID` field, and in step 6, we collect statistics for the `MY_TEST` table, generating histograms for the `ID` field with 10 buckets (more than the distinct values in the `ID` field). We compute the statistics on all the rows, as specified by the parameter `ESTIMATE_PERCENT`, set to 100.

In step 7, we get the histogram values from the data dictionary, as shown in the following screenshot:

In the steps that follow, we execute the same query over the MY_TEST table, verifying the execution plan when we change the ID value, for which we are querying, from 2 (only one record present in the table) to 1 (more than 50000 records).

In step 8, we define a bind variable, and in step 9, we set its value to 2. The corresponding execution plan, shown in the following screenshot, uses the index on the ID field, resulting in a quicker execution time:

In step 10, we change the parameter value to 1 and execute the same query again. In the following screenshot, we can see the output of this query:

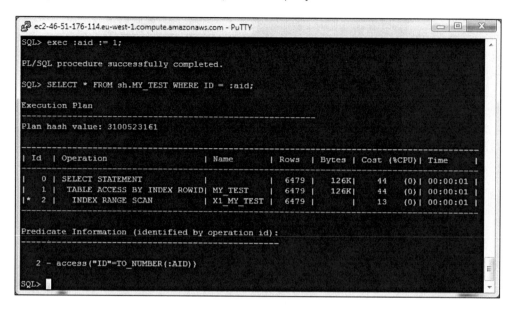

We can see that the execution plan hasn't changed, so we are accessing the table using the X1_MY_TEST index. This is not the fastest execution plan for this query, because we know that there are more than 50000 rows in the table (more than 99.99 percent of the total rows) that satisfy the query predicate; a full table scan is more efficient in such situations.

In step 11 and step 12, we execute the same queries as in step 9 and step 10, but without using the bind variable. When we query for value 2, we obtain the following execution plan that uses the same index as before:

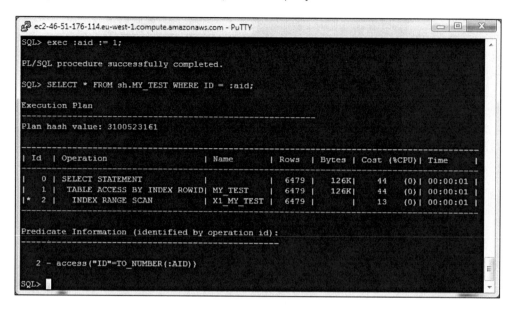

Instead, when we execute the query in step 12 (for records where the value for the ID field equals 1, without the use of bind variables), we obtain the following results:

```
ec2-46-51-176-114.eu-west-1.compute.amazonaws.com - PuTTY

SQL> SELECT * FROM sh.MY_TEST WHERE ID = 1;

Execution Plan
----------------------------------------------------------------
Plan hash value: 1615681525

----------------------------------------------------------------
| Id  | Operation          | Name    | Rows  | Bytes | Cost (%CPU)| Time     |
----------------------------------------------------------------
|   0 | SELECT STATEMENT   |         | 58305 | 1138K|    88   (0)| 00:00:02 |
|*  1 |  TABLE ACCESS FULL| MY_TEST | 58305 | 1138K|    88   (0)| 00:00:02 |
----------------------------------------------------------------

Predicate Information (identified by operation id):
----------------------------------------------------

   1 - filter("ID"=1)

SQL>
```

What happened? Without bind variables, we obtain a better execution plan, because the optimizer—thanks to statistics and histograms—knows that almost all records in the MY_TEST table have a value of 1 in the ID field, and therefore, that accessing the table with an index lookup would be a waste of time.

In previous recipes, we have repeatedly stated that not using bind variables is evil; in this situation, we have seen that not using bind variables gives us better performance.

To clarify the situation, let's examine the final part of the recipe. For a better understanding of what happens, we trace the execution of the queries. Therefore, in step 14, we connect as SYSDBA to the database, and in step 15, we prepare our session to generate a trace file.

In step 16, we execute the same query as in step 9, using bind variables; in step 17, we execute the query as in step 10. In step 18, we stop tracing.

In step 19, we query the data dictionary to know the SPID value of our session, to identify the trace file generated. In step 20, we call tkprof to format, in a human-readable text file, the result of the generated trace file. In our example, SPID has a value of 2324, as shown in the following screenshot, when we also invoke tkprof:

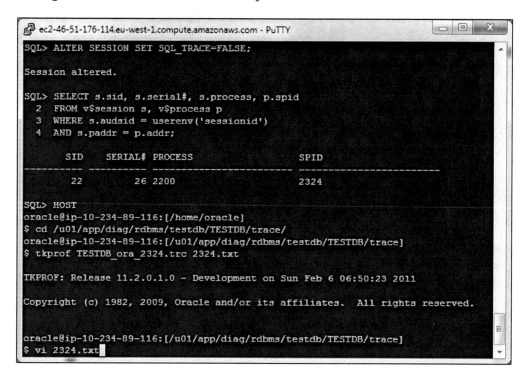

In the following screenshot, we can see an excerpt from the TKPROF output, which shows the execution plan for the query in step 16 (ID = 2):

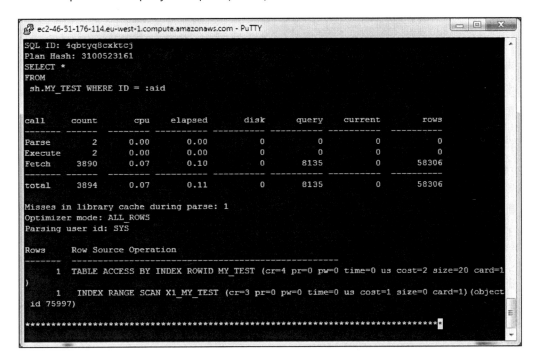

In the following screenshot, we can see an excerpt from the TKPROF output related to the query in step 17 (ID = 1):

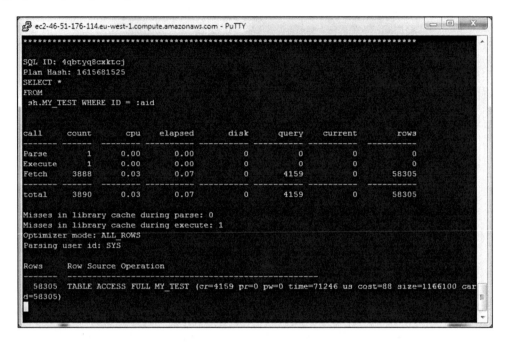

We can see that, regardless of the auto-trace results obtained earlier, TKPROF shows us the correct result. The optimizer has also chosen a different execution plan, when using bind variables, to obtain better performance using the index, when querying for an infrequent value. When the predicate discards only a few records of the table, a full table scan is used.

There's more...

Pre Oracle Database 10g, bind variables and histograms could not be used together. To use the histograms, the optimizer was required to know the actual value of the predicate and choose the appropriate execution plan for that particular value of the filter. To extend this feature in situations where both bind variables and histograms are used, the optimizer "peeks" the value used for bind variables the first time a statement is parsed—as if the user had used literals instead of bind variables—and the execution plan obtained is then used for subsequent executions of the same query.

However, this feature, called **Bind Variable Peeking**, can be disruptive in situations like the one in our example. When the statement was parsed, the actual value of the bind variable was 2, and for that particular case, the best choice was an index scan. Unfortunately, for the most part of the table, this isn't the best choice.

To avoid such a situation, where the execution plan depends upon the first value provided to bind variables, another feature was introduced in Oracle Database 11g, called **Adaptive Cursor Sharing**. This feature allows the optimizer to identify how an SQL statement can be satisfied by a different execution plan when different values for bind variables are used, as in our example.

> Adaptive Cursor Sharing is enabled by default. In **OnLine Transaction Processing** (**OLTP**) databases, there is often only one optimal execution plan, regardless of the actual value of binding variables. In this kind of database, we probably want to disable the Adaptive Cursor Sharing feature to eliminate the related overhead. To disable it, you need to set the CURSOR_SHARING initialization parameter to EXACT and the hidden _OPTIMIZER_EXTENDED_CURSOR_SHARING_REL initialization parameter to NONE, as follows:
>
> ALTER SYSTEM SET CURSOR_SHARING = EXACT SCOPE = BOTH;
>
> ALTER SYSTEM SET _OPTIMIZER_EXTENDED_CURSOR_ SHARING_REL = NONE SCOPE = BOTH;

With Adaptive Cursor Sharing multiple execution plans can be stored for a single SQL statement, resulting in the best plan for every value provided.

Please note that the SQL*Plus auto-trace feature is not aware of this situation, so the execution plan returned was the same. TKPROF, on the other hand, is more detailed and should be used whenever we want to seriously tune a statement or investigate what really happens under the hood.

See also

- For bind variables, see the *Using Bind Variables* recipe in *Chapter 4, Optimizing SQL Code*, and the *Using Bind Variables and Parsing* recipe in *Chapter 6, Optimizing PL/ SQL Code*

- For detailed information on the use of statistics to help the optimizer, see the *Collecting statistics* and *Using histograms* recipes in this chapter

- For details about using TKPROF, see the *Tracing SQL Activity* recipe in *Chapter 4, Optimizing SQL Code*

Creating SQL Tuning Sets

In this recipe, we will see how we can store a group of SQL statements along with their execution context and statistics, obtaining a so-called SQL Tuning Set.

Getting ready

To create a SQL Tuning Set, we need the `ADMINISTER SQL TUNING SET` privilege, so we grant this privilege to `SH` user, which will be used in this recipe.

```
CONNECT / AS SYSDBA
GRANT ADMINISTER SQL TUNING SET TO sh;
```

How to do it...

The following steps will demonstrate how to create and use SQL Tuning Sets:

1. Connect to `SH` schema:

    ```
    CONNECT sh@TESTDB/sh
    ```

2. Execute some queries to populate the cursor cache:

    ```
    SELECT CUST_FIRST_NAME, CUST_LAST_NAME, CUST_CITY
    FROM CUSTOMERS
    ORDER BY CUST_CITY;

    SELECT * FROM (
      SELECT
        CUST_ID, CUST_FIRST_NAME,
        CUST_LAST_NAME, CUST_YEAR_OF_BIRTH
      FROM CUSTOMERS
      ORDER BY CUST_YEAR_OF_BIRTH DESC
    )
    WHERE ROWNUM < 11;

    SELECT C.CUST_FIRST_NAME, C.CUST_LAST_NAME, N.COUNTRY_NAME
      FROM CUSTOMERS C, COUNTRIES N
      WHERE N.COUNTRY_ID BETWEEN C.COUNTRY_ID
        AND C.COUNTRY_ID + 10;

    SELECT AMOUNT_SOLD FROM sh.SALES S WHERE S.CUST_ID IN (
      SELECT C.CUST_ID FROM sh.CUSTOMERS C
      WHERE C.CUST_CREDIT_LIMIT IN (10000, 11000, 15000));

    SELECT prod_id, cust_id, time_id
    FROM sh.SALES
    ORDER BY amount_sold desc;
    ```

3. Create a tuning set named TEST_TUNING_SET:

```
BEGIN
  DBMS_SQLTUNE.CREATE_SQLSET(
    sqlset_name => 'test_tuning_set',
    description  => 'Demo tuning set');
END;
/
```

4. Load the TEST_TUNING_SET with the first five statements in cursor cache, ordered by elapsed time:

```
DECLARE
  sql_curs DBMS_SQLTUNE.SQLSET_CURSOR;
BEGIN
  OPEN sql_curs FOR
    SELECT VALUE(p)
      FROM TABLE (DBMS_SQLTUNE.SELECT_CURSOR_CACHE(
        RANKING_MEASURE1 => 'elapsed_time',
        RESULT_LIMIT => 5)) p;

  DBMS_SQLTUNE.LOAD_SQLSET(
    sqlset_name => 'test_tuning_set',
    populate_cursor => sql_curs);
END;
/
```

5. View the contents of the tuning set:

```
SELECT *
FROM TABLE(
  DBMS_SQLTUNE.SELECT_SQLSET('test_tuning_set', ''));
Clean the database—drop the tuning set and revoke privileges:
BEGIN
  DBMS_SQLTUNE.DROP_SQLSET(sqlset_name => 'test_tuning_set');
END;
/

CONNECT / AS SYSDBA
REVOKE ADMINISTER SQL TUNING SET FROM sh;
```

How it works...

In step 2, we simply execute some queries to populate the cursor cache (in this case we are in a single-user test environment).

In step 3, we create an SQL Tuning Set, by calling `test_tuning_set` and assigning a description to it. Then, in step 4, we populate the just-created tuning set, using the first five statements in the cursor cache, ordered by elapsed time. We can see the output in the following screenshot:

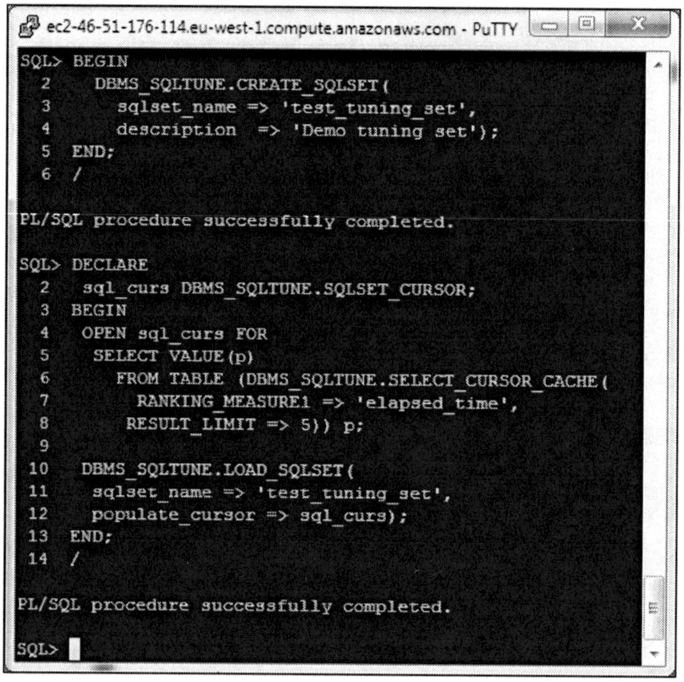

In step 5, we execute a query to view the statements that comprise our SQL Tuning Set, while in step 6, we drop the tuning set to clean the database, revoking the grant from the user SH.

There's more...

In this recipe, we have seen how to create an SQL Tuning Set, which can be used along with the SQL Tuning Advisor to tune a group of queries instead of a single query, or to create an SQL baseline.

We can load an SQL Tuning Set also from another tuning set, or from the Advanced Workload Repository. The SQL Tuning Set can be transported between different databases.

Defining the SQL Tuning Set helps in monitoring database performance after changes in configuration, for example, or to test in a separate database—transporting the tuning set to a different database—the effects of a change to a well-defined set of queries extracted from the typical workload.

See also

▸ The *Using the SQL Tuning Advisor* and *Configuring and using SQL Baselines* recipe in this chapter.

Using the SQL Tuning Advisor

In this recipe, we will see how to use the SQL Tuning Advisor to tune our queries.

Getting ready

To use the SQL Tuning Advisor, we need a special privilege; connect as SYSDBA and grant ADVISOR privilege to user SH:

```
CONNECT / AS SYSDBA
GRANT ADVISOR TO SH;
```

How to do it...

The following steps will demonstrate the SQL Tuning Advisor:

1. Connect to the SH schema:

   ```
   CONNECT sh@TESTDB/sh
   ```

2. Define an SQL Tuning Task for a single query:

   ```
   DECLARE
     l_task VARCHAR2(30);
     l_sql CLOB;
   BEGIN
     l_sql := 'SELECT AMOUNT_SOLD FROM sh.SALES S ' ||
       'WHERE S.CUST_ID IN ( '||
       'SELECT C.CUST_ID FROM sh.CUSTOMERS C ' ||
       'WHERE C.CUST_CREDIT_LIMIT IN (:l1, :l2, :l3))';
   ```

```
      l_task := DBMS_SQLTUNE.CREATE_TUNING_TASK(
       sql_text => l_sql,
       bind_list => sql_binds(anydata.ConvertNumber(10000),
         anydata.ConvertNumber(11000),
         anydata.ConvertNumber(15000)),
       user_name => 'SH',
       scope => 'COMPREHENSIVE',
       time_limit => 120,
       task_name => 'test_tuning_task',
       description => 'Specific SQL tuning');
      END;
      /
```

3. Execute the SQL Tuning Task just defined:

```
BEGIN
 DBMS_SQLTUNE.EXECUTE_TUNING_TASK(task_name => 'test_tuning_task');
END;
/
```

4. View the results of the tuning process:

```
SET LINESIZE 120
SET LONG 1000
SET LONGCHUNKSIZE 1000
SELECT DBMS_SQLTUNE.REPORT_TUNING_TASK('test_tuning_task')
FROM DUAL;
```

5. Drop the SQL Tuning Task and revoke grants from user SH:

```
EXEC DBMS_SQLTUNE.DROP_TUNING_TASK('test_tuning_task');
CONNECT / AS SYSDBA
REVOKE ADVISOR FROM SH;
```

How it works...

In step 2, we create an SQL Tuning Task, based on the following query:

```
SELECT AMOUNT_SOLD FROM sh.SALES S
WHERE S.CUST_ID IN (
 SELECT C.CUST_ID FROM sh.CUSTOMERS C
 WHERE C.CUST_CREDIT_LIMIT IN (:11, :12, :13)
)
```

We use the CREATE_TUNING_TASK procedure of the DBMS_SQLTUNE package, indicating—among other parameters—the SQL statement, the values for bind variables, and the task name and description.

In step 3, we execute the SQL Tuning Task just created, test_tuning_task, obtaining the following results:

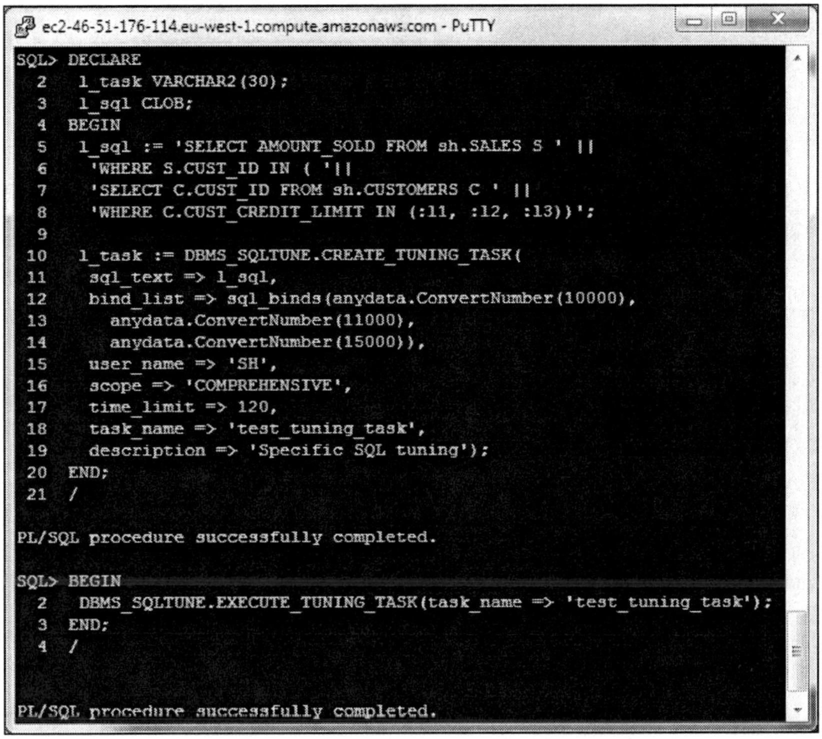

In step 4, we use the REPORT_TUNING_TASK function of the DBMS_SQLTUNE package to obtain the results of the tuning task execution.

In the following screenshot, we can see the report obtained in step 4, on a test environment, informing us that the optimizer statistics on the SALES_CUST_BIX bitmap index are stale. So, they need to be updated, in order to be sure that the execution plan of our query is optimal.

```
SQL> SELECT DBMS_SQLTUNE.REPORT_TUNING_TASK('test_tuning_task') FROM DUAL;

DBMS_SQLTUNE.REPORT_TUNING_TASK('TEST_TUNING_TASK')
-------------------------------------------------------------------------------
GENERAL INFORMATION SECTION
-------------------------------------------------------------------------------
Tuning Task Name       : test_tuning_task
Tuning Task Owner      : SH
Workload Type          : Single SQL Statement
Scope                  : COMPREHENSIVE
Time Limit(seconds)    : 120
Completion Status      : COMPLETED
Started at             : 02/06/2011 10:24:03
Completed at           : 02/06/2011 10:24:52


Schema Name: SH
SQL ID      : 3u0h1tb786wrt
SQL Text    : SELECT AMOUNT_SOLD FROM sh.SALES S WHERE S.CUST_ID IN ( SELECT
              C.CUST_ID FROM sh.CUSTOMERS C WHERE C.CUST_CREDIT_LIMIT IN (:11,
              :12, :13))

-------------------------------------------------------------------------------
FINDINGS SECTION (1 finding)
-------------------------------------------------------------------------------

1- Statistics Finding
---------------------
  Optimizer statistics for index "SH"."SALES_CUST_BIX" are stale.

  Recommend
```

In step 5, we clean the database by dropping the tuning task and revoking grants from the user SH.

There's more...

In this recipe, we have seen how to use SQL Tuning Advisor with a single SQL statement. The same tool can be executed over a single statement providing the sql_id, from the Automatic Workload Repository, or from an SQL Tuning Set. In the previous situation, we can use the following syntax to execute the SQL Tuning Advisor over the test_tuning_set SQL Tuning Set:

```
BEGIN
  DBMS_SQLTUNE.CREATE_TUNING_TASK( -
  sqlset_name => 'test_tuning_set', -
  rank1 => 'BUFFER_GETS', -
  time_limit => 3600, -
  description => 'Tuning a SQL Tuning Set');
END;
```

`test_tuning_set` is tuned ordered by buffer gets in the previous example.

We can query the view `USER_ADVISOR_TASK` to check the status of the task while it's running, or the view `V$ADVISOR_PROGRESS` to inspect the execution progress.

We can also interrupt a tuning task using the following procedure:

```
DBMS_SQLTUNE.INTERRUPT_TUNING_TASK( -
  task_name => 'test_tuning_set');
```

To resume an interrupted task, we have the following corresponding procedure:

```
DBMS_SQLTUNE.RESUME_TUNING_TASK( -
 task_name => 'test_tuning_set',
 basic_filter => NULL);
```

See also

> ▶ The *Creating SQL Tuning Sets* recipe in this chapter

Configuring and using SQL Baselines

We have seen the importance of execution plan stability in *Managing stored outlines*.

The disadvantage (by design) of using stored outlines is in the rigidity—we are sure that our execution plans don't change—so the performance doesn't deteriorate. However, due to schema or data changes, there could be a better execution plan. We are bound to our execution plan that is stored in the outlines, and we cannot benefit from the improvements.

SQL Plan Management with SQL Plan Baselines, a feature new to Oracle Database 11*g*, helps us in obtaining planning stability without losing the opportunity for performance improvements.

Getting ready

To create SQL Baselines we need the `ADMINISTER SQL MANAGEMENT OBJECT` privilege.

Connect as `SYSDBA` and grant permission to the user `SH`:

```
CONNECT / AS SYSDBA
GRANT ADMINISTER SQL MANAGEMENT OBJECT TO SH;
```

How to do it...

The following steps will show how to configure and use SQL Baselines:

1. Connect to the SH schema:

```
CONNECT sh@TESTDB/sh
```

2. Create a table MY_CUSTOMERS with some test data:

```
CREATE TABLE sh.MY_CUSTOMERS AS
  SELECT * FROM sh.CUSTOMERS NOLOGGING;
```

3. Obtain a column CUST_VALID containing skewed values (about 1 percent of rows contain value 'I', others containing value 'A'):

```
UPDATE sh.MY_CUSTOMERS SET CUST_VALID = 'I'
  WHERE CUST_VALID = 'A' AND MOD(CUST_ID,100) <> 0;
COMMIT;
```

4. Execute the query over the MY_CUSTOMERS data for which we want plan stability:

```
SELECT /* TEST */ COUNT(*) FROM sh.MY_CUSTOMERS
WHERE CUST_VALID = 'I';
```

Capture a baseline from the cursor cache for the previous query:

```
DECLARE
 l_sqlid VARCHAR2(13);
 l_plan PLS_INTEGER;
BEGIN
 SELECT SQL_ID INTO l_sqlid FROM V$SQL
  WHERE SQL_TEXT LIKE 'SELECT /* TEST */%';

 l_plan := dbms_spm.load_plans_from_cursor_cache(
  sql_id => l_sqlid);
END;
/
```

5. Create an index on the CUST_VALID field:

```
CREATE INDEX MY_CUSTOMERS_IX1 ON sh.MY_CUSTOMERS (CUST_VALID);
```

6. Execute the same query in step 4:

```
SELECT /* TEST */ COUNT(*) FROM sh.MY_CUSTOMERS
WHERE CUST_VALID = 'I';
```

7. Query the data dictionary to see if there are execution plans that are not yet accepted:

```
SELECT
   SQL_HANDLE, PLAN_NAME, ENABLED, ACCEPTED, FIXED
FROM DBA_SQL_PLAN_BASELINES;
Evolve the baseline with the new execution plan:
SET SERVEROUTPUT ON
SET LONG 10000
DECLARE
  l_report CLOB;
BEGIN
  l_report := DBMS_SPM.EVOLVE_SQL_PLAN_BASELINE(
     sql_handle => 'SYS_SQL_e6bd1707937cb2ca');
  DBMS_OUTPUT.PUT_LINE(l_report);
END;
/
```

8. Clean the database:

```
DECLARE
  l_plan pls_integer;
BEGIN
  l_plan := DBMS_SPM.DROP_SQL_PLAN_BASELINE( -
    sql_handle => 'SYS_SQL_e6bd1707937cb2ca');
END;
/
DROP TABLE sh.MY_CUSTOMERS;

CONNECT / AS SYSDBA
REVOKE ADMINISTER SQL MANAGEMENT OBJECT FROM SH;
```

How it works...

From step 1 to step 3, we create a table MY_CUSTOMERS to test SQL Baselines.

In step 4, we execute a query on the table to retrieve the invalid customers. We inserted a comment inside the query to easily identify it later.

In step 5, we retrieve the SQL_ID of the query executed in the preceding step and create a SQL Baseline using the procedure LOAD_PLANS_FROM_CURSOR_CACHE of the package DBMS_SPM, using SQL_ID. We can see the results of this operation in the following screenshot:

In step 6, we create an index over the CUST_VALID field, so accessing the MY_CUSTOMERS table using this index may be faster than a full table scan.

In step 7, we execute the same query as in step 4. The optimizer uses the execution plan stored in the SQL Baseline but elaborates a new execution plan and stores it in a **NOT ACCEPTED** state, as we can see when executing the query in step 8.

In step 9, we decide to **evolve our SQL Baseline**, executing the procedure EVOLVE_SQL_PLAN_BASELINE of the DBMS_SPM package, as we can see in the following screenshot:

The EVOLVE_SQL_PLAN_BASELINE procedure returns a report, from which we can see if the newly-generated execution plan passes the performance criterion. In other words, if it performs better (comparing the compound improvement ratio) than the previous baseline, it can be accepted.

The results of this operation can be seen in the following screenshot, which presents the results obtained evolving our baseline. As we can see, the results with the new execution plan are better than the previous baseline, so the execution plan is accepted:

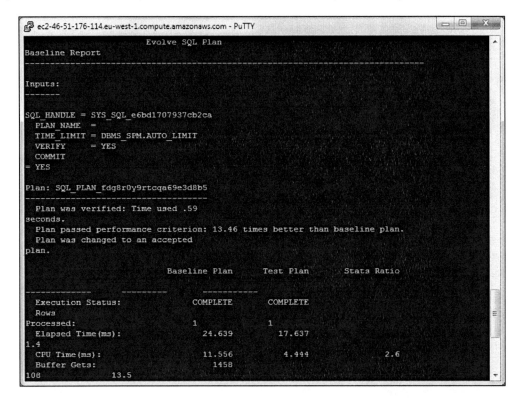

In step 10, we drop the baseline, accessing by SQL_HANDLE, then drop the MY_CUSTOMERS table and revoke the grant from user SH.

There's more...

We can also create a baseline using the snapshots taken from Automatic Workload Repository or using an SQL Tuning Set. In this case, we execute the following statement, to create a baseline from `test_tuning_set` (as created in the *Creating SQL Tuning Sets* recipe):

```
DECLARE
 l_plan pls_integer;
BEGIN
 l_plan := DBMS_SPM.LOAD_PLANS_FROM_SQLSET(
    sqlset_name => 'test_tuning_set');
END;
/
```

To control the SQL Plan Management there are two parameters:

- ► `OPTIMIZER_CAPTURE_SQL_PLAN_BASELINES`: If set to `TRUE`, automatic capturing of SQL Plans is enabled; the default value is `FALSE`
- ► `OPTIMIZER_USE_SQL_PLAN_BASELINES`: If set to `TRUE`, SQL Plan Management is enabled; this parameter is enabled by default

When we manually capture SQL Plans, the resulting plan is marked as accepted. However, when the plans are automatically captured, we need to perform the evolving SQL Plan baseline process, using the `DBMS_SPM.evolve_sql_plan_baseline` function.

By launching this function (it needs only one parameter, the `sql_handle` of the statement, which we can get from the `DBA_SQL_PLAN_BASELINES` view), the optimizer will determine if non-accepted plans in the baseline should be accepted. The function returns a CLOB containing a complete report of the results.

See also

- ► The *Managing stored outlines*, *Creating SQL Tuning Sets*, and *Using Tuning Advisor* recipes in this chapter

8
Other Optimizations

In this chapter, we will cover:

- ▶ Caching results with the client-side result cache
- ▶ Enabling parallel SQL
- ▶ Direct path inserting
- ▶ Using create table as select
- ▶ Inspecting indexes and triggers overhead
- ▶ Loading data with SQL*Loader and Data Pump

Introduction

In this chapter we will look at optimizations related to both queries and DML operations.

The first two recipes will show some features that can speed up a query; the following four recipes are focused on different techniques useful to load data in the database, from external sources and from other tables inside the database.

We will also focus on the overhead introduced by indexes and triggers. We have seen in past recipes that using indexes can speed up our queries, resulting in faster execution. However, in the recipes of this chapter, we will see how over-indexing a table can lead to poor DML performance.

About loading data, we will see how to use the SQL Loader and Data Pump to load our data faster. Direct path inserting and creating table using select will help us to populate some tables using data already available in the database.

Caching results with the client-side result cache

In this recipe we will see how to enable and use the client-side result cache to reach significant improvement in repeatedly executing complex queries.

Getting ready

To enable the client result cache feature in a database, we need to alter the CLIENT_RESULT_CACHE_SIZE parameter and set a size for caching larger than zero (the default value). This parameter specifies the size in bytes used by all the client processes as the maximum size of the client per-process result set cache.

To do so we need to execute the following commands, querying for the actual value of the parameter:

```
CONNNECT / AS SYSDBA
SHOW PARAMETER CLIENT_RESULT_CACHE_SIZE
```

If we need to alter the size, because it is set to zero, or if we want to change the actual size—we can use the following commands. Once we set the size for the client result cache to 5 MB, we restart the instance to enable the modifications:

```
ALTER SYSTEM SET CLIENT_RESULT_CACHE_SIZE=5M SCOPE=SPFILE;
SHUTDOWN IMMEDIATE
STARTUP OPEN
```

We are now ready to experiment with the client side result cache.

How to do it...

The following steps will demonstrate the client-side result cache:

1. Connect to the SH schema:

   ```
   CONNECT sh@TESTDB/sh
   ```

2. Enable the automatic explain plan and execute a query that joins CUSTOMERS and COUNTRIES tables:

   ```
   SET AUTOT TRACE EXP
   SELECT COUNTRY_NAME, CUST_LAST_NAME, COUNT(*)
   FROM CUSTOMERS C, COUNTRIES CT
   WHERE C.COUNTRY_ID = CT.COUNTRY_ID
   GROUP BY COUNTRY_NAME, CUST_LAST_NAME;
   ```

3. Enable the use of the result cache using a hint and execute the same query as in the previous step:

```
SELECT /*+ result_cache */
    COUNTRY_NAME, CUST_LAST_NAME, COUNT(*)
FROM CUSTOMERS C, COUNTRIES CT
WHERE C.COUNTRY_ID = CT.COUNTRY_ID
GROUP BY COUNTRY_NAME, CUST_LAST_NAME;
SET AUTOT OFF
```

How it works...

In step 2 we have executed a simple join query. The execution plan is represented in the following screenshot:

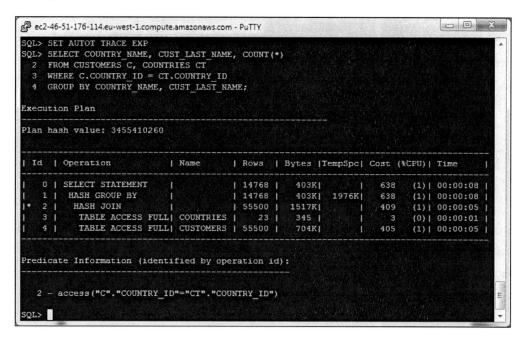

In step 3, we have used a specific hint `result_cache` to use the result cache (both client-side and server-side).

We can see in the next screenshot, the change in the execution plan for the same query mentioned above. However, to enable this behavior we have defined a size (greater than zero) for the `CLIENT_RESULT_CACHE_SIZE` parameter. In the next section we will see how to obtain the same behavior in a different way than just using hints in our queries.

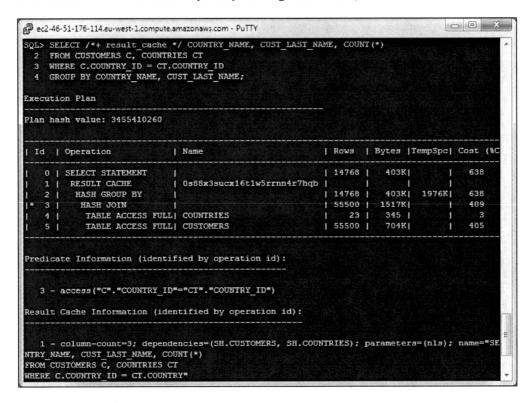

There's more...

We can enable client-side result cache in three different ways:

1. Using hints as in step 3 of our recipe.

2. Enabling the result cache at a session (or system) level:

    ```
    ALTER SESSION SET RESULT_CACHE_MODE = FORCE;
    ```

3. With table annotation, we can instruct the database to use the result cache for the queries against specific tables, using the following statement:

    ```
    ALTER TABLE CUSTOMERS RESULT_CACHE (MODE FORCE);
    ```

There are also two initialization parameters to take care of: RESULT_CACHE_MAX_SIZE, set to zero to disable the server-side cache and CLIENT_RESULT_CACHE_SIZE, set to a value greater than or equal to 32K to enable the client-side cache.

In the above statements, we have used the FORCE mode, which always enables the client-side result cache, except when the no_result_cache hint is specified in the query.

 Please note that table annotation takes precedence over session or system-wide settings.

The client-side result cache enables applications that use the **Oracle Call Interface** (**OCI**) to connect to the database to cache result sets on the client side. Memory will probably be less expensive on the client side than on the server side and it assures more locality by reusing the same query. This is more likely to happen on the same client with the same application. So caching on the client side results in a higher probability to find the data we need already in memory than when caching on the server side. Round-trips to the server are also avoided when the query can be answered using the client result cache.

Client-side result cache is always kept consistent with server data and metadata, eliminating the need for each application that uses OCI to implement its own custom caching mechanism.

 The client-side result cache is different from the server result cache. It's available from version 11.1 upward of OCI client libraries, connected to an Oracle database 11gR1 or above.

Configuring the client-side result cache

An important parameter in setting the client-side result cache is CLIENT_RESULT_CACHE_LAG.

This parameter allow us to define the number of milliseconds elapsed before flushing the cache. For example, if we set this parameter to 10000, as follows:

```
ALTER SYSTEM SET CLIENT_RESULT_CACHE_LAG=10000 SCOPE=SPFILE;
```

The client result cache can lag 10 seconds behind any changes in the database that affect its result sets.

Due to its static nature, this parameter needs to be set in the SPFILE and will be effective after the instance restarts.

See also

▸ The *Taking advantage of function result cache* recipe in *Chapter 6, Optimizing PL/ SQL Code*, to see the result cache applied in enhancing functions performance

Enabling parallel SQL

In the recent past, we have seen the passage from the megahertz era to the multi-core era in microprocessor design. Even laptops and small devices have multi-core CPUs available that can take advantage of applications accomplishing work in parallel.

In this recipe we will see how to enable parallel execution of queries to speed them up.

Getting ready

To observe a performance gain in this recipe, we obviously need a machine with a minimum of two cores. A single-core machine, using parallel SQL execution leads to a dip in performance when compared to using normal sequential execution.

How to do it...

In this recipe, we will use a query that returns about 1 million records. To avoid displaying this huge amount of data in our terminal, we will need to copy the code in a SQL script file, naming it TEST.SQL, for example, and then execute it using the @ operator from SQL*Plus:

```
@TEST.SQL
```

For clarity, the content of the script is split into the following steps:

1. Connect to the database as SYSDBA:

   ```
   CONNECT / AS SYSDBA
   ```

2. Empty the buffers from previous executions to be sure no data is already cached in memory:

   ```
   ALTER SYSTEM FLUSH BUFFER_CACHE;
   ```

3. Display the current date/time:

   ```
   SELECT TO_CHAR(SYSDATE,'YYYYMMDD_HH24MISS') TIMECOL FROM DUAL;
   ```

4. Disable the output to terminal and spool on the NULL device:

   ```
   SET TERMOUT OFF
   SPOOL /DEV/NULL
   ```

5. Execute a long query:

   ```
   SELECT
       S.PROD_ID, S.CUST_ID, S.TIME_ID
   FROM SH.SALES S
   ORDER BY S.AMOUNT_SOLD DESC;
   ```

6. Disable spooling:

   ```
   SPOOL OFF
   SET TERMOUT ON
   ```

7. Display the current date/time:

   ```
   SELECT TO_CHAR(SYSDATE,'YYYYMMDD_HH24MISS') TIMECOL FROM DUAL;
   ```

8. Empty the buffers from previous executions to be sure no data is already cached in memory:

   ```
   ALTER SYSTEM FLUSH BUFFER_CACHE;
   ```

9. Display the current date/time:

   ```
   SELECT TO_CHAR(SYSDATE,'YYYYMMDD_HH24MISS') TIMECOL FROM DUAL;
   ```

10. Disable output to terminal and spool on the NULL device:

    ```
    SET TERMOUT OFF
    SPOOL /DEV/NULL
    ```

11. Execute the same query in step 5 using a hint to use parallel SQL execution:

    ```
    SELECT /*+ PARALLEL (S, 2) */
       S.PROD_ID, S.CUST_ID, S.TIME_ID
    FROM SH.SALES S
    ORDER BY S.AMOUNT_SOLD DESC;
    ```

12. Disable spooling:

    ```
    SPOOL OFF
    SET TERMOUT ON
    ```

13. Display the current date/time:

    ```
    SELECT TO_CHAR(SYSDATE,'YYYYMMDD_HH24MISS') TIMECOL FROM DUAL;
    ```

How it works...

The script used in this recipe is made of two identical parts. In each part we initially flush the buffer cache to be sure that there are no data blocks in memory cached from previous executions of the same query.

We then enable the spool to a NULL device and we disable the terminal output to avoid viewing the rows returned from our query.

We need to focus on steps 5 and 11. In step 5 we execute the query in normal sequential steps, while in step 11 we add the /*+ PARALLEL (S, 2) */ hint. This hint requests parallel execution, using 2 processes/threads, on table S (the alias used for the SALES table in our query).

In the following screenshot we can see the results of this script executed in a single CPU core environment:

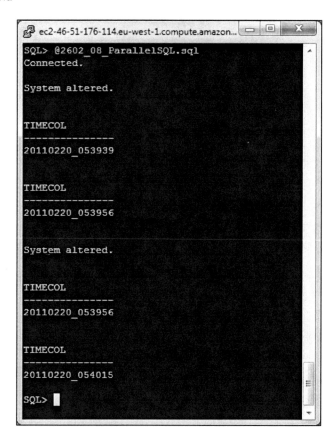

We can see, from the timestamp shown, that the execution time was about 17 seconds without the parallel hint and about 19 when using the parallel hint.

In the following screenshot we can see the results obtained executing the same script on a machine with a dual-core CPU:

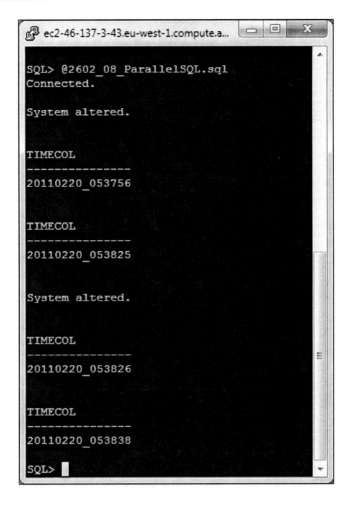

The execution time was about 29 seconds with the original query in step 5 and about 12 seconds using the parallel hint with the query in step 11.

 Please note that the results obtained in the previous screenshots on the single core and dual core machines cannot be used as a benchmark because they were obtained on two different machines.

There's more...

In the example there is a huge improvement in performance when using parallel queries on a machine with more than one CPU/core.

The hint in step 11 query suggests, to the database engine, the use of **degree of parallelism** of two. There will be two parallel processing streams, but the number of processes (or threads) involved will be probably more than two. This is because more steps are involved in answering the query (fetching data, sorting, returning results to the client).

To answer parallel requests there is a pool of parallel processes, which can range between PARALLEL_MIN_SERVERS and PARALLEL_MAX_SERVERS parameters.

If a request for a query (with a degree of parallelism that exceeds the number of parallel processes available in the pool) arrives, the request may be executed with a lower degree of parallelism—or even serially. From Oracle Database 11gR2, the request may be delayed until a sufficient number of parallel processes will be available.

Starting Oracle Database 11g, when setting the parameter PARALLEL_DEGREE_POLICY to AUTO, the degree of parallelism is automatically determined by the database, depending on the size of the objects involved in the query and the available resources. Setting this parameter is recommended only in data warehouse environments.

Parallel query and I/O

We have seen how simple it is to request the parallel execution of a query. However, the benefits of parallel SQL execution can be observed only when there is sufficient I/O throughput and a reduced contention on I/O devices. For some systems it also depends on network bandwidth. If we have a 16 core CPU and only one disk, and we use a degree of parallelism of 16, then we expect a dip in performance due to contention on disk segments. In such situations it's important that the accessed segments are spread on multiple disks to obtain maximum performance from parallel SQL execution.

When to use parallel SQL

Using a parallel SQL isn't always a good idea. In OLTP environments parallel executions cause too many locks and consume more resources—limiting the scalability of the application. Moreover, these systems are often very well used because there are many concurrent sessions working, so the parallelism is in use by multiple concurrent transactions.

As a rule of thumb, it's better to use parallel SQL for long running queries (batch working, reporting). For short-lived ones, the overhead needed to coordinate the parallel slave processes frustrates the performance gain obtained from parallel execution.

See also

▶ The *Disk Tuning and Strategies to distribute Oracle files* and *Object striping* recipes in *Chapter 10, Tuning I/O*, analyze useful techniques to avoid I/O bottlenecks and to get maximum advantage from parallel SQL execution

Direct path inserting

In this recipe we will see how to insert many rows in a table using a particular INSERT statement to boost performance.

How to do it...

The following steps demonstrates multiple row insertions in the same INSERT statement:

1. Connect to the SH schema:

    ```
    CONNECT sh@TESTDB/sh
    ```

2. Create an empty table MY_SALES with the SALES table structure:

    ```
    CREATE TABLE MY_SALES AS SELECT * FROM SALES WHERE ROWNUM < 1;
    ```

3. Insert all the rows from SALES table in the newly-created table:

    ```
    SET TIMING ON
    INSERT INTO MY_SALES SELECT * FROM SALES;
    COMMIT;
    SET TIMING OFF
    ```

4. Empty the MY_SALES table:

    ```
    TRUNCATE TABLE MY_SALES;
    ```

5. Insert all of the rows from the SALES table in the newly-created table using direct path inserting:

    ```
    SET TIMING ON
    INSERT /*+ APPEND */ INTO MY_SALES SELECT * FROM SALES;
    COMMIT;
    SET TIMING OFF
    ```

6. Show the execution plan for classical `INSERT` statement:

```
EXPLAIN PLAN FOR INSERT INTO MY_SALES SELECT * FROM SALES;
SELECT * FROM TABLE(
    DBMS_XPLAN.DISPLAY(null,null,'TYPICAL -BYTES'));
```

7. Show the execution plan for direct path insert statement:

```
EXPLAIN PLAN FOR INSERT /*+ APPEND */ INTO MY_SALES
    SELECT * FROM SALES;
SELECT * FROM TABLE(
    DBMS_XPLAN.DISPLAY(null,null,'TYPICAL -BYTES'));
```

8. Clean the database:

```
DROP TABLE MY_SALES;
```

How it works...

In step 2 we create a table `MY_SALES` with the same structure as the `SALES` table in the `SH` schema. In step 3 we execute an `INSERT` into the `MY_SALES` table, populating it with all of the rows in the `SALES` table (about 1 million rows). In the following screenshot we can see the results obtained:

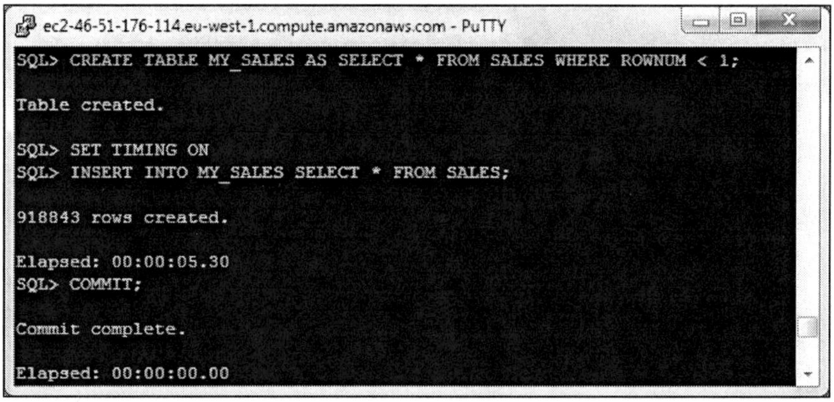

In step 4 we truncate the `MY_SALES` table, and then execute the same `INSERT` statement as above, using the `/*+ APPEND */` hint, forcing the database to use direct path insertion to execute the statement.

In the following screenshot we can see the results obtained:

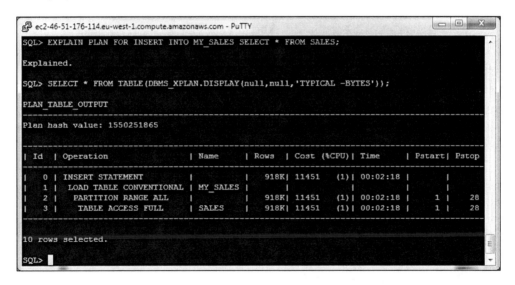

We can see that the execution time for the INSERT statement is **2.46** seconds instead of **5.30** as in step 3.

Let's observe the difference in the execution plans. The following screenshot shows the plan from step 6, related to the classical insert statement:

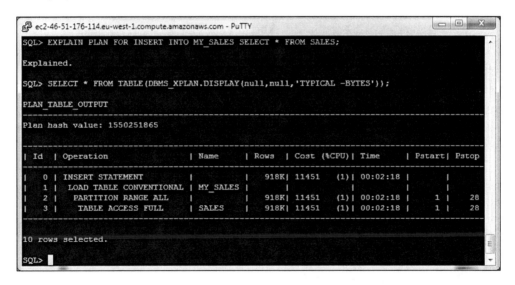

We can see that the statement uses LOAD TABLE CONVENTIONAL step to fill the MY_SALES table with data obtained from a FULL TABLE ACCESS of SALES table.

The following screenshot, instead, represents the execution plan for the INSERT in step 5, obtained with the statement in step 7:

We can see the change in the execution plan as a result of using the LOAD AS SELECT step to populate the data in the MY_SALES table; this is responsible for the speed-up measured above.

In step 8 we drop the MY_SALES table to clean the database schema.

There's more...

Direct path loading can be easily integrated in our INSERT statement using a simple hint. Let's see the magic behind this hint, which gave us an improvement in performance of about 50 percent.

The main difference between conventional and direct path loading is in the way the statement is executed. Conventional path loading uses the standard transactional SQL engine, so the rows are inserted in database blocks with free space in the buffer cache and the block is then asynchronously written to the disk by the database writer process. The available blocks below the High-Water Mark are used, using the space available in the table free-lists.

Direct path loading completely bypasses the transactional SQL engine. Data is composed in database blocks, which are directly written on the disk above the High-Water Mark. Free-lists and buffer cache are not used, and the transaction isn't recoverable, because only minimal redo log entries are generated.

However, there are some issues in using direct path loading; the table isn't accessible by other SQL within the same transaction. Other sessions can access the table on which an exclusive lock is held—DML activities are queued during the execution of the direct path loading.

Another issue can arise when using direct path insert—remember that conventional load inserts data in memory—and only the redo log is written to the disk on commit. The database writer works asynchronously and the direct path insert writes directly to the disk blocks. Hence, if I/O is a bottleneck in the database, direct path inserts could be slower than the conventional load counterpart.

See also

> ▶ The *Using create table as select* and *Loading data with SQL*Loader and Data Pump* recipes in this chapter

Using create table as select

In this recipe we will see how to create a table as the result of a selection from other tables or views in the database.

How to do it...

The following steps demonstrate how to use use selection to create a table:

1. Connect to the SH schema:

   ```
   CONNECT sh@TESTDB/sh
   ```

2. Create the empty table MY_SALES, and copy the SALES table structure:

   ```
   CREATE TABLE MY_SALES AS SELECT * FROM SALES WHERE ROWNUM < 1;
   ```

4. Insert all the rows from the SALES table into MY_SALES using direct path inserting :

   ```
   SET TIMING ON
   INSERT /*+ APPEND */ INTO MY_SALES SELECT * FROM SALES;
   SET TIMING OFF
   ```

5. Drop the MY_SALES table:

   ```
   DROP TABLE MY_SALES;
   ```

6. Create table MY_SALES as a selection from SALES table:

   ```
   SET TIMING ON
   CREATE TABLE MY_SALES AS SELECT * FROM SALES;
   SET TIMING OFF
   ```

7. Inspect the execution plan for the `INSERT` statement in step 3:

```
EXPLAIN PLAN FOR
 INSERT /*+ APPEND */ INTO MY_SALES
 SELECT * FROM SALES;
SELECT * FROM TABLE(
 DBMS_XPLAN.DISPLAY(null,null,'TYPICAL -BYTES'));
```

8. Drop the `MY_SALES` table:

```
DROP TABLE MY_SALES;
```

9. Inspect the execution plan for the `CREATE TABLE AS SELECT` statement in step 5:

```
EXPLAIN PLAN FOR
 CREATE TABLE MY_SALES AS SELECT * FROM SALES;
SELECT * FROM TABLE(
 DBMS_XPLAN.DISPLAY(null,null,'TYPICAL -BYTES'));
```

How it works...

In step 2 we create an empty table with the same structure as the `SALES` table and in step 3 we populate the newly-created `MY_SALES` table with all the rows of the `SALES` table.

We can see the results of this operation in the following screenshot:

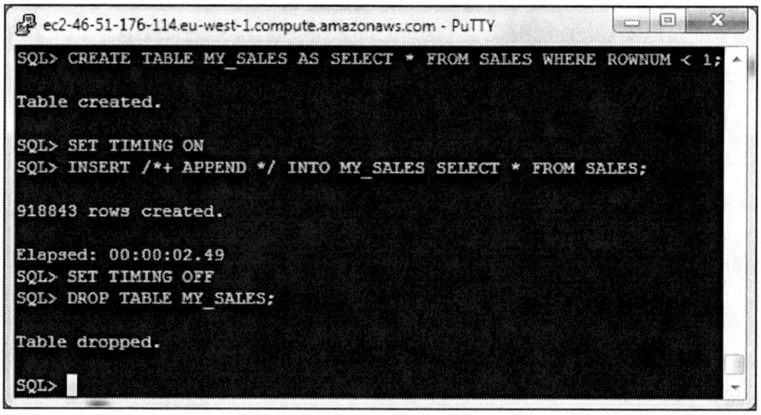

In step 4 we drop the `MY_SALES` table and recreate and populate it from the `SALES` table at the same time, using a `CREATE TABLE AS SELECT` statement in step 5.

In the following screenshot we can see the corresponding results:

We can see that the elapsed time is less in the `CREATE TABLE` when using the select statement rather than in the direct path loading insert.

In step 6 we inquire about the execution plan for the direct path insert statement in step 3. In the following screenshot you can see this execution plan:

```
SQL> EXPLAIN PLAN FOR INSERT /*+ APPEND */ INTO MY_SALES SELECT * FROM SALES;

Explained.

SQL> SELECT * FROM TABLE(DBMS_XPLAN.DISPLAY(null,null,'TYPICAL -BYTES'));

PLAN_TABLE_OUTPUT
---------------------------------------------------------------------------------
Plan hash value: 1315042658

---------------------------------------------------------------------------------
| Id  | Operation             | Name     | Rows  | Cost (%CPU)| Time     | Pstart| Pstop |
---------------------------------------------------------------------------------
|   0 | INSERT STATEMENT      |          |  918K| 11451     (1)| 00:02:18 |       |       |
|   1 |  LOAD AS SELECT       | MY_SALES |       |           |          |       |       |
|   2 |   PARTITION RANGE ALL |          |  918K| 11451     (1)| 00:02:18 |     1 |    28 |
|   3 |    TABLE ACCESS FULL  | SALES    |  918K| 11451     (1)| 00:02:18 |     1 |    28 |
---------------------------------------------------------------------------------

10 rows selected.

SQL>
```

In step 8 we retrieve the execution plan for the CREATE TABLE AS SELECT statement, and the corresponding result can be seen in the following screenshot:

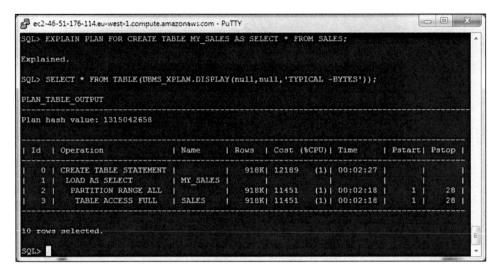

We can see that the execution plans related to both operations are identical in what concerns the load statement—they access the same rows in the same way. They differ only in the first part—the INSERT statement in the first case, the CREATE TABLE in the latter.

There's more...

We can use the CREATE TABLE AS SELECT statement to obtain a copy of a table, eventually filtering out some records that we don't want to keep in the table.

To further increase the performance of the CREATE TABLE AS SELECT statement, we can use the NOLOGGING and/or PARALLEL clause. The NOLOGGING clause doesn't write redo log entries for the operation, which is unrecoverable due to this behavior. The PARALLEL clause enables the database to use multiple parallel slave processes to execute the statement.

 Please note that using NOLOGGING can break other processes like Streams, Physical StandBy Databases, and GoldenGate among others. You need to consider all these implications when planning to use this clause in a production environment.

A typical use of this query is consolidating historic data or deleting them. If we want to delete a large amount of data from a table, it's better to create a new table by selecting the relevant record to keep in the table, truncating the old table, and then renaming the new table as the old one.

▶ The *Direct path inserting* and *Enabling parallel SQL* recipes earlier in this chapter

Inspecting indexes and triggers overhead

In this recipe we will see the overhead introduced by indexes and triggers on DML operations. We will explore alternative ways to implement calculated fields using virtual columns instead of triggers.

How to do it...

The following steps will demonstrate the index and trigger overheads:

1. Connect to the SH schema:

   ```
   CONNECT sh@TESTDB/sh
   ```

2. Create an empty table MY_CUSTOMERS, copying the CUSTOMERS table structure:

   ```
   CREATE TABLE MY_CUSTOMERS AS
     SELECT * FROM CUSTOMERS WHERE ROWNUM < 1;
   ```

3. Insert all of the records from CUSTOMERS to MY_CUSTOMERS, measuring time:

   ```
   SET TIMING ON
   INSERT INTO MY_CUSTOMERS SELECT * FROM CUSTOMERS;
   SET TIMING OFF
   ```

4. Truncate the MY_CUSTOMERS table:

   ```
   TRUNCATE TABLE MY_CUSTOMERS;
   ```

5. Add a unique index and three B-tree indexes on the MY_CUSTOMERS table:

   ```
   CREATE UNIQUE INDEX IX1_MY_CUSTOMERS
     ON MY_CUSTOMERS (CUST_ID);
   CREATE INDEX IX2_MY_CUSTOMERS
     ON MY_CUSTOMERS (CUST_LAST_NAME, CUST_FIRST_NAME);
   CREATE INDEX IX3_MY_CUSTOMERS
     ON MY_CUSTOMERS (COUNTRY_ID);
   CREATE INDEX IX4_MY_CUSTOMERS
     ON MY_CUSTOMERS (CUST_STREET_ADDRESS, CUST_POSTAL_CODE,
       CUST_CITY, CUST_STATE_PROVINCE);
   ```

6. Execute the same insert statement as in step 3 with the indexes in place, measuring elapsed time:

```
SET TIMING ON
INSERT INTO MY_CUSTOMERS SELECT * FROM CUSTOMERS;
SET TIMING OFF
```

7. Truncate the MY_CUSTOMERS table and drop indexes:

```
TRUNCATE TABLE MY_CUSTOMERS;
DROP INDEX IX1_MY_CUSTOMERS;
DROP INDEX IX2_MY_CUSTOMERS;
DROP INDEX IX3_MY_CUSTOMERS;
DROP INDEX IX4_MY_CUSTOMERS;
```

8. Add a MAX_CREDIT field to the MY_CUSTOMERS table:

```
ALTER TABLE MY_CUSTOMERS ADD MAX_CREDIT NUMBER;
```

9. Create a trigger on the MY_CUSTOMERS table to calculate the MAX_CREDIT value when inserting and updating records on MY_CUSTOMERS:

```
CREATE OR REPLACE TRIGGER TR_MY_CUSTOMERS_BINS
  BEFORE INSERT OR UPDATE ON MY_CUSTOMERS
  FOR EACH ROW
BEGIN
  IF ((:NEW.CUST_GENDER = 'M')
   AND (:NEW.CUST_YEAR_OF_BIRTH > 1975)) THEN
     :NEW.MAX_CREDIT := :NEW.CUST_CREDIT_LIMIT * 0.95;
  ELSE
     :NEW.MAX_CREDIT := :NEW.CUST_CREDIT_LIMIT * 1.05;
  END IF;
END;
/
```

10. Insert records in the MY_CUSTOMERS table, measuring elapsed time:

```
SET TIMING ON
INSERT INTO MY_CUSTOMERS (
  CUST_ID, CUST_FIRST_NAME, CUST_LAST_NAME,
  CUST_GENDER, CUST_YEAR_OF_BIRTH, CUST_MARITAL_STATUS,
  CUST_STREET_ADDRESS, CUST_POSTAL_CODE, CUST_CITY,
  CUST_CITY_ID, CUST_STATE_PROVINCE, CUST_STATE_PROVINCE_ID,
```

```
COUNTRY_ID, CUST_MAIN_PHONE_NUMBER, CUST_INCOME_LEVEL,
CUST_CREDIT_LIMIT, CUST_EMAIL, CUST_TOTAL, CUST_TOTAL_ID,
CUST_SRC_ID, CUST_EFF_FROM, CUST_EFF_TO, CUST_VALID)
SELECT CUST_ID, CUST_FIRST_NAME, CUST_LAST_NAME,
CUST_GENDER, CUST_YEAR_OF_BIRTH, CUST_MARITAL_STATUS,
CUST_STREET_ADDRESS, CUST_POSTAL_CODE, CUST_CITY,
CUST_CITY_ID, CUST_STATE_PROVINCE, CUST_STATE_PROVINCE_ID,
COUNTRY_ID, CUST_MAIN_PHONE_NUMBER, CUST_INCOME_LEVEL,
CUST_CREDIT_LIMIT, CUST_EMAIL, CUST_TOTAL, CUST_TOTAL_ID,
CUST_SRC_ID, CUST_EFF_FROM, CUST_EFF_TO, CUST_VALID
FROM CUSTOMERS;
SET TIMING OFF
```

11. Drop the trigger and the MAX_CREDIT column from the MY_CUSTOMERS table and truncate the table to empty data:

```
TRUNCATE TABLE MY_CUSTOMERS;
DROP TRIGGER TR_MY_CUSTOMERS_BINS;
ALTER TABLE MY_CUSTOMERS DROP COLUMN MAX_CREDIT;
```

12. Recreate the MAX_CREDIT field as a virtual column, reproducing the same effect as the previous trigger:

```
ALTER TABLE MY_CUSTOMERS ADD MAX_CREDIT AS (CASE
    WHEN CUST_GENDER = 'M' AND CUST_YEAR_OF_BIRTH > 1975 THEN
      CUST_CREDIT_LIMIT * 0.95
    ELSE CUST_CREDIT_LIMIT * 1.05
END);
```

13. Execute the same insert as in step 10, measuring elapsed time:

```
SET TIMING ON
INSERT INTO MY_CUSTOMERS (
 CUST_ID, CUST_FIRST_NAME, CUST_LAST_NAME,
 CUST_GENDER, CUST_YEAR_OF_BIRTH, CUST_MARITAL_STATUS,
 CUST_STREET_ADDRESS, CUST_POSTAL_CODE, CUST_CITY,
 CUST_CITY_ID, CUST_STATE_PROVINCE, CUST_STATE_PROVINCE_ID,
 COUNTRY_ID, CUST_MAIN_PHONE_NUMBER, CUST_INCOME_LEVEL,
 CUST_CREDIT_LIMIT, CUST_EMAIL, CUST_TOTAL, CUST_TOTAL_ID,
 CUST_SRC_ID, CUST_EFF_FROM, CUST_EFF_TO, CUST_VALID)
```

```
SELECT CUST_ID, CUST_FIRST_NAME, CUST_LAST_NAME,
 CUST_GENDER, CUST_YEAR_OF_BIRTH, CUST_MARITAL_STATUS,
 CUST_STREET_ADDRESS, CUST_POSTAL_CODE, CUST_CITY,
 CUST_CITY_ID, CUST_STATE_PROVINCE, CUST_STATE_PROVINCE_ID,
 COUNTRY_ID, CUST_MAIN_PHONE_NUMBER, CUST_INCOME_LEVEL,
 CUST_CREDIT_LIMIT, CUST_EMAIL, CUST_TOTAL, CUST_TOTAL_ID,
 CUST_SRC_ID, CUST_EFF_FROM, CUST_EFF_TO, CUST_VALID
FROM CUSTOMERS;
SET TIMING OFF
```

14. Clear the database schema:

```
DROP TABLE MY_CUSTOMERS;
```

How it works...

This recipe can be divided into two parts:

▶ The first from step 1 to step 7, which experiments with the overhead introduced in DML operations by indexes

▶ The second part from step 8 to step 14, where virtual columns are used to avoid the use of triggers to calculate field values

In step 2 we create a MY_CUSTOMERS table with the same structure of the CUSTOMERS table in the SH schema. In step 3 we load data from the CUSTOMERS table to the MY_CUSTOMERS table, using a conventional path insert, obtaining the following results:

In step 4 we wipe the data from the MY_CUSTOMERS table, and in step 5 we create four indexes on the same table.

In step 6 we execute the INSERT statement, as in step 3, and obtain the following result:

We can see that by executing the same INSERT statement with four indexes in place, the executing time has increased from less than 1 second to more than 6 seconds. There is a considerable dip in performance, due to the overhead involved in updating the indexes when inserting records.

In step 7 we empty the table and drop the indexes, returning to the initial state with the MY_CUSTOMERS table empty and without any index.

In step 8 we add a field MAX_CREDIT to the MY_CUSTOMERS table. We define a trigger, which fires before the insert or update on the MY_CUSTOMERS table to set the MAX_CREDIT field according to a business rule in step 9.

In step 10 we insert records in the MY_CUSTOMERS table, obtaining the following results:

In step 11 we drop the MAX_CREDIT column and the trigger used to set its value, and in step 12 we re-create the MAX_CREDIT field, defining it as a virtual column. Here, we specify the formula evaluated to implement the same fanciful business rule as implemented earlier in the trigger.

In step 13 we execute the same insert statement as in step 10. In the following screenshot the output of this operation can be observed. Then in step 14 we drop the MY_CUSTOMERS table to clear the SH database schema.

```
ec2-46-51-176-114.eu-west-1.compute.amazonaws.com - PuTTY

Trigger dropped.

SQL> ALTER TABLE MY_CUSTOMERS DROP COLUMN MAX_CREDIT;

Table altered.

SQL> ALTER TABLE MY_CUSTOMERS ADD MAX_CREDIT AS (CASE
  2        WHEN CUST_GENDER = 'M' AND CUST_YEAR_OF_BIRTH > 1975 THEN
  3           CUST_CREDIT_LIMIT * 0.95
  4        ELSE CUST_CREDIT_LIMIT * 1.05
  5   END);

Table altered.

SQL> SET TIMING ON
SQL> INSERT INTO MY_CUSTOMERS (CUST_ID, CUST_FIRST_NAME, CUST_LAST_NAME,
  2    CUST_GENDER, CUST_YEAR_OF_BIRTH, CUST_MARITAL_STATUS, CUST_STREET_ADDRESS,
  3    CUST_POSTAL_CODE, CUST_CITY, CUST_CITY_ID, CUST_STATE_PROVINCE,
  4    CUST_STATE_PROVINCE_ID, COUNTRY_ID, CUST_MAIN_PHONE_NUMBER, CUST_INCOME_LEVEL,
  5    CUST_CREDIT_LIMIT, CUST_EMAIL, CUST_TOTAL, CUST_TOTAL_ID, CUST_SRC_ID,
  6    CUST_EFF_FROM, CUST_EFF_TO, CUST_VALID)
  7   SELECT CUST_ID, CUST_FIRST_NAME, CUST_LAST_NAME,
  8    CUST_GENDER, CUST_YEAR_OF_BIRTH, CUST_MARITAL_STATUS, CUST_STREET_ADDRESS,
  9    CUST_POSTAL_CODE, CUST_CITY, CUST_CITY_ID, CUST_STATE_PROVINCE,
 10    CUST_STATE_PROVINCE_ID, COUNTRY_ID, CUST_MAIN_PHONE_NUMBER, CUST_INCOME_LEVEL,
 11    CUST_CREDIT_LIMIT, CUST_EMAIL, CUST_TOTAL, CUST_TOTAL_ID, CUST_SRC_ID,
 12    CUST_EFF_FROM, CUST_EFF_TO, CUST_VALID
 13   FROM CUSTOMERS;

55500 rows created.

Elapsed: 00:00:00.45
SQL>
```

In this example you can see that the insert statement with the virtual column needs half the time required by the insert on the same table, when the MAX_CREDIT field value is calculated using a trigger. The benefit in performance will vary due to the different amount of work needed in the trigger execution.

There's more...

In previous recipes we have encouraged the use of indexes to increase the execution speed of our queries.

In this recipe, instead, we are warned about over-indexing. In the first part of this recipe, you must have seen that when there are indexes on a table, insert (updating and deleting) operations on the table take long to execute.

When designing the database schema, it's important to balance the query speed obtained using indexes and the bottleneck in DML operations caused by the same indexes.

We have seen regular B-tree indexes in our example, but the same behavior applies to other types of indexes, especially when using bitmap indexes.

In the second part of the recipe there is a business rule that applies in our application. We decided to implement it in a trigger, which calculates the value for the maximum credit awarded to the customer based on his credit limit, age, and gender.

When we insert data in the table, the trigger fires and its body is executed, resulting in a slightly slower execution. Triggers are useful in many situations, but from Oracle 11g we have another tool to use, which can help us use fewer triggers to apply business rules when designing our application.

This new feature is called **virtual columns**. It allows us to define one or more columns in a table, whose value is the result of an expression. The actual value of the field is not stored on-disk, but is calculated when requested.

Using virtual columns we obtained an important gain in insert performance. As seen earlier, when we talked about using indexes—free lunch is over—there is a drawback when using virtual columns. The counterpart to the performance gain introduced in insert and update statement is a slightly slower query, when we ask for the virtual column value, which needs to be calculated on the fly.

 Result caching can be used also with tables containing virtual columns.

For the same reason, it's mandatory to avoid the use of `SELECT *` statements on tables that contain virtual columns, to avoid the useless calculation of values not required.

As always, in performance tuning there isn't a silver bullet, but a complex mix of pros and cons in every solution, which needs to be calibrated based on the application's requirements.

See also

- The *Reducing the number of requests to the database using materialized views* recipe in *Chapter 2, Optimizing Application Design*
- The *Indexing the correct way, Using bitmap indexes,* and *Migrating to index organized tables* recipes in *Chapter 3, Optimizing Storage Structures*

Loading data with SQL*Loader and Data Pump

In this recipe we will see how to load data from text files in the Oracle database using two different tools—SQL*Loader and External Tables. We will also see how to use the Data Pump to transfer data between different Oracle databases.

Getting ready

In order to test the functionalities provided by the SQL*Loader, we need some text files containing data. The text used in these recipes has the United States census participation rates data freely available at the following site:

`http://2010.census.gov/cgi-bin/staterates.cgi`

The direct link to the file used in the recipe is at:

`http://2010.census.gov/2010census/take10map/downloads/`
`participationrates2010.txt`

To test the recipe, download the file from the above link and save it to a directory accessible from the database server. In the recipe code we will use `/oracle/home/` as the path for the file.

In the same directory, create a text file, using your preferred text editor, naming it `loaddata.ldr`, and copy the following text in this file:

```
LOAD DATA
INTO TABLE MY_IMPORT_DATA
FIELDS TERMINATED BY ' ||'
(
GEO_ID,
PLACE_NAME,
TYPE,
PCT_2000,
PCT_2010
)
```

We will execute SQL*Plus from the `/oracle/home/` directory, to avoid specifying the complete path in our command line for `loaddata.ldr` and `participationrates2010.txt` files.

How to do it...

The following steps will demonstrate how to load data:

1. Connect to the SH schema:

   ```
   CONNECT sh@TESTDB/sh
   ```

2. Create the table MY_IMPORT_DATA to store the data loaded from the text file:

   ```
   CREATE TABLE MY_IMPORT_DATA (
     GEO_ID VARCHAR2(12),
     PLACE_NAME VARCHAR2(255),
     TYPE VARCHAR2(255),
     PCT_2000 NUMBER,
     PCT_2010 NUMBER);
   ```

3. Use SQL*Loader to import data from the participationrates2010.txt file to the MY_IMPORT_DATA table:

   ```
   !sqlldr userid=sh@TESTDB/sh control=loaddata.ldr
    data=participationrates2010.txt SILENT=ALL errors=10
   ```

4. Inspect the log file generated by the previous operation:

   ```
   !tail loaddata.log
   ```

5. Empty the table MY_IMPORT_DATA:

   ```
   TRUNCATE TABLE MY_IMPORT_DATA;
   ```

6. Use SQL*Loader to import data from the participationrates2010.txt file to the MY_IMPORT_DATA table using direct path load:

   ```
   !sqlldr userid=sh@TESTDB/sh DIRECT=TRUE control=loaddata.ldr
    data=participationrates2010.txt errors=10 SILENT=ALL
   ```

7. Inspect the log file generated by the previous operation:

   ```
   !tail loaddata.log
   ```

8. Drop the table MY_IMPORT_DATA:

   ```
   DROP TABLE MY_IMPORT_DATA;
   ```

9. Create the directory `TEST_DATA_DIR` to point to the folder containing the `participationrates2010.txt` file:

```
CREATE OR REPLACE DIRECTORY TEST_DATA_DIR AS '/home/oracle/';
```

10. Create the external table `MY_IMPORT_DATA`:

```
CREATE TABLE MY_IMPORT_DATA (
 GEO_ID VARCHAR2(12),
 PLACE_NAME VARCHAR2(255),
 TYPE VARCHAR2(255),
 PCT_2000 NUMBER,
 PCT_2010 NUMBER)
ORGANIZATION EXTERNAL(
 TYPE ORACLE_LOADER
 DEFAULT DIRECTORY TEST_DATA_DIR
 ACCESS PARAMETERS
 ( FIELDS TERMINATED BY ' ||' )
 LOCATION ('participationrates2010.txt')
);
```

11. Test the data in the external table:

```
SELECT COUNT(*) FROM MY_IMPORT_DATA;
```

12. Drop the external table `MY_IMPORT_DATA`:

```
DROP TABLE MY_IMPORT_DATA;
```

13. Export the CUSTOMERS and COUNTRIES tables using the Export Data Pump utility:

```
!expdp sh/sh DIRECTORY=TEST_DATA_DIR DUMPFILE=test_exp.dmp
 TABLES=customers,countries
```

14. Import the CUSTOMERS and COUNTRIES tables using the Import Data Pump utility:

```
!impdp sh/sh DIRECTORY=TEST_DATA_DIR DUMPFILE=test_exp.dmp
```

15. Connect as SYSDBA and drop the directory `TEST_DATA_DIR` created in the previous step:

```
CONNECT / AS SYSDBA
DROP DIRECTORY TEST_DATA_DIR;
```

How it works...

We have a text file, `participationrates2010.txt`, located in the `/home/oracle/` folder, and we want to load the data contained within it to a table in our Oracle database.

A small excerpt from the file is as follows:

```
06003 ||Alpine County, CA ||County ||0.71 ||0.22
06091 ||Sierra County, CA ||County ||0.50 ||0.45
06027 ||Inyo County, CA ||County ||0.79 ||0.78
06049 ||Modoc County, CA ||County ||0.62 ||0.57
06043 ||Mariposa County, CA ||County ||0.62 ||0.57
06011 ||Colusa County, CA ||County ||0.72 ||0.71
06105 ||Trinity County, CA ||County ||0.58 ||0.48
06021 ||Glenn County, CA ||County ||0.73 ||0.76
06015 ||Del Norte County, CA ||County ||0.71 ||0.74
06035 ||Lassen County, CA ||County ||0.55 ||0.67
06051 ||Mono County, CA ||County ||0.32 ||0.27
06063 ||Plumas County, CA ||County ||0.52 ||0.54
06069 ||San Benito County, CA ||County ||0.74 ||0.75
06005 ||Amador County, CA ||County ||0.72 ||0.71
06093 ||Siskiyou County, CA ||County ||0.72 ||0.72
```

In this text file, fields are delimited by a space followed by double pipes, containing both alphanumeric and numeric data.

The first step to load the data in the database is to create the destination table, as in step 2.

We also need to define the so-called **control file**, in order to instruct SQL*Loader on the file format and eventually, on filtering. In the *Getting ready* section of this recipe we defined the `loaddata.ldr` control file, in which we indicated the type of operation (load data into table `MY_IMPORT_DATA`), the file type (fields separated by), and the order of the fields in the file.

This is a very simple version of the control file. We will not investigate more details about different options available for filtering, formatting, and other more advanced features of SQL*Loader, which can be easily examined in the Oracle documentation.

In step 3, run the `sqlldr` executable, passing the credentials to log into the database, the name of the control file to use (the `control` parameter), the file containing data (parameter `data`), while suppressing on-screen messages. The parameter `ERRORS=10` will block the load process if 10 errors occur during the load process.

In step 4 we observe the last lines of the generated log file. The following screenshot shows the output of this procedure:

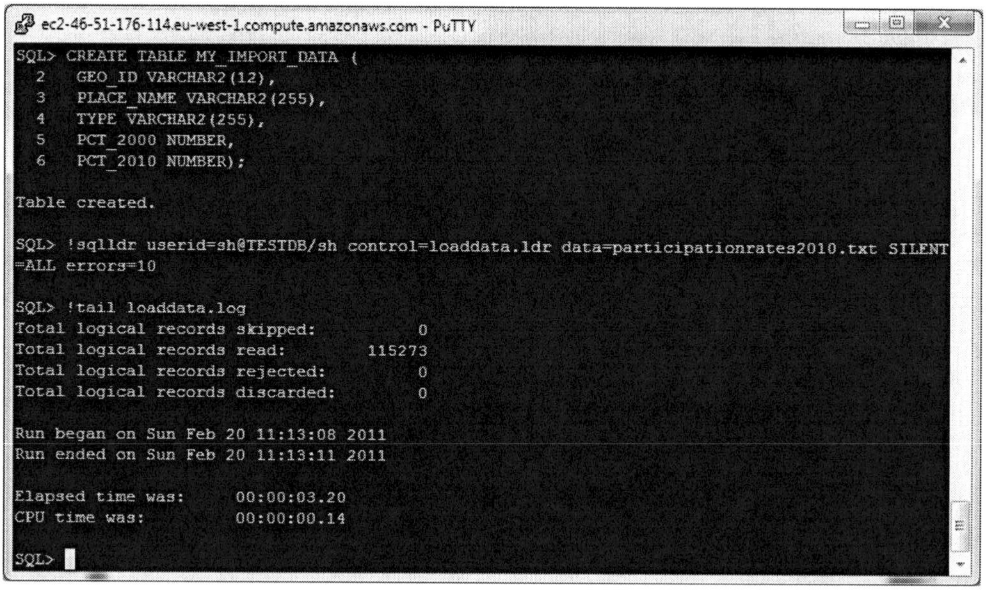

The log states that **115273** rows from the text file were loaded without errors in **3.20** seconds.

In step 5 we truncate the MY_IMPORT_DATA table, and in step 6 we execute another SQL*Loader session, using the same control file and data file, but adding the parameter DIRECT=TRUE. The loading process will use direct path loading—the data is loaded using a mechanism similar to direct path inserting—resulting in the following log, obtained from step 7:

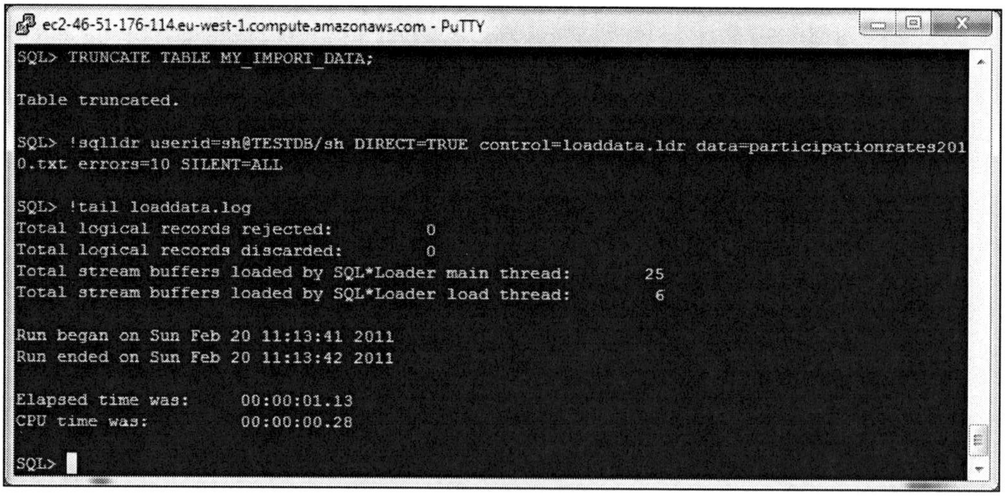

There were no errors while loading the file, and that there was a huge performance gain, resulting in a total elapsed time of 1.13 seconds, about half the time elapsed in step 3.

In step 8 we drop `MY_IMPORT_DATA` table and in step 9 we create a directory object in the database, which points to the `/home/oracle/` file-system folder. We need a **directory** object to create, in step 10, an **external table**. This object points to data outside the database, that is data not stored inside Oracle database datafiles—providing the same interface to manipulate the data, as if it was a regular database table.

When we create `MY_IMPORT_DATA` in step 10, we define the structure of the table—as it will be seen from the database and depending on how the data is structured in the external file. We specify the name of the data file to use and the directory object required to find the data file in the file-system.

After creating the external table, in step 11, we query against it to test whether we can easily access the data in the file as it was available in a regular database table.

We can see the result obtained from this operation in the following screenshot:

In step 11 we drop the `MY_IMPORT_DATA` table and in step 14 we drop the directory object `TEST_DATA_DIR`.

In step 12 we use the command line utility Export Data Pump (`expdp`) to export the data and metadata related to the `CUSTOMERS` and `COUNTRIES` tables in the `test_exp.dmp` file.

The Export and Import Data Pump utilities allow us to easily transport data between Oracle databases, even on different platforms. In our example we have exported two tables in a file, but we can export a schema or the whole database.

In step 13 we use the command line utility Import Data Pump (`impdp`) to import the data and metadata exported above in the database.

 If you are not the schema owner, the EXP_FULL_DATABASE privilege is needed.

In the following screenshot we can observe the output of the export process:

```
ec2-46-51-176-114.eu-west-1.compute.amazonaws.com - PuTTY

SQL> !expdp sh/sh DIRECTORY=TEST_DATA_DIR DUMPFILE=test_exp.dmp TABLES=customers,countries

Export: Release 11.2.0.1.0 - Production on Sun Feb 20 11:25:35 2011

Copyright (c) 1982, 2009, Oracle and/or its affiliates.  All rights reserved.

Connected to: Oracle Database 11g Enterprise Edition Release 11.2.0.1.0 - Production
With the Partitioning, OLAP, Data Mining and Real Application Testing options
Starting "SH"."SYS_EXPORT_TABLE_01":  sh/******** DIRECTORY=TEST_DATA_DIR DUMPFILE=test_exp.
dmp TABLES=customers,countries
Estimate in progress using BLOCKS method...
Processing object type TABLE_EXPORT/TABLE/TABLE_DATA
Total estimation using BLOCKS method: 12.06 MB
Processing object type TABLE_EXPORT/TABLE/TABLE
Processing object type TABLE_EXPORT/TABLE/GRANT/OWNER_GRANT/OBJECT_GRANT
Processing object type TABLE_EXPORT/TABLE/INDEX/INDEX
Processing object type TABLE_EXPORT/TABLE/CONSTRAINT/CONSTRAINT
Processing object type TABLE_EXPORT/TABLE/INDEX/STATISTICS/INDEX_STATISTICS
Processing object type TABLE_EXPORT/TABLE/COMMENT
Processing object type TABLE_EXPORT/TABLE/CONSTRAINT/REF_CONSTRAINT
Processing object type TABLE_EXPORT/TABLE/INDEX/FUNCTIONAL_AND_BITMAP/INDEX
Processing object type TABLE_EXPORT/TABLE/INDEX/STATISTICS/FUNCTIONAL_AND_BITMAP/INDEX_STATI
STICS
Processing object type TABLE_EXPORT/TABLE/STATISTICS/TABLE_STATISTICS
. . exported "SH"."CUSTOMERS"                          9.853 MB   55500 rows
. . exported "SH"."COUNTRIES"                          10.21 KB      23 rows
Master table "SH"."SYS_EXPORT_TABLE_01" successfully loaded/unloaded
******************************************************************************
Dump file set for SH.SYS_EXPORT_TABLE_01 is:
  /home/oracle/test_exp.dmp
Job "SH"."SYS_EXPORT_TABLE_01" successfully completed at 11:26:03
```

There's more...

SQL*Loader is a powerful command-line utility to load data into the database. However, the external table solution gives us more freedom and a very easy way to access our flat file data to load them in the database. Don't use external tables for purposes other than loading data in the database, which is the reason why they were designed.

With external tables we can also use a pre-processor program—which can range from shell-scripts to the user-generated binaries—to pre-process input data. The limit to the type of loadable formats relies on the user's ability to transform the original dataset.

Export and Import Data Pump utilities allow easy data and metadata transfer between databases.

Data Pump is a new feature in Oracle Database 10g, and in Enterprise Edition it also allows us to load or unload parallel multiple streams of data from the database.

There is also a network mode that allows remote export and import over the network. We can export data from a database directly to our local disks, or import data from a database to another database directly, without using any dump-file. The data is written directly from one database to another database using the network.

 You can find more on Data Pump in the Oracle Documentation: `http://download.oracle.com/docs/cd/E14072_01/` `server.112/e10701/part_dp.htm`.

See also

▶   The *Direct path inserting* recipe in this chapter

9
Tuning Memory

In this chapter, we will cover:

- ▸ Tuning memory to avoid Operating System paging
- ▸ Tuning the Library Cache
- ▸ Tuning the Shared Pool
- ▸ Tuning the Program Global Area and the User Global Area
- ▸ Tuning the Buffer Cache

Introduction

So far we have introduced various aspects of Oracle database performance tuning, mostly related to the application code and storage structures.

The last three chapters of this book, starting with this one, will focus on the tuning aspects related to the hardware environment and to the internal structure of the Oracle database, starting with memory tuning in this chapter.

We will see which structures are stored in the memory by the database and how to configure them to use the physical memory available optimally, and achieve the best performance from our hardware.

The first recipe covers some aspects related to the Operating System hosting our database.

Tuning memory to avoid Operating System paging

Tuning memory is a task common to both the database administrators and the system administrators. However, the DBA's task is to optimize the use of the memory available to the database instance, while the system administrator will focus on the overall memory available to the system and on how to divide it among the required applications and users.

It's common best practice to have a dedicated system to manage the database, not sharing it with other applications. The system administrator and DBA tasks are very similar, so this is often the same person.

In this recipe, we will see how to configure the total memory size of our database instance to avoid problems related to the use of virtual memory and pagination.

How to do it...

The following steps will demonstrate how to tune memory to avoid Operating System paging:

1. Connect to the database as SYSDBA using SQL*Plus:

   CONNECT / AS SYSDBA

2. Show the allocated memory to the **System Global Area** (**SGA**):

   SHOW SGA

3. Query the V$SGA view to obtain the same information as mentioned earlier:

   SELECT * FROM V$SGA;

4. Query the V$SGAINFO dynamic performance view to show more details about memory usage:

   SELECT * FROM V$SGAINFO;

5. Connect to Oracle Enterprise Manager as SYSDBA and go to **Advisor Central**.

6. Choose **Memory Advisors** to verify if **Automatic Memory Management** (**AMM**) is enabled, the total (and maximum) memory size configured, and the allocation history graph.

7. Click on the **Advice** button to see the **Memory Size Advice** graph, which helps us choose the right value for total memory size.

8. In SQL*Plus, verify if the SGA is locked querying the parameter LOCK_SGA:

```
SHOW PARAMETER LOCK_SGA
```

9. Query the V$PROCESS dynamic performance view to obtain a list of database processes:

```
SELECT PID, SPID, SERIAL#, PNAME FROM V$PROCESS;
```

How it works...

In this recipe, we explore the interactions between the Oracle database and the hosting Operating System, related to memory and processes. To do so, we use two tools: SQL*Plus command line interface and Oracle Enterprise Manager web interface. We use a SYSDBA account to log in using both the tools.

The first operation after logging in, in step 2, allows us to know the size of the SGA. The SGA represents the most important memory structure in the Oracle database, and it consists of different parts. The **Shared Pool**, the **Buffer Cache**, and the **Redo Log Buffer** are the most important ones. The SGA is shared among all the users of the database.

In the following screenshot, we can see the results of the command in step 2 and the query in step 3:

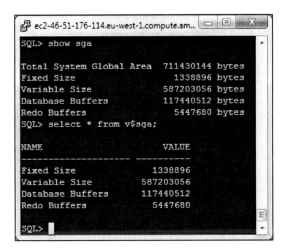

If you want to know more details about the size of the different SGA components, execute the query in step 4; you will obtain a more comprehensive view of the memory used by the database.

In the following screenshot, we can see the results of the query in step 4:

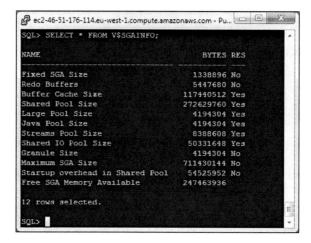

The last column queried, RESIZEABLE, indicates whether the element is resizable without a database restart or not.

We can also obtain this information using Oracle Enterprise Manager. Log in as SYSDBA, and navigate to **Advisor Central**, as shown in the following screenshot:

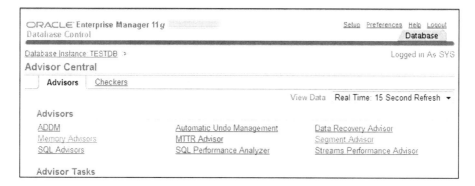

Choose Memory Advisors from the links in the Advisors. This will take you to the next screen, where you can see the AMM feature enabled and the memory space reserved for the Oracle Database. A graph shows the history of memory allocation. In the next screenshot, you can see this element in the Oracle Enterprise Manager:

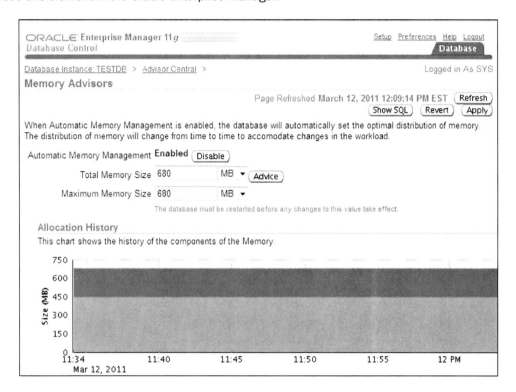

Clicking on the **Advice** button next to the **Total Memory Size**, you can see a graph showing the possible improvement in DB time for various sizes of **Total Memory**— this helps us choose the right memory size to get the best performance. As we can see in the following screenshot, over a certain threshold we cannot get a great improvement in DB time when we increase the memory further.

In the next screenshot, there is almost no difference between using 680 or 850 megabytes of memory:

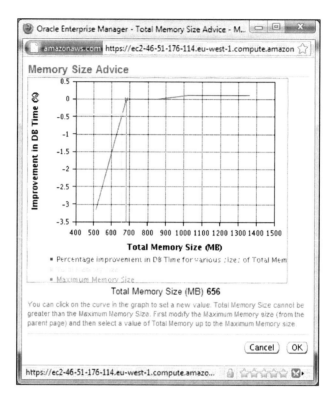

When we enable the **Automatic Memory Management** in the **Advisor Central**, we are asked to provide the **Total Memory Size**, as shown in the following screenshot:

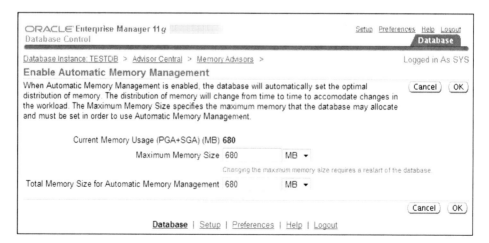

As suggested, to change the maximum memory size, we need to restart the database.

 Please note that Automatic Memory Management may not be optimal for every application; it should not be used on Linux systems with hugepages and with Oracle MultiThreaded Server.

When setting this parameter, using Oracle Enterprise Manager or the ALTER SYSTEM command, never exceed the limit of available physical memory, to avoid paging and swapping at the Operating System level.

Paging occurs when a process needs a block of memory (a page) that is not available in real memory but in virtual memory (on disk). The OS needs to read the requested page from disk to memory, writing the replaced memory page to virtual memory on disk.

Swapping is a process similar to paging, which involves all the memory of a process. Swapping arises when there are too many processes running in memory.

Both paging and swapping should be avoided to achieve best performance. On the same operating system, we can lock the allocation of SGA in real memory, avoiding the paging of SGA memory blocks to disk. In step 8, we verify whether our SGA is locked in the memory by querying the LOCK_SGA parameter, as shown in the following screenshot:

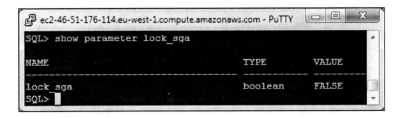

 Don't set the LOCK_SGA parameter to TRUE on Solaris platform in the server parameter file; it will not allow Oracle 11g database to function. See the documentation at the following site:

http://download.oracle.com/docs/cd/E18283_01/
server.112/e10839/appe_sol.htm

In step 9, we query the V$PROCESS dynamic performance view to collect information about the running processes. An excerpt of the results of the query is shown in the following screenshot:

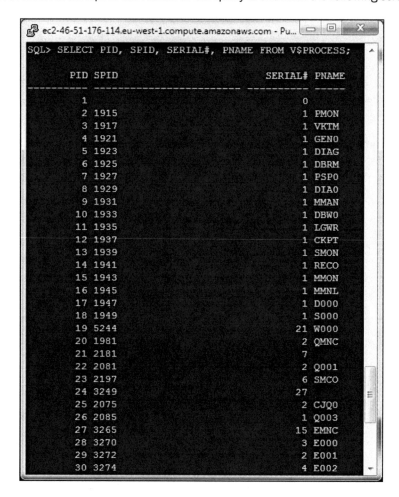

We see the PMON (Process MONitor) process, the DBW0 (DB Writer) process, and so on, running on the Windows systems. However, there is only one active ORACLE.EXE process, and each of the database processes mentioned earlier is implemented in a separate thread of the ORACLE.EXE process, as we can see using the task monitor and in the following screenshot:

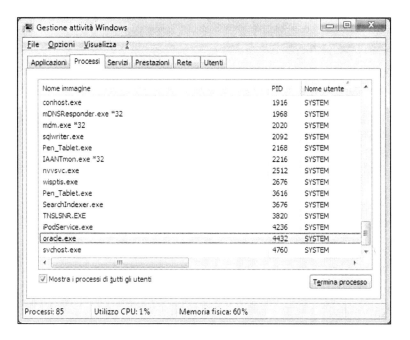

There's more...

To obtain maximum performance from Oracle database, a better option is to keep all the required memory structures in the physical memory, if enough memory is available. In order to do this, it is advisable to keep the SGA limit below the available physical memory. On Solaris systems, we can use **Intimate Shared Memory (ISM)**, a feature that allows multiple OS processes accessing the shared memory to use the same **Translation Lookaside Buffers**, saving a lot of kernel memory space.

On the Linux Platform, we can use **hugepages** to obtain a page size of 2 MB instead of the older 4 KB. The memory space used by hugepages is locked and cannot be paged out.

> For more details on using hugepages there is a good article on Metalink 361323.1.

See also

▶ Other optimizations at OS level—regarding I/O—are discussed in *Disk tuning and strategies to distribute Oracle files* and *Using Asynchronous I/O in Chapter 10, Tuning I/O*

Tuning the Library Cache

The **Library Cache** is part of the **Shared Pool**, inside the **System Global Area**. In this recipe, we will see how to inspect the use of the Library Cache, and how to tune it to obtain the best performance from our database.

How to do it...

The following steps will demonstrate how to tune the Library Cache:

1. Connect to the database as SYSDBA using SQL*Plus:

   ```
   CONNECT / AS SYSDBA
   ```

2. Query the V$LIBRARYCACHE dynamic performance view:

   ```
   COL NAMESPACE FOR A20
   SELECT NAMESPACE, GETS, GETHITRATIO, PINS, PINHITRATIO,
      RELOADS, INVALIDATIONS
   FROM V$LIBRARYCACHE;
   CLEAR COL
   ```

3. Calculate the library cache hit ratio:

   ```
   SELECT SUM(PINS - RELOADS)*100/SUM(PINS) AS "Hit Ratio"
   FROM V$LIBRARYCACHE;
   ```

4. Execute a sample query:

   ```
   SELECT /* TEST */ COUNT(*)
   FROM SH.CUSTOMERS
   WHERE CUST_YEAR_OF_BIRTH = 1975;
   ```

5. Inspect the execution details of a query:

   ```
   SELECT SUBSTR(SQL_TEXT,1,30), USERS_EXECUTING,
      EXECUTIONS, LOADS, HASH_VALUE
   FROM V$SQLAREA
   WHERE SQL_TEXT like 'SELECT /* TEST */ %';
   ```

6. Inspect cached execution plans:

   ```
   SELECT OPERATION, OBJECT_OWNER, OBJECT_NAME
   FROM V$SQL_PLAN
   WHERE HASH_VALUE = 3323436660;
   ```

How it works...

In step 1, we connect to the database as SYSDBA. In step 2, we query the V$LIBRARYCACHE dynamic performance view to obtain details about the current use of Library Cache. You can observe the output in the following screenshot:

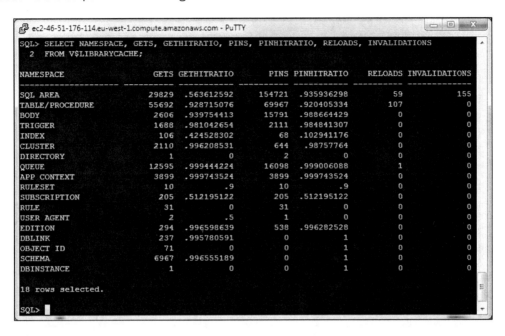

In step 3, we calculate the Library Cache Hit Ratio, an important parameter to evaluate the use of Library Cache—the result should be around 99.9 percent, as can be seen in the following screenshot:

Is it good to use ratios?

Throughout this chapter, we calculate and use various ratios as a simple way to see if there is a problem in a database which we can investigate further using other tools or reports.

The values suggested (as the 99.9 percent for the Library Cache hit ratio, see `http://raj_oracle90.tripod.com/sitebuildercontent/sitebuilderfiles/whya99percentbuffercacheratioisnotok-carymillsap.pdf`) have to be seen as optimal values to reach, but we can experience systems running slow even when we reach these ratios—or systems running very well with ratios far from the provided values.

Using ratios for a first estimate of problems is a fast and good way, but you should base your decisions also on more sophisticated reports and tools.

We can obtain the same information by executing a `statspack` report. In the following screenshot, you can see an excerpt from the report:

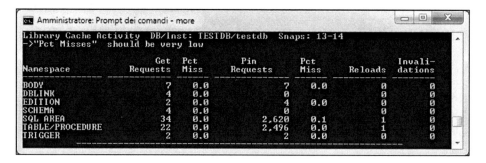

In this report, the `PctMiss` percentage values should be very low, because they identify how often the requested objects are not found in Library Cache.

In step 4, we execute a sample query to illustrate how to find the executions of a specific query using the `V$SQLAREA` dynamic performance view in step 5.

Using the results collected earlier, we query the `V$SQL_PLAN` dynamic performance view, in step 6, to see the cached execution plan.

In the following screenshot, we can see the results of the last three steps:

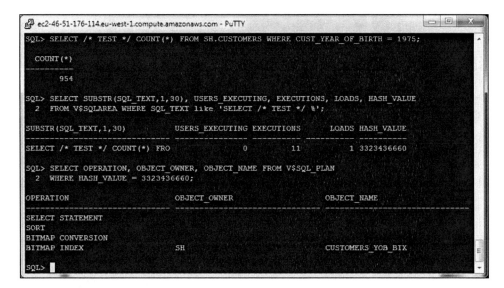

There's more...

The library cache stores parsed SQL statements, execution plans, PL/SQL blocks, and Java classes, ready to be executed. The application code shared in the Library Cache can be easily reused by different database sessions.

The reuse of a piece of code, already in the cache, is called a **Library Cache Hit**. A **Library Cache Miss** occurs when the execution of a piece of code can't find the already parsed code in the library cache.

 The Library Cache Hit is also called **soft parse**, while the Library Cache Miss is called **hard parse**.

The main reasons to tune the Library Cache are to minimize misses (reparsing) and avoid **invalidations**. They last occur when there are cached statements in the Library Cache that reference a database object which is modified, for example, a table altered to add a field.

The **reload** is executed when the corresponding parsed statement is not found in the Library Cache, due to invalidation or aging of the statement. The LRU (least recently used) algorithm determines which statements in the cache should be aged out to make room for newly-executed statements.

The result obtained in step 2 is now clear. We were presented with the number of GETS, PINS, RELOADS, and INVALIDATIONS, grouped according to the type of statement (the NAMESPACE column). The GETHITRATIO and PINHITRATIO are the parameters to inspect when checking the use of the Library Cache.

The query in step 3 summarized all the ratios mentioned earlier in a single parameter—the Library Cache Hit Ratio that is used to determine the average wealth of the Library Cache immediately.

> Even after using bind variables, shared SQLs, and so on, we still see heavy reloads, so now what do we do? You need to increase the size of the Library Cache. There is not a parameter to size the Library Cache, but we can increase the size of the SHARED_POOL_SIZE parameter.

How to minimize misses

To minimize misses in Library Cache (or reparsing, it's the same), we need to modify the applications, as shown in previous chapters, to make sure the statements are shared; for example, using bind variables and composing dynamic SQL statements in the same way. If we cannot modify our application, we can try the CURSOR_SHARING parameter, to determine when SQL statements are considered as identical, hence sharing the corresponding execution plan in the Library Cache.

See also

- The *Improving performance sharing reusable code* recipe in *Chapter 2, Optimizing Application Design*
- *Using bind variables* in *Chapter 4, Optimizing SQL Code*
- *Minimizing latches using bind variables* in *Chapter 11, Tuning Contention*

Tuning the Shared Pool

In the previous recipe, we have seen how to inspect and tune the Library Cache, which is a part of the Shared Pool. In this recipe, we will see the memory structures in the Shared Pool and how we can tune it by keeping PL/SQL blocks in it.

How to do it...

The following steps will demonstrate tuning of the Shared Pool:

1. Connect to the database as SYSDBA:

   ```
   CONNECT / AS SYSDBA
   ```

2. Inspect which objects can be shared by querying the V$DB_OBJECT_CACHE dynamic performance view:

   ```
   COL OWNER FOR A20
   COL NAME FOR A30
   COL TYPE FOR A20
   SELECT OWNER, NAME, TYPE, SHARABLE_MEM
   FROM V$DB_OBJECT_CACHE
   WHERE TYPE IN ('PACKAGE', 'PACKAGE BODY', 'PROCEDURE',
      'FUNCTION', 'TRIGGER')
   AND KEPT = 'NO'
   ORDER BY SHARABLE_MEM;
   ```

3. Force a package to be kept in the shared pool:

   ```
   EXEC SYS.DBMS_SHARED_POOL.KEEP('SYS.DBMS_SCHEDULER');
   ```

4. Show the objects in the shared pool with a certain size:

   ```
   SET SERVEROUTPUT ON
   EXEC SYS.DBMS_SHARED_POOL.SIZES(500);
   ```

5. Inspect the shared pool reserved memory:

   ```
   SELECT * FROM V$SHARED_POOL_RESERVED;
   ```

6. Inspect data dictionary cache statistics:

   ```
   COL PARAMETER FOR A20
   SELECT PARAMETER, GETS, GETMISSES,
      (GETS-GETMISSES)*100/GETS AS "Hit Ratio",
      MODIFICATIONS, FLUSHES
   FROM V$ROWCACHE WHERE GETS > 0;
   ```

7. Keep PL/SQL anonymous blocks in the shared pool:

```
DECLARE I NUMBER;
BEGIN
  /* BLOCK_TO_KEEP */
  I := 26;
END;
/

SELECT ADDRESS, HASH_VALUE
FROM V$SQLAREA
WHERE SQL_TEXT LIKE '%BLOCK_TO_KEEP%'
AND COMMAND_TYPE = 47;

EXEC SYS.DBMS_SHARED_POOL.KEEP ('3F0A8A14,1609869453);
```

How it works...

In the Shared Pool, it is possible to have fragmentation, because loading large objects requires more free space, so we need to unload many small objects to free the required space. The freed space may be not contiguous, leading to fragmentation. To avoid this situation, we can reserve some space for large objects and keep them in this reserved space.

We can also "pin" some objects in the Shared Pool using the DBMS_SHARED_POOL.KEEP procedure. The pinned objects are removed from the Least Recently Used list, so they are never aged out and removed from the Shared Pool.

You can experience ORA-4031 error (unable to allocate "x" bytes of shared memory) if there is no free block with the required memory in the shared pool, due to fragmentation.

You can find a good place to start investigating ORA-4031 error on Oracle Blogs at the following site:

```
http://blogs.oracle.com/db/entry/ora-4031_
troubleshooting
```

In step 2, we query the `V$DB_OBJECT_CACHE` dynamic performance view, in order to inspect what database objects are actually cached in the Shared Pool. The output of this query is shown in the following screenshot:

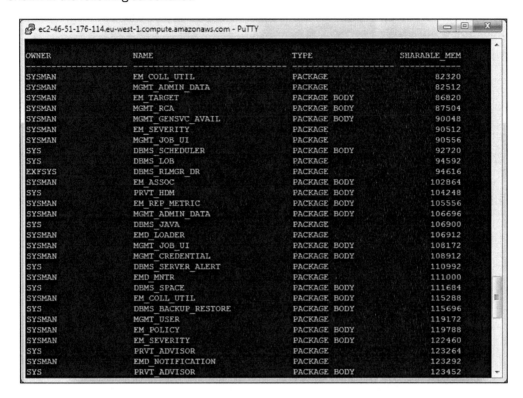

This query can help us decide what objects to keep in memory, based on the memory requirement (the `SHARABLE_MEM` column). We can also query the `EXECUTIONS` column to see objects that are used most often.

In step 3, we use the `DBMS_SHARED_POOL` package to keep the `SYS.DBMS_SCHEDULER` package in the Shared Pool. There is no public synonym to this package, so you have to reference it with the `SYS` schema. The pinned package has to be fully qualified—as in our example `SYS.DBMS_SCHEDULER`.

 If the `DBMS_SHARED_POOL` was not created during the installation, the `$ORACLE_HOME/rdbms/admin/dbmspool.sql` script—executed as `SYSDBA`—will create it.

In step 4, we have used the SIZES procedure of DBMS_SHARED_POOL to show objects that are larger than the size given in the shared pool, as shown in the following screenshot:

```
ec2-46-51-176-114.eu-west-1.compute.amazonaws.com - PuTTY

SQL> EXEC SYS.DBMS_SHARED_POOL.KEEP('SYS.DBMS_SCHEDULER');

PL/SQL procedure successfully completed.

SQL> SET SERVEROUTPUT ON
SQL> EXEC SYS.DBMS_SHARED_POOL.SIZES(500);
SIZE(K) KEPT    NAME
------- ------  --------------------------------------------------------------
889           /* OracleOEM */  SELECT * FROM ( SELECT /*+ ordered */  1 "OBJE
CT_TYPE", u.name "USER_NAME", o.name "OBJECT_NAME", ' ' "PA
RTITION",   ' ' "LOB_COLUMN", 1 "SEG_TYPE", tts.name "TABLE
SPACE",   decode (s.extpct, 0, 0, 1) + decode(mod(s.extsize
, s.iniexts), 0, 0, 2) "PROBLEM" FROM   (SELECT ts#,name
FROM sys.ts$    WHERE (bitmapped = 0 OR (bitmapped !
(3F22A644,78007361)         (CURSOR)
876          ./* OracleOEM */  SELECT * FROM ( SELECT /*+ ordered */  1 "OBJ
ECT_TYPE", u.name "USER_NAME", o.name "OBJECT_NAME", ' ' "P
ARTITION",   ' ' "LOB_COLUMN", 1 "SEG_TYPE", tts.name "TABL
ESPACE",   decode (s.extpct, 0, 0, 1) + decode(mod(s.extsiz
e, s.iniexts), 0, 0, 2) "PROBLEM" FROM   (SELECT ts#,name
FROM sys.ts$    WHERE (bitmapped = 0 OR (bitmapped != 0
AND bitand(flags,3)=0))        AND bitand(flags,2048) != 20
48          AND online$ != 3       AND name != 'SYSTEM' AND na
me != 'SYSAUX'       AND dflextpct = 0       AND (dflinit =
0 OR MOD(dflincr, dflinit) = 0)) tts,   sys.tab$ t, sys.se
g$ s, sys."_CURRENT_EDITION_OBJ" o, sys.user$ u WHERE o.own
er# = u.user#   AND u.type# !=2   AND o.obj# = t.obj#   AND
t.ts# = tts.ts#     AND t.file# = s.file#     AND t.block#
= s.block#      AND t.ts# = s.ts#   AND (s.extpct > 0 OR (s
.iniexts > 0 AND (mod(s.extsize, s.iniexts) != 0) ) )     A
ND decode (bitand (t.property, 1), 1, 1, 0) = 0   AND dec
ode (bitand (t.property, 32), 32, 1, 0) = 0    AND d(CURSO
R)
```

In step 5, querying the V$SHARED_POOL_RESERVED dynamic performance view, we inspect the statistics about the use of reserved space in the Shared Pool. Our goal is to minimize the REQUEST_MISSES and REQUEST_FAILURES, similar to the Library Cache. If the number of failed requests is increasing, we need to expand the Reserved Pool (and probably also the Shared Pool).

> To size the Reserved Pool, we use the SHARED_POOL_RESERVED_SIZE initialization parameter. The value of this parameter cannot exceed 50 percent of the SHARED_POOL_SIZE parameter.

In the following screenshot, you can observe the results obtained on our test database:

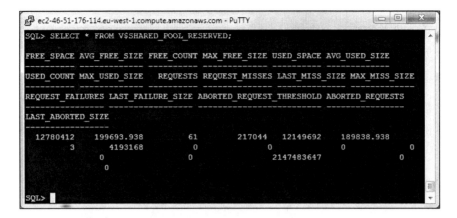

In step 6, we query the V$ROWCACHE dynamic performance view to obtain **Dictionary Cache** statistics, also calculating the Hit Ratio.

In the following screenshot, you can observe the output:

```
SQL> SELECT PARAMETER, GETS, GETMISSES, (GETS-GETMISSES)*100/GETS AS "Hit Ratio",
  2  MODIFICATIONS, FLUSHES
  3  FROM V$ROWCACHE WHERE GETS > 0;

PARAMETER                   GETS  GETMISSES  Hit Ratio MODIFICATIONS    FLUSHES
-------------------- ---------- ---------- ---------- ------------- ----------
dc_rollback_segments       5577         21 99.6234535            31         30
dc_segments               17391       1292   92.57087            31         31
dc_tablespaces           193771          9 99.9953553             0          0
dc_files                    108          6 94.4444444             0          0
dc_users                 318206         94 99.9704594             0          0
dc_objects               122589       3716 96.9687329           237         79
dc_global_oids            31156        117 99.6244704             0          0
dc_sequences                 36         16 55.5555556            36         36
dc_histogram_defs         65043       6441 90.0973202            49          0
dc_profiles                1128          2  99.822695             0          0
global database name      16730          1 99.9940227             0          0

PARAMETER                   GETS  GETMISSES  Hit Ratio MODIFICATIONS    FLUSHES
-------------------- ---------- ---------- ---------- ------------- ----------
outstanding_alerts          220         15 93.1818182            16         16
dc_awr_control              444          1 99.7747748            13         13
sch_lj_objs                   1          1          0             0          0
sch_lj_oids                  47          9 80.8510638             0          0
dc_users                    686          5  99.271137             0          0
dc_object_grants           4882        105 97.8492421             0          0
dc_histogram_data         22328       1462 93.4521677             0          0
dc_histogram_data         21025        475 97.7407848             0          0
dc_users                  10142         12 99.8816801             0          0

20 rows selected.

SQL>
```

In step 7, we execute a (simple) anonymous PL/SQL block and then query V$SQLAREA to identify the ADDRESS and HASH_VALUE of the statement. We then use these values as parameters for the KEEP procedure of DBMS_SHARED_POOL package to pin the anonymous block in the Shared Pool.

The complete execution of the steps mentioned earlier is represented in the following screenshot:

There's more...

Due to the LRU algorithm, blocks of code can be aged out of the shared pool. When a large block is aged out to make room for a small piece of code, and is needed again, then the large block is reloaded. There can be fragmentation in the Shared Pool, which causes performance degradation.

To avoid fragmentation, we can separate the memory required to store frequently used large blocks of code from other blocks, using the Shared Pool Reserved Space.

We need to set the SHARED_POOL_RESERVED_SIZE initialization parameter. Querying the V$SHARED_POOL_RESERVED dynamic performance view, we can inspect the Reserved Pool statistics.

In this view, we need to lower the value for REQUEST_MISSES and REQUEST_FAILURES. Using the V$DB_OBJECT_CACHE, we can inquire for large objects that are not kept in the Shared Pool and decide to keep them in the reserved pool using the KEEP procedure of the DBMS_SHARED_POOL package. Doing so also prevents flushing of the pinned object when executing the ALTER SYSTEM FLUSH SHARED_POOL command.

The SIZES procedure of the same package allows us to identify the objects that exceed the defined size in the Shared Pool.

A problem may arise when there are large PL/SQL anonymous blocks. In these situations, we have two alternatives—the first, as explained in the recipe, is to keep the anonymous block in the Reserved Pool, using the ADDRESS and HASH_VALUE to identify the statement to keep; these values are obtained from the V$SQLAREA dynamic performance view.

The second alternative, to improve performance when we have large PL/SQL anonymous blocks, is to divide large blocks into smaller blocks that execute stored procedures.

We can use the V$SHARED_POOL_ADVICE dynamic performance view to obtain information about estimated parse time in the shared pool for different shared pool sizes, with a range from 10 percent to 200 percent of the current shared pool size, in equal intervals.

The column ESTD_LC_TIME_SAVED indicate the estimated elapsed parse time saved in seconds, while the ESTD_LC_LOAD_TIME column contains estimated elapsed time in seconds for parsing.

Tuning the Dictionary Cache

Another task to tune the Shared Pool is to tune the Dictionary Cache. This is the memory structure, where the statements related to the Data Dictionary, the logical structures stored in the database, are cached. The Data Dictionary is queried often, for example, to retrieve information about the database objects involved in a query, grants to the user, this data should be accessed very fast.

The V$ROWCACHE dynamic performance view enables us to query for updated statistics on the Dictionary Cache. The data in this view is cumulative since instance start-up. The PARAMETER column identifies the data dictionary item, the total number of requests, GETMISSES identifies the number of requests not satisfied by the cache, MODIFICATIONS identifies the number of times the data (related to the item) was updated, and FLUSHES identifies the number of times the item was flushed to the disk.

An instance and a database are two different items. The database is a collection of physical files or disks, while an instance is a set of Oracle background processes/threads and a shared memory area. An instance can mount and open only a single database; a database may be mounted and opened by one or more instances at a time (as in Oracle Real Application Cluster).

In this recipe, we also calculate the **Hit Ratio** for each item. We can also calculate a cumulative **Hit Ratio for the Dictionary Cache**, as done for the Library Cache:

```
SELECT SUM(GETS—GETMISSES) / SUM(GETS) AS "Hit Ratio"
FROM V$ROWCACHE;
```

We need to keep this value above 85 percent.

 Please note that the first time objects need to be loaded into the cache, so there can never be a 100 percent value for the Hit Ratio.

To improve the Dictionary Cache, we can reduce DDL activities and, if we use sequences, use the CACHE option to avoid a get for each NEXTVAL call to the sequence.

The size of the Dictionary Cache cannot be changed; it's a part of the Shared Pool and is automatically maintained by the database. The database uses an algorithm that prefers to keep dictionary data than library cache data in the shared pool, because the performance benefits achieved by using the former approach are more significant. We can only size the Shared Pool using the SHARED_POOL_SIZE initialization parameter.

See also

- The *Tuning the Library Cache* recipe in this chapter
- The *Reducing the number of requests to the database using sequences* recipe in *Chapter 2, Optimizing Application Design*, for more details on sequences

Tuning the Program Global Area and the User Global Area

In this recipe, we will see the **Program Global Area** (**PGA**) and the **User Global Area** (**UGA**) and how to tune them for maximum performance.

The PGA is used to store real values of bind variables, sort areas, and cursor state information. In a dedicated server environment this area is in private user memory. Only in a shared-server environment the session stack space remains in the PGA, while session data and cursor state are moved into the shared pool.

How to do it...

The following steps will demonstrate tuning the PGA and UGA:

1. Connect to Oracle Enterprise Manager as SYSDBA.
2. Go to **Advisor Central**.
3. Choose **Memory Advisors**.
4. Choose the **PGA** palette to show or change the size of PGA.
5. Connect to SQL*Plus as SYSDBA:

    ```
    CONNECT / AS SYSDBA
    ```

6. Show the parameters related to cursors:

    ```
    SHOW PARAMETER CURSOR
    ```

7. Query for the total session memory:

    ```
    SELECT SUM(VALUE) AS "session uga memory"
    FROM V$MYSTAT, V$STATNAME
    WHERE V$STATNAME.NAME = 'session uga memory'
    AND V$MYSTAT.STATISTIC# = V$STATNAME.STATISTIC#;
    ```

8. Query for the session UGA memory:

    ```
    SELECT SUM(VALUE) AS "session uga memory max"
    FROM V$SESSTAT, V$STATNAME
    WHERE V$STATNAME.NAME = 'session uga memory max'
    AND V$SESSTAT.STATISTIC# = V$STATNAME.STATISTIC#;
    ```

How it works...

Private information about the user session, such as private data and cursor state are stored in the **UGA**. The UGA is located in the **PGA** when using dedicated server environments, and inside the Shared Pool when using shared servers.

We can size the PGA using Oracle Enterprise Manager, following steps 1 through 4, where we get the following page, allowing us to size the PGA:

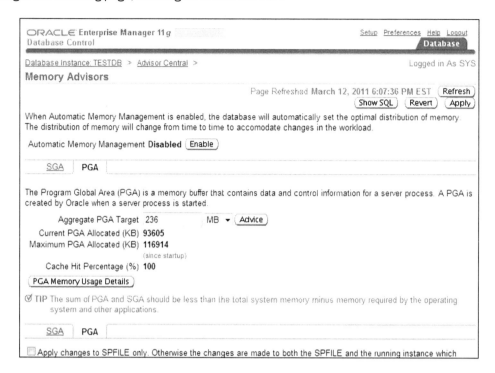

As for **System Global Area (SGA),** we have the **ADVICE** button to see the performance improvement that could be obtained by varying the PGA size.

In step 5, we query for the parameters related to cursors. The results are shown in the following screenshot:

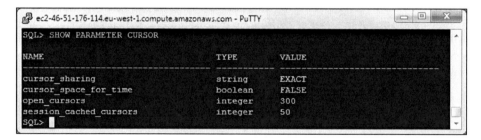

In step 6 and step 7, we query the statistics to see the space used by the current session and the maximum UGA space used by all users, respectively.

The following is an output of these queries:

```
SQL> SELECT SUM(VALUE) AS "session uga memory"
  2  FROM V$MYSTAT, V$STATNAME
  3  WHERE V$STATNAME.NAME = 'session uga memory'
  4  AND V$MYSTAT.STATISTIC# = V$STATNAME.STATISTIC#;

session uga memory
------------------
           1367996

SQL> SELECT SUM(VALUE) AS "session uga memory max"
  2  FROM V$SESSTAT, V$STATNAME
  3  WHERE V$STATNAME.NAME = 'session uga memory max'
  4  AND V$SESSTAT.STATISTIC# = V$STATNAME.STATISTIC#;

session uga memory max
----------------------
           9961620

SQL>
```

There's more...

In step 5, we have seen the parameters related to cursor management. Let's explain their use. OPEN_CURSORS defines the number of concurrent cursors that a user process can use to reference private SQL areas. Increasing the value associated to this parameter allows the user to use more cursors simultaneously, but the memory consumption will be greater.

SESSION_CACHED_CURSORS allows defining the number of session cursors cached. Setting this parameter to a value greater than zero results in a performance gain, where there are repeated parse calls to the same SQL statements. Closed cursors will be cached within the session, ready to be reused.

The last parameter, CURSOR_SHARING, allows us to define whether the cursors are shared only when they match exactly (using EXACT) or also in other situations (using FORCE and SIMILAR).

See also

- ▶ More details on CURSOR_SHARING parameter and on parsing in PL/SQL code can be found in the *Using bind variables and parsing* recipe in *Chapter 6, Optimizing PL/SQL Code*, and in the *Improving performance sharing reusable code* recipe in *Chapter 2, Optimizing Application Design*.

Tuning the Buffer Cache

In this recipe, we will see how to tune the use of Buffer Cache to obtain the best performance.

How to do it...

The following steps will demonstrate how to tune the Buffer Cache:

1. Connect to the database as SYSDBA using SQL*Plus:

   ```
   CONNECT / AS SYSDBA
   ```

2. Show the size of the Buffer Cache:

   ```
   SHOW PARAMETER CACHE_SIZE
   ```

3. Change the buffer cache size for 16K DB blocks to 24 MB:

   ```
   ALTER SYSTEM SET DB_16K_CACHE_SIZE = 24M;
   ```

4. Query the statistics related to the Buffer Cache:

   ```
   SELECT NAME, VALUE FROM V$SYSSTAT WHERE NAME LIKE '%buffer%';
   ```

5. Verify if the parameter DB_CACHE_ is enabled:

   ```
   SHOW PARAMETER DB_CACHE_ADVICE
   ```

6. Estimate the performance with various sizes for the Buffer Cache and different database block sizes:

   ```
   SELECT BLOCK_SIZE, SIZE_FOR_ESTIMATE,
     BUFFERS_FOR_ESTIMATE, ESTD_PHYSICAL_READS
   FROM V$DB_CACHE_ADVICE
   ORDER BY BLOCK_SIZE, SIZE_FOR_ESTIMATE;
   ```

7. Evaluate the **Buffer Cache Hit Ratio** from statistics:

   ```
   SELECT
     PR.VALUE AS "phy. reads",
     PRD.VALUE AS "phy. reads direct",
     PRDL.VALUE AS "phy. reads direct (lob)",
     SLR.VALUE AS "session logical reads",
     1 - (PR.VALUE - PRD.VALUE - PRDL.VALUE) / SLR.VALUE
       AS "hit ratio"
   FROM V$SYSSTAT PR, V$SYSSTAT PRD,
     V$SYSSTAT PRDL, V$SYSSTAT SLR
   ```

```
WHERE PR.NAME = 'physical reads'
AND PRD.NAME = 'physical reads direct'
AND PRDL.NAME = 'physical reads direct (lob)'
AND SLR.NAME = 'session logical reads';
```

8. Enable the KEEP and RECYCLE Buffer Cache:

```
SHOW PARAMETER DB_KEEP_CACHE_SIZE
SHOW PARAMETER DB_RECYCLE_CACHE_SIZE
ALTER SYSTEM SET DB_KEEP_CACHE_SIZE=16M;
ALTER SYSTEM SET DB_RECYCLE_CACHE_SIZE=16M;
```

9. Evaluate the size of the CUSTOMERS table in the SH schema:

```
SELECT TABLE_NAME, BLOCKS FROM DBA_TABLES
WHERE OWNER = 'SH' AND TABLE_NAME = 'CUSTOMERS';
```

10. Evaluate the size of two indexes in the SH schema:

```
SELECT INDEX_NAME, LEAF_BLOCKS FROM DBA_INDEXES
WHERE OWNER = 'SH'
AND INDEX_NAME IN ('CUSTOMERS_YOB_BIX', 'CUSTOMERS_PK');
```

11. Move a table and two indexes to the KEEP Buffer Cache:

```
ALTER TABLE SH.CUSTOMERS STORAGE (BUFFER_POOL KEEP);
ALTER INDEX SH.CUSTOMERS_YOB_BIX STORAGE (BUFFER_POOL KEEP);
ALTER INDEX SH.CUSTOMERS_PK STORAGE (BUFFER_POOL KEEP);
```

12. Evaluate the statistics and Hit Ratio for various Buffer Pools:

```
SELECT
  NAME,
  PHYSICAL_READS AS "physical reads",
  DB_BLOCK_GETS AS "DB block gets",
  CONSISTENT_GETS AS "consistent gets",
  1 - (PHYSICAL_READS / (DB_BLOCK_GETS + CONSISTENT_GETS))
    AS "hit ratio"
FROM V$BUFFER_POOL_STATISTICS
WHERE DB_BLOCK_GETS + CONSISTENT_GETS > 0;
```

13. Query the objects in the Buffer Cache:

```
COL OBJECT_NAME FOR A30
COL OBJECT_TYPE FOR A20
```

```
SELECT OBJECT_NAME, OBJECT_TYPE, COUNT(*) AS "buffers"
FROM SYS.X$BH XBH, SYS.DBA_OBJECTS OBJ
WHERE XBH.OBJ = OBJ.OBJECT_ID
AND OWNER = 'SH'
GROUP BY OBJECT_TYPE, OBJECT_NAME
ORDER BY OBJECT_TYPE, OBJECT_NAME;

CLEAR COL
```

14. Clean the database, moving the altered objects in the SH schema to the default Buffer Cache:

```
ALTER TABLE SH.CUSTOMERS STORAGE (BUFFER_POOL DEFAULT);
ALTER INDEX SH.CUSTOMERS_YOB_BIX STORAGE
   (BUFFER_POOL DEFAULT);
ALTER INDEX SH.CUSTOMERS_PK STORAGE (BUFFER_POOL DEFAULT);
```

How it works...

In step 2, we show the parameters related to the Buffer Cache. In our database, we have defined only a Buffer Cache for a **16K** database block size, as can be seen in the following screenshot:

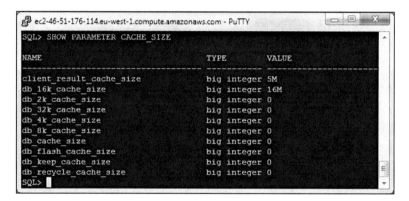

In step 3, we alter this size to **24M**, as shown in the following screenshot:

In step 4, we query for detailed statistics on how the buffer is used. In the following screenshot, you can see the result of this query:

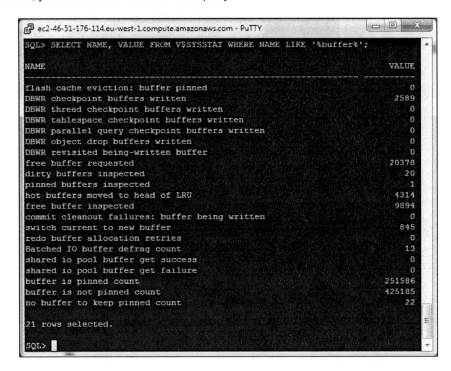

In step 5, we verify that the parameter DB_CACHE_ADVICE is set. The output is as follows:

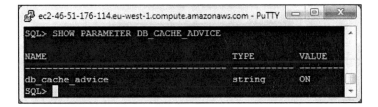

The parameter `DB_CACHE_ADVICE` set to `ON` allows us to obtain, in step 6, an estimate of performance varying the Buffer Cache size for 8K and 16K database block sizes. We can see the results obtained in the following screenshot:

```
ec2-46-51-176-114.eu-west-1.compute.amazonaws.com - PuTTY

SQL> SELECT BLOCK_SIZE, SIZE_FOR_ESTIMATE, BUFFERS_FOR_ESTIMATE, ESTD_PHYSICAL_READS
  2  FROM V$DB_CACHE_ADVICE ORDER BY BLOCK_SIZE, SIZE_FOR_ESTIMATE;

BLOCK_SIZE SIZE_FOR_ESTIMATE BUFFERS_FOR_ESTIMATE ESTD_PHYSICAL_READS
---------- ----------------- -------------------- -------------------
      8192                 8                  992               35698
      8192                16                 1984               28751
      8192                24                 2976               26661
      8192                32                 3968               25378
      8192                40                 4960               22576
      8192                48                 5952               21721
      8192                56                 6944               20616
      8192                64                 7936               19476
      8192                72                 8928               18669
      8192                80                 9920               18110
      8192                88                10912               18051
      8192                96                11904               17885
      8192               104                12896               17849
      8192               112                13888               17790
      8192               120                14880               17766
      8192               128                15872               17766
      8192               136                16864               17766
      8192               144                17856               17766
      8192               152                18848               17766
      8192               160                19840               17766
     16384                 4                  250                   0
     16384                 8                  500                   0
     16384                12                  750                   0
     16384                16                 1000                   0
     16384                20                 1250                   0
     16384                24                 1500                   0
     16384                28                 1750                   0
     16384                32                 2000                   0
```

Observing the `ESTD_PHYSICAL_READS` column, increasing the Buffer Cache for 8K database blocks over 112 Megabytes doesn't enhance the performance of the system, so we can use this value to set the appropriate size for the Buffer Cache.

In step 7, we calculate the **Buffer Cache Hit Ratio**, using statistics, to see how many reads are resolved in the Buffer Cache. The results are shown in the following screenshot:

```
ec2-46-51-176-114.eu-west-1.compute.amazonaws.com - PuTTY                    —   □   X

SQL> SELECT
  2      PR.VALUE AS "phy. reads",
  3      PRD.VALUE AS "phy. reads direct",
  4      PRDL.VALUE AS "phy. reads direct (lob)",
  5      SLR.VALUE AS "session logical reads",
  6      1 - (PR.VALUE - PRD.VALUE - PRDL.VALUE) / SLR.VALUE AS "hit ratio"
  7  FROM V$SYSSTAT PR, V$SYSSTAT PRD, V$SYSSTAT PRDL, V$SYSSTAT SLR
  8  WHERE PR.NAME = 'physical reads'
  9  AND PRD.NAME = 'physical reads direct'
 10  AND PRDL.NAME = 'physical reads direct (lob)'
 11  AND SLR.NAME = 'session logical reads';

phy. reads phy. reads direct phy. reads direct (lob) session logical reads  hit ratio
---------- ----------------- ----------------------- --------------------- ----------
    259739              5020                      20               6635431 .961615304

SQL>
```

 We can use the previous query to obtain a simple representation of how the Buffer Cache is performing. To obtain more accurate information, we can check the value for buffer gets in the AWR report.

We can also use other two Buffer Pools, other than the default one, named KEEP and RECYCLE. The former allows us to keep the buffers in the pool as long as possible, while the latter can be used to store segments that are not allowed to interfere with other segments in the Buffer Cache; this is used when they are only temporarily required.

In step 8, we query and alter the size of the KEEP and RECYCLE buffer pools, setting them both to 16 Megabytes. The following screenshot shows the corresponding output:

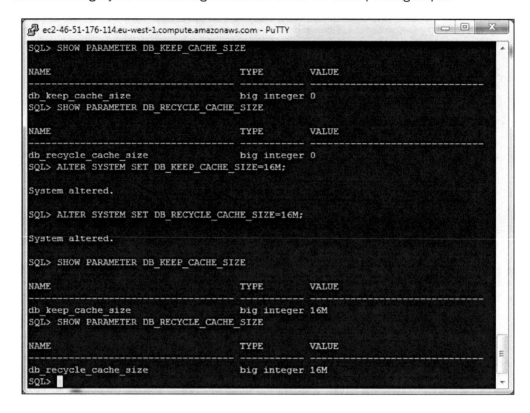

In step 9 and step 10, we query the size, expressed in database blocks, of the CUSTOMERS table in the SH schema and of two indexes, CUSTOMERS_YOB_BIX and CUSTOMERS_PK, to be sure that they can be stored inside the KEEP Buffer Cache.

In step 11, we move the objects queried earlier to the KEEP Buffer Cache. In the following screenshot, we can see the output of these executions:

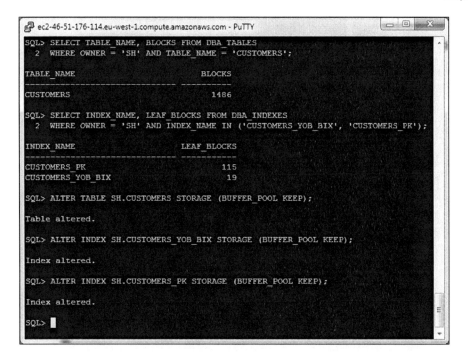

In step 12, we calculate a **Buffer Cache hit ratio** for each different Buffer Pool, as shown in the following screenshot (only the DEFAULT and RECYCLE pool have been used at that time):

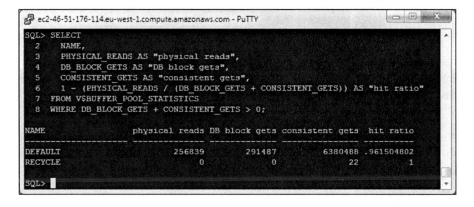

In step 13, we investigate the objects of the SH schema present in the Buffer Cache, obtaining the following output:

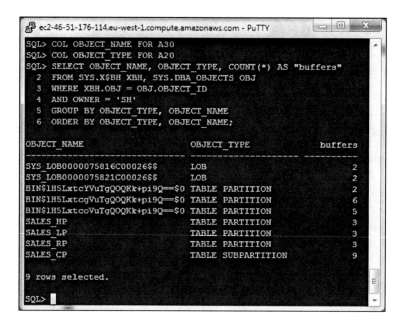

There's more...

To understand the operations discussed in this recipe, we need to provide more details about the Buffer Cache operations.

Buffer Cache is used to store the data read from disk onto the database blocks. Due to the I/O operation, which is slower on-disk than on-memory, it's obviously preferable that the database makes a few I/O operations on-disk. This result is achievable when most of the requests are satisfied by the data already in the Buffer Cache.

The Buffer Cache operates using an LRU list in order to keep track of the database blocks most often used and a dirty list. The dirty list stores the modified blocks that are required to be written to the disks.

The main use of the LRU list is to add blocks to the LRU end using a full table scan, while the normal operations add blocks to the MRU end of the list, and hence they are quickly replaced by the blocks required for subsequent operations.

In this recipe, we have seen various statistics of the on-buffer Cache. We can also obtain this data and the **Buffer Cache Hit Ratio** from STATSPACK reports, as shown in the excerpt in the following screenshot:

```
Buffer Pool Statistics  DB/Inst: TESTDB/testdb  Snaps: 13-14
-> Standard block size Pools  D: default,  K: keep,  R: recycle
-> Default Pools for other block sizes: 2k, 4k, 8k, 16k, 32k
-> Buffers: the number of buffers.  Units of K, M, G are divided by 1000


                                                      Free Writ
           Pool          Buffer     Physical   Physical  Buffer Comp
P   Buffers Hit%           Gets        Reads     Writes   Waits Wait
--- ------- ---- --------------- ------------ ------------ ------- ---- ---
D      51K   98           3,006           64            0        0    0
                -------------------------------------------------------
```

To obtain optimal performance, we can configure multiple Buffer Pools for different segment usage needs, as we have seen with the KEEP and RECYCLE pools.

The KEEP pool is specifically designed for situations where we want to store some data in the Buffer Cache because it is used very often. We can also store small tables, typically subject to full table scans in the KEEP pool. We will use the RECYCLE pool, instead, to store segments rarely accessed or (almost) never reused, so they don't contribute to the age out of other segments in the Buffer Pool.

See also

▶   The *Avoiding Full Table Scans* recipe in *Chapter 4, Optimizing SQL Code*

10
Tuning I/O

In this chapter, we will cover:

- ▸ Tuning at the disk level and strategies to distribute Oracle files
- ▸ Striping objects across multiple disks
- ▸ Choosing different RAID levels for different Oracle files
- ▸ Using asynchronous I/O
- ▸ Tuning checkpoints
- ▸ Tuning redo logs

Introduction

In the previous chapter, we have seen some methods to tune the memory used by Oracle processes to obtain best performance from our hardware.

The database is made up of datafiles on disks; typically, I/O time from disk is slower by one order of magnitude than I/O from memory. So, tuning the disk I/O subsystem can gain significant performance improvements for the database.

In this chapter, we will see the different types of files used by the Oracle database and the available options to tune each of them. Due to their specific use, we can see that there is a different solution to be implemented to optimize the I/O.

At the end of this chapter, you will also see how to tune checkpoints and redo logs to optimize according to their related disk activities.

Tuning at the disk level and strategies to distribute Oracle files

There are many Oracle background and foreground processes involved in a database instance; each of them specializes in a certain operation. In this recipe we will see what operations are executed by each process and what type of interaction takes place between files. On this basis, we will establish a strategy to distribute the Oracle files on different disks to help improve performance.

In *Chapter 9, Tuning Memory*, we have seen that the Oracle database uses different O/S processes on *nix machines, and different threads inside the same process on Windows machines, to obtain the same functionalities. In this chapter, when we refer to processes, we are talking about either *nix O/S processes or Windows threads.

Getting ready

To monitor and diagnose I/O performance issues, we need to enable timed statistics in the database, by setting the appropriate initialization parameter:

```
ALTER SYSTEM SET TIMED_STATISTICS = TRUE;
```

Without enabling this parameter we will not be able to see, in the statistics, the time required to complete an I/O operation; this value is needed to tune the I/O subsystem.

An appropriate Oracle Tuning Management Pack license is required.

How to do it...

The following steps will show how to destribute Oravle files to increase performance:

1. Connect to the database as SYSDBA:

   ```
   CONNECT / AS SYSDBA
   ```

2. Read the statistics about I/O on data files querying V$FILESTAT dynamic performance view:

```
COL FILE_NAME FOR A40
SELECT DF.FILE_NAME, FS.PHYRDS,
   FS.PHYWRTS, FS.READTIM, FS.WRITETIM
FROM V$FILESTAT FS, DBA_DATA_FILES DF
WHERE FS.FILE# = DF.FILE_ID;
```

3. Read the statistics about I/O on temporary files querying V$TEMPSTAT dynamic performance view:

```
SELECT DF.FILE_NAME, FS.PHYRDS,
   FS.PHYWRTS, FS.READTIM, FS.WRITETIM
FROM V$TEMPSTAT FS, DBA_DATA_FILES DF
WHERE FS.FILE# = DF.FILE_ID;
```

4. Identify the log files by querying V$LOGFILE dynamic performance view:

```
COL MEMBER FOR A40
SELECT * FROM V$LOGFILE;
CLEAR COL
```

5. Put redo log files on disk without other activities; to move log files perform the following steps, otherwise go to step 10. Shut down the database:

```
SHUTDOWN IMMEDIATE
```

6. Move the log files using the O/S commands:

```
!mv /u01/oradata/TESTDB/redo01.log
   /u01/oradata/TESTDB2/redo01.log
!mv /u01/oradata/TESTDB/redo02.log
   /u01/oradata/TESTDB2/redo02.log
!mv /u01/oradata/TESTDB/redo03.log
   /u01/oradata/TESTDB2/redo03.log
```

7. Mount the database:

```
STARTUP MOUNT
```

8. Alter the location of the log files:

```
ALTER DATABASE RENAME FILE '/u01/oradata/TESTDB/redo01.log'
    TO '/u01/oradata/TESTDB2/redo01.log';
ALTER DATABASE RENAME FILE '/u01/oradata/TESTDB/redo02.log'
    TO '/u01/oradata/TESTDB2/redo02.log';
ALTER DATABASE RENAME FILE '/u01/oradata/TESTDB/redo03.log'
    TO '/u01/oradata/TESTDB2/redo03.log';
```

9. Open the database:

```
ALTER DATABASE OPEN;
```

10. Separate redo log files and archived redo logs, placing them on separate disks. To change the destination of archived redo logs, execute the following steps; otherwise, go to step 14. Shut down the database:

```
SHUTDOWN IMMEDIATE
```

11. Mount the database:

```
STARTUP MOUNT
```

12. Alter the parameter for archived redo log locations:

```
ALTER SYSTEM SET LOG_ARCHIVE_DEST_1 =
    'LOCATION=/u01/oradata/disk1/archive';
ALTER SYSTEM SET LOG_ARCHIVE_DEST_2 =
    'LOCATION=/u01/oradata/disk2/archive';
ALTER SYSTEM SET LOG_ARCHIVE_DEST_3 =
    'LOCATION=/u01/oradata/disk3/archive';
```

13. Open the database:

```
ALTER DATABASE OPEN;
```

14. Move heavily-accessed files to a separate disk. If you want to move the EXAMPLE tablespace to another disk, perform steps similar to step 5 through step 9. Take the tablespace offline:

```
ALTER TABLESPACE EXAMPLE OFFLINE;
```

15. Move the data files using the O/S commands:

```
!mv /u01/oradata/TESTDB/example01.dbf
    /u01/oradata/TESTDB2/example01.dbf
```

16. Alter the location of the data files:

```
ALTER DATABASE RENAME FILE '/u01/oradata/TESTDB/example01.dbf'
    TO '/u01/oradata/TESTDB2/example01.dbf';
```

17. Take the tablespace online:

```
ALTER TABLESPACE EXAMPLE ONLINE;
```

18. Remember to keep on separate disks data that is not related to the database.

The last step may seem obvious, but, in many installations, the same disks are shared with other applications, such as web or application servers. The disks used by the database should not be shared among other applications to ensure optimal performance.

How it works...

In step 2, we query the I/O statistics on data files, obtaining the result shown in the following screenshot:

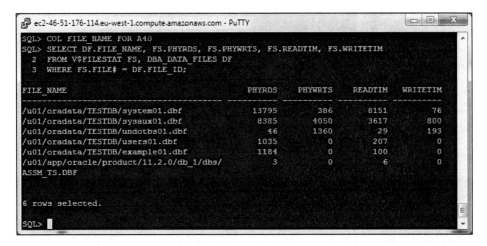

For each file, we can see the number of physical reads and writes performed and the time spent (in milliseconds) for these operations. By observing this, we can identify heavily-accessed data files.

In step 3, we execute a query similar to the one previously mentioned (regarding temporary files), obtaining the results shown in the following screenshot:

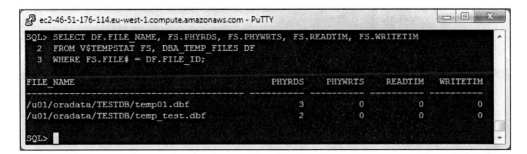

For good performance we need to distribute the online redo log files on different disks, on which little or no other I/O is performed. To do so, in step 4, we retrieve their current position, as shown in the following screenshot:

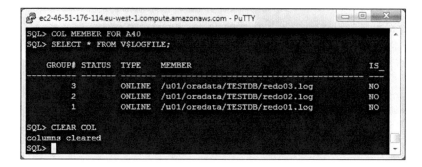

In step 5 through step 9, we moved the online redo log files to another disk, mounted in /u01/oradata/TESTDB2. We need to stop the database by executing a SHUTDOWN command and then use the mv command to physically move the redo log files identified in step 4.

In step 7, we mounted the database and, before opening it, informed the system of the new redo log file positions, by executing the ALTER statements in step 8.

In the following screenshot, we can see the result of all these operations:

When we execute the database in ARCHIVELOG mode (the norm for a production environment), we need to separate the disks in which online redo logs and archived redo logs are stored. If we want to change the location of our archived redo logs, we can follow step 10 through step 13.

Also, in this situation, we need to shut down the database and open and mount it, as in step 10 and step 11. In step 12, we set three different locations for our archived redo logs, storing them on three different disks. In step 13 we open the database and start using the new destinations for archived redo log.

>
> Please note that when we change the archived redo log file locations, we need to change backup procedures accordingly, to reflect the changes made to the locations. We could obtain a RMAN-06207 error, and to fix it we can execute the CROSSCHECK COPY command in the RMAN prompt.

You can see the output of the preceding operations in the following screenshot:

```
ec2-46-51-176-114.eu-west-1.compute.amazonaws.com - PuTTY

SQL> SHUTDOWN IMMEDIATE
Database closed.
Database dismounted.
ORACLE instance shut down.
SQL> STARTUP MOUNT
ORACLE instance started.

Total System Global Area  464519168 bytes
Fixed Size                  1337240 bytes
Variable Size             339740776 bytes
Database Buffers          117440512 bytes
Redo Buffers                6000640 bytes
Database mounted.
SQL> ALTER SYSTEM SET LOG_ARCHIVE_DEST_1 = 'LOCATION=/u01/oradata/disk1/archive';

System altered.

SQL> ALTER SYSTEM SET LOG_ARCHIVE_DEST_2 = 'LOCATION=/u01/oradata/disk2/archive';

System altered.

SQL> ALTER SYSTEM SET LOG_ARCHIVE_DEST_3 = 'LOCATION=/u01/oradata/disk3/archive';

System altered.

SQL> ALTER DATABASE OPEN;

Database altered.

SQL>
```

In step 14 through step 17, we have seen how to move data files to different disks. When we heavily access data files and we know which file is executing the query against the statistics (shown in step 2 and step 3), we can gain in performance by separating the heavily-accessed data files on different disks.

In production environments, we usually check the disk controller-level information to see if the same disk controller is handling both the file systems. We distribute the data files based on disk controller allocation—distributing them on different mount points managed by the same disk controller brings no performance improvement.

The operations to be performed are similar to those executed when moving the online redo log files, but, this time, we don't need to shut down the database. We can take the tablespace offline, and move the desired data files to the new locations using O/S commands—we used `mv` in the example, inform the database about the new data file locations, as in step 17, and then bring the tablespace back online.

By executing the all the steps until now, you can see the following output:

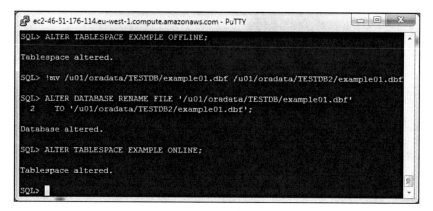

In step 19, there is a final tip about distributing Oracle files on machines where the Oracle database shares resources with other applications. We need to keep separate disks for the database to avoid possible issues and slowing down of simultaneous access to the disk by other applications.

There's more...

When we discuss different disks, we obviously refer to different physical disks, possibly using different controllers. It's important to know which process uses which type of database file.

Data files are written mostly by DBWn processes; the CKPT process reads and writes only data file headers. Server processes read data from data files.

Redo log files are sequentially written by the LGWR process and read by ARCn processes, when the database is in ARCHIVELOG mode. Archived redo logs are only written by ARCn processes, under the same conditions.

The CKPT, LGWR, and ARCn processes can only read and write control files.

LGWR writes online redo logs sequentially, using a RAID 5 on the disks, where online redo logs are stored. This can lead to poor performance due to the slower write times that characterize this type of disk array—using RAID 0+1 is preferable.

See also

▶ The *Choosing different RAID levels for different Oracle files* recipe in this chapter

Striping objects across multiple disks

In the previous recipe, we have seen how to distribute Oracle files on different disks to obtain better performance. In this recipe, we will see how to stripe objects using different tablespaces or data files, to improve performance.

How to do it...

The following steps will demonstrate how to stripe objects across multiple disks:

1. Connect to the database as SYSDBA:

   ```
   CONNECT / AS SYSDBA
   ```

2. Create a new tablespace, EXAMPLE2, on a different disk:

   ```
   CREATE TABLESPACE EXAMPLE2
     DATAFILE '/u01/oradata/TESTDB2/example2.dbf' SIZE 100M;
   ```

3. Move the CUSTOMERS table of the SH schema to the newly-created tablespace:

   ```
   ALTER TABLE SH.CUSTOMERS MOVE TABLESPACE EXAMPLE2 NOLOGGING;
   ```

4. Identify the indexes that need to be rebuilt:

   ```
   SELECT INDEX_NAME, STATUS FROM ALL_INDEXES
     WHERE TABLE_OWNER = 'SH' AND TABLE_NAME = 'CUSTOMERS';
   ```

5. Rebuild the indexes:

   ```
   ALTER INDEX SH.CUSTOMERS_PK REBUILD;
   ALTER INDEX SH.CUSTOMERS_GENDER_BIX REBUILD;
   ALTER INDEX SH.CUSTOMERS_MARITAL_BIX REBUILD;
   ALTER INDEX SH.CUSTOMERS_YOB_BIX REBUILD;
   ```

6. Add a data file to the EXAMPLE tablespace on a different disk:

```
ALTER TABLESPACE EXAMPLE ADD
    DATAFILE '/u01/oradata/TESTDB2/example_DISK2.dbf' SIZE 100M;
```

7. Allocate an extent for the COUNTRIES table of the SH schema on the newly-created data file:

```
ALTER TABLE SH.COUNTRIES ALLOCATE EXTENT
    (DATAFILE '/u01/oradata/TESTDB2/example_DISK2.dbf' SIZE 1M);
```

How it works...

We want to spread our objects to different disks, to obtain better performance. To do so, we can use multiple tablespaces, allocating them to different disks and distributing objects among different tablespaces, or we can add multiple data files—spread among different disks—to the same tablespace and allocate extents for our objects to these data files. In this recipe, we have followed both the methods.

 We can use the DBA_HIST_SEG_STAT view to identify the most-accessed segments from instance startup.

In step 2, we created a new tablespace, named EXAMPLE2, made by a single data file on a disk mounted under the /u01/oradata/TESTDB2/ path.

In step 3, we moved the CUSTOMERS table of the SH schema from tablespace EXAMPLE to tablespace EXAMPLE2. We have used the NOLOGGING option to avoid logging all the data movements—only the change in a data dictionary is logged.

We can see the results of these operations in the following screenshot:

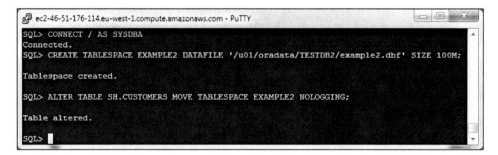

As always, be careful when executing NOLOGGING operations. To avoid possible data loss, plan this operation with the database backup administrators.

In step 4, we have queried the status of indexes on the moved table. As seen in the following screenshot, all the indexes on the CUSTOMERS table are showing the UNUSABLE status, so they need to be rebuilt:

```
ec2-46-51-176-114.eu-west-1.compute.amazonaws.com - PuTTY

SQL> SELECT INDEX_NAME, STATUS FROM ALL_INDEXES
  2    WHERE TABLE_OWNER = 'SH' AND TABLE_NAME = 'CUSTOMERS';

INDEX_NAME                      STATUS
------------------------------- ----------
CUSTOMERS_PK                    UNUSABLE
CUSTOMERS_GENDER_BIX            UNUSABLE
CUSTOMERS_MARITAL_BIX           UNUSABLE
CUSTOMERS_YOB_BIX               UNUSABLE

SQL>
```

In step 5, we rebuild the indexes, obtaining the following output:

```
ec2-46-51-176-114.eu-west-1.compute.amazonaws.com - ...

SQL> ALTER INDEX SH.CUSTOMERS_PK REBUILD;

Index altered.

SQL> ALTER INDEX SH.CUSTOMERS_GENDER_BIX REBUILD;

Index altered.

SQL> ALTER INDEX SH.CUSTOMERS_MARITAL_BIX REBUILD;

Index altered.

SQL> ALTER INDEX SH.CUSTOMERS_YOB_BIX REBUILD;

Index altered.

SQL>
```

From step 6 onwards, we follow a different strategy—adding a data file to an existing tablespace and storing it on a different disk. In step 6, we add the new data file to the EXAMPLE tablespace.

In step 7, we allocate an extent for the COUNTRIES table of the SH schema, on the newly created data file. From now onwards, the data in the COUNTRIES table will be stored on a different disk.

The results of these operations can be seen in the following screenshot:

```
ec2-46-51-176-114.eu-west-1.compute.amazonaws.com - PuTTY

SQL> ALTER TABLESPACE EXAMPLE ADD
  2      DATAFILE '/u01/oradata/TESTDB2/example_DISK2.dbf' SIZE 100M;

Tablespace altered.

SQL> ALTER TABLE SH.COUNTRIES ALLOCATE EXTENT
  2      (DATAFILE '/u01/oradata/TESTDB2/example_DISK2.dbf' SIZE 1M);

Table altered.

SQL>
```

There's more...

In the latter steps of the recipe, we have manually striped the objects. But if we have many objects in our database, manual striping can be a nightmare. In such situations, consider moving objects to different tablespaces or using partitions.

We can also distribute tables and related indexes on different disks, to obtain performance gain in both read and write operations. If we have tables and indexes on the same disk, we need to read and write in two different places on the same disk. By dividing the work between two disks, we can perform an index range scan faster than when the index and the table are on the same disk.

See also

► The *Using partitioning* recipe in *Chapter 3, Optimizing Storage Structures*

Choosing different RAID levels for different Oracle files

In this recipe, we will see the characteristics of different RAID levels available in the market and learn what to choose for each different Oracle file type.

RAID is the acronym for **Redundant Arrays of Inexpensive Disks**, a common configuration in a storage subsystem. It is used to obtain low-cost, fault-tolerant configurations for high performance in the non-mainframe market, by using multiple "inexpensive" disks in different configurations.

Getting ready

Despite the "I" in RAID, we need a minimum of two or three drives, depending on the RAID level we want to implement.

Every RAID level has different requirements and offers different performance and data integrity levels. In this recipe, we will illustrate these requirements for each RAID level.

There is a common requirement, that is, the RAID controller; it can be software-based at the operating system, firmware level, or hardware-based. The latter offers guaranteed performance and no overhead on the CPU.

How to do it...

The following steps will demonstrate the various RAID levels; you can chose the right RAID level by considering the following:

1. RAID 0+1 is preferable for your Oracle database installations.
2. RAID 5 has significant write penalty, so don't use it for storing write-intensive data files (if RAID 0+1 is available), redo log files, archived redo log files, and undo segments. You can use it for control files and for data files with a moderate write activity.

How it works...

This recipe has only two steps, which are simple tips to choose the right hardware to obtain better performance. More than a buy list it's a no-buy list:

1. Starting with step 1, in terms of performance the best RAID level for an Oracle database is RAID 0+1, also known as RAID 10. The drawback of this option is the cost of the solution, because it is twice the cost of storage due to mirroring. Additionally, it uses more complex procedures and hardware to manage the striping.
2. In step 2, we warn against RAID 5. There is a significant write penalty when using this RAID level, so storing frequently-updated data is not a good choice. Also, redo log files and archived redo logs don't fit well in this environment, because, on OLTP databases, there is an intense write activity on these files, and also because undo segments experience heavy load.

There's more...

To understand different RAID levels better, we will cover the differences between the most common RAID configurations, highlighting performance considerations related to storing Oracle database files.

RAID level 0

This is the simplest RAID level, and it's **not** recommended to use it in any production environment by Oracle itself.

In this RAID level only non-redundant striping is implemented, that is, the data is striped across multiple disks to obtain better read/write performance. However, this is a non-redundant solution, so any disk failure causes the outage of the entire array and hence data loss. It's very cheap because it doesn't need more storage capacity than the actual space required.

RAID level 1

RAID level 1 implements a disk mirroring strategy. For each disk drive there is at least one identical disk drive on which an exact copy of the data is maintained. There can be *n-1* outages, where *n* is the number of drives on which the data is simultaneously stored, without any data loss. If hot-swappable drives are used there could be no application outage even after *n-1* outages in different disks.

The main defect of this implementation is the cost per megabyte, because for each megabyte of data stored we need *n* megabytes of storage to ensure the design redundancy.

Performance, as compared to the performance of a single drive, is slightly better in read times if the controller can choose the disk from which to read the data considering the least I/O cost.

We can use RAID level 1 to store control files, system tablespace, flashback recovery area, undo segments, and data files. It's not a good idea to store redo logs and temporary segments on RAID level 1 configurations, because redo logs should be multiplexed on different disks, and there is no need to protect temporary segments from failures.

RAID level 5

RAID level 5 introduces the concepts of Block-interleave and distributed parity.

In a RAID 3 array, there is one disk dedicated to the storage of parity data for the other disks in the array, and data is striped using a strip of 1 bit. RAID 5 introduces two variations of the schema—stripes size is configurable and parity data is not stored on a single drive but is distributed among all disks of the array.

The reason to choose RAID level 5 is to obtain a redundant storage solution, cheaper than RAID level 1. Due to storage of parity data, however, write operation performance suffers. This is because, when writing some data, we need to read the old data and parity value, and write the new data and parity value, resulting in four I/O operations.

Read performance is excellent when the data fits in a single striping segment, allowing a heavy concurrency on data. Except undo segments and intensive-write data files, all other Oracle files can be stored in a RAID level 5 array—when you cannot use RAID level 0+1, especially with read-only data files.

RAID level 0+1

RAID level 0+1 is also known as RAID level 10; it's the result of RAID level 0 and RAID level 1 arrays being used together. So, we have a striping and mirroring solution that allows excellent performance in read operations and very good performance in write operations, due to the additional write operation required by mirroring. RAID level 0+1 ensures optimal protection against failures, thanks to mirroring.

The only defect of RAID level 0+1 subsystems is the cost of this solution, but it can be used to store every type of Oracle database file with optimal performance.

See also

> ▸ The *Tuning memory to avoid Operating System paging* recipe in *Chapter 9, Tuning Memory*

Using asynchronous I/O

In this recipe we will see how to use asynchronous I/O to obtain better performance from our I/O subsystem.

How to do it...

The following steps will describe the use of asynchronous I/O:

1. Connect to the database as SYSDBA:

   ```
   CONNECT / AS SYSDBA
   ```

2. Verify whether asynchronous I/O is enabled:

   ```
   SHOW PARAMETER FILESYSTEMIO_OPTIONS
   ```

3. Enable asynchronous I/O, if it is not enabled:

   ```
   ALTER SYSTEM SET FILESYSTEMIO_OPTIONS=SETALL SCOPE=SPFILE;
   ```

4. Shut down the database instance:

   ```
   SHUTDOWN IMMEDIATE
   ```

5. Start and open the database:

   ```
   STARTUP OPEN
   ```

6. Verify the change in system configuration:

   ```
   SHOW PARAMETER FILESYSTEMIO_OPTIONS
   ```

How it works...

The Oracle database may use synchronous or asynchronous I/O calls. With synchronous I/O, when an I/O request is submitted to the Operating System, the write process will block until the operation is completed.

Using asynchronous I/O, while the I/O request is still executing, the calling process continues its work without blocking. This is the reason why asynchronous I/O can lead to performance gain in processing writes to Oracle database files.

 There is an important downside to keep in mind while using asynchronous writes—the blocks may not get written immediately to the file system, and this behavior may lead to missing data, or corruption, in case of a failure.

In step 2, we verify if the asynchronous I/O option is enabled in our database instance. In step 3, we set the value to `SETALL`, enabling both asynchronous and **direct I/O** on system files. Using direct I/O allows the process to bypass the Operating System cache. The Oracle database already uses the database buffer cache, so we can access database files directly, without consuming resources required by the OS cache.

In steps 4 and 5, we restart the database to set the new parameters, and, in step 6, we verify the new value for the `FILESYSTEMIO_OPTIONS` parameter.

In the following screenshot, we can see the output for the previous operations:

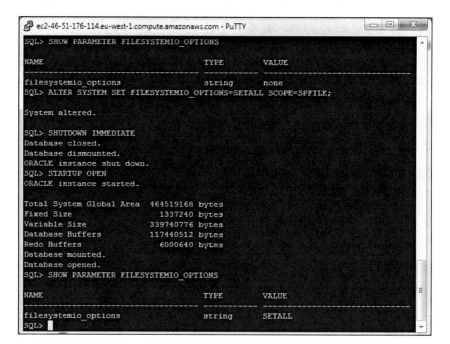

There's more...

Other options for the FILESYSTEMIO_OPTIONS parameter include:

- ▸ NONE: this disables both asynchronous I/O and direct I/O
- ▸ ASYNCH: this enables asynchronous operations
- ▸ DIRECTIO: this enables only the direct I/O option, thus bypassing the O/S cache

On Windows systems the OS cache is never used, so every request will bypass the Operating System cache and go directly to the disk.

On Windows systems, starting from Oracle 10g, asynchronous I/O is supported for all files on Windows Server 2003 x64 bit upward.

On *nix systems we need to pay attention to certain operations that don't use database buffer cache. Using direct I/O option may lead to a performance dip. Those operations include I/O on the temporary tablespace, using NOCACHE LOBs, and parallel query slaves reading data.

Asynchronous I/O is important for DBWn and LGWR processes, because it allows DBWn to use the available hardware bandwidth completely. The LGWR writes to multiple log file members and can overlap multiple writes due to rapidly subsequent committed transactions occurring simultaneously.

Using asynchronous I/O on redo log files and temp files eliminates some contention related to the file system read/write locks, resulting in increased performance. Using asynchronous I/O on data files instead doesn't affect performance but scalability, that is, the database can handle more requests at a time. The DBWn processes, responsible for writing to the data files, work asynchronously, so the performance of user processes is not affected by the use of asynchronous I/O. However, using asynchronous I/O allows DBWn processes to use all the available bandwidth, and use it in a more efficient way, so higher workloads can be managed by the system when asynchronous I/O is enabled.

On platforms that don't support asynchronous I/O, we can enable **multiple database writer slave processes**. A single DBWR process will use multiple slave processes to write data on disks, simulating something similar to asynchronous I/O. Please note that multiple DBWn processes and multiple DBWR slaves cannot be run together, and the last option takes precedence.

> To enable multiple database writer slave processes, you need to set the initialization parameter DBWR_IO_SLAVES to a non-zero value, setting the number of slave processes to use.

See also

- ▸ Refer to the *Tuning the buffer cache* recipe in *Chapter 9, Tuning Memory*

Tuning checkpoints

A **checkpoint** is used to ensure consistency in the database; during this operation, all data files are synchronized with the data blocks in memory.

The process responsible for signaling a checkpoint is the CKPT process, which signals the DBWn processes to write the dirty (modified) buffers from database buffer cache in memory to the data files.

During this operation data, file headers and control files are updated to store the last **System Change Number** (**SCN**), to ensure data block consistency.

In this recipe, we will see how to tune checkpoints in an Oracle database, to optimize all these write operations involved in checkpoints, balancing the trade-off between the redo log size and recovery time, in case of instance failure.

How to do it...

The following steps will demonstrate checkpoints in an Oracle database:

1. Connect to the database as SYSDBA:

   ```
   CONNECT / AS SYSDBA
   ```

2. Verify the value for the LOG_CHECKPOINTS_TO_ALERT parameter:

   ```
   SHOW PARAMETER LOG_CHECKPOINTS_TO_ALERT
   ```

3. Alter the LOG_CHECKPOINTS_TO_ALERT parameter to trace checkpoints to the alert log:

   ```
   ALTER SYSTEM SET LOG_CHECKPOINTS_TO_ALERT=TRUE SCOPE=SPFILE;
   ```

4. Switch the log file to force a checkpoint to occur:

   ```
   ALTER SYSTEM SWITCH LOGFILE;
   ```

5. Verify the checkpoint event has been traced in the alert log:

   ```
   !tail /u01/app/diag/rdbms/testdb/TESTDB/trace/alert_TESTDB.log
   ```

6. Query the V$SYSSTAT dynamic performance view to monitor checkpoint process activity:

   ```
   SELECT NAME, VALUE FROM V$SYSSTAT
   WHERE NAME LIKE 'background check%';

   SELECT NAME, VALUE FROM V$SYSSTAT
   WHERE NAME LIKE 'DBWR check%';
   ```

7. Verify other parameters involved in the checkpoint:

   `SHOW PARAMETER LOG_CHECKPOINT`

8. List parameters related to Fast-Start checkpointing:

   `SHOW PARAMETER FAST_START`

9. Query the `V$INSTANCE_RECOVERY` dynamic performance view to obtain estimations on recovery time:

```
SELECT
    RECOVERY_ESTIMATED_IOS,
    ESTIMATED_MTTR,
    TARGET_MTTR,
    LOG_FILE_SIZE_REDO_BLKS,
    LOG_CHKPT_INTERVAL_REDO_BLKS,
    LOG_CHKPT_TIMEOUT_REDO_BLKS
FROM V$INSTANCE_RECOVERY;
```

How it works...

In step 2, we verify the value for the `LOG_CHECKPOINTS_TO_ALERT` parameter, and in step 3 we set it to `TRUE`, to record checkpoint information to the alert log. In step 4, we force a checkpoint to occur by switching log files.

In the following screenshot, you can see the output of the previous operations:

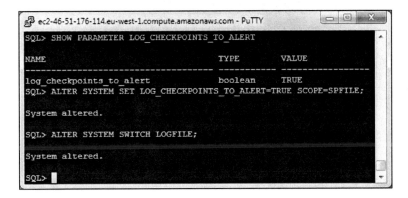

In step 5, we verify the content of the alert log to be sure that the checkpoint information is being stored in it.

In the following screenshot, you can see that the checkpoint information was written to the alert log:

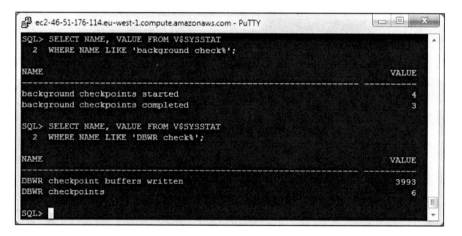

In step 6, we query `V$SYSSTAT` to monitor some statistics related to the redo log files and checkpoint. The result of the query is shown in the following screenshot:

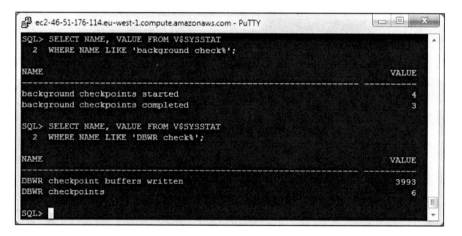

If the number of started checkpoints is greater than the value of completed checkpoints by more than one, in the first query, you need to enlarge redo log file size. In this situation, checkpoints are not completed between log file switches, because the log file switches occur too often, as log files are very small. Increasing redo log file size will limit the number of log switches required, allowing checkpoints to complete between them.

A redo log switch should occur every 15 to 30 minutes (as a rule of thumb); switching too often leads to performance issues, whilst switching not often enough often may cause a recovery operation to take longer.

The second query shows the number of data blocks written by DBWR and the number of checkpoints. This is useful for monitoring the number of blocks written by DBWR during checkpoints.

In step 7, we view the actual value of parameters, that influence checkpoints, obtaining the following output:

We have seen the use of the LOG_CHECKPOINTS_TO_ALERT parameter in step 2 and step 3.

You can set LOG_CHECKPOINT_INTERVAL to the maximum number of redo log blocks—equivalent to the size of O/S file blocks. It will be left in the redo log before a checkpoint occurs. This value cannot exceed 90 percent of the number of redo blocks that can be stored in the smallest redo log file, to ensure that there won't be log switch between checkpoints.

The LOG_CHECKPOINT_TIMEOUT is used to set the maximum number of seconds for which a dirty block can stay in the memory before it's written to disk. The default value is 1800 seconds. In step 8, we show other initialization parameters related to **Fast-Start checkpointing**. The output of this operation is shown in the following screenshot:

Fast-Start checkpointing is configured to assure that the instance recovery time is acceptable; this target can be achieved by setting one of the parameters, as shown in the previous image.

We can set the FAST_START_MTTR_TARGET parameter to the expected *Mean Time To Recover*, that is, the number of seconds required to recover the instance after a crash.

When you set FAST_START_MTTR_TARGET, you cannot use the parameters LOG_CHECKPOINT_INTERVAL and LOG_CHECKPOINT_TIMEOUT, shown earlier.

In step 9, we query the V$INSTANCE_RECOVERY view to obtain an estimate of recovery time, collecting data required to choose the correct values for the parameters shown earlier. In the following screenshot, you can observe the output of this query:

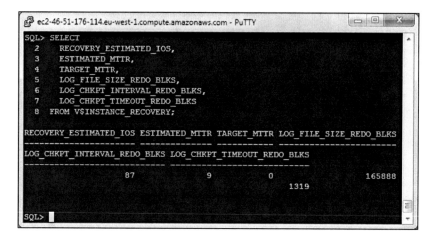

You can find the description for each field in V$INSTANCE_RECOVERY view in *Appendix A, Dynamic Performance Views*.

There's more...

In this recipe, we have seen how different parameters can influence the checkpoint behavior.

The **checkpoint queue** is a list of dirty buffers (that is, blocks in the buffer cache modified and not already written to the disk) waiting to be written to the disk by the DBWR processes.

There is a trade-off between a short checkpoint queue that ensures faster recovery times in case of instance crash, and a long checkpoint queue which avoids frequent DBWR writes that can affect performance.

As always, we need to evaluate the ideal configuration to satisfy our Service Level Agreements. If we assure the maximum recovery time, we will shorten the checkpoint queue, resulting in some more DBWR writes.

The last query of this recipe helps us to obtain RECOVERY_ESTIMATED_IOS. This is an estimate of the number of data blocks to be processed during recovery. ESTIMATED_MTTR indicates the estimated recovery time, based on the current system load. TARGET_MTTR is based on the value of the FAST_START_MTTR_TARGET parameter and on the system performance and limitations. LOG_FILE_SIZE_REDO_BLKS is the number of redo blocks required to make sure that a log switch doesn't occur before the checkpoint completes.

The value for LOG_CHKPT_INTERVAL_REDO_BLKS and LOG_CHKPT_TIMEOUT_REDO_BLKS indicates the number of redo blocks that will be processed during recovery to satisfy the LOG_CHECKPOINT_INTERVAL and LOG_CHECKPOINT_TIMEOUT parameters, respectively.

See also

> ▸ The *Tuning redo logs* recipe that follows

Tuning redo logs

In this recipe, we will see how to monitor redo logs.

How to do it...

The following steps will demonstrate monitoring of redo logs:

1. Connect to the database as SYSDBA:

    CONNECT / AS SYSDBA

2. Verify possible problems by inspecting the V$SYSTEM_EVENT dynamic performance view:

    SELECT EVENT, TOTAL_WAITS, TIME_WAITED FROM V$SYSTEM_EVENT

    WHERE EVENT LIKE 'log file%';

3. Query the data dictionary about the redo log files:

    COL MEMBER FOR A40

    SELECT * FROM V$LOGFILE;

    CLEAR COL

4. Query the data dictionary about redo log details:

    SELECT * FROM V$LOG;

5. Query the historical log switch data:

    SELECT * FROM V$LOG_HISTORY ORDER BY RECID;

How it works...

In step 2, we query the V$SYSTEM_EVENT dynamic performance view to inspect problems related to redo logs. In the following screenshot, we can see the results obtained on a test database:

```
SQL> SELECT EVENT, TOTAL_WAITS, TIME_WAITED FROM V$SYSTEM_EVENT
WHERE EVENT LIKE 'log file%';
  2
EVENT                                    TOTAL_WAITS TIME_WAITED
---------------------------------------- ----------- -----------
log file sequential read                          10          10
log file single write                             10           1
log file parallel write                         4594        2662
log file switch completion                         1           7
log file sync                                    349         620

SQL>
```

The important events to be observed are **log file sync** and **log file parallel write**. Often, a high value for the latter statistic is not evidence of a problem. It indicates a wait in LGWR activity, but doesn't specify whether waits affect user processes or not.

The **log file sync** statistic is more reliable. The symptoms of I/O issues, related to slow disks on which redo log files are written, are highlighted by a high value for **log file sync** statistic. Often a high value for the **log file parallel write** is confirmed by a high value for this parameter. In these situations, you need to solve the issue—the high waits—related to redo log file writes.

In step 3, we query the V$LOGFILE to know the redo log files in our database and some information on their status. We can see the results obtained in the following screenshot:

```
SQL> SELECT * FROM V$LOGFILE;

    GROUP# STATUS  TYPE    MEMBER                               IS_
---------- ------- ------- ------------------------------------ ---
         3         ONLINE  /u01/oradata/TESTDB2/redo03.log      NO
         2         ONLINE  /u01/oradata/TESTDB2/redo02.log      NO
         1         ONLINE  /u01/oradata/TESTDB2/redo01.log      NO

SQL>
```

We can see that there are three redo log groups in the database, with only one member each. In a production database, you need at least two members for each group, and, according to the transaction load on the database, more redo log groups could be required.

In step 4, we query the V$LOG dynamic performance view, in which we can find more details regarding redo logs, as in the following screenshot:

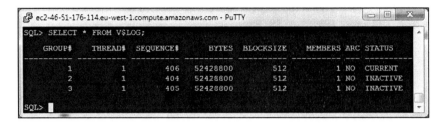

In the excerpt shown in the previous screenshot, you can see the redo log group (**GROUP#**), the sequence number (the first SCN, System Change Number) in each group (**SEQUENCE#**), the size of each group's members (**BYTES**), the status (**STATUS**), and whether the log is archived or not (**ARC**).

In step 5, finally, we query the V$LOG_HISTORY dynamic performance view, obtaining a row for each log switch. This view is useful to verify the log switch frequency, and indicates the first and last change numbers in the log file.

This information is stored in the control file; the MAXLOGHISTORY clause, specified when the control file was created, indicates the length of time for which the information is retained in the control file itself.

In the following screenshot, you can see an excerpt of the results obtained by the query executed in step 5:

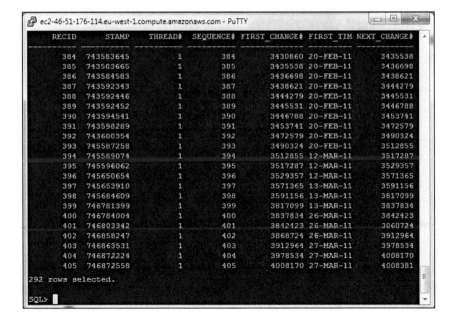

There's more...

We can also execute a statspack report and search for the **File IO Stats** section or for **log file parallel write** wait events in the **Event** section.

See also

- ► The *Tuning checkpoints* recipe in this chapter
- ► The *Analyzing data using Statspack report* recipe in *Chapter 1, Starting with Performance Tuning*

11
Tuning Contention

In this chapter, we will cover:

- ▶ Detecting and preventing lock contention
- ▶ Investigating transactions and concurrency
- ▶ Tuning latches
- ▶ Tuning resources to minimize latch contention
- ▶ Minimizing latches using bind variables

Introduction

In this chapter we will focus on preventing, detecting, and tuning contention-related issues.

In a database, as in any information system, there is a limited amount of resources to be shared among many users. When more than one user asks for a resource—which can be a file, a row in a table, a block in the buffer cache—there is a need for a synchronization mechanism to avoid the contemporary use of the resource itself by more than one user at a time.

In this chapter we will investigate two different synchronization mechanisms used in Oracle databases: **locks** and **latches**.

Locks are used to regulate access to a shared resource, such as a row or a table, while latches protect shared data structures and shared memory allocations in the System Global Area.

The main difference between locks and latches is that latches are held for a short time, while the purpose of locks is to protect resources for a relatively long time. Another difference is that locks involve a queuing mechanism and prioritization, whereas latches don't.

Detecting and preventing lock contention

If databases were used by a single user there would be no need for locks, because other users are not accessing the same data at the same time. In this recipe we will see how two concurrent sessions experience wait time due to locks, and how to diagnose them and what to do to resolve and avoid these situations.

Getting ready

In this recipe we use three concurrent SQL*Plus sessions to simulate two concurrent users in the first two sessions, while querying dynamic performance views in a third session. We will use the TESTDB database in the rest of this book.

How to do it...

The following steps will show how to detect and prevent lock contention:

1. Connect SESSION1 as user SH:

   ```
   -- SESSION 1
   CONNECT sh@TESTDB/sh
   ```

2. Update a row in SESSION1, not completing the transaction with a COMMIT or ROLLBACK statement:

   ```
   UPDATE CUSTOMERS SET
     CUST_FIRST_NAME = 'TEST1'
     WHERE CUST_ID = 26;
   ```

3. Connect SESSION2 as user SH:

   ```
   -- SESSION 2
   CONNECT sh@TESTDB/sh
   ```

4. Update the same row SESSION2 as in SESSION1:

   ```
   UPDATE CUSTOMERS SET
     CUST_FIRST_NAME = 'TEST2'
     WHERE CUST_ID = 26;
   ```

5. Connect SESSION3 as SYSDBA:

   ```
   -- SESSION 3
   CONNECT / AS SYSDBA
   ```

6. Inspect the active locks:

```
SELECT SID, ID1, ID2, BLOCK, TYPE, LMODE, REQUEST, CTIME
   FROM V$LOCK
MINUS
SELECT SID, ID1, ID2, BLOCK, TYPE, LMODE, REQUEST, CTIME
   FROM V$ENQUEUE_LOCK;
```

7. Verify the object on which the lock is held:

```
SELECT OWNER, OBJECT_NAME, OBJECT_TYPE
FROM ALL_OBJECTS
WHERE OBJECT_ID = 74136;
```

8. Query the V$LOCKED_OBJECT dynamic performance view:

```
SELECT * FROM V$LOCKED_OBJECT;
```

9. Query DBA_WAITERS to see which sessions are waiting due to a lock held by another session:

```
SELECT * FROM DBA_WAITERS;
```

10. Query DBA_BLOCKERS to see which sessions are holding a lock that is blocking another session:

```
SELECT * FROM DBA_BLOCKERS;
```

11. Execute the utllockt.sql script to view a tree representation of the current state of the locks:

```
@$ORACLE_HOME/rdbms/admin/utllockt.sql
```

12. View the object, file, block, and row locked:

```
SELECT
   SUBSTR(F.NAME, 1, 40) AS FILE_NAME,
   O.OWNER, O.OBJECT_NAME, O.OBJECT_TYPE,
   S.ROW_WAIT_BLOCK#, S.ROW_WAIT_ROW#
FROM V$SESSION S, V$DATAFILE F, ALL_OBJECTS O
WHERE S.SID = 17
AND S.ROW_WAIT_FILE# = F.FILE#
AND S.ROW_WAIT_OBJ# (+)= O.OBJECT_ID;
```

13. Acquire the `SERIAL#` and `SID` of the locked session (`SESSION2`):

    `SELECT SERIAL# FROM V$SESSION WHERE SID = 17;`

14. Kill the locked session:

    `ALTER SYSTEM KILL SESSION '17, 15';`

15. Complete the transaction in `SESSION1` to avoid other locking:

    `-- SESSION 1`

    `ROLLBACK;`

How it works...

We use two sessions of SQL*Plus connected as user `SH` to simulate the concurrent use of the same table/row by different users. In step 1 we connect the first session.

In step 2 the user updates one record in the `CUSTOMERS` table, not committing the transaction that is left open. In this situation a lock is held by the user in session 1 on the updated row until the transaction ends.

In step 3 we connect the second session as user `SH` and in step 4 we try to update the same record in step 2. By doing so, our session gets locked, waiting for the transaction in session 1 to be committed or rolled-back. We can see this situation in the following screenshot, where the terminal on the left is for session 1 and the terminal on the right is for session 2:

In the previous screenshot we can see that session 2 on the right is waiting.

In step 5 we connect another session to the database as `SYSDBA`, and in step 6 we execute a query to see the locks in the database, obtaining the following output:

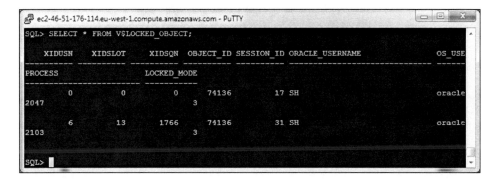

In the previous screenshot we can see the `SID`, identifying the session, and which session is locking (`BLOCK=1`) other sessions. In our example, session `31` (our `SESSION 1`) is blocking session `17` (our `SESSION 2`).

The `TYPE` field indicates that two different types of locks are held by session `31`: a `TM`, or **Table Level Lock**. This prevents DDL operations on the object with `ID 74136`, and a `TX`, or **Row Level Lock**, which ensures that at the same time no two transactions modify the same row.

In the previous screenshot we can also see the result for the query in step 7, which tells us that the object on which the `TM` lock is held is the `SH.CUSTOMERS` table.

In step 8 we query the `V$LOCKED_OBJECT` dynamic performance view, obtaining the following results:

Using this view we can see the undo segment number (**XIDUSN**), the slot number (**XIDSLOT**), and the sequence number (**XIDSQN**) by the session specified. The view also shows the object ID, the username (`SH` in our example), and other information about the locks acquired in the system.

The XIDUSN, XIDSLOT, and XIDSQN values can be used to identify a transaction, for example when using LogMiner to query online and archived redo log files.

In step 9 we query the `DBA_WAITERS` dynamic performance view, which is useful to correlate the blocked transactions to the blocking one, as we can see in the following screenshot:

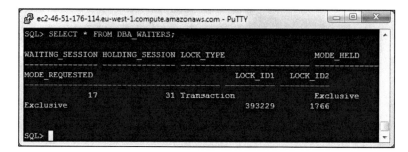

In the above screenshot observe that session 17 is blocked by session 31, the type of lock, and IDs of the objects involved.

The `DBA_BLOCKERS` dynamic performance view queried in step 10 is very simple, because there is only one column returned with the session IDs of the sessions holding locks, in our example session 31, as shown in the following screenshot:

In step 11 we execute the script `utllockt.sql`, located in the `/rdbms/admin` subfolder of our `ORACLE_HOME`; this returns a tree representation of the data we have queried in the dynamic performance views above, merged together. In the next screenshot you can see the results obtained by the script in this situation:

We can acquire data on locking from the V$SESSION dynamic performance view also, as in step 12. Here we join the V$DATAFILE and ALL_OBJECTS views to see the data files and objects responsible for the lock. In the following screenshot we can see the results obtained by executing this query:

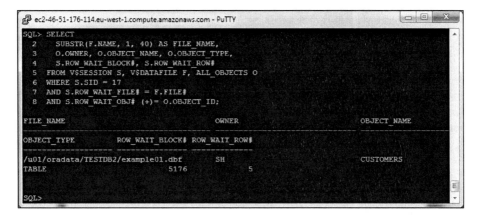

When we are in situations like the one analyzed in this recipe we can solve the issue by killing the blocked or the blocking session. To do so we need to know the SID and the Serial# of the session to kill, so in step 13 we query for this data from V$SESSION and in step 14 we kill the blocked session (SESSION 2). We can see the results of these operations in the next screenshot, where on the left side you will see the session in which we are connected as SYSDBA and on the right side you can see the output of the killed session:

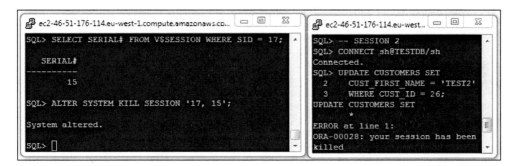

In the above screenshot you can see that, in the killed session, an error message informs us about what happened.

Another way to solve this issue is to terminate the blocking transactions by executing a COMMIT or a ROLLBACK. In step 15 we execute the ROLLBACK of the update, terminating the transaction and leaving the data in the table unchanged.

There's more...

In this recipe we have seen how to detect a lock in the system and retrieve more information about the locks.

There are many possible causes of contention. We have seen what happens when we have uncommitted changes like in our example. The same behavior can happen when there are long-running transactions, such as long batch jobs, or unnecessary high level locking.

The Oracle database automatically ensures the appropriate level of locking for DML and DDL operations, ensuring maximum availability and scalability. However, there are many products on the market that were not specifically designed for the Oracle database. They can require unnecessary high locking level; sometimes this behavior is also found in frameworks or APIs used in a multilayer application, which the developer is unaware of, causing locking problems.

As a rule of thumb, in developing applications for Oracle databases, always write code that acquires locks in the same order and don't use excessive locking for operations such as UPDATE and SELECT FOR UPDATE. Long-running batch jobs in OLTP environments should be scheduled in off-peak hours to avoid issues.

See also

See *Investigating transactions and concurrency* in this chapter.

Investigating transactions and concurrency

In this recipe we will see more details on locking and, specifically, on **deadlocks**.

Getting ready

In this recipe we will use two SQL*Plus sessions, to simulate two users concurrently accessing the database.

How to do it...

This recipe deals wits transactions and concurrency. Follow these steps:

1. Connect SESSION 1 to the database as SH user:

    ```
    -- SESSION 1
    CONNECT sh@TESTDB/sh
    ```

2. Update a row on the CUSTOMERS table in SESSION 1:

```
UPDATE CUSTOMERS SET
  CUST_FIRST_NAME = 'TEST1-1'
  WHERE CUST_ID = 26;
```

3. Connect SESSION 2 to the database as SH user:

```
-- SESSION 2
CONNECT sh@TESTDB/sh
```

4. Update a row on the CUSTOMERS table in SESSION 2, different from the one updated in step 2 by SESSION 1:

```
UPDATE CUSTOMERS SET
  CUST_FIRST_NAME = 'TEST2-1'
  WHERE CUST_ID = 30;
```

5. Try to update, in SESSION 1, the same row updated in step 4 by SESSION 2:

```
-- SESSION 1
UPDATE CUSTOMERS SET
  CUST_FIRST_NAME = 'TEST1-2'
  WHERE CUST_ID = 30;
```

6. Try to update, in SESSION 2, the same row updated in step 2 by SESSION 1:

```
-- SESSION 2
UPDATE CUSTOMERS SET
  CUST_FIRST_NAME = 'TEST2-2'
  WHERE CUST_ID = 26;
```

7. Rollback transaction in SESSION 1:

```
-- SESSION 1
ROLLBACK;
```

8. Rollback transaction in SESSION 2:

```
-- SESSION 2
ROLLBACK;
```

9. Connect to the database as SYSDBA:

```
-- SESSION 3
CONNECT / AS SYSDBA
```

10. Show the parameter USER_DUMP_DEST:

```
SHOW PARAMETER USER_DUMP_DEST
```

11. Use OS commands to see the trace file and the alert log in which the deadlock is recorded:

```
HOST
cd /u01/app/diag/rdbms/testdb/TESTDB/trace/
ls -ltr TESTDB_ora*.trc
more < TESTDB_ora_5997.trc
tail alert_TESTDB.log
exit
```

How it works...

In steps 2 and 4 we update two different rows in the CUSTOMERS table from two different sessions. As we can see in the following screenshots, the transactions are not locked due to this operation:

In step 5 we try to update, in SESSION 1, the same row updated above in SESSION 2. The transaction in SESSION 2 is still active, so the SESSION 1 will wait until the SESSION 2 transaction ends, as shown in the following screenshot:

In step 6 we try to update, in SESSION 2, the first row that was updated earlier in SESSION 1. The transaction in SESSION 1 is still active, so SESSION 2 should wait until the SESSION 1 transaction ends, as shown in the following screenshots:

In this situation, the transaction in SESSION 1 is waiting for a resource (the row in the CUSTOMERS table with CUST_ID = 30) locked by SESSION 2 which, in turn, is waiting for a resource (the row in CUSTOMERS table with CUST_ID = 26) locked by SESSION 1. This is a **deadlock**, and due to its cyclic nature there is no chance for the transactions involved to end regularly because they are blocking each other.

When the Oracle database detects a deadlock it automatically rolls back the statement causing the deadlock. You can see this in the following screenshot, where we have SESSION 1 on the left and SESSION 2 on the right:

It is the user's responsibility to rollback the whole transaction involved in the deadlock, as we do in step 7. The output is as follows:

In step 8 we also rollback the transaction in SESSION 2, to leave the data unchanged (but this is not mandatory; as we can see in the previous screenshot, the transaction in SESSION 2 is not locked and no errors are signaled, so we can continue our work).

In step 9 we connect a third session to the database and in step 10 we query the parameter USER_DUMP_DEST, which shows us the path in which trace files and the alert log are written. In our example database the location is /u01/app/diag/rdbms/testdb/TESTDB/trace/.

In step 11 we move to that directory using OS commands and list the trace files contained, sorted by date in reverse order. The result of this operation is shown in the next screenshot:

We identify the TESTDB_ora5997.trc as the trace file containing the trace regarding the detected deadlock, so we use the more OS command to inspect the contents of the trace file. The first excerpt can be seen in the following screenshot, which displays the DEADLOCK DETECTED ORA-00060 error at the end of the page:

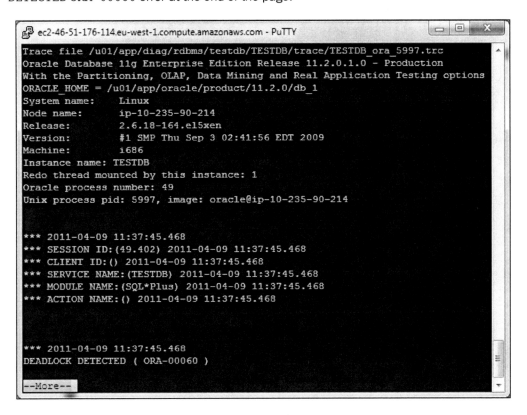

```
ec2-46-51-176-114.eu-west-1.compute.amazonaws.com - PuTTY

Trace file /u01/app/diag/rdbms/testdb/TESTDB/trace/TESTDB_ora_5997.trc
Oracle Database 11g Enterprise Edition Release 11.2.0.1.0 - Production
With the Partitioning, OLAP, Data Mining and Real Application Testing options
ORACLE_HOME = /u01/app/oracle/product/11.2.0/db_1
System name:    Linux
Node name:      ip-10-235-90-214
Release:        2.6.18-164.el5xen
Version:        #1 SMP Thu Sep 3 02:41:56 EDT 2009
Machine:        i686
Instance name: TESTDB
Redo thread mounted by this instance: 1
Oracle process number: 49
Unix process pid: 5997, image: oracle@ip-10-235-90-214


*** 2011-04-09 11:37:45.468
*** SESSION ID:(49.402) 2011-04-09 11:37:45.468
*** CLIENT ID:() 2011-04-09 11:37:45.468
*** SERVICE NAME:(TESTDB) 2011-04-09 11:37:45.468
*** MODULE NAME:(SQL*Plus) 2011-04-09 11:37:45.468
*** ACTION NAME:() 2011-04-09 11:37:45.468



*** 2011-04-09 11:37:45.468
DEADLOCK DETECTED ( ORA-00060 )

--More--
```

On the next page of the trace file that is reported in the following screenshot, you can see the processes and resources that caused the deadlock, along with information on the rows that caused the deadlock. This can help us to identify the possible causes:

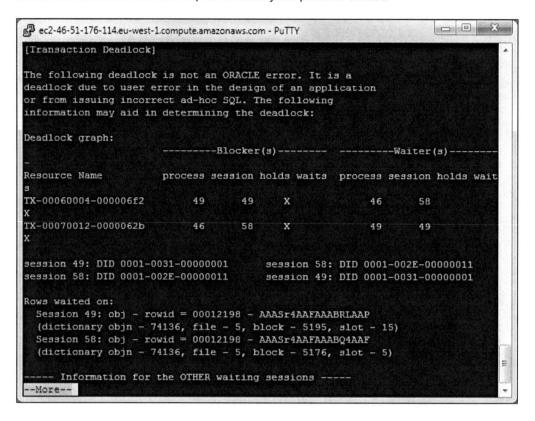

The information provided by the trace file also contains the session, the process, and the SQL statement that caused the deadlock for each process involved. In the following screenshot you can observe the UPDATE statement executed in SESSION 2 and the UPDATE statement executed in SESSION 1, for our example:

```
ec2-46-51-176-114.eu-west-1.compute.amazonaws.com - PuTTY
Session 58:
  sid: 58 ser: 617 audsid: 851306 user: 88/SH flags: 0x45
  pid: 46 O/S info: user: oracle, term: UNKNOWN, ospid: 6076
    image: oracle@ip-10-235-90-214
  client details:
    O/S info: user: oracle, term: pts/1, ospid: 6067
    machine: ip-10-235-90-214 program: sqlplus@ip-10-235-90-214 (TNS V1-V3)
    application name: SQL*Plus, hash value=3669949024
  current SQL:
  UPDATE CUSTOMERS SET
  CUST_FIRST_NAME = 'TEST2-2'
  WHERE CUST_ID = 26

----- End of information for the OTHER waiting sessions -----

Information for THIS session:

----- Current SQL Statement for this session (sql_id=7n8tt3g0a9pwa) -----
UPDATE CUSTOMERS SET
  CUST_FIRST_NAME = 'TEST1-2'
  WHERE CUST_ID = 30
========================================================================
PROCESS STATE
-------------
Process global information:
    process: 0x3bbd70d4, call: 0x387a8418, xact: 0x3a7d8324, curses: 0x3b270d
54, usrses: 0x3b270d54
--More--
```

These details are useful in identifying the statements that caused the issue, and you can change the application accordingly.

When a deadlock occurs it is also logged in the database alert log. In the next screenshot you can see the line in the alert log that identifies the trace file in which the details about the issue are saved, in our example TESTDB_ora_6424.trc:

```
ec2-46-51-176-114.eu-west-1.compute.amazonaws.com - PuTTY
$ tail alert_TESTDB.log
Sat Apr 09 11:40:46 2011
ORA-00060: Deadlock detected. More info in file /u01/app/diag/rdbms/testdb/TESTD
B/trace/TESTDB_ora_6424.trc.
Sat Apr 09 11:47:48 2011
Incremental checkpoint up to RBA [0x197.11231.0], current log tail at RBA [0x197
.11587.0]
Sat Apr 09 12:00:06 2011
Beginning log switch checkpoint up to RBA [0x198.2.10], SCN: 4048098
Thread 1 advanced to log sequence 408 (LGWR switch)
  Current log# 3 seq# 408 mem# 0: /u01/oradata/TESTDB2/redo03.log
Sat Apr 09 12:05:09 2011
Completed checkpoint up to RBA [0x198.2.10], SCN: 4048098
oracle@ip-10-235-90-214:[/u01/app/diag/rdbms/testdb/TESTDB/trace]
$
```

There's more...

A deadlock is a situation where two or more transactions are waiting for data locked by each other and none of these transactions can acquire the locks.

The database automatically detects the deadlocks and rolls back the statement causing it in a transaction when a deadlock is detected. It is the user's responsibility to rollback the remainder of the transaction.

Deadlocks are caused by excessive locking used by applications—which means that explicit locking was requested, overriding the default database behavior—or by statements that update data using different orders, as we have done in our example.

To avoid the latter cause of deadlocks, use shared code in your application to accomplish the same task. This way you can be sure that operations will always be executed in the same order, limiting the possibility of a deadlock.

See also

See *Detecting and preventing lock contention* in this chapter.

Tuning latches

In this recipe we will see what latches are, and how (and if) we can tune latches. We will discover that we don't tune latches, but we tune resources that can cause issues related to latches.

How to do it...

The following steps will demonstrate how to tune latches:

1. Connect to the database as `SYSDBA`:

   ```
   CONNECT / AS SYSDBA
   ```

2. Investigate system events related to latches:

   ```
   SELECT
      EVENT, TIME_WAITED, TOTAL_WAITS
   FROM V$SYSTEM_EVENT
   WHERE EVENT LIKE '%latch%';3
   ```

3. Query information about **willing-to-wait latch** requests:

```
COL NAME FOR A20
SELECT * FROM (
 SELECT
   NAME, GETS, MISSES, SLEEPS, SPIN_GETS, WAIT_TIME
 FROM V$LATCH
 ORDER BY GETS DESC
)
WHERE ROWNUM < 11;
```

4. Query information about **immediate latch** requests:

```
COL NAME FOR A40
SELECT * FROM (
 SELECT
   NAME, IMMEDIATE_GETS, IMMEDIATE_MISSES
 FROM V$LATCH
 ORDER BY IMMEDIATE_GETS DESC
)
WHERE ROWNUM < 11;
```

How it works...

In step 2 we query the V$SYSTEM_EVENT dynamic performance view to see if latch contention causes high waits on the system. Inspecting the value for the TIME_WAITED column, expressed in hundredths of a second, we obtain the following results:

If we have experienced a high value for the `latch free` event—we know that the value is high if we encounter a latch free event in the top timed events in a statspack or AWR report—we need to investigate the causes for latch contention in our database.

We can do this by querying the `V$LATCH` dynamic performance view. In step 3 we query for information about willing-to-wait latches, obtaining the results shown in the following screenshot:

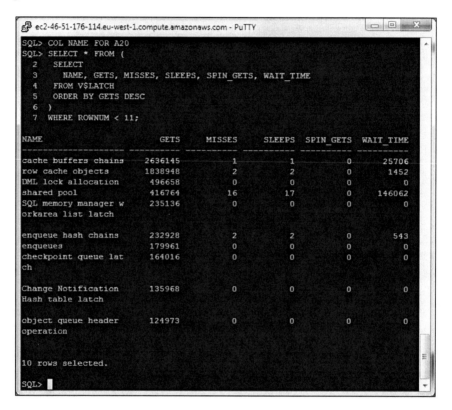

In the example results, we can see that there is a high wait time (and some misses and sleeps) for shared pool latches, so we can identify the area of the database that needs to be tuned.

In step 4 we query the same dynamic performance view as above, this time investigating immediate latch requests.

We can see the results of the query in the following screenshot:

Obviously, we can obtain the same results in a single query; here we preferred to split the results into two queries for graphical reasons.

There's more...

Latches are lightweight synchronization mechanisms that implement serialization in an efficient and low-level way. They don't support queuing, so when a latch request is not satisfied, the request fails and the process can only retry to acquire the busy latch, by polling.

The internal implementation of latches is related to the OS and platform. Often it's implemented using a single memory location and a single atomic instruction to test and set the latch. Busy latches are usually identified by a non-zero value.

When more latches are needed to access a specific data structure, for example the library cache, there is a parent-child latch relationship, so the database needs to acquire the parent latch to access the child latch.

In single processor machines (are there any more?), when a latch was busy the process requesting the latch would release the CPU and sleep for a brief time, to allow other processes to acquire the CPU. This event was logged as a **latch free** wait event.

Single processor machines are being replaced by multi-core machines. However, when using Instance Caging, we can have single processor/core assigned to a database instance. In these situations, the considerations made for single processor machine are still valid.

On multiprocessor/multicore systems, another mechanism is in place. The requesting process can "spin", which means it holds the CPU and counts to a specific number, consuming CPU cycles but not releasing the CPU, avoiding a costly context switch. This behavior allows processes executed on other machine cores to proceed and eventually release the required latch. Obviously, a high number of "spins" affects performance, and the maximum number of spins a process can execute when waiting for a latch before releasing the CPU is platform and OS specific. In single core/processor systems, spinning makes no sense (when a process "spins" no other processes are executed, which results only in wasting CPU time).

We have referred to two different types of latches: willing-to-wait latch requests and immediate latch requests. The difference is in the behavior of the process when the latch is in use. In willing-to-wait requests the process sleeps and then acquires the latch again, when it becomes available. In immediate requests, the process not acquiring the latch will eventually release the latches already acquired—to avoid deadlocks—and releases the CPU before trying to acquire the latches again.

The query used in this recipe investigates the top 10 requested latches, showing the misses for both willing-to-wait and immediate (also referred as no-wait) latch requests.

The answer to the question titling this recipe is "NO", we don't tune latches; we investigate possible latch contentions using the statement in this recipe and then we tune the resources causing latch contention.

See also

▸ *Tuning resources to minimize latch contention* in this chapter
▸ *Minimizing latches using bind variables* in this chapter

Tuning resources to minimize latch contention

In this recipe we will see how to identify the resources that need to be tuned to minimize latch contention.

Getting ready

In this recipe we will present how to diagnose a latch contention problem using a Statspack report, obtained with the procedures used in *Chapter 1*.

How to do it...

To identify the resources to be tuned to avoid latch contention we need to:

1. Execute a Statspack report.

2. See in the **Instance Efficiency Indicators** section the value for **Latch Hit %**.

3. See in the **Top 5 Timed Events** section if there is a **latch free** wait event.

4. Verify the **Latch Activity** section to identify the kind of latches that are eventually experiencing misses (and sleeps for willing-to-wait requests).

5. Verify the **Latch Sleep breakdown** section to identify the type of latches with the highest misses.

6. Verify the **Latch Miss Sources** section to identify, among the latch requests experiencing sleeps, where the latch misses occur.

How it works...

After executing a statspack report, we can go to the **Instance Efficiency Indicators** section to see the value for the **Latch Hit %**, to see the Hit percentage of latches, as in step 2. The following screenshot shows the report for a database with small Latch Misses (the value for **Latch Hit %** is **100.00**):

```
Instance Efficiency Indicators
~~~~~~~~~~~~~~~~~~~~~~~~~~~~~~~~~~~~
            Buffer Nowait %:  100.00      Redo NoWait %:  100.00
            Buffer  Hit   %:   99.81  Optimal W/A Exec %:  100.00
            Library Hit   %:   91.42       Soft Parse %:    2.92
         Execute to Parse %:    0.50        Latch Hit %:  100.00
Parse CPU to Parse Elapsd %:   97.34     % Non-Parse CPU:    8.42
```

In step 3 we investigate the section **Top 5 Timed Events**, in which a latch-related **Latch Free** wait event can indicate an issue in latch contention. In the next screenshot we can see the result for our test database, resulting in latch-related problems:

```
Top 5 Timed Events                                          Avg %Total
~~~~~~~~~~~~~~~~~~~                                          wait  Call
Event                            Waits   Time (s)   (ms)    Time
----------------------------- ------------ ------------ ------ ------
CPU time                                        73             98.5
latch free                         16            0     24       .5
direct path write                 462            0      1       .4
db file sequential read            32            0      5       .2
direct path read                    8            0      9       .1
                              ------------ ------------ ------ ------
```

In step 4 we verify the **Latch Activity** section of the report, an excerpt of which is represented in the next screenshot, where we can find values on sleeps and misses from willing-to-wait and no-wait latches:

```
              Latch Activity  DB/Inst: TESTDB/testdb  Snaps: 2-3
->"Get Requests", "Pct Get Miss" and "Avg Slps/Miss" are statistics for
  willing-to-wait latch get requests
->"NoWait Requests", "Pct NoWait Miss" are for no-wait latch get requests
->"Pct Misses" for both should be very close to 0.0

                                   Pct   Avg   Wait
                            Get    Get   Slps  Time          NoWait
Latch                     Requests Miss  /Miss  (s)         Requests
------------------------- --------------- ------ ------ ------ ------------
active checkpoint queue       491   0.0            0             0
active service list           677   0.0            0           454
AQ deq hash table latch         1   0.0            0             0
ASM db client latch           245   0.0            0             0
ASM map operation hash t        1   0.0            0             0
ASM network state latch         5   0.0            0             0
buffer pool                     3   0.0            0             0
business card                   1   0.0            0             0
cache buffer handles          278   0.0            0             0
cache buffers chains       31,361   0.0            0         6,472
cache buffers lru chain     4,531   0.0   0.0      0         6,179
```

In this section, for each type of latch, we have the statistics for willing-to-wait latch get requests (**Pct Get Miss** and **Avg Slps/Miss**) and for no-wait latch get requests (**NoWait Requests** and **Pct NoWait Miss**). For both types of latches the Pct Misses should be very close to 0.0, as stated in the heading of this section.

In steps 5 and 6 we observe the **Latch Sleep breakdown** and **Latch Miss Sources** to get information on the events with the highest misses and the related source, as shown in the next screenshot:

```
Latch Sleep breakdown  DB/Inst: TESTDB/testdb  Snaps: 3-4
-> ordered by misses desc

                                 Get
Latch Name                    Requests       Misses       Sleeps
------------------------  ---------------  ------------  ----------  ---
shared pool                    4,410,310          341          56
row cache objects             31,315,577          149           2
enqueues                          99,984            1           1
qmn task queue latch                  12            1           1
                          --------------------------------------------------

Latch Miss Sources  DB/Inst: TESTDB/testdb  Snaps: 3-4
-> only latches with sleeps are shown
-> ordered by name, sleeps desc

                                                 NoWait
Latch Name               Where                   Misses      Sleeps
------------------------  ------------------------  -------  ----------
enqueues                 ksqgel: create enqueue        0           1
qmn task queue latch     kwqmnmvtsks: delay to read    0           1
row cache objects        kqrpre: find obj              0           1
row cache objects        kqreqd                        0           1
shared pool              kghalo                        0          43
shared pool              kghupr1                       0           9
shared pool              kghalp                        0           4
                          --------------------------------------------------
```

Using this section of the statspack report we can identify the events that are causing the highest misses. In the above example, there were 341 misses (and 56 sleeps) on requests involving latches on the shared pool, and 149 misses (and 2 sleeps) on requests for latches on row cache objects.

There's more...

There are several types of latches on which we may experience contention. The most common are the **shared pool latches**, identifying a problem related to the application. Maybe the cursor cache is too small or we are explicitly closing cursors too soon—for example after each execution.

The **library cache latches** are used when finding SQL statements in the library cache. High wait time values for this type of latch requests are caused by unnecessary parses and not using bind variables, as we will see in the next recipe.

Cache buffers (LRU) chain latches are used to protect data blocks and LRU lists in the buffer cache. When we experience contention on these latches, we probably need to tune large full table or index scans in our application to minimize them. Increasing the buffer cache size or the number of DBWn processes may help if there is too much buffer cache activity. Contention also indicates that a data block is heavily accessed. This can be identified by the following query, where 'X' is the address of the child latch; we can get this from the V$LATCH_CHILDREN dynamic performance view:

```
SELECT * FROM X$BH
WHERE HLADDR = 'X'
```

We can then join the DBA_EXTENTS view to identify the segment, to which the heavily accessed data block belongs.

The **redo copy** and **redo allocation latches** are used to write into the redo log buffer. Experiencing contention on this latch, requests can be avoided from executing, when possible, statements using the NOLOGGING option or increasing the LOG_BUFFER parameter.

See also

- The *Analyzing data using Statspack report* recipe in *Chapter 1*
- *Tuning latches* in this chapter
- *Minimizing latches using bind variables* in this chapter

Minimizing latches using bind variables

In this recipe we will see how not using bind variables leads to latch contentions.

Getting ready

We will use the same package used in *Chapter 4*, where we have discussed using bind variables in our application code, to compare the execution with and without the use of bind variables.

How to do it...

The following steps will show how we can minimize latches by using bind variables:

1. Connect to the database as `SYSDBA`:

   ```
   CONNECT / AS SYSDBA
   ```

2. Query the V$SYSTEM_EVENT dynamic performance view to monitor latch-related events:

   ```
   COL EVENT FOR A37

   SELECT EVENT, TOTAL_WAITS, TIME_WAITED, AVERAGE_WAIT,
     TOTAL_TIMEOUTS

   FROM V$SYSTEM_EVENT WHERE EVENT LIKE 'latch:%' ORDER BY EVENT;
   ```

3. Connect to the SH schema and create the package CHAPTER4 containing a test workload:

   ```
   -- FROM CHAPTER 4 EXAMPLE...

   CONNECT sh@TESTDB/sh

   CREATE OR REPLACE PACKAGE sh.CHAPTER4 AS

      PROCEDURE WORKLOAD_NOBIND;

      PROCEDURE WORKLOAD_BIND;

      PROCEDURE WORKLOAD_BIND_STATIC;

      PROCEDURE TEST_INJECTION(

         NAME IN sh.customers.cust_last_name%TYPE);

      PROCEDURE TEST_INJECTION2(

         NAME IN sh.customers.cust_last_name%TYPE);

   END;
   /

   CREATE OR REPLACE PACKAGE BODY sh.CHAPTER4 AS

      PROCEDURE TEST_NOBIND(CUSTID IN sh.customers.cust_id%TYPE) IS

      BEGIN

         DECLARE aRow sh.customers%ROWTYPE;

         l_stmt VARCHAR2(2000);

         BEGIN

            l_stmt :=

            'SELECT * FROM sh.customers s WHERE s.cust_id = ' ||

            TO_CHAR (CUSTID);

         EXECUTE IMMEDIATE l_stmt INTO aRow;

         END;
   ```

```
       END TEST_NOBIND;

       PROCEDURE TEST_BIND(CUSTID IN sh.customers.cust_id%TYPE) IS
       BEGIN
         DECLARE aRow sh.customers%ROWTYPE;
         l_stmt VARCHAR2(2000);
         BEGIN
           l_stmt := 'SELECT * FROM sh.customers s WHERE s.cust_id =
             :p_cust_id';
         EXECUTE IMMEDIATE l_stmt INTO aRow USING CUSTID;
         END;
       END TEST_BIND;

       PROCEDURE TEST_BIND_STATIC(
         CUSTID IN sh.customers.cust_id%TYPE) IS
       BEGIN
         DECLARE aRow sh.customers%ROWTYPE;
         BEGIN
         SELECT * INTO aROW FROM sh.customers s
           WHERE s.cust_id = CUSTID;
           EXCEPTION
           WHEN NO_DATA_FOUND THEN
           NULL;
         END;
       END TEST_BIND_STATIC;

       PROCEDURE WORKLOAD_NOBIND IS
       BEGIN
         FOR i IN 1..50000
         LOOP
         TEST_NOBIND(i);
         END LOOP;
       END WORKLOAD_NOBIND;

       PROCEDURE WORKLOAD_BIND IS
       BEGIN
         FOR i IN 1..50000
```

```
      LOOP
        TEST_BIND(i);
      END LOOP;
    END WORKLOAD_BIND;

    PROCEDURE WORKLOAD_BIND_STATIC IS
    BEGIN
      FOR i IN 1..50000
      LOOP
      TEST_BIND_STATIC(i);
      END LOOP;
    END WORKLOAD_BIND_STATIC;

    PROCEDURE TEST_INJECTION(
      NAME IN sh.customers.cust_last_name%TYPE) IS
    BEGIN
      DECLARE l_stmt VARCHAR2(2000); res NUMBER;
      BEGIN
      l_stmt := 'SELECT COUNT(*) FROM sh.customers s WHERE
          s.cust_last_name = ''' || NAME || '''';
      EXECUTE IMMEDIATE l_stmt INTO res;
      DBMS_OUTPUT.PUT_LINE('Count: ' || TO_CHAR(res));
      END;
    END TEST_INJECTION;

    PROCEDURE TEST_INJECTION2(
      NAME IN sh.customers.cust_last_name%TYPE) IS
    BEGIN
      DECLARE l_stmt VARCHAR2(2000);
      BEGIN
      l_stmt := 'BEGIN DBMS_OUTPUT.PUT_LINE (''You passed ' ||
          NAME || '''); END;';
      EXECUTE IMMEDIATE l_stmt;
      END;
    END TEST_INJECTION2;
  END;
/
```

4. Connect as SYSDBA and execute the WORKLOAD_NOBIND procedure, executing the query in step 2 before and after the procedure execution to monitor latch contention:

```
CONNECT / AS SYSDBA
ALTER SYSTEM FLUSH SHARED_POOL;

SELECT
   EVENT, TOTAL_WAITS,
   TIME_WAITED, AVERAGE_WAIT, TOTAL_TIMEOUTS
FROM V$SYSTEM_EVENT
WHERE EVENT LIKE 'latch:%' ORDER BY EVENT;

exec sh.CHAPTER4.WORKLOAD_NOBIND;

SELECT
   EVENT, TOTAL_WAITS,
   TIME_WAITED, AVERAGE_WAIT, TOTAL_TIMEOUTS
FROM V$SYSTEM_EVENT
WHERE EVENT LIKE 'latch:%' ORDER BY EVENT;
```

5. Execute the WORKLOAD_BIND procedure as in step 2 and compare the results obtained with the ones in step 4:

```
ALTER SYSTEM FLUSH SHARED_POOL;

SELECT
   EVENT, TOTAL_WAITS,
   TIME_WAITED, AVERAGE_WAIT, TOTAL_TIMEOUTS
FROM V$SYSTEM_EVENT
WHERE EVENT LIKE 'latch:%' ORDER BY EVENT;

exec sh.CHAPTER4.WORKLOAD_BIND;

SELECT
   EVENT, TOTAL_WAITS,
   TIME_WAITED, AVERAGE_WAIT, TOTAL_TIMEOUTS
FROM V$SYSTEM_EVENT
WHERE EVENT LIKE 'latch:%' ORDER BY EVENT;
```

6. Drop the package CHAPTER4:

```
DROP PACKAGE sh.CHAPTER4;
```

How it works...

In step 2 we query the `V$SYSTEM_EVENT` dynamic performance view for events related to latches, and we obtain the following results:

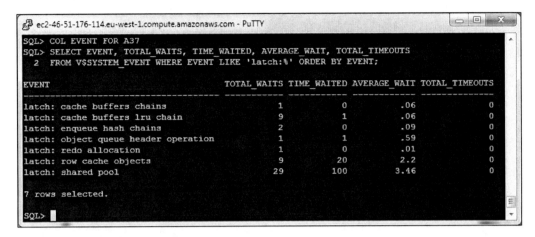

We can see 29 waits on **shared pool latches** and a `TIME_WAITED` of 100.

In step 3 we create a test package and in step 4 we execute a workload procedure that does not use bind variables. Before and after the execution we query the view as in step 2, to compare the results obtained.

In the following screenshot we can see that there is an increase in shared pool latch waits from **29** to **58**, and a TIME_WAITED value raised from **100** to **135**:

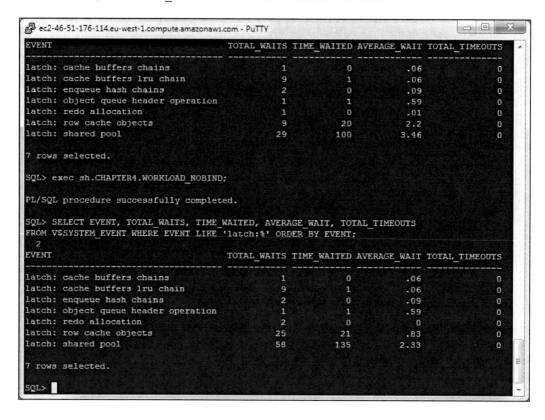

In step 5 we execute an analogous workload as in step 4, this time using bind variables. As in the previous step, we query the V$SYSTEM_EVENT immediately before and after the execution of the package procedure, obtaining the results shown in the following screenshot. No additional shared pool latch waits have been added, to those already reported:

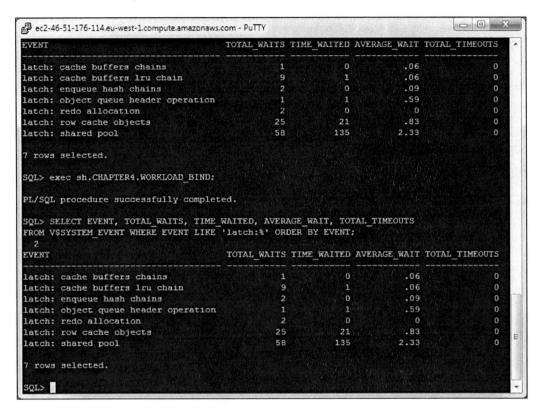

In step 6 we drop the package created in step 3.

There's more...

In previous recipes we have seen that not using bind variables led to performance and scalability problems, not sharing SQL statements.

In this recipe we have also seen that when we don't use bind variables, there are latch contentions on the library cache. We can see this behavior by inspecting the V$SYSTEM_EVENT dynamic performance view.

As stated in previous recipes, we don't tune latch contention, but the presence of these types of issues in the database is an alert signal that something else is wrong and it needs to be tuned.

See also

- ▶ *Chapter 4, Using bind variables*
- ▶ *Tuning latches* in this chapter
- ▶ *Tuning resources to minimize latch contention* in this chapter

Dynamic Performance Views

In this book, we have been presented with many dynamic performance views, used to access a wide spread of details about an Oracle database, regarding different aspects from the sessions to the SQL statement executed.

In this appendix, we present a summary of these views, in alphabetical order, which can be used as a reference. For each view, there is a brief description and a list of the most useful fields of the view.

ALL_OBJECTS

This view lists all the database objects the current user can access. As for many ALL_ views, there are similar DBA_OBJECTS and USER_OBJECTS views; they have the same fields but DBA_OBJECTS shows all the objects in the database, while USER_OBJECTS shows information only on the objects of the current user.

This view is often joined to other dynamic performance views, for example, V$LOCKED_OBJECT, by OBJECT_ID to obtain the object name and owner.

Fields

The most relevant view fields are as follows:

- OWNER: The owner of the object
- OBJECT_NAME: The name of the object
- OBJECT_ID: The unique ID associated to the object in the data dictionary

- ▶ OBJECT_TYPE: The object type, such as TABLE, INDEX, and so on
- ▶ CREATED: The timestamp for the creation of the object
- ▶ STATUS: The status of the object, such as VALID, INVALID, or N/A

DBA_BLOCKERS

This view returns the session IDs of the sessions holding locks.

Fields

There is only one field in this view, namely, HOLDING_SESSION.

See also

- ▶ The DBA_WAITERS and V$SESSION sections in this appendix

DBA_DATA_FILES

This view returns all datafiles. It's often joined with other views by the FILE_ID field, sometimes named as FILE# in other views.

Fields

The most relevant view fields are as follows:

- ▶ FILE_ID: A unique ID associated with the file
- ▶ FILE_NAME: The name of the database file
- ▶ TABLESPACE_NAME: The name of the tablespace to which the file belongs
- ▶ BYTES: The size in bytes
- ▶ BLOCKS: The size in database blocks
- ▶ STATUS: The status of the file, related to its availability; can be AVAILABLE or INVALID (for example, a file in a dropped tablespace)
- ▶ ONLINE_STATUS: The online status of the file, can be SYSOFF, SYSTEM, OFFLINE, ONLINE, or RECOVER

See also

- ▶ The DBA_EXTENTS, FILE$, V$DATAFILE, V$LOGFILE, DBA_TEMP_FILES, and V$CONTROLFILE sections in this appendix

DBA_EXTENTS

This view returns the extents which build the database files. No extent information is showed for offline datafiles in locally managed tablespaces.

Fields

The most relevant view fields are as follows:

- ▸ SEGMENT_TYPE: The type of the segment, such as INDEX (PARTITION), or TABLE (PARTITION)
- ▸ OWNER: The owner of the associated segment
- ▸ SEGMENT_NAME: The name of the associated segment
- ▸ TABLESPACE_NAME: The name of the tablespace containing the extent
- ▸ BYTES: The size in bytes
- ▸ BLOCKS: The size in database blocks
- ▸ FILE_ID: The file identifier of the file containing the extent
- ▸ EXTENT_ID: The extent number in the segment

See also

- ▸ The DBA_DATA_FILES section in this appendix

DBA_INDEXES

In this view are listed all the indexes in the database. There are the corresponding ALL_INDEXES and USER_INDEXES, showing, respectively, the indexes which the current user can access and the indexes the current user owns.

Fields

The most relevant view fields are as follows:

- ▸ OWNER: The owner of the index
- ▸ INDEX_NAME: The name of the index
- ▸ TABLE_OWNER: The owner of the table on which the index is built
- ▸ TABLE_NAME: The name of the table on which the index is built
- ▸ TABLESPACE_NAME: The name of the tablespace in which the index is stored
- ▸ STATUS: This can be VALID or UNUSABLE

- ▶ INDEX_TYPE: The type of the index; can be NORMAL, BITMAP, FUNCTION-BASED NORMAL, FUNCTION-BASED BITMAP, or DOMAIN
- ▶ TABLE_TYPE: The type of the indexed object (TABLE or CLUSTER)
- ▶ UNIQUENESS: Whether the index is UNIQUE or NONUNIQUE
- ▶ COMPRESSION: If the index is compressed then the value is ENABLED, else DISABLED
- ▶ PREFIX_LENGTH: The number of columns in the compressed prefix of the key
- ▶ LEAF_BLOCKS: The number of leaf blocks in the index

DBA_SQL_PLAN_BASELINES

Displays information about the SQL Plan baselines created for a specific SQL statement.

Fields

The most relevant view fields are as follows:

- ▶ SQL_HANDLE: A unique identifier
- ▶ SQL_TEXT: The un-normalized SQL text
- ▶ PLAN_NAME: A unique plan identifier
- ▶ ENABLED: This indicates whether the plan baseline is enabled (YES/NO)
- ▶ ACCEPTED: This indicates if the plan baseline is accepted (YES/NO)
- ▶ FIXED: This indicates if the plan baseline is fixed (YES/NO)
- ▶ EXECUTIONS: The number of executions at the time the plan baseline was created

DBA_TABLES

This view lists all the tables in the database. There are the corresponding ALL_TABLES and USER_TABLES, showing, respectively, the tables which the current user can access and the tables the current user owns.

Fields

The most relevant view fields are as follows:

- ▶ OWNER: The owner of the table
- ▶ TABLE_NAME: The name of the table
- ▶ TABLESPACE_NAME: The name of the tablespace in which the table is stored
- ▶ STATUS: This can be VALID or UNUSABLE

- ▶ LOGGING: This indicates whether changes to the table are logged or not (YES/NO)
- ▶ NUM_ROWS: The number of rows in the table
- ▶ BLOCKS: The number of used database blocks in the table
- ▶ EMPTY_BLOCKS: The number of empty database blocks in the table
- ▶ AVG_SPACE: The average free space in bytes for allocated data blocks
- ▶ CHAIN_CNT: The number of chained rows in the table
- ▶ AVG_ROW_LEN: The average length of a row in the table
- ▶ AVG_SPACE_FREELIST_BLOCKS: The average free space of all blocks on a freelist
- ▶ NUM_FREELIST_BLOCKS: The number of blocks in a freelist
- ▶ SAMPLE_SIZE: The sample size used when analyzing the table
- ▶ GLOBAL_STATS: For partitioned tables, this indicates whether the statistics were made on all the partitions (YES) or estimated (NO)
- ▶ USER_STATS: This indicates whether the statistics were entered by the user (YES/NO)
- ▶ LAST_ANALYZED: The date on which the table was last analyzed

DBA_TEMP_FILES

This view shows all temporary files in the database.

Fields

The most relevant view fields are as follows:

- ▶ FILE_ID: A unique ID associated to the file
- ▶ FILE_NAME: The name of the temporary file
- ▶ TABLESPACE_NAME: The name of the tablespace to which the file belongs
- ▶ BYTES: The size in bytes
- ▶ BLOCKS: The size in database blocks

See also

- ▶ The DBA_EXTENTS, FILE$, V$DATAFILE, V$LOGFILE, DBA_DATA_FILES, and V$CONTROLFILE sections in this appendix

DBA_VIEWS

This view shows all the views in the database. There are the corresponding ALL_VIEWS and USER_VIEWS, that show, respectively, the views which the current user can access and the views the current user owns.

Fields

The most relevant view fields are as follows:

- OWNER: The owner of the view
- VIEW_NAME: The name of the view
- TEXT: The text of the view

DBA_WAITERS

This view shows all the sessions waiting for a lock. It correlates a blocked transaction to the blocking one.

Fields

The most relevant view fields are as follows:

- WAITING_SESSION: The ID of the waiting session
- HOLDING_SESSION: The ID of the session holding the lock
- LOCK_TYPE: The type of lock
- MODE_HELD: The locking mode held
- MODE_REQUESTED: The locking mode requested

See also

- The DBA_BLOCKERS, V$LOCK, and V$LOCKED_OBJECT sections in this appendix

INDEX_STATS

This view collects information from index statistics (after an ANALYZE INDEX).

Fields

The most relevant view fields are as follows:

- ▸ NAME: The name of the index
- ▸ HEIGHT: The height of the B-tree index
- ▸ BLOCKS: The number of allocated database blocks
- ▸ BTREE_SPACE: The total space allocated
- ▸ USED_SPACE: The total space used
- ▸ DISTINCT_KEYS: The number of distinct keys in the index
- ▸ OPT_CMPR_COUNT: The optimal key compression length
- ▸ OPT_CMPR_PCTSAVE: Space saving corresponding to the adoption of the optimal key compression length

See also

- ▸ The DBA_INDEXES section in this appendix

DBA_SEQUENCES

This lists all the user sequences. It's a synonym for USER_SEQUENCES.

Fields

The most relevant view fields are as follows:

- ▸ SEQUENCE_OWNER: The owner of the sequence
- ▸ SEQUENCE_NAME: The name of the sequence
- ▸ MIN_VALUE: The minimum value of the sequence
- ▸ MAX_VALUE: The maximum value of the sequence
- ▸ INCREMENT_BY: The value by which the sequence is incremented
- ▸ CYCLE_FLAG: This indicates whether the sequence numbering restarts after it has reached the upper limit
- ▸ ORDER_FLAG: This indicates whether the sequence is ordered (numbers generated in order) or not; this is useful in an RAC environment
- ▸ CACHE_SIZE: The number of sequence numbers to cache
- ▸ LAST_NUMBER: The last number written to disk; if caching is enabled, it is the last number placed in the sequence cache

DBA_TABLESPACES

This is a dynamic performance view equivalent to the `SYS.TS$` table containing information on all tablespaces; the only difference is that `DBA_TABLESPACES` doesn't list dropped tablespaces.

Fields

The most relevant view fields are as follows:

- `TABLESPACE_NAME`: The name of the tablespace
- `BLOCK_SIZE`: The database block size used in the tablespace
- `STATUS`: This can be `ONLINE`, `OFFLINE`, or `READ ONLY`
- `CONTENTS`: This can be `UNDO`, `PERMANENT`, or `TEMPORARY`
- `LOGGING`: This can be `LOGGING` or `NOLOGGING`
- `EXTENT_MANAGEMENT`: This can be `DICTIONARY` for dictionary managed or `LOCAL` for locally managed tablespaces
- `ALLOCATION_TYPE`: This can be `SYSTEM`, `USER`, or `UNIFORM`

DBA_TAB_HISTOGRAMS

This view describes histograms on all the tables and views generated when collecting statistics using the `ANALYZE` statement or `DBMS_STATS` package. There are the equivalent views `ALL_TAB_HISTOGRAMS` and `USER_TAB_HISTOGRAMS`; the first contains information on all the objects accessible by the current user, the last on the current user objects in the database.

Fields

The most relevant view fields are as follows:

- `OWNER`: The owner of the table
- `TABLE_NAME`: The name of the table
- `COLUMN_NAME`: The name of the column
- `ENDPOINT_NUMBER`: The histogram bucket number
- `ENDPOINT_VALUE`: The normalized endpoint value for the bucket
- `ENDPOINT_ACTUAL_VALUE`: The actual endpoint value (not normalized) for the bucket

V$ADVISOR_PROGRESS

This view inspects the execution progress of a SQL Tuning Advisor set.

Fields

The most relevant view fields are as follows:

- `SID`: The session ID
- `SERIAL#`: The session serial number
- `USERNAME`: The Oracle username
- `OPNAME`: The operation name
- `ADVISOR_NAME`: The advisor name
- `TASK_ID`: The task ID
- `SOFAR`: The amount of work done so far
- `TOTALWORK`: The total work to be done
- `TIME_REMAINING`: The estimated remaining time in seconds

V$BUFFER_POOL_STATISTICS

This displays statistics about buffer pools in the database instance.

Fields

The most relevant view fields are as follows:

- `ID`: The buffer pool identifier
- `NAME`: The name of the buffer pool
- `FREE_BUFFER_WAIT`: The free buffer wait statistic
- `WRITE_COMPLETE_WAIT`: The write complete wait statistic
- `BUFFER_BUSY_WAIT`: The buffer busy wait statistic
- `DB_BLOCK_GETS`: The number of database blocks gotten statistic
- `CONSISTENT_GETS`: The number of consistent gets statistic
- `PHYSICAL_READS`: The number of physical reads statistic
- `PHYSICAL_WRITES`: The number of physical writes statistic

See also

> ▸ The `V$DB_CACHE_ADVICE` section to get advice in sizing the buffer pools

V$CONTROLFILE

This lists the names of the control files.

Fields

The most relevant view fields are as follows:

> ▸ `STATUS`: This is null if the name can be determined, `INVALID` otherwise
>
> ▸ `NAME`: The control filename
>
> ▸ `IS_RECOVERY_DEST_FILE`: This indicates whether the control file was created in the fast recovery area (`YES`) or not (`NO`)
>
> ▸ `BLOCK_SIZE`: The control file block size
>
> ▸ `FILE_SIZE_BLKS`: The control file size in blocks

See also

> ▸ The `V$DATAFILE`, `DBA_TEMP_FILES`, `V$FILESTAT`, `V$LOGFILE`, and `V$TEMPFILE` sections in this appendix

V$DATAFILE

This lists datafile information taken from the control file.

Fields

The most relevant view fields are as follows:

> ▸ `FILE#`: The file identification number
>
> ▸ `NAME`: The filename
>
> ▸ `CREATION_TIME`: The timestamp of file creation
>
> ▸ `TS#`: The tablespace identification number

- ▸ STATUS: The datafile status; can be OFFLINE, ONLINE, SYSTEM, RECOVER, or SYSOFF
- ▸ ENABLED: This describes if the file is accessible; the possible values are DISABLED, READ ONLY, READ WRITE, or UNKNOWN
- ▸ BYTES: The datafile size in bytes
- ▸ BLOCKS: The datafile size in database blocks

See also

- ▸ The V$FILESTAT, V$LOGFILE, and V$TEMPFILE sections in this appendix

V$DB_CACHE_ADVICE

This view contains predictions on the number of physical reads obtained when varying the cache size.

Fields

The most relevant view fields are as follows:

- ▸ ID: The buffer pool identifier
- ▸ NAME: The buffer pool name
- ▸ BLOCK_SIZE: The size of the database block for this pool
- ▸ SIZE_FOR_ESTIMATE: The cache size for prediction in megabytes
- ▸ BUFFERS_FOR_ESTIMATE: The cache size for prediction in number of buffers
- ▸ ESTD_PHYSICAL_READS: The estimated number of physical reads for the cache size evaluated
- ▸ ESTD_PHYSICAL_READ_FACTOR: The estimated physical read factor for the cache size evaluated, a ratio to the number of reads in the cache

See also

- ▸ The V$BUFFER_POOL_STATISTICS and V$DB_OBJECT_CACHE sections in this appendix

V$DB_OBJECT_CACHE

This view lists objects currently cached in the library cache.

Fields

The most relevant view fields are as follows:

- OWNER: The owner of the object
- NAME: The object name
- TYPE: The object type, for example, INDEX, TABLE, VIEW, CLUSTER, SEQUENCE, PROCEDURE, FUNCTION, PACKAGE, TRIGGER, or CLASS
- SHARABLE_MEM: The amount of memory in the shared pool used by the object
- KEPT: If the object was pinned in the library cache using the DBMS_SHARED_POOL. KEEP procedure, the value is YES, otherwise NO
- LOADS: The number of times the object was loaded
- LOCKS: The number of users locking the object
- PINS: The number of users pinning the object
- INVALIDATIONS: The number of times the object was marked invalid because a dependent object was modified

See also

- The ALL_OBJECTS section in this appendix

V$ENQUEUE_LOCK

This view shows the locks owned by enqueue state objects.

Fields

The most relevant view fields are as follows:

- ADDR: The address of the lock state object
- KADDR: The address of the lock
- SID: The identifier for the session holding or acquiring the lock
- TYPE: The type of lock
- ID1: Lock identifier #1 (depends on TYPE)

- ▸ ID2: Lock identifier #2 (depends on TYPE)
- ▸ LMODE: A lock mode in which the session holds the lock; values can be:
  - ❏ NONE
  - ❏ NULL (NULL)
  - ❏ ROW-S (SS)
  - ❏ ROW-X
  - ❏ SHARE (S)
  - ❏ S/ROW-X (SSX)
  - ❏ EXCLUSIVE (X)
- ▸ REQUEST: A lock mode in which the process request locks; values are the same as for LMODE fields
- ▸ CTIME: The time since the current mode was grant
- ▸ BLOCK: Whether this lock is blocking another lock

See also

- ▸ The V$LOCK, V$LOCKED_OBJECT, DBA_WAITERS, and DBA_BLOCKERS sections in this appendix

V$FILESTAT

This view displays statistics about I/O operations on files.

Fields

The most relevant view fields are as follows:

- ▸ FILE#: The file identification number
- ▸ PHYRDS: The number of physical reads done
- ▸ PHYWRTS: The number of physical writes done
- ▸ READTIM: The time spent doing reads (in hundredths of a second)
- ▸ WRITETIM: The time spent doing writes (in hundredths of a second)

See also

- ▸ The V$DATAFILE section in this appendix

V$FIXED_TABLE

This view lists all V$ and X$ Dynamic Performance Views.

Fields

The most relevant view fields are as follows:

- NAME: The object name
- OBJECT_ID: The object identification number
- TYPE: The object type; can be TABLE or VIEW
- TABLE_NUM: If the type is TABLE, it identifies the dynamic performance table

V$INSTANCE_RECOVERY

This view monitors the mechanisms available to the user/DBA to limit the I/O needed for recovery.

Fields

The most relevant view fields are as follows:

- RECOVERY_ESTIMATED_IOS: The estimated number of data blocks to process during recovery
- ESTIMATED_MTTR: The estimated time recovery based on the current system load
- TARGET_MTTR: The **Mean Time To Recover** (**MTTR**) target value in seconds
- LOG_FILE_SIZE_REDO_BLKS: The number of redo blocks required to be sure that a log switch won't occur before the checkpoint completes
- LOG_CHKPT_INTERVAL_REDO_BLKS: The number of redo blocks that will be processed during recovery to satisfy the LOG_CHECKPOINT_INTERVAL parameter
- LOG_CHKPT_TIMEOUT_REDO_BLKS: The number of redo blocks that will be processed during recovery to satisfy the LOG_CHECKPOINT_TIMEOUT parameter
- ACTUAL_REDO_BLKS: The current number of redo blocks needed to recover
- TARGET_REDO_BLKS: The current target number of redo blocks that must be processed for recovery

V$LATCH

This view displays aggregate latch statistics.

Fields

The most relevant view fields are as follows:

- LATCH#: The latch number
- NAME: The latch name
- GETS: The number of times the latch is requested in the willing-to-wait mode
- MISSES: The number of times the latch is requested in willing-to-wait mode and the requestor had to wait
- SLEEPS: The number of times a willing-to-wait latch request resulted in a session sleeping
- SPIN_GETS: The number of times a willing-to-wait latch request was satisfied only after a spin
- WAIT_TIME: The elapsed time spent waiting for the latch in microseconds
- IMMEDIATE_GETS: The number of times the latch is requested in no-wait mode
- IMMEDIATE_MISSES: The number of times a no-wait latch request was unsatisfied

See also

- The V$LATCH_CHILDREN recipe in this appendix

V$LATCH_CHILDREN

This view displays statistics about child latches.

Fields

The most relevant view fields are:

- CHILD#: The child latch number
- LATCH#: The parent latch number
- NAME: The latch name
- GETS: The number of times the latch is requested in willing-to-wait mode

- ▸ MISSES: The number of times the latch is requested in willing-to-wait mode, and the requestor had to wait

- ▸ SLEEPS: The number of times a willing-to-wait latch request resulted in a session sleeping

- ▸ SPIN_GETS: The number of times a willing-to-wait latch request was satisfied only after a spin

- ▸ WAIT_TIME: The elapsed time spent waiting for the latch in microseconds

- ▸ IMMEDIATE_GETS: The number of times the latch is requested in no-wait mode

- ▸ IMMEDIATE_MISSES: The number of times a no-wait latch request was unsatisfied

See also

- ▸ The V$LATCH section in this appendix

V$LIBRARYCACHE

Displays statistics on library cache activity.

Fields

The most relevant view fields are:

- ▸ NAMESPACE: The library cache namespace

- ▸ GETS: The number of times a lock was requested for objects in the namespace

- ▸ GETHITRATIO: The number of times the object's handle was found in memory

- ▸ PINS: The number of times a PIN was requested for objects in the namespace

- ▸ PINHITRATIO: The number of times the object's metadata were found in memory

- ▸ RELOADS: Any PIN of the object, following the first after object creation, which requires loading the object from disk

- ▸ INVALIDATIONS: The number of times objects in the namespace were marked invalid due to dependent object modifications

V$LOCK

This view lists the locks held by the database.

Fields

The most relevant view fields are:

▸ SID: An identifier for the session holding or acquiring the lock

▸ ID1: Lock identifier #1 (depends on TYPE)

▸ ID2: Lock identifier #2 (depends on TYPE)

▸ TYPE: The type of lock; user locks can be TM (DML enqueue), TX (transaction enqueue), or UL (user supplied)

▸ LMODE: A lock mode in which the session holds the lock; values can be:

- ❑ NONE
- ❑ NULL (NULL)
- ❑ ROW-S (SS)
- ❑ ROW-X
- ❑ SHARE (S)
- ❑ S/ROW-X (SSX)
- ❑ EXCLUSIVE (X)

▸ REQUEST: A lock mode in which the process request locks; values are the same as for the LMODE field

▸ CTIME: The time since current mode was granted

▸ BLOCK: If the lock is blocking another lock the value is 1, otherwise the value is 0

See also

▸ The DBA_BLOCKERS, DBA_WAITERS, V$ENQUEUE_LOCK, and V$LOCKED_OBJECT sections in this appendix

V$LOCKED_OBJECT

This view shows which sessions are holding DML locks and on what objects.

Fields

The most relevant view fields are:

- XIDUSN: The undo segment number
- XIDSLOT: The slot number
- XIDSQN: The sequence number
- OBJECT_ID: The object ID being locked
- SESSION_ID: The session identifier number
- ORACLE_USERNAME: The Oracle username
- OS_USER: The operating system user
- PROCESS: The operating system process identifier
- LOCKED_MODE: The lock mode

See also

- The DBA_BLOCKERS, DBA_WAITERS, V$ENQUEUE_LOCK, and V$LOCK sections in this appendix

V$LOG

This view displays information on log files from the control file.

Fields

The most relevant view fields are:

- GROUP#: The log group number
- THREAD#: The log thread number
- SEQUENCE#: The log sequence number
- BYTES: The size of the log in bytes
- BLOCKSIZE: The block size of the log file

- ▸ MEMBERS: The number of members in the log group
- ▸ ARCHIVED: The archive status (YES or NO)
- ▸ STATUS: The log status; it can be UNUSED, CURRENT, ACTIVE, CLEARING, CLEARING_CURRENT, or INACTIVE
- ▸ FIRST_CHANGE#: The lowest system change number stored in the log
- ▸ FIRST_TIME: The time of the first system change number in the log

See also

- ▸ The V$LOG_HISTORY and V$LOGFILE sections in this appendix

V$LOG_HISTORY

This view shows the log history from the control file.

Fields

The most relevant view fields are:

- ▸ RECID: The control file record ID
- ▸ STAMP: The control file record stamp
- ▸ THREAD#: The thread number of the archived log
- ▸ SEQUENCE#: The sequence number of the archived log
- ▸ FIRST_CHANGE#: The lowest system change number in the log
- ▸ FIRST_TIME: The time of the first entry in the log
- ▸ NEXT_CHANGE#: The highest system change number in the log
- ▸ RESETLOGS_CHANGE#: The *resetlogs change number* of the database when the log was written
- ▸ RESETLOGS_TIME: The *resetlogs time* of the database when the log was written

See also

- ▸ The V$LOG and V$LOGFILE sections in this appendix

V$LOGFILE

This view contains information about redo log files.

Fields

The most relevant view fields are as follows:

- GROUP#: The redo log group identification number
- STATUS: The status of the log member; it can be INVALID, STALE, DELETED, or NULL when the file is in use
- TYPE: The type of the log file, it can be ONLINE or STANDBY
- MEMBER: The redo log member name
- IS_RECOVERY_DEST_FILE: This indicates whether the file was created in the fast recovery area (YES) or not (NO)

See also

- The V$LOG and V$LOG_HISTORY recipes in this appendix

V$MYSTAT

This view contains statistics on the current session.

Fields

The most relevant view fields are as follows:

- SID: The session identifier for the current session
- STATISTIC#: The number of the STATISTIC
- VALUE: The value of the STATISTIC

See also

- The V$STATNAME, V$SESSTAT, and V$SYSSTAT sections in this appendix

V$PROCESS

This view displays information about the currently active processes.

Fields

The most relevant view fields are as follows:

- ▸ `PID`: An Oracle process identifier
- ▸ `SPID`: The operating system process identifier
- ▸ `ADDR`: The address of the process state object
- ▸ `SERIAL#`: The process serial number
- ▸ `PNAME`: The name of the process
- ▸ `USERNAME`: The operating system process username
- ▸ `TERMINAL`: The operating system terminal identifier
- ▸ `PROGRAM`: The program currently in progress

See also

- ▸ The `V$SESSION` section in this appendix

V$ROLLSTAT

This view contains rollback segments statistics.

Fields

The most relevant view fields are as follows:

- ▸ `USN`: The rollback segment number
- ▸ `LATCH`: The latch for the rollback segment
- ▸ `EXTENTS`: The number of extents in the rollback segment
- ▸ `RSSIZE`: The size of the rollback segment in bytes

- ▶ WRITES: The number of bytes written to the rollback segment
- ▶ XACTS: The number of active transactions
- ▶ GETS The number of header gets
- ▶ WAITS: The number of header waits
- ▶ STATUS: The rollback segment status, it can be ONLINE, OFFLINE, PENDING OFFLINE, or FULL

V$ROWCACHE

This view displays statistics about the data dictionary activity.

Fields

The most relevant view fields are as follows:

- ▶ PARAMETER: The name of the initialization parameter that determines the number of entries in the data dictionary cache
- ▶ GETS: The total number of requests for information on the data object
- ▶ GETMISSES: The number of data requests resulting in cache misses
- ▶ MODIFICATIONS: The number of inserts, updates, and deletions
- ▶ FLUSHES: The number of times flushed to disk

V$SESSION

This view displays information on each current session.

Fields

The most relevant view fields are as follows:

- ▶ SID: The session identifier
- ▶ SADDR: The session address
- ▶ SERIAL#: The session serial number
- ▶ PROCESS: The operating system client process ID
- ▶ PADDR: The address of the process that owns this session
- ▶ AUDSID: The auditing session ID

- ▸ EVENT: The resource or event for which the session is waiting
- ▸ P1, P2, P3: Wait event parameters
- ▸ WAIT_TIME: This is set to:
    - ❑ -2 if TIMED_STATISTICS is set to false
    - ❑ -1 if the last wait duration was less than a hundredth of a second
    - ❑ 0 if the session is currently waiting
    - ❑ A value greater than zero, which is the duration of the last wait in hundredths of a second
- ▸ LAST_CALL_ET: The elapsed time in seconds since the session has become active/inactive
- ▸ SQL_ID: The identifier of the currently executed SQL statement
- ▸ PREV_SQL_ID: The identifier of the last SQL statement executed
- ▸ ROW_WAIT_BLOCK#: The identifier for the block containing the row specified in ROW_WAIT_ROW#
- ▸ ROW_WAIT_ROW#: The current row being locked
- ▸ ROW_WAIT_FILE#: The file identifier for the datafile containing the row specified in ROW_WAIT_ROW#
- ▸ ROW_WAIT_OBJ#: The object ID for the table containing the row specified in ROW_WAIT_ROW#

See also

- ▸ The V$SESSION_EVENT and V$SESSTAT sections in this appendix

V$SESSION_EVENT

This view displays information on waits for an event by a session.

Fields

The most relevant view fields are as follows:

- ▸ SID: The session identifier
- ▸ EVENT: The name of the wait event
- ▸ TOTAL_WAITS: The total number of waits for the event in the session
- ▸ TOTAL_TIMEOUTS: The total number of timeouts for the event in the session

- ▸ TIME_WAITED: The total amount of time waited, in hundredths of a second for the event in the session
- ▸ AVERAGE_WAIT: The average amount of time waited, in hundredths of a second for the event in the session
- ▸ MAX_WAIT: The maximum time waited, in hundredths of a second for the event in the session
- ▸ EVENT_ID: The wait event identifier

See also

- ▸ The V$SESSION and V$SESSTAT sections in this appendix

V$SESSTAT

This view displays statistics on the sessions.

Fields

The most relevant view fields are as follows:

- ▸ SID: The session identifier
- ▸ STATISTIC#: The statistic number
- ▸ VALUE: The statistic value

See also

- ▸ The V$STATNAME section in this appendix

V$SGA

This view displays summary information about the **System Global Area (SGA)**.

Fields

The most relevant view fields are as follows:

- ▸ NAME: The SGA component group
- ▸ VALUE: The memory size of the SGA component group in bytes

See also

▸ The V$SGAINFO section in this appendix

V$SGAINFO

This view displays detailed information about the SGA components.

Fields

The most relevant view fields are as follows:

▸ NAME: The name of the SGA component

▸ BYTES: The size in bytes

▸ RESIZEABLE: This indicates whether the component is resizable (YES) or not (NO)

See also

The V$SGA section in this appendix

V$SHARED_POOL_RESERVED

This view displays statistics useful in tuning the shared pool.

Fields

The most relevant view fields are as follows:

▸ FREE_SPACE: The amount of free space on the reserved list

▸ USED_SPACE: The amount of used memory on the reserved list

▸ REQUESTS: The number of times that the reserved list was searched for a free piece of memory

▸ REQUEST_MISSES: The number of times the reserved list did not have a free piece of memory to satisfy the request, and started flushing objects from the LRU list

▸ REQUEST_FAILURES: The number of times that no memory was found to satisfy a request

V$SORT_SEGMENT

This view displays information about every sort segment in a given instance.

Fields

The most relevant view fields are as follows:

- ▸ TABLESPACE_NAME: The name of the tablespace
- ▸ CURRENT_USERS: The active users of the segment
- ▸ TOTAL_BLOCKS: The total number of blocks in the segment
- ▸ USED_BLOCKS: The number of blocks in the segment allocated to active sorts
- ▸ FREE_BLOCKS: The number of blocks in the segment not allocated to any sort
- ▸ MAX_BLOCKS: The maximum number of blocks ever used
- ▸ MAX_USED_BLOCKS: The maximum number of blocks used by all sorts
- ▸ MAX_SORT_BLOCKS: The maximum number of blocks used by an individual sort
- ▸ EXTENT_SIZE: The extent size
- ▸ TOTAL_EXTENTS: The total number of extents in the segment
- ▸ USED_EXTENTS: The extents allocated to active sorts
- ▸ FREE_EXTENTS: The extents not allocated to any sort
- ▸ EXTENT_HITS: The number of times an unused extent was found in the pool

V$SQL

This view lists statistics on shared SQL areas.

Fields

The most relevant view fields are as follows:

- ▸ SQL_ID: The identifier of the parent cursor in the library cache
- ▸ SQL_TEXT: The first thousand characters of the SQL text
- ▸ SQL_FULLTEXT: The full text of the SQL statement
- ▸ EXECUTIONS: The number of executions that took place on this object since it was brought into the library cache

- ▸ INVALIDATIONS: The number of times this child cursor has been invalidated

- ▸ PARSE_CALLS: The number of parse calls for this child cursor

- ▸ IS_BIND_SENSITIVE: This indicates whether the cursor is bind sensitive (Y) or not (N). A query is considered bind-sensitive if the optimizer peeked at one of its bind variable values when computing predicate selectivity and where a change in a bind variable value may cause the optimizer to generate a different plan

- ▸ IS_BIND_AWARE: This indicates whether the cursor is bind aware (Y) or not (N); a query is considered bind-aware if it has been marked to use extended cursor sharing

- ▸ IS_SHAREABLE: This indicates whether the cursor can be shared (Y) or not (N)

See also

- ▸ The V$SESSION, V$SQL_PLAN, and V$SQLAREA sections in this appendix

V$SQL_PLAN

This view contains information on execution plans for each child cursor loaded in the library cache.

Fields

The most relevant view fields are as follows:

- ▸ OPERATION: The name of the internal operation performed in the step

- ▸ OBJECT_OWNER: The owner of the object (table or index)

- ▸ OBJECT_NAME: The name of the object (table or index)

- ▸ HASH_VALUE: The hash value of the parent statement in the library cache

- ▸ SQL_ID: The SQL identifier of the parent cursor in the library cache

- ▸ PLAN_HASH_VALUE: The hash value representing the SQL plan for the cursor, useful to compare two plans

See also

The V$SQL and V$SQLAREA sections in this appendix

V$SQLAREA

This view displays statistics on shared SQL areas, containing one row per SQL string.

Fields

The most relevant view fields are as follows:

- SQL_ID: The identifier of the parent cursor in the library cache
- SQL_TEXT: The first thousand characters of the SQL text
- SQL_FULLTEXT: The full text of the SQL statement
- USERS_EXECUTING: The total number of users executing the statement
- LOADS: The number of times the object was loaded or reloaded
- HASH_VALUE: The hash value for the parent statement in the library cache
- ADDRESS: The address of the handle for the parent cursor
- COMMAND_TYPE: The Oracle command type definition
- EXECUTIONS: The number of executions that took place on this object since it was brought into the library cache
- INVALIDATIONS: The number of times this child cursor has been invalidated
- PARSE_CALLS: The number of parse calls for this child cursor
- IS_BIND_SENSITIVE: This indicates whether the cursor is bind sensitive (Y) or not (N). A query is considered bind-sensitive if the optimizer peeked at one of its bind variable values when computing predicate selectivity and where a change in a bind variable value may cause the optimizer to generate a different plan
- IS_BIND_AWARE: This indicates whether the cursor is bind aware (Y) or not (N); a query is considered bind-aware if it has been marked to use extended cursor sharing

See also

- The V$SQL and V$SQL_PLAN recipes in this appendix

V$STATNAME

This view is used to decode a statistic identifier to its description.

Fields

The most relevant view fields are as follows:

- ▸ STATISTIC#: The statistic number (may change across different database versions)
- ▸ NAME: The statistic name
- ▸ CLASS: A number representing one or more STATISTIC classes ORed together; this can be:
  - ❑ 1: User
  - ❑ 2: Redo
  - ❑ 4: Enqueue
  - ❑ 8: Cache
  - ❑ 16: OS
  - ❑ 32: Real Application Clusters
  - ❑ 64: SQL
  - ❑ 128: Debug
- ▸ STAT_ID: The identifier of the STATISTIC

See also

- ▸ The V$MYSTAT, V$SESSTAT, and V$SYSSTAT sections in this appendix

V$SYSSTAT

This view displays system statistics.

Fields

The most relevant view fields are as follows:

- ▸ STATISTIC#: The statistic number
- ▸ NAME: The statistic name
- ▸ CLASS: A number representing one or more statistic classes ORed together; the values are same as those mentioned in the previous section
- ▸ VALUE: The statistic value
- ▸ STAT_ID: The identifier of the statistic

See also

▸ The V$MYSTAT, V$SESSTAT, and V$STATNAME sections in this appendix

V$SYSTEM_EVENT

This view displays information on total waits for an event.

Fields

The most relevant view fields are as follows:

▸ EVENT: The name of the wait event

▸ EVENT_ID: The identifier of the wait event

▸ TOTAL_WAITS: The total number of waits for the event

▸ TIME_WAITED: The total amount of time waited in hundredths of a second for the event

▸ AVERAGE_WAIT: The average amount of time waited in hundredths of a second for the event

▸ TOTAL_TIMEOUTS: The total number of timeouts for the event

V$TEMPFILE

This view displays temporary file information.

Fields

The most relevant view fields are as follows:

▸ FILE#: The file identifier number

▸ NAME: The filename

▸ STATUS: The file status; it can be ONLINE or OFFLINE

▸ ENABLED: This is enabled for read and/or write

▸ BYTES: The size of the file in bytes

▸ BLOCKS: The size of the file in blocks

▸ BLOCK_SIZE: The block size for the file

V$TEMPSTAT

This view displays statistics about I/O operations on temporary files.

Fields

The most relevant view fields are as follows:

- ▶ FILE#: The file identification number
- ▶ PHYRDS: The number of physical reads performed
- ▶ PHYWRTS: The number of physical writes performed
- ▶ READTIM: The time spent doing reads in hundredths of a second
- ▶ WRITETIM: The time spent doing writes in hundredths of a second

See also

- ▶ The V$TEMPFILE section in this appendix

V$WAITSTAT

This view displays block contention statistics.

Fields

The most relevant view fields are as follows:

- ▶ CLASS: The class of the block
- ▶ COUNT: The number of waits for this CLASS of block
- ▶ TIME: The sum of all wait times for this CLASS of block

See also

- ▶ The V$SESSION and V$SESSION_EVENT sections in this appendix

X$BH

This view displays the status and number of pings for every buffer in the SGA.

Fields

The most relevant view fields are as follows:

- OBJ: The object identifier
- HLADDR: The address of the child latch
- TS#: The tablespace identifier number
- FILE#: The file identifier number
- BLOCK#: The database block identifier number

A Summary of Oracle Packages Used for Performance Tuning

In this book we have used various Oracle tools and packages to investigate and solve performance issues.

There are also many tools in the market, made by third-party software vendors, which can help DBAs and developers in many fields, from coding PL/SQL packages and procedures to analyzing data warehouses or tuning the database I/O.

In this appendix we present a brief summary of these packages, providing a small reference from which we can start when we want to solve a performance problem. The packages are presented in alphabetical order.

DBMS_ADDM

This package provides procedures to manage Oracle Automatic Database Diagnostic Monitor.

Procedures

The most relevant procedures are:

- ▸ ANALYZE_DB: creates an ADDM task to analyze the database and execute it
- ▸ ANALYZE_INST: creates an ADDM task for analyzing in instance analysis mode and executes it
- ▸ GET_REPORT: retrieves the default text report of an executed ADDM task

DBMS_ADVISOR

This package helps in managing the Advisors, a set of expert systems that identify and help resolve performance problems related to various database server components.

Procedures

The most relevant procedures are:

- ▸ SET_DEFAULT_TASK_PARAMETER: sets the default values for task parameters
- ▸ QUICK_TUNE: performs an analysis on a single SQL statement
- ▸ EXECUTE_TASK: executes the specified task

DBMS_JOB

Schedules and manages jobs in the database job queue.

 Oracle recommends using the DBMS_SCHEDULER package.

Procedures

The most relevant procedures are:

- ▸ SUBMIT: submits a new job to the job queue
- ▸ RUN: forces a specified job to run
- ▸ NEXT_DATE: alters the next execution time for a specified job
- ▸ BROKEN: deletes a job execution
- ▸ REMOVE: removes the specified job from the job queue

DBMS_LOB

This package provides procedures to work with BLOBs, CLOBs, NCLOBs, BFILEs, and temporary LOBs.

Procedures

The most relevant procedures are:

- GET_LENGTH: gets the length of the LOB value
- FILEOPEN: opens a file
- LOADFROMFILE: loads LOB data from a file
- APPEND: appends the contents of a source LOB to a destination LOB
- OPEN: opens an LOB
- READ: reads data from the LOB starting at the specified offset
- WRITE: writes data to the LOB from a specified offset
- CLOSE: closes a previously opened LOB

DBMS_MVIEW

This package helps the management of Materialized Views, refreshes them and helps understanding the capabilities for materialized views and potential materialized views.

Procedures

The most relevant procedures are:

- EXPLAIN_MVIEW: explains what is possible with a materialized view or potential materialized view
- EXPLAIN_REWRITE: explains why a query failed to rewrite or why the optimizer chose to rewrite a query with a particular materialized view(s)
- REFRESH: refreshes one or more materialized views
- REFRESH_ALL_MVIEWS: refreshes all the materialized views

DBMS_OUTLN

This package contains the functional interface to manage stored outlines.

To use this package the EXECUTE_CATALOG_ROLE role is needed. There is also a public synonym OUTLN_PKG.

Procedures

The most relevant procedures are:

- CLEAR_USED: clears the outline "used" flag
- DROP_BY_CAT: drops outlines which belong to a specific category
- UPDATE_BY_CAT: updates the category of outlines to a new category
- DROP_UNUSED: drops outlines never applied in the compilation of a SQL statement

DBMS_OUTLN_EDIT

This package contains the functional interface to manage stored outlines.

The public role has execute privileges on DBMS_OUTLN_EDIT, which is defined with invoker's rights.

Procedures

The most relevant procedures are:

- CREATE_EDIT_TABLES: creates outline editing tables in calling a user's schema; beginning from Oracle 10g, you will not need to use this procedure because the outline editing tables are part—as temporary tables—of the SYSTEM schema
- REFRESH_PRIVATE_OUTLINE: refreshes the in-memory copy of the outline, synchronizing its data with the edits made to the outline hints
- DROP_EDIT_TABLES: drops the outline editing tables from the calling user's schema

DBMS_SHARED_POOL

This package allows access to information about sizes of the objects stored in the shared pool and marks them for keeping or not-keeping.

Procedures

The most relevant procedures are:

- KEEP: keeps an object in the shared pool, so it isn't subject to aging
- UNKEEP: unkeeps an object from the shared pool
- PURGE: purges the object
- SIZES: shows objects in the shared pool larger than the specified size

DBMS_SPACE

This package enables the analysis of segment growth and space requirements.

Procedures

The most relevant procedures are:

- CREATE_TABLE_COST: determines the size of a table
- CREATE_INDEX_COST: determines the size of an index
- FREE_BLOCKS: returns information about free blocks in an object
- SPACE_USAGE: returns information about free blocks in a segment managed by automatic space management

DBMS_SPM

This package provides an interface to manipulate plan history and SQL plan baselines.

Procedures

The most relevant procedures are:

- LOAD_PLANS_FROM_CURSOR_CACHE: loads one or more plans from the cursor cache for a SQL statement
- LOAD_PLANS_FROM_SQLSET: loads plans stored in a SQL tuning set into SQL plan baselines
- EVOLVE_SQL_PLAN_BASELINE: evolves SQL plan baselines associated with one or more SQL statements, changing them to accepted if they are found to be better than the SQL plan baseline performance and if the user asks such action
- DROP_SQL_PLAN_BASELINE: drops a single plan or all the plans associated with a SQL statement

DBMS_SQL

This package provides an interface to use dynamic SQL to parse both DML and DDL statements using PL/SQL.

Procedures

The most relevant procedures are:

- ▸ EXECUTE: executes a cursor
- ▸ OPEN_CURSOR: returns the cursor ID number of the new cursor
- ▸ PARSE: parses the given statement
- ▸ BIND_VARIABLE: binds a given value to a given variable
- ▸ CLOSE_CURSOR: closes a given cursor and frees associated memory

DBMS_SQLTUNE

This package provides an interface to tune SQL statements.

Procedures

The most relevant procedures related to the SQL tuning set are:

- ▸ CREATE_SQLSET: creates a SQL tuning set object in the database
- ▸ DROP_SQLSET: drops a SQL tuning set if not active
- ▸ SELECT_SQLSET: collects SQL statements from an existing SQL tuning set
- ▸ LOAD_SQLSET: populates the SQL tuning set with a set of selected SQL statements
- ▸ SELECT_CURSOR_CACHE: collects SQL statements from the cursor cache

The most relevant procedures to manage SQL tuning tasks are:

- ▸ CREATE_TUNING_TASK: creates a tuning of a single statement or tuning set
- ▸ EXECUTE_TUNING_TASK: executes a previously created tuning task
- ▸ REPORT_TUNING_TASK: displays the results of a tuning task
- ▸ INTERRUPT_TUNING_TASK: interrupts the currently executing tuning task
- ▸ RESUME_TUNING_TASK: resumes a previously interrupted tuning task

DBMS_STATS

This package allows you to view and modify optimizer statistics.

Procedures

The most relevant procedures are:

- ► GATHER_SCHEMA_STATS: gathers optimizer statistics for a schema class
- ► GATHER_DATABASE_STATS: gathers optimizer statistics for a database class
- ► GATHER_TABLE_STATS: gathers table statistics
- ► GATHER_INDEX_STATS: gathers index statistics
- ► CREATE_STAT_TABLE: creates the user statistics table
- ► DROP_STAT_TABLE: drops the user statistics table
- ► EXPORT_SCHEMA_STATS: exports schema statistics to a user statistics table
- ► IMPORT_SCHEMA_STATS: import schema statistics from a user statistics table

DBMS_UTILITY

This package provides various utility subprograms.

Procedures

The most relevant procedures are:

- ► ANALYZE_SCHEMA: analyzes all the tables, indexes, and clusters in a schema
- ► ANALYZE_DATABASE: analyzes all the tables, indexes, and clusters in a database
- ► GET_TIME: returns the current time in hundredths of a second

DBMS_WORKLOAD_REPOSITORY

This package allows management of Workload Repository.

Procedures

The most relevant procedures are:

- ► CREATE_SNAPSHOT: creates a manual snapshot
- ► MODIFY_SNAPSHOT_SETTINGS: modifies the snapshot settings
- ► CREATE_BASELINE: creates a single baseline

Index

Symbols

$ROWCACHE view 490

A

adaptive cursor sharing
  about 327
  for bind variable peeking 317, 320-327
ADDM
  about 15, 32
  running, in database mode 32
  running, in partial mode 33
  used, for analyzing data 32-36
ADMINISTER SQL MANAGEMENT OBJECT
      privilege 335
Advice button 376
alert log
  used, for diagnosing performance
      issues 28, 29
ALL_OBJECTS view 469
ALL_ROWS 296
ALTER INDEX REBUILD command 130
ALTER OUTLINE statement 316
ALTER SYSTEM FLUSH SHARED_POOL
      command 394
ANALYZE command 21
ANALYZE_DATABASE procedure 507
ANALYZE_DB procedure 502
ANALYZE_INST procedure 502
ANALYZE_SCHEMA procedure 507
anti-join query 195
APPEND 297
APPEND procedure 503

array processing
  about 257
  demonstrating 257, 258
  working 259-262
arrays
  about 181
  direct path load, using 185, 186
  used for inserting data, in tables 181-185
asynchronous I/O
  about 425
  FILESYSTEMIO_OPTIONS parameter 427
  using 425-427
  working 426
AUTOALLOCATE option 252
Automatic Database Diagnostic Monitor.
      See **ADDM**
Automatic Memory Management (AMM) 376
Automatic Memory Management
      enhancement 215
AUTOMATIC policy 211
Automatic Segment Space Management
      (ASSM) 172
Automatic Workload Repository. *See* **AWR**
AWR
  used, for analyzing data 29-31

B

batch processing 47
BEFORE INSERT trigger 134
BIG_ROWS table 87
bind variable peeking
  adaptive cursor sharing 317, 320-327
BIND_VARIABLE procedure 506

bind variables
about 254, 255
security 161
testing 157
used, for minimizing latches 460, 464-468
using 154
working 158, 159, 256, 257
bitmap indexes
bitmap join index 140
CUST_GENDER column 139
FULL TABLE SCAN operation 139
using 136-138
working 138, 139
bitmap join index 140
BLOB field 101
BROKEN procedure 502
B-Tree Index
about 119
index entries 120
leaf nodes 120
Buffer Cache hit ratio 407
buffer cacher
Buffer Cache hit ratio 407
KEEP buffer cache 406
KEEP pool 409
RECYCLE pool 409
tuning 400
tuning, steps 400, 402
working 402-405
bulk-collect
about 257
working 259-262

C

Cache buffers (LRU) chain latches 460
CACHE (table_name) 297
c_file BLOB field 101
checkpoint
about 428
checkpoint queue 432, 433
tuning 428
working 429-432
checkpoint queue 432
CHUNK parameter 101
CL_DEPARTMENTS table 111

CLEAR_USED procedure 504
CL_EMPLOYEES table 111
CLIENT_RESULT_CACHE_LAG 345
CLIENT_RESULT_CACHE_SIZE
    parameter 342-345
client-side result cache
configuring 345
used, for caching results 342-345
CLOSE_CURSOR procedure 506
CLOSE procedure 503
cluster
about 103, 192
and truncating 108
index 108
size 108
CLUSTER (table_name) 296
composite partitioning 150, 151
COMPRESS parameter 130
COND_FIELD parameters 257
configuration, temporary
    tablespaces 248, 249
connection management
dedicated server versus shared server 46
optimizing 42
optimizing, steps 42-45
working 45
control file 369
control parameter 369
COUNT(*) function 218
COUNTRY_ID attribute 106
CREATE_BASELINE procedure 507
CREATE CLUSTER statement 112
CREATE_EDIT_TABLES procedure 504
CREATE INDEX command 130
CREATE_INDEX_COST procedure 505
CREATE_SNAPSHOT procedure 507
CREATE_SQLSET procedure 506
CREATE_STAT_TABLE procedure 301, 507
create table
using, as select 355-358
CREATE TABLE AS SELECT statement 357
CREATE_TABLE_COST procedure 505
CREATE_TUNING_TASK procedure 333, 506
CROSSCHECK COPY command 417
cursor management, performance
    issues 8-10

CURSOR_SHARING parameter 388, 399
CUSTOMERS table 293
CUSTOMERS_YOB_BIX bitmap
 index 294, 301

D

data
 acquiring, data dictionary used 20-23
 analyzing, ADDM used 32-36
 analyzing, AWR used 29-31
 analyzing, Statspack report used 23-25
 collecting 26
 loading, data pump used 366-373
 loading, SQL*Loader used 366-373
database
 sort operations, managing 214
database memory architecture 214
database request
 reducing, materialized views used 65-68
 reducing, sequences used 59-65
 reducing, stored procedures used 54-59
data compression 102
data dictionary
 used, for acquiring data 20-23
datafile parameter 23
Data Manipulation Language (DML) 153
data pump
 URL 373
 used, for loading data 366, 369-373
DBA_BLOCKERS dynamic performance
 view 442
DBA_BLOCKERS view 470
DBA_DATA_FILES view 470
DBA_EXTENTS view 471
DBA_INDEXES view 471
DBA_SEQUENCES view 475
DBA_SQL_PLAN_BASELINES view 472
DBA_TAB_HISTOGRAMS view 476
DBA_TABLES dictionary view 300
DBA_TABLESPACES view 476
DBA_TABLES view 472, 473
DBA_TEMP_FILES view 473
DBA_VIEWS view 474
DBA_WAITERS dynamic
 performance view 442

DBA_WATERS view 474
DBMS_ADDM package
 about 501
 ANALYZE_DB procedure 502
 ANALYZE_INST procedure 502
 GET_REPORT procedure 502
 procedures 502
DBMS_ADVISOR package
 EXECUTE_TASK procedure 502
 procedures 502
 QUICK_TUNE procedure 502
 SET_DEFAULT_TASK_PARAMETER
  procedure 502
DBMS_JOB package
 BROKEN procedure 502
 NEXT_DATE procedure 502
 procedures 502
 REMOVE procedure 502
 RUN procedure 502
 SUBMIT procedure 502
DBMS_LOB package
 APPEND procedure 503
 CLOSE procedure 503
 FILEOPEN procedure 503
 GET_LENGTH procedure 503
 LOADFROMFILE procedure 503
 OPEN procedure 503
 procedures 503
 READ procedure 503
 WRITE procedure 503
DBMS_MVIEW package
 EXPLAIN_MVIEW procedure 503
 EXPLAIN_REWRITE procedure 503
 procedures 503
 REFRESH_ALL_MVIEWS procedure 503
 REFRESH procedure 503
DBMS_OUTLN_EDIT package
 CREATE_EDIT_TABLES procedure 504
 DROP_EDIT_TABLES procedure 504
 procedures 504
 REFRESH_PRIVATE_OUTLINE procedure 504
DBMS_OUTLN package
 CLEAR_USED procedure 504
 DROP_BY_CAT procedure 504
 DROP_UNUSED procedure 504
 procedures 504
 UPDATE_BY_CAT procedure 504

DBMS_SHARED_POOL package
about 391
KEEP procedure 504
procedures 504
PURGE procedure 504
SIZES procedure 504
UNKEEP procedure 504
DBMS_SPACE package
about 95
CREATE_INDEX_COST procedure 505
CREATE_TABLE_COST procedure 505
FREE_BLOCKS procedure 505
procedures 505
SPACE_USAGE procedure 505
DBMS_SPM.MIGRATE_STORED_OUTLINE
    procedure 312
DBMS_SPM package
DROP_SQL_PLAN_BASELINE procedure 505
EVOLVE_SQL_PLAN_BASELINE
    procedure 505
LOAD_PLANS_FROM_CURSOR_CACHE
    procedure 505
LOAD_PLANS_FROM_SQLSET procedure 505
procedures 505
DBMS_SQL package
BIND_VARIABLE procedure 506
CLOSE_CURSOR procedure 506
EXECUTE procedure 506
OPEN_CURSOR procedure 506
PARSE procedure 506
procedures 506
DBMS_SQLTUNE package
about 333
CREATE_SQLSET procedure 506
CREATE_TUNING_TASK procedure 506
DROP_SQLSET procedure 506
EXECUTE_TUNING_TASK procedure 506
INTERRUPT_TUNING_TASK procedure 506
LOAD_SQLSET procedure 506
procedures 506
REPORT_TUNING_TASK procedure 506
RESUME_TUNING_TASK procedure 506
SELECT_CURSOR_CACHE procedure 506
SELECT_SQLSET procedure 506
DBMS_STATS.GATHER_SCHEMA_STATS
    procedure 303

DBMS_STATS.IMPORT_SCHEMA_STATS
    procedure 302
DBMS_STATS package
about 300, 305
CREATE_STAT_TABLE procedure 507
DROP_STAT_TABLE procedure 507
EXPORT_SCHEMA_STATS procedure 507
GATHER_DATABASE_STATS procedure 507
GATHER_INDEX_STATS procedure 507
GATHER_SCHEMA_STATS procedure 507
GATHER_TABLE_STATS procedure 507
IMPORT_SCHEMA_STATS procedure 507
procedures 305, 507
DBMS_UTILITY function 21
DBMS_UTILITY package
ANALYZE_DATABASE procedure 507
ANALYZE_SCHEMA procedure 507
GET_TIME procedure 507
procedures 507
DBMS_WORKLOAD_REPOSITORY package
CREATE_BASELINE procedure 507
CREATE_SNAPSHOT procedure 507
MODIFY_SNAPSHOT_SETTINGS
    procedure 507
procedures 507
DBW0 (DB Writer) process 382
deadlocks
about 444-452
UPDATE statement 451
dedicated server versus shared server 46
DELETE operation 127
DELETE_SCHEMA_STATS procedure 301
denormalization 192
DENSE_RANK() function 225, 228
dictionary cache
tuning 395, 396
V$ROWCACHE dynamic performance 395
direct I/O 426
direct path inserting 351-354
DISTINCT keyword 224
DMBS_STATS procedure 304
DROP_BY_CAT procedure 316, 504
DROP_EDIT_TABLES procedure 504
DROP_SQL_PLAN_BASELINE procedure 505
DROP_SQLSET procedure 506
DROP_STAT_TABLE procedure 507

DROP_UNUSED procedure 316, 504
dynamic performance views
  about 20-23
  ALL_OBJECTS 469
  DBA_BLOCKERS 470
  DBA_DATA_FILES 470
  DBA_EXTENTS 471
  DBA_INDEXES 471, 472
  DBA_SEQUENCES 475
  DBA_SQL_PLAN_BASELINES 472
  DBA_TAB_HISTOGRAMS 476
  DBA_TABLES 472
  DBA_TABLESPACES 476
  DBA_TEMP_FILES 473
  DBA_VIEWS 474
  DBA_WAITERS 474
  INDEX_STATS 474
  V$ADVISOR_PROGRESS 477
  V$BUFFER_POOL_STATISTICS 477
  V$CONTROLFILE 478
  V$DATAFILE 478
  V$DB_CACHE_ADVICE 479
  V$DB_OBJECT_CACHE 480
  V$ENQUEUE_LOCK 480
  V$FILESTAT 481
  V$FIXED_TABLE 482
  V$INSTANCE_RECOVERY 482
  V$LATCH 483
  V$LATCH_CHILDREN 483
  V$LIBRARYCACHE 484
  V$LOCK 485
  V$LOCKED_OBJECT 486
  V$LOG 486
  V$LOGFILE 488
  V$LOG_HISTORY 487
  V$MYSTAT 488
  V$PROCESS 489
  V$ROLLSTAT 489
  V$ROWCACHE 490
  V$SESSION 490
  V$SESSION 491
  V$SESSION_EVENT 491, 492
  V$SESSTAT 492
  V$SGA 492
  V$SGAINFO 493
  V$SHARED_POOL_RESERVED 493

  V$SORT_SEGMENT 494
  V$SQL 494
  V$SQLAREA 496
  V$SQL_PLAN 495
  V$STATNAME 496
  V$SYSSTAT 497
  V$SYSTEM_EVENT 498
  V$TEMPFILE 498
  V$TEMPSTAT 499
  V$WAITSTAT 499
  X$BH 500
dynamic sampling 304
dynamic SQL
  avoiding 79
  avoiding, steps 79-82

E

EMP_DEPARTMENT_IX index 111
EMP_DEPT_CLUSTER cluster 111
ENDPOINT_VALUE 308
ESTIMATE_PERCENT parameter 303
estimator 292
EVOLVE_SQL_PLAN_BASELINE
            procedure 339, 505
example database
  exploring 17
  preparing, steps 17-19
  working 19
EXECUTE procedure 506
EXECUTE_TASK procedure 502
EXECUTE_TUNING_TASK procedure 506
EXPLAIN_MVIEW procedure 503
EXPLAIN_REWRITE procedure 503
EXPORT_SCHEMA_STATS procedure 301,
            507
external table 371

F

Fast-Start checkpointing 431
FAST_START_MTTR_TARGET parameter 431
FILEOPEN procedure 503
FILESYSTEMIO_OPTIONS parameter 427
filters
  using, in group-by queries 232-238
FIRST_ROWS (n) 296

FORALL statement 184
FORCE mode 345
FOR EACH ROW
  avoiding, in triggers 289
FREE_BLOCKS procedure 505
FTS. *See* full table scan
FULL (table_name) 296
full table scan
  avoiding 164, 165
  working 166-168
FULL TABLE SCAN operation 139
function-based index 119
function inlining technique 283
function result cache
  about 276
  using 276-279
  working 279, 280

G

GATHER_DATABASE_STATS procedure 507
GATHER_INDEX_STATS procedure 507
GATHER_SCHEMA_STATS procedure 507
GATHER_TABLE_STATS procedure 507
GET_LENGTH procedure 503
GET_REPORT procedure 502
GET_TIME procedure 507
group-by queries
  filters, using in 232-238
GROUP BY query 216

H

hash clusters
  about 109
  CL_DEPARTMENTS table 111
  CL_EMPLOYEES table 111
  CREATE CLUSTER statement 112
  custom hash function 112
  EMP_DEPARTMENT_IX index 111
  EMP_DEPT_CLUSTER cluster 111
  HASHKEYS parameters 111
  single-table 112
  sorted 111
  TABLE ACCESS HASH operation 111
  using 109, 110
  working 111

HASH GROUP BY operation 224
HASHKEYS parameters 111
hash partitioning 149, 150
HASH (table_name) 296
HASH UNIQUE operation 224
HAVING clause 233, 238
height-based histograms 310
High-Water Mark (HWM)
  about 171
  resetting 172
High-Water Mark (HWM), resetting
  ALTER TABLE MOVE 172
  EXPORT + DROP + IMPORT 172
  TRUNCATE 172
histograms
  about 305
  ENDPOINT_VALUE 308
  height-based histograms 310
  skewed values 309
  value-based histograms 310
  working 307, 308
home directory 208
hugepages 383

I

ID field 321
ID value 321
immediate latch requests 456
IMPORT_SCHEMA_STATS procedure 507
INCLUDING option 145
index clusters
  COUNTRY_ID attribute 106
  Multi-Table Index Cluster Tables 107
  using 103, 105
index entries 120
indexes
  about 113
  ALTER INDEX REBUILD command 130
  B-Tree Index 119
  compressing 128
  compressing, steps 128-130
  COMPRESS parameter 130
  CREATE INDEX command 130
  DELETE operation 127
  function-based index 119
  INDEX FAST FULL SCAN 121

INSERT operation 127
inspecting 359-365
ONLINE options 127
PARALLEL option 127
prefix length 130
rebuild and statistics 127
rebuilding 123-126
rebuilding in offline mode, drawbacks 126
reverse key indexes, using 130-134
UPPER function 119
used, for avoiding sort operations 215-222
using 113-117
where condition 121
working 118
index lookup
example 173
exploring 173
function, using 177
NULL values, searching for 177
steps 173, 174
working 174-176
Index Organized Table. *See* **IOT**
index range-scan
and index skip-scan, differences 177-181
Index Range Scan operation 176
index skip-scan
and index range-scan, differences 177-181
INDEX_STATS view 474
INDEX (table_name index_name) 297
INDEX UNIQUE SCAN operation 135
in-memory sort operation
versus on-disk sort operation 208-214
INSERT operation 127
INSERT statement 181, 351
Instance Efficiency Indicators section 457
INTERRUPT_TUNING_TASK procedure 506
INTERSECT operator 241, 244
Intimate Shared Memory (ISM) 383
I/O performance issues
monitoring 412-414
working 415-418
IOT
about 142-144
INCLUDING option 145
Logical ROWID 146
PCTTHRESHOLD parameter 145, 146
USER tablespace 145

J

Java DataBase Connectivity. *See* **JDBC**
JDBC 257
JOIN operator 245
joins
optimizing 187
types 187
working 188-191

K

k-combinations 272
KEEP buffer cache 406
KEEP pool 409
KEEP procedure 504

L

Large OBjects. *See* **LOBs**
Latch Activity section 458
latch contention
minimizing, by tuning resources 457-459
latches
about 455
Cache buffers (LRU) chain latches 460
immediate latch requests 456
Instance Efficiency Indicators section 457
Latch Activity section 458
latch free event 454
latch free wait event 455
library cache latches 460
minimizing, bind variables
used 460, 464-468
redo allocation latches 460
redo copy latches 460
shared pool latches 459
TIME_WAITED column 453
tuning 452
V$LATCH_CHILDREN dynamic
performance view 460
V$LATCH dynamic performance view 454
V$SYSTEM_EVENT dynamic
performance view 453, 465, 468
willing-to-wait latch requests 456
WORKLOAD_BIND procedure 464
WORKLOAD_NOBIND procedure 464

latch free event 454
latch free wait event 455
LEADING (table_name1 table_name2) 297
leaf nodes 120
library cache
  CURSOR_SHARING parameter 388
  misses, minimizing 388
  tuning 384
  tuning, steps 384
  working 385-388
library cache latches 460
list partitioning 148, 149
LOADFROMFILE procedure 503
LOAD_PLANS_FROM_CURSOR_CACHE
    procedure 505
LOAD_PLANS_FROM_SQLSET procedure 505
LOAD_SQLSET procedure 506
LOBs
  BLOB data, encryption 103
  BLOB field 101
  c_file BLOB field 101
  CHUNK parameter 101
  data compression 102
  NOLOGGING parameters 103
  SecureFile (s) 102
  using 96-100
  working 100, 101
lock contention
  DBA_BLOCKERS 439
  DBA_BLOCKERS dynamic
    performance view 442
  DBA_WAITERS 439
  DBA_WAITERS dynamic
    performance view 442
  detecting 438-443
  preventing 438-443
  Row Level Lock 441
  Table Level Lock 441
  V$LOCKED_OBJECT dynamic
    performance view 439, 441
  V$SESSION dynamic performance view 443
LOCK_SGA parameter 381
log file sync statistic 434
Logical ROWID 146

M

MANUAL policy 211, 212
materialized views 192
  used, for reducing database requests 65-69
MAX_CREDIT column 364
MAX_CREDIT field 364
MAX_CREDIT field value 364
memory
  tuning, to avoid operating system
    paging 376-383
min/max aggregates
  computing 232-238
MIN/MAX query 232
MINUS operator 241
MODIFY_SNAPSHOT_SETTINGS
    procedure 507
multi-pass sort 213, 215
multiple block sizes
  advantages 88
multiple database writer slave processes 427
multiple disks
  objects, stripping 419, 420
Multi-Table Index Cluster Tables 107
Multi-Threaded Server (MTS) 46
MY_SALES table 184
MYSTATS table 299

N

native compilation
  about 271
  using 272-274
  working 274-276
NEXT_DATE procedure 502
NOCOPY
  parameters, passing to functions 262-264
  using, issues 266
  working 264-266
NO_INDEX (table_name index_name) 297
NOLOGGING clause 358
NOLOGGING parameters 103
no_result_cache 345
NULL device 347

O

objects
stripping, across multiple disks 420-422
OF
using 287, 288
on-disk sort operation
versus in-memory sort operation 208-214
ONLINE options 127
OnLine Transaction Processing (OLTP) 47, 327
OPEN_CURSOR procedure 506
OPEN procedure 503
operating system paging
avoiding, by tuning memory 376-383
optimal sort 213, 214
optimal storage parameters, temporary tablespaces 252
OPTIMIZER_DYNAMIC_SAMPLING parameter 304
Oracle
packages 501
Oracle Call Interface (OCI) 345
Oracle database
features 15
Oracle Database Configuration Assistant (DBCA) 17
Oracle Enterprise Manager (OEM) 16
Oracle Real Application Cluster (RAC) 25
ORDER BY clause 210
ORDER BY query 216
ORDERED 297
OTHER_SALES partition 149
OUTLN_PKG package 316

P

package, Oracle
DBMS_ADDM package 501
DBMS_ADVISOR package 502
DBMS_JOB package 502
DBMS_LOB package 503
DBMS_MVIEW package 503
DBMS_OUTLN_EDIT package 504
DBMS_OUTLN package 503
DBMS_SHARED_POOL package 504
DBMS_SPACE package 505
DBMS_SPM package 505
DBMS_SQL package 505
DBMS_SQLTUNE package 506
DBMS_STATS package 506
DBMS_UTILITY package 507
DBMS_WORKLOAD_REPOSITORY package 507
PARALLEL clause 358
PARALLEL (DEFAULT | AUTO | MANUAL | n) 297
PARALLEL option 127
parallel SQL
degree of parallelism of two 350
enabling 346
need for 350
parallel query and I/O 350
working 347-349
PARAMETER column 395
PARSE procedure 506
parsing
about 254, 255
working 256, 257
partitioning
composite partitioning 150, 151
hash partitioning 149, 150
list partitioning 148, 149
OTHER_SALES partition 149
PARTITION KEY 147
partition pruning 148
TIME_ID field 147
using 146, 147
PARTITION KEY 147
partition pruning 148
PCTFREE parameter
about 94, 172
CREATE_TABLE_COST package 95
DBMS_SPACE package 95
table size, estimating 95, 96
PCTINCREASE parameter 252
PCTTHRESHOLD parameter 145, 146
PCTUSED parameter 172
performance issues diagnosing, alert log used
about 28, 29
steps 28

performance issues, Oracle database
about 7, 8
cursor management, issues 8-10
poor session management 8
relational design, issues 11
storage structures, improper usage 11
performance, optimizing
schema denormalization used 71-79
performance sharing
improving, reusable code used 48, 50
PL/SQL and parsing 52
working 50, 51
performance tuning
about 7
database, creating for examples 17-19
process, reviewing 12, 13
performance tuning, example
about 36
demonstrating, SH schema used 36-40
performance tuning, process
issues, solving 12
reviewing 12
working 13-16
PGA
about 46, 215
tuning 396-399
PGA_AGGREGATE_TARGET
   parameter 211, 215
PGA size 210
plan generator
about 292
hints, issues 298
PL/SQL code
about 281
function inlining technique 283
inlining 281, 282
working 283
PMON (Process MONitor) proces 382
prefix length 130
private stored outlines 316, 317
Program Global Area. *See* **PGA**
public stored outlines 316, 317
PURGE procedure 504

Q

query optimizer
about 291
hints, exploring 292-297
query transformation 292
QUICK_TUNE procedure 502

R

RAID level 0+1 425
RAID level 5 424
RAID levels
choosing, for different Oracle files 422, 423
RAID level 0 424
RAID level 0+1 425
RAID level 1 424
RAID level 5 424
working 423
RANK() function 225, 227
READ procedure 503
recursive functions
about 269
avoiding 269-271
working 270, 271
RECYCLE pool 409
redo allocation latches 460
redo copy latches 460
redo logs
monitoring 433
working 434, 435
redo log switch 430
Redundant Arrays of Inexpensive Disks. *See*
   RAID levels
REFRESH_ALL_MVIEWS procedure 503
REFRESH_PRIVATE_OUTLINE procedure 504
REFRESH procedure 503
relational design, performance issues 11
REMOVE procedure 502
REPORT_TUNING_TASK function 333
REPORT_TUNING_TASK procedure 506
resources
tuning, to minimize latch contention 457-459
RESULT_CACHE_MAX_SIZE parameter 345

RESULT_CACHE option 280
results
    caching, client-side result
        cache used 342-345
RESUME_TUNING_TASK procedure 506
reusable code
    used, for improving performance
        sharing 48-52
reverse key B-Tree index 134
reverse key indexes
    BEFORE INSERT trigger 134
    INDEX UNIQUE SCAN operation 135
    reverse key B-Tree index 134
    REVERSE keyword 134
    TABLE ACCESS BY INDEX ROWID
        operation 135
    using 130-134
REVERSE keyword 134
REWRITE (materialized_view) 297
row
    BIG_ROWS table 87
    changing, avoiding 84-86
    counting 232-238
    migration, avoiding 89-94
    multiple block sizes, advantages 88
    PCTFREE parameter 94
    working 87
Row Level Lock 441
RUN procedure 502

S

schema denormalization
    used, for optimizing performance 71-79
select
    create table, using 355-358
SELECT_CURSOR_CACHE procedure 506
SELECT DISTINCT query 216
SELECT_SQLSET procedure 506
SESSION_CACHED_CURSORS 399
session management, performance issues 8
SET_DEFAULT_TASK_PARAMETER
        procedure 502
set operations
    sort, avoiding in 240-247

set operators 247
set theory 247
SGA 398
shared pool
    ALTER SYSTEM FLUSH SHARED_POOL
        command 394
    DBMS_SHARED_POOL.KEEP
        procedure 390
    DBMS_SHARED_POOL package 391
    SHARED_POOL_RESERVED_SIZE
        initialization parameter 394
    SHARED_POOL_SIZE parameter 392
    SIZES procedure 395
    tuning 388
    tuning, steps 389
    V$ROWCACHE dynamic performance 393
    V$SHARED_POOL_ADVICE dynamic
        performance 395
    working 390-394
shared pool latches 459
SHARED_POOL_RESERVED_SIZE
        initialization parameter 394
SHARED_POOL_SIZE parameter 392
short-circuit IF statements
    about 266
    using, steps 266, 267
    working 268, 269
SH schema 36, 209
SIMPLE_FUNCTION function 281
single-pass sort 213, 215
SIZES procedure 395, 504
skewed values 309
SORT_AREA_SIZE parameter 252
SORT GROUP BY operation 224, 238
sorting
    about 207
    avoiding, in set operations 240-247
sort operations
    about 223
    avoiding, indexes used 215-222
    managing 214
SORT UNIQUE operation 224, 242, 243
SPACE_USAGE procedure 505
spcreate.sql script 24
SQL Access Advisor 15

SQL activity
tracing, with SQL trace 201-205
tracing, with TKPROF 201-205
SQL baselines
configuring 336, 337
creating 335
working 337-339
SQL*Loader
used, for loading data 366, 369-373
SQL*Plus environment 208
SQL script 208
SQL Trace
used, for tracing SQL activity 201-205
SQL Tuning Advisor
about 15
using 331
working 333, 334
SQL tuning sets
about 327
creating 328-330
STAR_TRANSFORMATION 297
statistics
collecting 298-302
computation 303
table statistics, locking for highly volatile
tables 304
Statspack report
data, collecting 26
report on specific SQL, producing 26, 27
snapshot generation, automating 27
Statspack, maintenance 27
used, for analyzing data 23-25
storage structures, performance issues
improper usage 11
stored outlines
managing 310-316
private stored outlines 316, 317
public stored outlines 316, 317
stored procedures
used, for reducing database
requests 54-62
SUBMIT procedure 502
subqueries
using 192, 193
working 193-198
System Change Number (SCN) 428
System Global Area. *See* **SGA**

T

table
data inserting, arrays used 181-185
**TABLE ACCESS BY INDEX ROWID operation
135**
TABLE ACCESS HASH operation 111
Table Level Lock 441
temporary tablespaces
configuring 248, 249
optimal storage parameters 252
troubleshooting 248-251
TEST_TUNING_SET 329
TIMED_STATISTICS parameter 20
TIME_ID field 147
TIME_WAITED column 453
TKPROF
used, for tracing SQL activity 201-205
top n queries
ranking, demonstrating 224-230
retrieving 224-230
triggers
about 284
FOR EACH ROW, avoiding 289
OF, using 287, 288
WHEN, using 287, 288
triggers overhead
inspecting 359-365

U

UGA
tuning 396-399
UNION ALL operation 243
UNION-ALL operation 242
UNION operator 240, 242
UNKEEP procedure 504
UPDATE_BY_CAT procedure 316, 504
UPDATE statement 451
UPPER function 119
USE_HASH (table_name1 table_name2) 297
**USE_MERGE (table_name1 table_name2)
297**
USE_NL (table_name1 table_name2) 297
User Global Area. *See* **UGA**
User Global Area (UGA) 215
USER_TAB_HISTOGRAMS 307
USER tablespace 145

V

V$ADVISOR_PROGRESS view 477
V$BUFFER_POOL_STATISTICS view 477
V$CONTROLFILE view 478
V$DATAFILE view 478
V$DB_CACHE_ADVICE view 479
V$DB_OBJECT_CACHE view 480
V$ENQUEUE_LOCK view 480
V$FILESTAT view 481
V$FIXED_TABLE view 482
V$INSTANCE_RECOVERY view 482
V$LATCH_CHILDREN dynamic
    performance view 460
V$LATCH_CHILDREN view 483, 484
V$LATCH dynamic performance view 454
V$LATCH view 483
V$LIBRARYCACHE view 484
V$LOCKED_OBJECT dynamic
    performance view 439, 441
V$LOCKED_OBJECT view 486
V$LOCK view 485, 486
V$LOGFILE view 488
V$LOG_HISTORY view 487
V$LOG view 486
V$MYSTAT view 488
V$PROCESS dynamic performance view 382
V$PROCESS view 489
V$ROLLSTAT view 489
V$ROWCACHE dynamic performance 393,
    395
V$SESSION dynamic performance view 443
V$SESSION_EVENT view 491, 492
V$SESSION view 490, 491
V$SESSTAT view 492
V$SGAINFO dynamic performance view 376
V$SGAINFO view 493
V$SGA view 492
V$SHARED_POOL_ADVICE
    dynamic performance 395
V$SHARED_POOL_RESERVED view 493
V$SORT_SEGMENT view 494
V$SQLAREA view 496
V$SQL_PLAN view 495
V$SQL view 494, 495
V$STATNAME view 496
V$SYSSTAT view 497
V$SYSTEM_EVENT dynamic
    performance view 453, 465, 468
V$SYSTEM_EVENT view 498
V$TEMPFILE view 498
V$TEMPSTAT view 499
V$WAITSTAT view 499
value-based histograms 310
virtual columns
  about 284, 365
  using 284, 286
  working 286, 287

W

web application 46, 47
WHEN
  using 287
WHERE clause 233
where condition 121
willing-to-wait latch requests 456
WORKLOAD_BIND procedure 464
WORKLOAD_NOBIND procedure 158, 464
WRITE procedure 503

X

X$BH view 500
X1_MY_TEST index 322

Thank you for buying
Oracle Database 11gR2 Performance Tuning Cookbook

About Packt Publishing

Packt, pronounced 'packed', published its first book "*Mastering phpMyAdmin for Effective MySQL Management*" in April 2004 and subsequently continued to specialize in publishing highly focused books on specific technologies and solutions.

Our books and publications share the experiences of your fellow IT professionals in adapting and customizing today's systems, applications, and frameworks. Our solution-based books give you the knowledge and power to customize the software and technologies you're using to get the job done. Packt books are more specific and less general than the IT books you have seen in the past. Our unique business model allows us to bring you more focused information, giving you more of what you need to know, and less of what you don't.

Packt is a modern, yet unique publishing company, which focuses on producing quality, cutting-edge books for communities of developers, administrators, and newbies alike. For more information, please visit our website: www.PacktPub.com.

About Packt Enterprise

In 2010, Packt launched two new brands, Packt Enterprise and Packt Open Source, in order to continue its focus on specialization. This book is part of the Packt Enterprise brand, home to books published on enterprise software – software created by major vendors, including (but not limited to) IBM, Microsoft and Oracle, often for use in other corporations. Its titles will offer information relevant to a range of users of this software, including administrators, developers, architects, and end users.

Writing for Packt

We welcome all inquiries from people who are interested in authoring. Book proposals should be sent to author@packtpub.com. If your book idea is still at an early stage and you would like to discuss it first before writing a formal book proposal, contact us; one of our commissioning editors will get in touch with you.

We're not just looking for published authors; if you have strong technical skills but no writing experience, our experienced editors can help you develop a writing career, or simply get some additional reward for your expertise.

Oracle 11g R1/R2 Real Application
Clusters Essentials

Design, implement, and support complex Oracle 11g RAC
environments for real-world deployments

Ben Prusinski
Syed Jaffer Hussain

Oracle 11*g* R1/R2 Real Application Clusters Essentials

ISBN: 978-1-84968-266-4 Paperback: 552 pages

Design, implement, and support complex Oracle 11*g*
RAC environments for real world deployments

1. Understand sophisticated components that make up
   your Oracle RAC environment such as the role of High
   Availability, the RAC architecture required, the RAC
   installation and upgrade process, and much more!

2. Get hold of new Oracle RAC components such
   as the new features of Automatic Storage
   Management (ASM), performance tuning, and
   troubleshooting.

3. Packed with practical, real-world examples,
   expert tips and troubleshooting advice on how to
   administer a complex Oracle 11*g* RAC environment.

OCA Oracle Database 11g: SQL
Fundamentals I: A Real-World
Certification Guide

Ace the 1Z0-051 SQL Fundamentals I exam and become a
successful DBA by learning how SQL concepts work in the
real world

Steve Ries

OCA Oracle Database 11*g*: SQL Fundamentals I: A Real World Certification Guide

ISBN: 978-1-84968-364-7 Paperback: 500 pages

Ace the 1Z0-051 SQL Fundamentals I exam and become
a successful DBA by learning how SQL concepts work in
the real world

1. Successfully clear the first stepping stone
   towards attaining the Oracle Certified Associate
   Certification on Oracle Database 11*g*.

2. This book uses a real world example-driven
   approach that is easy to understand and
   makes engagin.

3. Complete coverage of the prescribed syllabus.

4. Learn from a range of self-test questions to fully
   equip you with the knowledge to pass this exam.

Please check **www.PacktPub.com** for information on our titles

Oracle Database 11*g* – Underground Advice for Database Administrators

ISBN: 978-1-849680-00-4   Paperback: 348 pages

A real-world DBA survival guide for Oracle 11*g* database implementation

1. A comprehensive handbook aimed at reducing the day-to-day struggle of Oracle 11*g* Database newcomers.

2. Real-world reflections from an experienced DBA—what novice DBAs should really know.

3. Implement Oracle's Maximum Availability Architecture with expert guidance.

4. Extensive information on providing high availability for Grid Control.

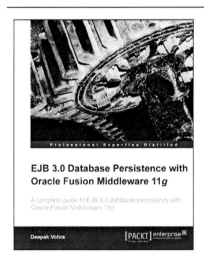

EJB 3.0 Database Persistence with Oracle Fusion Middleware 11*g*

ISBN: 978-1-849681-56-8   Paperback: 448 pages

A complete guide to building EJB 3.0 database persistent applications with Oracle Fusion Middleware 11*g*

1. Integrate EJB 3.0 database persistence with Oracle Fusion Middleware tools: WebLogic Server, JDeveloper, and Enterprise Pack for Eclipse.

2. Automatically create EJB 3.0 entity beans from database tables.

3. Learn to wrap entity beans with session beans and create EJB 3.0 relationships.

4. Apply JSF and ADF Faces user interfaces (UIs) to EJB 3.0 database persistence.

Please check **www.PacktPub.com** for information on our titles

CPSIA information can be obtained at www.ICGtesting.com
Printed in the USA
BVOW081232250112

281299BV00003B/36/P